A HISTORY OF PHILOSOPHY

VOLUME II

Renaissance, Enlightenment, and Modern

WILHELM WINDELBAND

HARPER TORCHBOOKS

HARPER & BROTHERS, PUBLISHERS
New York

A HISTORY OF PHILOSOPHY: II—Renaissance, Enlightenment, and Modern

Printed in the United States of America

Reprinted by arrangement with The Macmillan Company, New York, from the revised edition of 1901, translated by James H. Tufts.

First HARPER TORCHBOOK edition published 1958

Library of Congress catalog card number: LC-58-7114—Vol. II

HARPER TORCHBOOKS / The Cloister Library

(Continued on next page)

HARPER TORCHBOOKS / The Academy Library

HARPER TORCHBOOKS / The Science Library

CONTENTS.

PART VII.

THE PHILOSOPHY OF THE NINETEENTH CENTURY.

A
HISTORY
OF
PHILOSOPHY

VOLUME II

PART IV.

THE PHILOSOPHY OF THE RENAISSANCE.

J. E. Erdmann, *Versuch einer wissenschaftlichen Darstellung der Geschichte der neueren Philosophie.* 3 pts., in 6 vols. Riga and Leips. 1834–53.

H. Ulrici, *Geschichte und Kritik der Principien der neueren Philosophie.* 2 vols. Leips. 1845.

Kuno Fischer, *Geschichte der neueren Philosophie.* 4th ed. Heidelb. 1897 ff. [Eng. tr. of Vol. I., *Descartes and His School,* by J. P. Gordy, N.Y. 1877.]

Ed. Zeller, *Geschichte der deutschen Philosophie seit Leibniz.* 2d ed., Berlin, 1875.

W. Windelband, *Geschichte der neueren Philosophie.* 2 vols. Leips. 2d ed. 1899.

R. Falckenberg, *Geschichte der neueren Philosophie.* Leips. 1886. [Eng. tr. by A. C. Armstrong, N.Y. 1893.]

J. Schaller, *Geschichte der Naturphilosophie seit Bacon.* 2 vols. Leips. 1841–44.

J. Baumann, *Die Lehren von Raum, Zeit und Mathematik in der neueren Philosophie.* 2 vols. Berlin, 1868 f.

F. Vorländer, *Geschichte der philosophischen Moral-, Rechts-, und Staatslehre der Engländer und Franzosen.* Marburg, 1855.

F. Jodl, *Geschichte der Ethik in der neueren Philosophie.* 2 vols. Stuttgart, 1882–89.

B. Pünjer, *Geschichte der christlichen Religionsphilosophie seit der Reformation.* 2 vols. Braunschweig, 1880–83. [Eng. tr. of Vol. I., *History of the Christian Philosophy of Religion from the Reformation to Kant,* by W. Hastie, Edin. and N.Y. 1887.]

[B. F. Burt, *History of Modern Philosophy.* 2 vols. Chicago, 1892.]

THE antitheses which make their appearance in mediæval philosophy at the time of its close have a more general significance; they show in theoretical form the self-conscious strengthening of secular civilisation by the side of that of the Church. The undercurrent, which for a thousand years had accompanied the religious main movement of the intellectual life among the Western peoples, swelling here and there to a stronger potency, now actually forced its way to the surface, and in the centuries of transition its slowly wrested victory makes the essential characteristic for the beginning of modern times.

Thus gradually developing and constantly progressing, modern science freed itself from mediæval views, and the intricate process in which it came into being went hand in hand with the multifold activity with which modern life in its entirety began. For modern life begins everywhere with the vigorous development of details; the tense (*lapidare*) unity into which mediæval life was concentrated, breaks asunder in the progress of time, and primitive vigour bursts the band of common tradition with which history had encircled the mind of the nations. Thus the new epoch announces itself by the awakening of national life; the time of the world-empire is past in the intellectual realm also, and the wealth and variety of decentralisation takes the place of the unitary concentration in which the Middle Ages had worked. Rome and Paris cease to be the controlling centres of Western civilisation, Latin ceases to be the sole language of the educated world.

In the religious domain this process showed itself first in the fact that Rome lost its sole mastery over the Church life of Christianity. Wittenberg, Geneva, London, and other cities became new centres of religion. The inwardness of faith, which in Mysticism had already risen in revolt against the secularisation of the life of the Church, rose to victorious deliverance, to degenerate again at once into the organisation which was indispensable for it in the outer world. But the process of splitting into various sects, which set in in connection with this external organisation, wakened all the depths of religious feeling, and stirred for the following centuries the passion and fanaticism of confessional oppositions. Just by this means, however, the dominance at the summit of scientific life of a complete and definitive religious belief was broken. What had been begun in the age of the Crusades by the contact of religions was now completed by the controversy between Christian creeds.

It is not a matter of accident that the number of centres of scientific life in addition to Paris was also growing rapidly. While Oxford had already won an importance of its own as a seat of the Franciscan opposition, now we find first Vienna, Heidelberg, Prague, then the numerous academies of Italy, and finally the wealth of new universities of Protestant Germany, developing their independent vital forces. But at the same time, by the invention of the art of printing, literary life gained such an extension and such a widely ramifying movement that, following its inner impulse, it was able to free itself from its rigid connection with the schools, strip off the fetters of learned tradition, and expand unconstrained in the forms shaped out for it by individual personalities. So philosophy in the Renaissance loses its corporate character, and becomes in its best achievements the free deed of individuals; it

seeks its sources in the broad extent of the real world of its own
time, and presents itself externally more and more in the garb of
modern national languages.

In this way science became involved in a powerful fermentation.
The two-thousand-year-old forms of the intellectual life seemed to
have been outlived and to have become unusable. A passionate, and
at the first, still unclear search for novelty filled all minds, and
excited imagination gained the mastery of the movement. But, in
connection with this, the whole multiplicity of interests of secular
life asserted themselves in philosophy, — the powerful development
of political life, the rich increase in outward civilisation, the extension of European civilisation over foreign parts of the world, and
not least the world-joy of newly awakened art. And this fresh and
living wealth of new content brought with it the result that philosophy became pre-eminently subject to no one of these interests, but
rather took them all up into itself, and with the passing of time
raised itself above them again to the free work of knowing, to the
ideal of knowledge for its own sake.

The *new birth of the purely theoretical spirit* is the true meaning of
the scientific " Renaissance," and in this consists also its *kinship of
spirit with Greek thought,* which was of decisive importance for its
development. The subordination to ends of practical, ethical, and
religious life which had prevailed in the whole philosophy of the
Hellenistic-Roman period and of the Middle Ages, decreased more
and more at the beginning of the modern period, and knowledge of
reality appeared again as the absolute end of scientific research.
Just as at the beginnings of Greek thought, so now, this theoretical
impulse turned its attention essentially to natural science. The
modern mind, which had taken up into itself the achievements of
later antiquity and of the Middle Ages, appears from the beginning
as having attained a stronger self-consciousness, as internalised, and
as having penetrated deeper into its own nature, in comparison
with the ancient mind. But true as this is, its first independent
intellectual activity was the return to a disinterested conception of Nature. The whole philosophy of the Renaissance pressed
toward this end, and in this direction it achieved its greatest
results.

Feeling such a relationship in its fundamental impulse, the
modern spirit in its passionate search for the new seized at first
upon the oldest. The knowledge of ancient philosophy brought out
by the humanistic movement was eagerly taken up, and the systems of
Greek philosophy were revived in violent opposition to the mediæval
tradition. But from the point of view of the whole movement of

history this return to antiquity presents itself as but the instinctive preparation for the true work of the modern spirit,[1] which in this Castalian bath attained its youthful vigour. By living itself into the world of Greek ideas it gained the ability to master in thought its own rich outer life, and thus equipped, science turned from the subtility of the inner world with full vigour back to the investigation of Nature, to open there new and wider paths for itself.

The history of the philosophy of the Renaissance is therefore in the main the history of the process in which the natural science mode of regarding the world is gradually worked out from the humanistic renewal of Greek philosophy. It falls, therefore, appropriately into two periods, the *humanistic* period and the *natural science* period. As a boundary line between the two we may perhaps regard the year 1600. The first of these periods contains the supplanting of mediæval tradition by that of genuine Grecian thought, and while extremely rich in interest for the history of civilisation and in literary activity, these two centuries show from a philosophical point of view merely that shifting of earlier thoughts by which preparation is made for the new. The second period includes the beginnings of modern natural research which gradually conquered their independence, and following these the great metaphysical systems of the seventeenth century.

The two periods form a most intimately connected whole. For the inner impelling motive in the philosophical movement of Humanism was the same urgent demand for a radically new knowledge of the world, which ultimately found its fulfilment in the process in which natural science became established and worked out according to principles. But the manner in which this work took place, and the forms of thought in which it became complete, prove to be in all important points dependent upon the stimulus proceeding from the adoption of Greek philosophy. *Modern natural science is the daughter of Humanism.*

---

[1] In this respect the course of development of science in the Renaissance ran exactly parallel to that of art. The line which leads from Giotto to Leonardo, Raphael, Michael Angelo, Titian, Dürer, and Rembrandt, passes gradually from the reanimation of classical forms to independent and immediate apprehension of Nature. And Goethe is likewise proof that for us moderns the way to Nature leads through Greece.

CHAPTER I.

THE HUMANISTIC PERIOD.

Jac. Burckhardt, *Die Cultur der Renaissance in Italien.* 4th ed., Leips. 1886.
[*The Civilisation of the Renaissance.* Tr. by S. G. C. Middlemore, Lond. 1878 and 1890.

Mor. Carrière, *Die philosophische Weltanschauung der Reformationszeit.* 2d ed., Leips. 1887.

A. Stöckl, *Geschichte der Philosophie des Mittelalters.* 3d vol., Mainz, 1866.

[J. A. Symonds, *The Renaissance in Italy.* 5 pts. in 7 vols., 1875–86.]

THE continuity in the intellectual and spiritual development of European humanity manifests itself nowhere so remarkably as in the Renaissance. At no time perhaps has the want for something completely new, for a total and radical transformation, not only in the intellectual life, but also in the whole state of society, been felt so vigorously and expressed so variously and passionately as then, and no time has experienced so many, so adventurous, and so ambitious attempts at innovation as did this. And yet, if we look closely, and do not allow ourselves to be deceived, either by the grotesque self-consciousness or by the naïve grandiloquence which are the order of the day in this literature, it becomes evident that the whole multiform process goes on within the bounds of ancient and mediæval traditions, and strives in obscure longing toward a goal which is an object rather of premonition than of clear conception. It was not until the seventeenth century that the process of fermentation became complete, and this turbulent mixture clarified.

The essential ferment in this movement was the opposition between the inherited philosophy of the Middle Ages, which was already falling into dissolution, and the original works of Greek thinkers which began to be known in the fifteenth century. A new stream of culture flowed from Byzantium by the way of Florence and Rome, which once more strongly diverted the course of Western thought from its previous direction. In so far the humanistic Renaissance, the so-called re-birth of classical antiquity, appears as a continuation and completion of that powerful process of appropriation presented by the Middle Ages (cf. pp. 264 ff., 310 f.); and if this process consisted in retracing in reverse order the ancient movement of thought, it now reached its end, inasmuch as essentially all of the original ancient Greek literature which is accessible to-day, now became known.

The becoming known of the Greek originals, and the spread of *humanistic culture*, called out a movement of opposition to Scholasticism, at first in Italy, then also in Germany, France, and England. As regards subject-matter, this opposition was directed against the mediæval interpretations of Greek metaphysics; as regards method, against authoritative deduction from conceptions taken as assumptions; as regards form, against the tasteless stiffness of monastic Latin: and with the wonderful restoration of ancient thought, with the fresh imaginative nature of a life-loving race, with the refinement and wit of an artistically cultivated time for its aids this opposition won a swift victory.

But this opposition was divided within itself. There were *Platonists*, who for the most part would better be called Neo-Platonists; there were *Aristotelians*, who, in turn, were again divided into different groups, vigorously combating one another, according to their attachment to one or another of the ancient interpreters. There, too, were the reawakened older doctrines of Greek cosmology, of the Ionians and *Pythagoreans;* the conception of Nature held by *Democritus* and *Epicurus* rose to new vigour. *Scepticism* and the mixed *popular and philosophical Eclecticism* lived again.

While this humanistic movement was either religiously indifferent or even engaged together with open "heathenism" in warfare against Christian dogma, an equally violent controversy between transmitted doctrines was in progress in the life of the Church. The *Catholic* Church intrenched itself against the assault of thought more and more firmly behind the bulwark of *Thomism,* under the leadership of the *Jesuits.* Among the *Protestants, Augustine* was the leading mind — a continuation of the antagonism observed in the Middle Ages. But when dogmas were thrown into philosophical form in the Protestant Church, the *Reformed* branch remained nearer to Augustine, while in the *Lutheran* Church, in consequence of the influence of Humanism, a tendency toward the original form of the Aristotelian system prevailed. In addition to these tendencies, however, German *Mysticism*, with all the widely ramified traditions which united in it (cf. § 26, 5), maintained itself in the religious need of the people, to become fruitful and efficient for the philosophy of the future, more vigorous in its life than the Church erudition that sought in vain to stifle it.

The new which was being prepared in these various conflicts was the consummation of that movement which had begun with Duns Scotus at the culmination of mediæval philosophy, viz. the separation of philosophy from theology. The more philosophy established itself by the side of theology as an independent secular science, the more its peculiar task was held to be the *knowledge of Nature.* In this result all lines of the philosophy of the Renaissance meet. Philosophy shall be natural science, — this is the watchword of the time.

The carrying out of this purpose, nevertheless, necessarily moved at first within the traditional modes of thought; these, however, had their common element in the *anthropocentric* character of their *Weltanschauung*, which had been the consequence of the development of philosophy as a theory and art of life. For this reason the natural philosophy of the Renaissance in all its lines takes for its starting-point, in constructing its problems, *man's position in the cosmos;* and the revolution in ideas which took place in this aspect, under the influence of the changed conditions of civilisation, became of decisive importance for shaping anew the whole theory of the world. At this point metaphysical imagination and fancy was most deeply stirred, and from this point of view it produced its cosmical poetry, prototypal for the future, in the doctrines of *Giordano Bruno* and *Jacob Boehme.*

The following treat in general the *revival of ancient philosophy:* L. Heeren, *Geschichte der Studien der classischen Litteratur* (Göttingen, 1797–1802); G. Vogt, *Die Wiederbelebung des classischen Alterthums* (Berlin, 1880 f.).

The main seat of **Platonism** was the *Academy of Florence*, which was founded by **Cosmo de' Medici**, and brilliantly maintained by his successors. The impulse for this had been given by Georgius Gemistus **Pletho** (1355–1450), the author of numerous commentaries and compendiums, and of a treatise in Greek on the difference between the Platonic and the Aristotelian doctrine. Cf. Fr. Schultze, *G. G. P.* (Jena, 1874). — **Bessarion** (born 1403 in Trebizond, died as Cardinal of the Roman church in Ravenna, 1472) was his influential pupil. Bessarion's main treatise, *Adversus Calumniatorem Platonis*, appeared at Rome, 1469. Complete Works in Migne's coll. (Paris, 1866). — The most important members of the Platonic circle were **Marsilio Ficino** of Florence (1433–1499), the translator of the works of Plato and Plotinus, and author of a *Theologia Platonica* (Florence, 1482), and at a later time, **Francesco Patrizzi** (1529–1597), who brought the natural philosophy of this movement to its completest expression in his *Nova de Universis Philosophia* (Ferrara, 1591).

A similar instance of Neo-Platonism alloyed with Neo-Pythagorean and ancient Pythagorean motives is afforded by **John Pico of Mirandola** (1463–94).

The study of **Aristotle** in the original sources was promoted in Italy by **Georgius of Trebizond** (1396–1484; *Comparatio Platonis et Aristotelis*, Venice, 1523) and **Theodorus Gaza** (died 1478), in Holland and Germany by **Rudolf Agricola** (1442–1485), and in France by **Jacques Lefèvre** (Faber Stapulensis, 1455–1537).

The Aristotelians of the Renaissance (aside from the churchly-scholastic line) divided into the two parties of the **Averroists** and the **Alexandrists** The University of Padua, as the chief seat of Averroism, was also the place of the liveliest controversies between the two.

As representatives of **Averroism** we mention **Nicoletto Vernias** (died 1499), especially **Alexander Achillini** of Bologna (died 1518 ; works, Venice, 1545) ; further, **Augostino Nifo** (1473–1546 ; main treatise, *De Intellectu et Dæmonibus; Opuscula,* Paris, 1654), and the Neapolitan **Zimara** (died 1532).

To the **Alexandrists** belong **Ermolao Barbaro** of Venice (1454–1493 ; *Compendium Scientiæ Naturalis ex Aristotele,* Venice, 1547), and the most important Aristotelian of the Renaissance, **Pietro Pomponazzi** (born 1462 in Mantua, died 1524 in Bologna. His most important writings are *De Immortalitate Animæ* with the *Defensorium* against Niphus, *De fato libero arbitrio prædestinatione providentia dei libri quinque;* cf. L. Ferri, *La Psicologia di P. P.,* Rome, 1877), and his pupils, **Gasparo Contarini** (died 1542), **Simon Porta** (died 1555), and Julius Cæsar **Scaliger** (1484–1558).

Among the later Aristotelians, **Jacopo Zabarella** (1532–1589), **Andreas Cæsalpinus** (1519–1603), **Cesare Cremonini** (1552–1631) and others seem rather to have adjusted the above oppositions.

Of the renewals of other Greek philosophers, the following are especially to be mentioned : —

Jœst Lips (1547–1606), *Manuductio ad Stoicam Philosophiam* (Antwerp, 1604), and other writings ; and **Caspar Schoppe,** *Elementa Stoicæ Philosophiæ Moralis* (Mainz, 1606).

Dav. **Sennert** (1572–1637), *Physica* (Wittenberg, 1618) ; Sebastian **Basso** (*Philosophia Naturalis adversus Aristotelem,* Geneva, 1621) ; and Johannes **Magnenus,** *Democritus Reviviscens* (Pavia, 1646).

Claude de Bérigard as renewer of the Ionic natural philosophy in his *Cerculi Pisani* (Udine, 1643 ff.).

Pierre **Gassendi** (1592–1655), *De Vita Moribus et Doctrina Epicuri* (Leyden, 1647) [works, Lyons, 1658], and lastly

Emanuel **Maignanus** (1601–1671), whose *Cursus Philosophicus* (Toulouse, 1652) defends Empedoclean doctrines.

The following wrote in the spirit of the ancient **Scepticism : Michel de Montaigne** (1533–1592 ; *Essais,* Bordeaux, 1580, new editions, Paris, 1865, and Bordeaux, 1870) [Eng. tr. by Cotton, ed. by Hazlitt, Lond. 1872 ; also by Florio, ed. by Morley, Lond. 1887], **François Sanchez** (1562–1632, a Portuguese who taught in Toulouse, author of the *Tractatus de multum nobili et prima universali scientia quod nihil scitur,* Lyons, 1581 ; cf. L. Gerkrath, *F. S.,* Vienna, 1860), **Pierre Charron** (1541–1603 ; *De la Sagesse,* Bordeaux, 1601) : later François de la Motte le **Vayer** (1586–1672, *Cinq Dialogues,* Mons, 1673), Samuel **Sorbière** (1615–1670, translator of Sextus Empiricus), and Simon **Foucher** (1644–96, author of a history of the Academic Sceptics, Paris, 1690).

The sharpest polemic against Scholasticism proceeded from those Humanists who set against it the Roman **eclectic popular philosophy** of sound common sense in an attractive form, and as far as possible in *rhetorical* garb. Agricola is to be mentioned here also, with his treatise *De Inventione Dialectica* (1480). Before him was **Laurentius Valla** (1408–1457 ; *Dialecticæ Disputationes contra Aristoteleos,* Ven. 1499), **Ludovico Vives** (born in Valencia, 1492, died in Brügge, 1546 ; *De Disciplinis,* Brügge, 1531, works, Basel, 1555 ; cf. A. Lange in Schmidt's *Encyclopädie der Pädagogik,* Vol. IX.), **Marius Nizolius** (1498–1576 ; *De veris principiis et vera ratione philosophandi,* Parma, 1553), finally **Pierre de la Ramée** (Petrus Ramus, 1515–1572, *Institutiones Dialecticæ,* Paris, 1543 ; cf. Ch. Waddington, Paris, 1849 and 1855).

The tradition of **Thomistic Scholasticism** maintained itself most strongly at the *Spanish* universities. Among its supporters the most prominent was Francis **Suarez** of Granada (1548–1617 ; *Disputationes Metaphysicæ,* 1605, works, 26 vols., Paris, 1856–66 ; cf. K. Werner, *S. und die Scholastik der letzten Jahrhunderte,* Regensburg, 1861) ; the collective work of the Jesuits of Coimbra, the so-called *Collegium Conembricense,* is also to be mentioned.

Protestantism stood from the beginning in closer relation to the humanistic movement. In Germany especially the two went frequently hand in hand ; cf. K. Hagen, *Deutschlands litterarische und religiöse Verhältnisse im Reformationszeitalter,* 3 vols., Frankfort, 1868.

At the Protestant universities Aristotelianism was introduced principally by **Philip Melancthon**. In the edition of his works by Bretschneider and Bindseil the philosophical works form Vols. 13. and 16. Of chief importance among them are the text-books on logic (dialectic) and ethics. Cf. A. Richter, *M.'s Verdienste um den philosophischen Unterricht* (Leips. 1870); K. Hartfelder, *M. als Præceptor Germaniæ* (Berlin, 1889).

Luther himself stood much nearer the position of Augustinianism (cf. Ch. Weisse, *Die Christologie Luther's*, Leips. 1852). This was still more the case with **Calvin**, while **Zwingli** was friendlier inclined toward contemporaneous philosophy, especially the Italian Neo-Platonism. The scientific importance of all three great reformers lies, however, so exclusively in the theological field that they are to be mentioned here only as essential factors of the general intellectual movement in the sixteenth century.

Protestant Aristotelianism found its opponents in **Nicolaus Taurellus** (1547–1606, Professor in Basel and Altorf; *Philosophiæ Triumphus*, Basel, 1573; *Alpes Cæsæ*, Frankfort, 1597; cf. F. X. Schmidt-Schwarzenberger, *N. T., Der erste deutsche Philosoph*, Erlangen, 1864), further in **Socinianism** founded by **Lelio Sozzini** of Sienna (1525–1562) and his nephew **Fausto** (1539–1604; cf. A. Fock, *Der Socinianismus*, Kiel, 1847, and the article *S.* by Herzog in his *Theol. Enc.*, 2d ed., XIV. 377 ff), and especially in the popular movement of *Mysticism*. Among the representatives of this movement are prominent **Andreas Osiander** (1498–1552), **Caspar Schwenckfeld** (1490–1561), **Sebastian Franck** (1500–1545; cf. K. Hagen, *op. cit.*, III. chap. 5) and especially **Valentine Weigel** (1553–1588; *Libellus de Vita Beata*, 1606, *Der guldne Griff*, 1613, *Vom Ort der Welt*, 1613, *Dialogus de Christianismo*, 1614, Γνῶθι σαυτόν, 1615; cf. J. O. Opel, *V. W.*, Leips. 1864).

The tendency toward **natural philosophy** in attachment to Nic. Cusanus appears more strongly in Charles **Bouillé** (Bovillus, 1470–1553; *De Intellectu* and *De Sensibus; De Sapientia*. Cf. J. Dippel, *Versuch einer system. Darstellung der Philos. des C. B.*, Würzburg, 1862), and **Girolamo Cardano** (1501–1576; *De Vita Propria, De Varietate Rerum, De Subtilitate;* works, Lyons, 1663). Cf. on this and the following, Rixner und Siber, *Leben und Lehrmeinungen berühmter Physiker im 16. und 17. Jahrhundert*, 7 Hefte, Sulzbach, 1819 ff.).

The most brilliant among the Italian natural philosophers is **Giordano Bruno** of Nola, in Campania. Born in 1548, and reared in Naples, he met so much suspicion in the Dominican Order, into which he had entered, that he fled, and from that time on, led an unsettled life. He went by way of Rome and upper Italy to Genoa, Lyons, Toulouse, held lectures in Paris and Oxford, then in Wittenberg and Helmstädt, visited also Marburg, Prague, Frankfort, and Zurich, and finally, in Venice, met the fate of coming into the hands of the Inquisition by treachery. He was delivered to Rome, and there, after imprisonment for several years, was burned, 1600, on account of his steadfast refusal to retract. His Latin works (3 vols., Naples, 1880–91) concern partly the Lullian art (esp. *De Imaginum Signorum et Idearum Compositione*), and in part are didactic poems or metaphysical treatises (*De Monade Numero et Figura; De Triplici Minimo*): the Italian writings (ed. by A. Wagner, Leips. 1829, new ed. by P. de Lagarde, 2 vols., Göttingen, 1888) are partly satirical compositions (*Il Candelajo, La Cena delle Cineri, Spaccio della Bestia Trionfante*, German by Kuhlenbeck, Leips. 1890, *Cabala del Cavallo Pegaseo*), and on the other hand, the most complete expositions of his doctrines: *Dialoghi della Causa Principio ed Uno*, German by Lasson (Berlin, 1872); *Degli Eroici Furori; Dell' Infinito, Universo e Dei Mondi*. Cf. Bartholmèss, *G. B.* (Paris, 1816 f.); Dom. Berti, *Vita di G. B.* (Turin, 1867), and *Documenti Intorno a G. B.* (Turin, 1880); Chr. Sigwart in *Kleine Schriften*, I. (Freiburg, 1889); H. Brunnhofer, *G. B.'s Weltanschauung und Verhängniss* (Leips. 1882). [*G. Bruno*, by I. Frith, Lond., Trübner; T. Whitaker in *Mind*, Vol. IX.].

Another tendency is represented by **Bernardino Telesio** (1508–1588; *De rerum natura juxta propria principia*, Rome, 1565 and Naples, 1586. On him see F. Fiorentino, Florence, 1872 and 1874; L. Ferri, Turin, 1873), and his more important successor, **Tommaso Campanella**. Born 1568, in Stilo of Calabria, he early became a Dominican, was rescued and brought to France after many persecutions and an imprisonment of several years. There he became intimate with the Cartesian circle, and died in Paris. 1639. before the completion of the full edition of his writings, which was to be called *Instauratio Scientiarum.* A new edition, with biographical introduction by d'Ancona has appeared (Turin, 1854). Of his very numerous writings may be mentioned: *Prodromus Philosophiæ Instaurandæ,* 1617 ; *Realis Philosophiæ Partes Quatuor* (with the appendix, *Civitas Solis*), 1623 ; *De Monarchia Hispanica,* 1625 ; *Philosophiæ Rationalis Partes Quinque,* 1638 ; *Universalis Philosophiæ seu metaphysicarum rerum juxta propria principia partes tres,* 1638. Cf. Baldachini, *Vita e Filosofia di T. C.* (Naples, 1840 and 1843) ; Dom. Berti, *Nuovi Documenti di T. C.* (Rome, 1881).

Theosophical-magical doctrines are found with **John Reuchlin** (1455–1522 ; *De Verbo Mirifico, De Arte Cabbalistica*), **Agrippa of Nettesheim** (1487–1535 ; *De Occulta Philosophia ; De Incertitudine et Vanitate Scientiarum*), **Francesco Zorzi** (1460–1540, *De Harmonia Mundi,* Paris, 1549).

A more important and independent thinker is Theophrastus Bombastus **Paracelsus** of Höhenheim (born 1493 at Einsiedeln, he passed an adventurous life, was Professor of Chemistry in Basel, and died in Salzburg, 1541). Among his works (ed. by Huser, Strassburg, 1616–18), the most important are the *Opus Paramirum, Die grosse Wundarznei,* and *De Natura Rerum.* Cf. R. Eucken, *Beiträge zur Gesch. der neueren Philos.,* Heidelberg, 1886. Of his numerous pupils the most important are **Johann Baptist van Helmont** (1577–1644 ; German ed. of his works, 1683), and his son, Franz Mercurius, also **Robert Fludd** (1574–1637, *Philosophia Mosaica,* Guda, 1638), and others.

The most noteworthy deposit of these movements is formed by the doctrine of **Jacob Boehme.** He was born, 1575, near Görlitz, absorbed all kinds of thoughts in his wanderings, and quietly elaborated them. Settled as a shoemaker at Görlitz, he came forward, 1610, with his main treatise *Aurora,* which at a later time after he had been temporarily forced to keep silence, was followed by many others, among them especially *Vierzig Fragen von der Seele* (1620), *Mysterium Magnum* (1623), *Von der Gnadenwahl* (1623). He died 1624. Coll. works ed. by Schiebler, Leips. 1862. Cf. H. A. Fechner, *J. B., sein Leben und seine Schriften,* Görlitz, 1853 ; A. Peip, *J. B. der deutsche Philosoph,* Leips. 1860.

§ 28. The Struggle between the Traditions.

The immediate attachment to the Greek philosophy which became prevalent in the Renaissance, was not entirely without its precedent in the Middle Ages, and men like Bernard of Chartres and William of Conches (cf. p. 302) were prototypes of the union of an increasing interest for knowledge of Nature with the humanistic movement. It is noteworthy, and characteristic of the changing fortune of transmitted doctrines, that now, as then, the union between Humanism and natural philosophy attaches itself to Plato, and stands in opposition to Aristotle.

1. In fact, the revival of ancient literature showed itself at first in the form of a strengthening of *Platonism.* The humanistic movement had been flowing on since the days of Dante, Petrarch, and Boccaccio, and arose from the interest in Roman secular literature which was closely connected with the awakening of the Italian national consciousness; but this current could not become a victorious stream until it received the help of the impulse from without which proceeded from the removal of the Byzantine scholars to Italy. Among these the Aristotelians were of like number and importance with the Platonists, but the latter brought that which was

relatively less known, and therefore more impressive. In addition to this, Aristotle was regarded in the West as the philosopher who was in agreement with the Church doctrine, and thus the opposition, which longed for something new, hoped much more from Plato; and still further there was the æsthetic charm that comes from the writings of the great Athenian, and for which no time was more keenly susceptible than this. Thus Italy first became intoxicated with an enthusiasm for Plato that matched that of departing antiquity. As if to connect itself immediately with this latter period, the Academy was again to live in Florence, and under the protection of the Medicis a rich scientific activity actually developed here, in which a reverence was paid to the leaders like Gemistus Pletho and Bessarion which was not less than that once given to the Scholarchs of *Neo-Platonism.*

But the relationship with this latter system of thought went deeper; the Byzantine tradition, in which the Platonic doctrine was received, was the Neo-Platonic tradition. What at that time was taught in Florence as Platonism was in truth Neo-Platonism. Marsilio *Ficino* translated Plotinus as well as Plato, and his "Platonic Theology" was not much different from that of Proclus. So, too, the fantastic natural philosophy of Patrizzi is in its conceptional basis nothing but the Neo-Platonic system of emanation; but it is significant that in this case the dualistic elements of Neo-Platonism are entirely stripped off, and the monistic tendency brought out more purely and fully. On this account the Neo-Platonist of the Renaissance places in the foreground the *beauty of the universe;* on this account even the deity, the Unomnia (One-all) is for him a sublime world-unity which includes plurality harmoniously within itself; on this account he is able to glorify even the infinity of the universe in a way to fascinate the fancy.

2. The pantheistic tendency, which is so unmistakable in this, was enough to make this Platonism an object of suspicion to the Church, and thus to give its Peripatetic opponents a welcome instrument with which to combat it; and an instrument that was used not only by the scholastic Aristotelians, but also by the others. On the other hand, to be sure, the Platonists could reproach the new humanistic Aristotelianism for its naturalistic tendencies, and praise their own tendency toward the super-sensuous, as allied to Christianity. Thus the two great traditions of Greek philosophy fought their battle over again, while each charged the other with its unchristian character.[1] In this spirit Pletho, in his νόμων συγ-

---

[1] Quite the same relation is repeated in the case of the different groups of Aristotelians, each of which wished to be regarded orthodox, — even at the price

γραφή, conducted his polemic against the Aristotelians, and incurred thereby condemnation from the Patriarch Gennadios in Constantinople; in this spirit George of Trebizond attacked the Academy, and in the same spirit, though milder, Bessarion answered him. Thus the animosity between the two schools, and the literary stir it produced in antiquity, were transferred to the Renaissance, and it was in vain that men like Leonicus Thomæus of Padua (died 1533) admonished the combatants to understand the deeper unity that subsists between the two heroes of philosophy.

3. Meanwhile there was absolutely no unity among the *Aristotelians* themselves. The Grecian interpreters of the Stagirite and their adherents looked down with as much contempt upon the Averroists as upon the Thomists. Both passed for them in like manner as barbarians; they themselves, however, were for the most part prepossessed in favour of that interpretation of the Master which was closely allied to Stratonism, and which was best represented among the commentators by *Alexander of Aphrodisias.* Here, too, one transmitted theory stood in opposition to the others. The conflict was especially severe in Padua, where the *Averroists* saw their fortress threatened by the successful activity of *Pomponatius* as a teacher. The main point of controversy was the problem of immortality. Neither party admitted a full, individual immortality, but Averroism believed that it possessed at least a compensation for this in the unity of the intellect, while the *Alexandrists* attached even the rational part of the soul to its animal conditions, and regarded it as perishable with them. Connected with this were the discussions on theodicy, providence, destiny and freedom of the will, miracles and signs, in which Pomponazzi frequently inclined strongly to the Stoic doctrine.

In the course of time this dependence upon commentators and their oppositions was also stripped off, and the way prepared for a pure, immediate apprehension of Aristotle. This succeeded best with Cæsalpinus, who avowed his complete allegiance to Aristotle. An equally correct understanding of the Peripatetic system was gained by the German Humanists from a philological standpoint, but following Melancthon's precedent they adopted this in their own doctrine only in so far as it agreed with Protestant dogma.

4. In all these cases the adoption of Greek philosophy led to an opposition to Scholasticism as regards the real content or matter of

---

of the "twofold truth." In this the Averroists, especially, were ready, and so it came about that one of them, Nifo, had himself entrusted by the Pope with the refutation of Pomponazzi's doctrine of immortality. The latter, indeed, also covered himself with the same shield.

the opposing systems. Another line of Humanism, which was more in sympathy with Roman literature, inclined to a predominantly *formal* opposition, of which John of Salisbury may be regarded as a mediæval forerunner. The taste of the Humanists rebelled against the barbarous outward form of mediæval literature. Accustomed to the polished refinement and transparent clearness of the ancient writers, they were not able to value rightly the kernel so full of character, which lay within the rough shell of the scholastic terminology. The minds of the Renaissance, with their essentially æsthetic disposition, had no longer any feeling for the abstract nature of that science of abstract conceptions. Thus they opened the battle in all directions, with the weapons of jest and of earnest; *instead of conceptions they demanded things;* instead of artificially constructed words, the language of the cultivated world; instead of subtle proofs and distinctions, a tasteful exposition that should speak to the imagination and heart of the living man.

Laurentius Valla was the first to make this cry resound. *Agricola* took it up in lively controversy, and Erasmus also joined in. The models of these men were Cicero and Quintilian, and when at their hand the method of philosophy was to be changed, the scholastic dialectic was dislodged and in its place were introduced the principles of rhetoric and grammar. The true dialectic is the science of discourse.[1] The "Aristotelian" logic therefore becomes the object of most violent polemic; the doctrine of the syllogism is to be simplified and driven from its commanding situation. The syllogism is incapable of yielding anything new; it is an unfruitful form of thought. This was later emphasised by Bruno, Bacon, and Descartes, as strongly as by these Humanists.

But the more closely the dominance of the syllogism was connected with dialectical "Realism," the more nominalistic and terministic motives connected themselves with the humanistic opposition. This shows itself in the cases of *Vives* and *Nizolius.* They are zealous against the reign of universal conceptions; in this, according to Vives, lies the true reason for the mediæval corruption of the sciences. Universals, Nizolius teaches,[2] are collective names which arise by "comprehension," not by abstraction; individual things with their qualities constitute reality. It concerns us to apprehend these, and the secondary activity of the understanding which compares, is to be carried out as simply and unartificially as possible. Hence all metaphysical assumptions, which have made so great a

---

[1] Petr. Ramus, *Dialect. Instit.*, at the beginning.
[2] Mar. Nizolius, *De Ver. Princ.*, I. 4–7; III. 7.

difficulty in previous dialectic, must be banished from logic. Empiricism can use only a *purely formal logic.*

The "natural" dialectic, however, was sought in rhetoric and grammar, for, *Ramus* held, it should teach us only to follow in our voluntary thinking the same laws which, according to the nature of reason, control also our involuntary thinking, and present themselves spontaneously in the correct expression of this involuntary process of thought. In all reflection, however, the essential thing is to discover the point of view that is determinative for the question, and then to apply this correctly to the subject. Accordingly Ramus, following a remark of Vives,[1] divides his new dialectic into the doctrines of *Inventio* and *Judicium.* The first part is a kind of general logic, which yet cannot avoid introducing again in the form of the "*loci*" the categories, such as Causality, Inherence, Genus, etc., and thus, enumerating them without system, falls into the naïve metaphysics of the ordinary idea of the world. The doctrine of *judgment* is developed by Ramus in three stages. The first is the simple decision of the question by subsuming the object under the discovered point of view ; here the doctrine of the syllogism has its place, which is accordingly much smaller than formerly. In the second place the judgment is to unite cognitions that belong together to a systematic whole, by definition and division ; its highest task, however, it fulfils only when it brings all knowledge into relation to God, and finds it grounded in him. Thus natural dialectic culminates in theosophy.[2]

Slight as was the depth and real originality of this rhetorical system, it yet excited great respect in a time that was eager for the new. In Germany, especially, Ramists and anti-Ramists engaged in vehement controversy. Among the friends of the system, *Johannes Sturm* is especially worthy of note, a typical pedagogue of Humanism, who set the task for education of bringing the scholar to the point where he knows things, and how to judge concerning them from a correct point of view, and to speak in cultivated manner.

5. A characteristic feature of this movement is its cool relation toward metaphysics; this very fact proves its derivation from the Roman popular philosophy. Cicero, to whom it especially attached itself, was particularly influential by virtue of his Academic Scepticism or Probabilism. Surfeit of abstract discussions alienated a considerable part of the Humanists from the great systems of

---

[1] Lud. Vives, *De Causis Corr. Art.* (first part of *De Disciplinis*), III. 5.
[2] Cf. E. Laas, *Die Pädagogik des J. St. kritisch und historisch beleuchtet* (Berlin, 1872).

antiquity also. The extension of religious unbelief or indifferent ism was an additional motive to make *scepticism* appear in many circles as the right temper for the cultivated man. The charm of outer life, the glitter of refined civilisation, did the rest to bring about indifference toward philosophical subtleties.

This scepticism of the man of the world was brought to its complete expression by *Montaigne*. With the easy grace and fineness of expression of a great writer, he thus gave French literature a fundamental tone which has remained its essential character. But this movement also runs in the ancient track. Whatever of philosophical thought is found in the "Essays" arises from Pyrrhonism. Hereby a thread of tradition which had for a long time been let fall is again taken up. The relativity of theoretical opinions and ethical theories, the illusions of the senses, the cleft between subject and object, the constant change in which both are involved, the dependence of all the work of the intellect upon such doubtful data,—all these arguments of ancient Scepticism meet us here, not in systematic form, but incidentally in connection with the discussion of individual questions, and thus in a much more impressive manner.

Pyrrhonism was at the same time revived in a much more scholastic form by *Sanchez*, and yet in a lively manner, and not without hope that a sure insight might yet at some time be allowed to man. He concludes individual chapters, and the whole work, with "*Nescis? At ego nescio. Quid?*" To this great "Quid?" he has indeed given no answer, and guidance to a true knowledge was a debt that he did not discharge. But he left no doubt as to the direction in which he sought it. It was the same which Montaigne also pointed out: science must free itself from the word-lumber of the wisdom of the schools, and put its questions directly to things themselves. Thus Sanchez demands a new knowledge, and has, indeed, a dim foreboding of it, but where and how it is to be sought he is not prepared to say. In many passages it seems as though he would proceed to empirical investigation of Nature, but just here he cannot get beyond the sceptical doctrine of outer perception, and if he recognises the greater certainty of inner experience, this inner experience in turn loses its value because of its indefiniteness.

Charron comes forward with firmer step, since he keeps before him the practical end of wisdom. Like his two predecessors he doubts the possibility of certain theoretical knowledge; in this respect all three set up the authority of the Church and of faith: a metaphysics can be revealed only; the human power of knowledge is not sufficient for it. But, proceeds Charron, the human knowing faculty is all the more sufficient for that *self-knowledge* which is requisite for the moral life. To this self-knowledge belongs, above all, the humility of the sceptic who has no confidence that he knows anything truly, and in this humility is rooted the freedom of spirit with which he everywhere withholds his theoretical judgment. On the other hand, the ethical command of righteousness and of the fulfilment of duty is known without a doubt in this self-knowledge.

This diversion toward the practical realm, as might be expected from the general tendency of the time, was not permanent. The later Sceptics turned the theoretical side of the Pyrrhonic tradition again to the front, and the effect which resulted from this tendency for the general tone of the time applied ultimately, for the most part, to the certainty of dogmatic convictions.

6. The *Church doctrine* could no longer master these masses of thought which now made their way so powerfully into the life of this period, as it had succeeded in doing with the Arabian-Aristotelian invasion: this new world of ideas was too manifold and too full of antitheses, and, on the other hand, the assimilative power of the Church dogma was too far exhausted. The Roman Church limited itself, therefore, to defending its spiritual and external power with all the means at its disposal, and was only concerned to fortify its own tradition and make it as sure as possible within itself. In this changed form the Jesuits now performed the same task that in the thirteenth century had fallen to the mendicant orders. With their help the definitive and complete form of Church dogma was fixed against all innovations at the Council of Trent (1563), and *Thomism* declared to be authoritative in essentials for philosophical doctrine. Thereafter there could be no more any question as to changes of principle, but only as to more skilful presentations and occasional insertions. In this way the Church excluded itself from the fresh movement of the time, and the philosophy dependent upon it fell into unavoidable stagnation for the next following centuries. Even the short after-bloom which Scholasticism experienced about 1600 in the universities of the Iberian peninsula bore no real fruit. *Suarez* was an important writer, clear, acute, accurate, and with a great capacity for a luminous disposition of his thoughts; he surpasses also, to a considerable degree, most of the older Scholastics in the form of his expression; but in the content of his doctrine he is bound by tradition, and a like constraint will be understood as a matter of course in the case of the collective work of the Jesuits of Coimbra.

Over against this form of religious tradition, another now made its appearance in the *Protestant churches.* Here, too, the opposition claimed the older tradition, and put aside its mediæval modifications and developments. The Reformation desired to renew original Christianity as against Catholicism. It drew the circle of the canonical books narrower again; putting aside the Vulgate, it recognised only the Greek text as authoritative; it returned to the Nicene creed. The controversy over dogmas in the sixteenth century — theoretically considered — hinges upon the question, which tradition of Christianity shall be the binding one.

But the theological antithesis drew the philosophical antithesis after it, and here again a relation was repeated which had appeared at many points during the Middle Ages. In the doctrine of *Augustine,* the religious need found a deeper, richer satisfaction, and a more immediate expression than in the conceptions worked out by the Scholastics. Earnestness in the consciousness of sin, passionate longing for redemption, faith that was internal in its source and its nature, — all these were traits of Augustine's nature which repeated themselves in *Luther* and *Calvin.* But it is only in the doctrine of Calvin that the permanent influence of the great Church Father is shown; and yet just by this means an *antagonism between Thomism and Augustinianism* was once more created, which evinced itself as especially important in the French literature of the seventeenth century (cf. § 30 f.). For the Catholics under the guidance of Jesuitism, Thomas was the ruling authority; for the Reformed Churches, and for the freer tendencies in Catholicism itself, Augustine held the same position.

German Protestantism followed other courses. In the development of the Lutheran dogma, Luther's genius was aided by the cooperation of *Melancthon* and thus of *Humanism.* Little as the theoretico-æsthetical and religiously indifferent nature of the Humanists[1] might accord with the mighty power of Luther's soul with its profound faith, he was, nevertheless, obliged, when he would give his work scientific form, to accommodate himself to the necessity of borrowing from philosophy the conceptions with which to lay his foundations. Here, however, Melancthon's harmonising nature came in, and while Luther had passionately rejected scholastic Aristotelianism, his learned associate introduced *humanistic Aristotelianism* as the *philosophy of Protestantism,* here, too, opposing the older tradition to the remodelled tradition. This original Aristotelianism had to be corrected in many passages, to be sure, by

---

[1] On the relation of the Reformation and Humanism cf. Th. Ziegler, *Gesch. der Ethik*, II. 414 ff.

means of the Scriptures, and the combination of doctrines could not reach such an organic union as had been attained by the slow ripening of Thomism in the Middle Ages; but the Peripatetic system was in this instance treated rather as but a supplement to theology in the department of profane science, and for this end, Melancthon knew how to sift, arrange, and set forth the material in his text-books with so great skill that it became the basis for a doctrine which was in the main one in its nature, and as such was taught at the Protestant universities for two centuries.

7. But in Protestantism there were still other traditional forces active. Luther's work of liberation owed its origin and its success not least to *Mysticism,* — not indeed to that sublime, spiritualised form of viewing the world to which the genius of Master Eckhart had given expression, but to the movement of deepest piety which, as " practical Mysticism," had spread from the Rhine in the "League of the Friends of God," and in the "Brothers of the Common Life." For this Mysticism, the disposition, purity of heart, and the imitation of Christ were the sole content of religion; assent to dogmas, the external works of holiness, the whole worldly organisation of Church life, appeared to be matters of indifference and even hindrances: the believing soul demands only the freedom of its own religious life, — a demand that transcends all these outward works. This was the inner source of the Reformation. Luther himself had not only searched Augustine, he had also edited the *"German Theology"*: and his word let loose the storm of this religious longing, with which, in the conflict against Rome, an impulse of national independence was also mingled.

But when the Protestant State Church became again consolidated in the fixed forms of a theoretical system of doctrine, and clung to this the more anxiously in proportion as it was obliged to struggle for its existence in the strife of Confessions, then the supra-confessional impulse of Mysticism became undeceived, as did also the national consciousness. The theological fixation of the thought of the Reformation appeared as its ruin, and as Luther had once waged his warfare against the "sophistry" of the Scholastics, so now a movement of Mysticism that was quietly stirring farther and wider among the people, directed itself against his own creation. In men like *Osiander* and *Schwenckfeld* he had to contend against parts of his own nature and its development. But in this movement it became evident that the doctrines of mediæval Mysticism had been quietly maintained and continued in legendary form amid all kinds of fantastic ideas and obscure imagery. The Mysticism which comes to light in the teachings of men like *Sebastian Franck,* or in the secretly circulated tracts of *Valentine Weigel,* has its support in the idealism of Eckhart, which transformed all the outer into the inner, all the historical into the eternal, and saw in the process of Nature and history but the symbol of the spiritual and divine. This constituted, though frequently in strange form, the deeper ground of the battle which the Mystics of the sixteenth century waged in Germany against the "letter" of theology.

8. Look where we will in the intellectual movement of the fifteenth and sixteenth centuries, we see everywhere tradition arrayed against tradition, and every controversy is a battle between transmitted doctrines. The spirit of the Western peoples has now taken up into itself the entire material which the past offers for its culture, and in the feverish excitement into which it is finally put by direct contact with the highest achievements of ancient science, it struggles upward to the attainment of complete independence. It feels sufficiently hardened to execute work of its own, and overflowing with its wealth of thought, it seeks new tasks. One feels the impulsive blood of youth pulsate in its literature, as though something unheard of, something which had never before been, must now come into being. The men of the Renaissance announce to us nothing less than the approach of a total renovation of science and of the state of humanity. The warfare between the transmitted doctrines leads to a surfeit of the past; learned research into the old wisdom ends with throwing aside all book-rubbish, and full of the youthful joy of dawning, growing life, the mind goes forth into the cosmic life of Nature ever young.

The classical portrayal of this temper of the Renaissance is the first monologue in Goethe's *Faust.*

§ 29. Macrocosm and Microcosm.

By Scotism and Terminism the faith-metaphysics of the Middle Ages had become disintegrated and split in twain: everything supersensuous had been given to dogma, and as the object of philosophy there remained the world of experience. But before thought had as yet had time to become clear as to the methods and special problems of this secular knowledge, Humanism, and with it above all, the Platonic *Weltanschauung,* burst in. No wonder that the solution of the problem, which was itself at first seen but dimly, was first sought in connection with this theory: and this doctrine must have been the more welcome, especially in its Neo-Platonic form, as it showed the world of the supersensuous presageful in the background, but made the particulars of the world of sense stand out distinctly in purposefully defined outlines. The supersensuous itself, and all therein that was connected with man's religious life, might be cheerfully set off to theology; philosophy could dedicate itself to the task of being natural science, with all the calmer conscience in proportion as it followed the Neo-Platonic precedent of apprehending Nature as a product of spirit, and thus believed that in the conception of the deity it retained a point of unity for the diverging branches of science, the spiritual and the secular. Did theology teach how God reveals himself in the *Scripture*, it was now the business of philosophy to apprehend with admiration his revelation in *Nature*. On this account the beginnings of modern natural science were *theosophical* and thoroughly *Neo-Platonic*.

1. The characteristic fact, however, is that in this revival of Neo-Platonism, the last dualistic motives which had belonged to the same were also completely set aside. They disappeared together with the specifically religious interest which had supported them, and the theoretical element of recognising in Nature the creative divine power came forward pure and unmixed.[1] The fundamental tendency in the natural philosophy of the Renaissance was therefore the fanciful or imaginative conception of the *divine unity of the living All*, the admiration of the *macrocosm*: the fundamental thought of Plotinus of the *beauty of the universe* has been taken up by no other time so sympathetically as by this; and this beauty was now also regarded as a manifestation of the divine Idea. Such a view is expressed in almost entirely Neo-Platonic forms by Patrizzi, in a more original form and with strongly poetical quality by Giordano *Bruno*, and likewise by Jacob *Boehme*. With Bruno the symbol of the all-forming and all-animating primitive light is still dominant (cf. p. 245); with Boehme, on the contrary, we find that of the organism; the world is a tree which from root to flower and fruit is permeated by one life-giving sap, and which is formed and ordered from within outward by its own germinal activity.[2]

In this inheres naturally the inclination to complete monism and *pantheism*. Everything must have its cause, and the last cause can be but one, — God.[3] He is, according to Bruno, at the same time the formal, the efficient, and the final cause; according to Boehme he is at once the rational ground and efficient cause ("*Urgrund*" and "*Ursache*") of the world (*principium* and *causa* with Bruno).

---

[1] In a certain sense this might also be expressed by saying that thereby the Stoic elements of Neo-Platonism came with controlling force into the foreground.

[2] Cf. the remarkable agreement between Bruno, *Della Causa Pr. e. U.*, II. (Lag. I. 231 f.) and Boehme, *Aurora*, Vorrede.

[3] *Aurora*, Chap. III.

Hence the universe is also nothing but "the essential nature of God himself made creatural."[1] And yet the idea of the transcendence of God is here, too, connected with this view, as it had been in Neo-Platonism. Boehme holds that God should be thought not as a force devoid of reason and "science," but as the "all-knowing, all-seeing, all-hearing, all-smelling, all-tasting" spirit: and Bruno adds another analogy; for him God is the artist who works unceasingly and shapes out his inner nature to rich life.

Harmony is accordingly, for Bruno also, the inmost nature of the world, and he who can apprehend it with the gaze of enthusiasm (as does the philosopher in the dialogues and poetic inventions *Degli Eroici Furori*), for him the apparent defects and imperfections of detail vanish in the beauty of the whole. He needs no special theodicy; the world is perfect because it is the life of God, even down to every detail, and he only complains who cannot raise himself to a view of the whole. The world-joy of the æsthetic Renaissance sings philosophical dithyrambs in Bruno's writings. A *universalistic optimism* that carries everything before it prevails in his poetic thought.

2. The conceptions which lie at the basis of this unfolding of the metaphysical fantasy in Bruno had their source in the main in *Nicolaus Cusanus*, whose teachings had been preserved by Charles Bouillé, though in his exposition they had to some degree lost their vivid freshness. Just this the Nolan knew how to restore. He not only raised the principle of the *coincidentia oppositorum* to the artistic reconciliation of contrasts, to the harmonious total action of opposing partial forces in the divine primitive essence, but above all he gave to the conceptions of the *infinite and the finite* a far wider reaching significance. As regards the deity and its relation to the world, the Neo-Platonic relations are essentially retained. God himself, as the unity exalted above all opposites, cannot be apprehended through any finite attribute or qualification, and therefore is unknowable in his own proper essence (negative theology); but at the same time he is still thought as the inexhaustible, *infinite* world-force, as the *natura naturans,* which in eternal change forms and "unfolds" itself purposefully and in conformity with law, into the *natura naturata.* This identification of the essence of God and the world is a general doctrine of the natural philosophy of the Renaissance; it is found likewise in Paracelsus, in Sebastian Franck, in Boehme, and finally also with the whole body of the "Platonists." That it could also assume an extremely naturalistic form, and could

---

[1] *Aurora*, Chap. II.

lead to the denial of all transcendence, is proved by the agitative and boastfully polemical doctrine of Vanini.[1]

For the *natura naturata,* on the other hand, for the "universe" — the sum-total of creatures — the characteristic of true "infinity" is not claimed, but rather that of *unlimitedness* in space and time. This conception gained an incomparably clearer form and more fixed significance by the *Copernican theory.* The spherical form of the earth and its revolution about its axis had been a familiar idea to Cusanus as well as to the old Pythagoreans, perhaps, indeed, through them; but only the victoriously proved hypothesis of the motion of the earth about the sun could furnish a rational basis for the completely new view of *man's position in the universe,* which is peculiar to modern science. The anthropocentric idea of the world which had ruled the Middle Ages became out of joint. Man, as well as the earth, must cease to be regarded as centre of the universe and centre of the world. Men like Patrizzi and Boehme also raised themselves above such "restriction" on the basis of the teaching of Copernicus, which for that reason was condemned by the dogmatic authorities of all confessions; but the fame of having thought out the Copernican system to its end, both in natural philosophy and in metaphysics, belongs to *Giordano Bruno.*

He developed from this system the theory that the universe forms a system of countless worlds, each of which moves about its central sun, leads its own proper life, grows from chaotic conditions to clear and definite formation, and again yields to the destiny of dissolution. The tradition of Democritus and Epicurus had perhaps a share in the formation of this conception of a plurality of worlds arising and perishing again; but it is the peculiar feature of Bruno's doctrine, that he regarded the plurality of solar systems not as a mechanical juxtaposition, but as an organic living whole, and regarded the process of the growth and decay of worlds as maintained by the pulse-beat of the one divine All-life.

3. While in this way universalism, with its bold flight into spatial and temporal boundlessness, threatened to claim the fantasy entirely for its own, there was an effective counterpoise in the Peripatetic-Stoic doctrine of the *analogy between macrocosm and microcosm,* which found in man's nature the sum, the "quintessence" of the cosmical powers. We see this doctrine reviving in the most varied

---

[1] Lucilio *Vanini* (born 1585 at Naples, burned 1619 at Toulouse), a dissolute adventurer, wrote *Amphitheatrum Æternæ Providentiæ* (Lyons, 1615) and *De admirandis naturæ reginæ deæque mortalium arcanis* (Paris, 1616).

[2] Nicolaus Copernicus, *De Revolutionibus Orbium Cœlestium* (Nuremberg, 1543).

forms during the Renaissance ; it controls entirely the theory of
knowledge at this period, and moreover the Neo-Platonic triple
division is almost universally authoritative in connection with it,
furnishing a scheme for a *metaphysical anthropology.* One can know
only what one himself is, is the mode in which this was expressed
by *Valentine Weigel :* man knows the all in so far as he is the all.
This was a pervading principle of Eckhart's Mysticism. But this
idealism now took on a definite form. As body, man belongs to the
material world ; indeed, he unites within himself, as *Paracelsus,* and
following him *Weigel* and *Boehme* teach, the essence of all material
things in finest and most compact form. Just on this account he is
competent to understand the corporeal world. As intellectual being,
however, he is of " sidereal " origin, and is therefore able to know
the intellectual world in all its forms. Finally, as a divine " spark,"
as *spiraculum vitæ,* as a partial manifestation of the highest principle of life, he is also able to become conscious of the divine nature
whose image he is.

A more abstract application of this same principle, according to
which all knowledge of the world is rooted in *man's knowledge of
himself,* is found in the thought of *Campanella,* involving not the
Neo-Platonic separation of world-strata (although this too is present
in Campanella), but the fundamental categories of all reality. Man
— is the thought here too — knows in the proper sense only himself,
and knows all else only from and through himself. All knowledge
is perception (*sentire*), but we perceive, not the things, but only
the states into which these set us. In this process, however, we
learn by experience that inasmuch as we are, we can do something,
we know something and will something, and further, that we find
ourselves limited by corresponding functions of other beings. From
this it follows that power, knowledge, and will are the " primalities " of all reality, and that if they belong to God in an unlimited
degree, he is known as all-powerful, all-knowing, and all-good.

4. The doctrine that all knowledge of God and of the world is
ultimately locked up in man's knowledge of himself, is nevertheless
only an epistemological inference from the more general metaphysical principle according to which the divine nature was held to be
fully and entirely contained in each of its finite manifestations.
Giordano Bruno follows the Cusan also in holding that God is the
smallest as well as the greatest, as truly the vital principle of the
individual being as that of the universe. And accordingly every
individual thing, and not merely man, becomes a " mirror " of the
world-substance. Each without exception is according to its essential nature the deity itself, but each in its own way, which it

different from all the rest. This thought Bruno incorporated in his conception of the *monad*. He understood by this the individual substance (*Einzelwesen*), which, as continually "formed" matter, constitutes one of the partial manifestations of the world-force, in the interaction of which the world-life consists. It is living from the beginning, and is imperishable; it is corporeal as well as spiritual in its nature. Each monad is a form in which the Divine Being finds individual existence, a finite existence-form of the infinite essence. Since, now, there is nothing but God and the monads, the universe is *animated* even to the smallest nook and corner, and the infinite all-life individualises itself at every point to a special and peculiar nature. It results from this that each thing, in the movements of its life, follows in part the law of its special nature, and in part a more general law, just as a planet or heavenly body moves at the same time on its own axis and about its sun. Campanella, who took up this doctrine also in connection with the Copernican system, designated this striving toward the whole, this tendency toward the original source of all reality, as religion, and spoke in this sense of a "natural" religion, that is of religion as "natural impulse,"—one would now perhaps say centripetal impulse,—which he with logical consistency ascribed to all things in general, and which in man was held to assume the special form of "rational" religion; that is, of the striving to become one with God by love and knowledge.

This principle of the infinite variability of the divine ground of the world which presents itself in a special form in every particular thing, is found in a similar form also with Paracelsus. Here, as with Nicolaus Cusanus, it is taught that all substances are present in everything, that each thing therefore presents a microcosm, and yet that each has also its special principle of life and activity. This special mind or spirit of the individual is called by Paracelsus the Archeus; Jacob Boehme, to whom this doctrine passed over, calls it the Primus.

With Bruno the conception of the monad connects itself in a very interesting manner, though without further effect upon his physical views, with that of the *atom*, which was brought to him, as to the earlier period, by the Epicurean tradition through Lucretius. The "smallest"—in metaphysics the monad, in mathematics the point —is in physics the atom, the indivisible spherical element of the corporeal world. Memories of the Pythagorean and Platonic theory of the elements, and of the related atomic theory of Democritus, became thus alive in the midst of Neo-Platonism; they found also an independent revival with men like Basso, Sennert, and others, and so led to the so-called *corpuscular theory*, according to which the corporeal world consists of inseparable atom-complexes, the corpuscles. In the atoms themselves, the theory assumed in connection with their mathematical form an original and unchangeable law of action, to which, it held, the mode of action of the corpuscles is also to be traced.[1]

5. Here the workings of *mathematics* assert themselves in the old Pythagorean form, or as modified by Democritus and Plato. The ultimate constituents of physical reality are determined by their geometrical form, and the qualitative determinations of experience must be traced back to this. The combination of elements presupposes numbers and their order as the principle of multiplicity.[2] Thus spatial forms and number-relations again make their appearance as the essential and original in the physical world, and thereby the Aristotelian-Stoic doctrine of the qualitatively determined forces, of the inner Forms of things, of the *qualitates occultæ*, was displaced. As this latter doctrine had formerly gained the victory over the principle of Pythagoras, Democritus, and Plato, so it must in turn yield to this: and herein lies one of the most important preparations for the origin of modern natural science.

The beginnings of this are found already with Nicolaus Cusanus; but now they receive an essential strengthening from the same source from which their presence in his thought is explained: namely, from the old literature, and in particular from the Neo-Pythagorean writings. Just for this reason, however, they still have the fantastic metaphysical garb of *number-mysticism* and *number-symbolism*. The book of Nature is written in numbers; the harmony of things is that of the number-system. All is arranged by God according to measure and number; all life is an unfolding of mathematical relations. But just as in antiquity, so here, this thought is unfolded at first as an arbitrary interpretation of conceptions, and a mysterious speculation. The procedure of the world forth from God, from the construction of the Trinity on, — as, for example, in the attempt of Bouillé, — is again to be conceived as the process of the transformation of unity into the number-system. Such fantasies were followed by men like Cardan and Pico. Reuchlin added further the mythological creations of the Jewish Cabbala.

6. Thus the principle which was destined for the most fruitful development made its entrance into the new world wrapped again in the old metaphysical fantasticalness, and fresh forces were

---

[1] Cf. K. Lasswitz, *Geschichte des Atomismus*, I. pp. 359 ff. (Hamburg and Leips. 1890).

[2] Cf. for this especially G. Bruno, *De Triplici Minimo*.

needed to strip off this covering, and free it for its right working. Meanwhile, however, it became mingled with quite other efforts, which likewise had their origin in the Neo-Platonic tradition. To the idea of a universal psychical life, to the fanciful spiritualisation of Nature, belonged also the impulse to interfere in the course of things with mysterious means, with conjurations and magic arts, and so to guide it according to the will of man. Here, too, a higher thought hovered before the fantastic impulse of the excited age, — the thought of mastering Nature by a knowledge of the forces working in it. But this thought was also received in the wrappings of ancient superstition. If, as was the case with the Neo-Platonists, the life of Nature was regarded as a dominance of spirits, as a mysteriously connected system of internal forces, it was a proper aim to make these subject by knowledge and will. Thus *magic* became a favourite subject of thought in the Renaissance, and science again concerned itself with the task of bringing system into superstition.

Astrology, with its influences of the stars upon human life, the interpretation of dreams and signs, necromancy, with its conjurations of spirits, the predictions of persons in the ecstatic state, — all these elements of the Stoic and Neo-Platonic divination were then in most luxuriant bloom. Pico and Reuchlin brought them into connection with the number-mysticism; Agrippa of Nettesheim adopted all the sceptical attacks against the possibility of rational science, in order to seek help in mystical illuminations and secret magic arts. Cardan proceeded with all seriousness to the task of determining the laws of these operations, and Campanella conceded them an unusually wide space in his idea of the world.

Physicians especially, whose vocation demanded an interference in the course of Nature and might seem permitted to expect special advantage in secret arts, showed an inclination toward these magic arts. From this point of view *Paracelsus* desired to reform medicine. He also proceeds from the sympathy of all things, from the idea of the universe as a spiritually connected system. He finds the essence of disease in the injuring of the individual vital principle, the Archeus, by foreign powers, and seeks the means wherewith to free and strengthen the Archeus. Since this latter process must come about by a corresponding composition of materials, all sorts of magical drinks, tinctures, and other secret remedies must be brewed, and thus the arts of *alchemy* were set in motion, which, in spite of all its fantastic performances, ultimately yielded a number of useful results for chemical knowledge in the course of its incredibly extended pursuits.

In this connection the fundamental metaphysical presupposition of the unity of all vital force led of itself to the thought that there must be also a simple, most efficacious, universal remedy for the strengthening of every Archeus whatever, a panacea against all diseases and for the maintenance of all the vital forces; and connection with the macrocosmic efforts of magic nourished the hope that the possession of this secret would lend the highest magic power, and afford the most desirable treasures. All this was to be achieved by the "philosopher's stone"; it was to heal all diseases, transmute all substances into gold, conjure all spirits into the power of its possessor. And thus the purposes which it was thought would be satisfied in the ventures of alchemy, were ultimately very real and sober.

7. The introduction of this magical view of Nature into the subtle religious system of German Mysticism constitutes the peculiar feature of *Boehme's* philosophy. He, too, is seized by the thought that philosophy should be knowledge of Nature; but the deep earnestness of the religious need which lay at the basis of the German Reformation did not allow him to content himself with the separation of religious metaphysics and natural science, customary at his time, and he sought to work the two into one again. Similar efforts which tended to transcend the dogmatic, fixed form of Protestantism, and hoped to solve the problems of the new science with the aid of a Christian metaphysics, throve also by the side of the official Peripatetic system. *Taurellus* aimed to produce such a supra-confessional philosophy of Christianity, and with a true instinct for his purpose, adopted many elements of the Augustinian doctrine of the will, but was not able to work enough real material from the interests of his time into these thoughts, and so came ultimately rather to a complete separation of empirical research from all metaphysics. A similar process went on in the mystical movement, which grew with the popular opposition against the new orthodoxy all the more in proportion as the latter dried and hardened within itself. The mystical doctrines also remained suspended in vague generality until the teaching of Paracelsus was brought to them, at first by Weigel, and then completely by Boehme.

In Boehme's doctrine Neo-Platonism assumes again a completely religious colouring. Here, too, man is regarded as the microcosm from and by which the bodily, the "sidereal," and the divine worlds can be known, if one follows the right illumination and is not misled by learned theories. Self-knowledge, nevertheless, is religious knowledge, which finds the opposition of good and evil as a fundamental trait of human nature. The same opposition fills the whole world; it rules in heaven as on earth, and since God is the sole cause of all, this opposition must be sought in him also. Boehme extends the *coincidentia oppositorum* to the extreme limit, and finds the ground of duality in the necessity of the self-revelation of the divine Primordial Ground. As light can be revealed only in connection with darkness, so God's goodness can be revealed only in connection with his anger. Thus Boehme portrays the process of the *eternal self-generation of God*, describing how from the dark ground of Being within him the urgent impulse (*" Drang "*), or will, which has only itself for its object, attains self-revelation in the divine wisdom, and how that which has thus become revealed forms itself into the world. While the theogonic development thus passes over immediately into the cosmogonic, the effort is everywhere shown in this latter development to carry the fundamental religious antithesis into the physical categories of the system of Paracelsus. Thus three kingdoms of the world and seven forms, or *"qualia"* (*" Qualen "*), are constructed, which ascend from the material forces of attraction and repulsion to those of light and warmth, and from there on to those of the sensible and intellectual functions. To this portrayal of the eternal nature of things is then attached the history of the earthly world, which begins with the fall of Lucifer and the process of rendering the spiritual essence perceptible to the senses, and ends with the overcoming of the proud infatuation (*" Vergafftsein "*) for the creature, with the mystical devotion of man to the deity, and ultimately with the restoration of the spiritual nature. All this is presented by Boehme in prophetic discourse, full of deep conviction, with a unique mingling of profundity and dilettantism. It is the attempt of the Eckhartian Mysticism to become master of the modern interests of science, and the first still tentatively uncertain step toward raising natural science into an idealistic metaphysics. But because this is made from the standpoint of the deepest religious life, the intellectualistic features of the older Mysticism retreat, with Boehme, more into the background. While with Eckhart, the world-process both in its arising and in its passing was regarded as a knowing process, with Boehme it is rather a struggling of the will between good and evil.

8. In all these ways the result of the separation of philosophy from dogmatic theology always was that the knowledge of Nature that was sought took on the form of the older metaphysics. This procedure was inevitable so long as the desire for a knowledge of Nature could provide neither a material of facts which it had itself acquired, nor new conceptions to serve as forms for the elaboration of this material. As a prerequisite for this, it was necessary to see the inadequacy of metaphysical theories, and putting them aside,

to turn to *empiricism*. This service was rendered to the genesis of modern thought by the tendencies of *Nominalism* and *Terminism*, in part, also, by the rhetorical and grammatical opposition to the science of the schools, and also by the revival of ancient *Scepticism*.

The writings of Ludovico *Vives* must be regarded as a common starting-point for these various efforts; but they prove also that the importance of these endeavours is essentially negative in character. In place of the obscure words and arbitrary conceptions of metaphysics, a demand is made in nominalistic fashion for the immediate, intuitive apprehension of things themselves by experience: but the remarks as to the manner in which this should be scientifically set about are meagre and uncertain; he speaks of experiment, but without any very deep insight into its nature. Quite so lies the case at a later time with Sanchez. And if the artificial subtleties of the syllogistic method were attacked with great hue and cry, this line of thought had ultimately only the Ramistic fancies of "natural logic" to put in their stead.

Further, this empiricism, just by virtue of its origin from Terminism, could move only with a very uncertain step in the presence of external Nature. It could not deny the background of Occam's dualism. Sense-perception was held to be, not a copy of a thing, but an inner state of the subject corresponding to the presence of the thing. These scruples could be only strengthened by the theories of ancient Scepticism, for this added the doctrine of the deceptions of the senses and the consideration of the relativity and change of all perceptions. Hence this empiricism of the Humanists now also threw itself more upon inner perception, which was universally regarded as much surer than outer perception. Vives is most fortunate where he speaks the language of empirical psychology; men like Nizolius, Montaigne, and Sanchez shared this view, and Charron gave it practical significance. Strenuously as all these urge toward looking at things themselves, outer perception ultimately turns out comparatively empty.

How little certain of itself, and how little fruitful in principles this empiricism was at that time, is shown best of all by its two main representatives in Italy, — *Telesio* and Campanella. The former, one of the most stirring and influential opponents of Aristotelianism, is everywhere famous even in his own time (and also with Bruno and Bacon), as he who demanded most strongly that science should build only on the basis of facts perceived by the senses. He founded in Naples an academy which he called the Academia *Cosentina*, after the name of his home, and, in fact, contributed much toward the cultivation of the sense for empirical natural science.

But if we look to see how he treats Nature *"juxta propria principia,"* we are met by genuinely physical theories which from few observations hastily leap over to most general metaphysical principles quite after the fashion of the ancient Ionics.   The dry-warm and the moist-cold are set forth as the two opposing fundamental forces, out of whose conflict both the macrocosmic and the microcosmic life are to be explained.   This same inner contradiction appears almost more prominent still in *Campanella.*   He teaches the most pronounced sensualism.   All knowledge is for him a "feeling" (*sentire*) ;   even recollection, judgment, and inference are for him but modified forms of that feeling.   But in his case also, sensualism tilts over into psychological idealism ; he is far too good a Nominalist not to know that all perception is but a feeling of the states of the percipient himself.   Thus he takes his starting-point in inner experience, and following the principle of the analogy of macrocosmus and microcosmus, builds upon a simple *aperçu* (cf. above) an extended ontology.   Into this he then draws also the quite scholastic antithesis of Being and Non-being (*ens* and *non-ens*), which, following the Neo-Platonic example, is identified with that of the perfect and imperfect, and between the two he spreads the variegated metaphysical picture of a world-system arranged in successive strata.

So tenaciously do the long-wonted habits of metaphysical thought cling everywhere to the beginnings of the new research.

CHAPTER II.

THE NATURAL SCIENCE PERIOD.

Damiron, *Essai sur l'Histoire de la Philosophie au 17ᵐᵉ Siècle.* Paris, 1846.
Kuno Fischer, *Francis Bacon und seine Nachfolger.* 2d ed., Leips. 1875.
Ch. de Rémusat, *Histoire de la Philosophie en Angleterre depuis Bacon jusqu'à Locke.* 2 vols., Paris, 1875.

Natural science acquired its decisive influence upon the development of modern philosophy by first gaining its own independence with the aid of a conscious use of a scientific method, and then from this position being able to determine the general movement of thought as regards both form and content. In so far the development of the method of natural science from Kepler and Galileo down to Newton is not indeed itself the evolution of modern philosophy, but is yet that series of events in reference to which this evolution constantly proceeds.

For this reason the positive beginnings of modern philosophy are in general to be sought, not so much in new conceptions with new content, as in *methodical reflection,* out of which, with the progress of time, there resulted of course new material and so new points of view for the treatment of both theoretical and practical problems. But at first the points of departure of modern thought were in all cases where permanently fruitful conceptions of the task and thereby conditioned procedure of the new science grew out of the humanistic opposition against Scholasticism, and out of the excited metaphysical fantasies of the transitional period.

In this consists from the outset an essential difference between modern and ancient philosophy. The former is as reflective in its beginning as the latter was naïve, and this is self-explaining, since the former must develop out of those traditions which the latter created. In this way it is characteristic of the greater number of the systems of modern philosophy to seek the path to the real or "material" problems by considering the science of method and the theory of knowledge ; and in particular the *seventeenth century* with respect to its philosophy may be characterised as a *strife of methods*

378

While, however, the movement of the humanistic period had in the main taken place in Italy and Germany, the cooler and more considerate temper of the two western civilised peoples now became prominent. Italy was made dumb by the counter-reformation, Germany was crippled by the ruinous war between the confessions. *England* and *France,* on the contrary, experienced in the seventeenth century the bloom of their intellectual civilisation, and between them the *Netherlands* became a flourishing seat of art and science.

In the development of the method of natural science the lines of *empiricism* and of *mathematical theory* converged: in philosophical generalisation the two came forward in an independent attitude. The programme of the *experience philosophy* was laid down by *Bacon,* but the method which formed its fundamental thought was not carried out by him in the fruitful manner which he had anticipated. Much more comprehensive was the form in which *Descartes* brought together the scientific movement of his time to establish rationalism anew, by filling the scholastic system of conceptions with the rich content of the Galilean research. From this resulted far-reaching metaphysical problems, which in the second half of the seventeenth century called forth an extraordinarily vigorous movement of philosophical thought, — a movement in which the new principles entered into manifold antithetical combinations with the principles of mediæval philosophy. Out of the *Cartesian school* rose *Occasionalism,* of which *Geulincx* and *Malebranche* are the chief representatives. But the complete issue of this development was found in the two great philosophical systems brought forward by *Spinoza* and *Leibniz.*

The influence which the powerful development of theoretical philosophy exercised also upon the treatment of *practical* problems shows itself principally in the field of the *philosophy of law (or right).* In this department *Hobbes,* who was in like measure a disciple of Bacon and of Descartes, and as such marks an important point in the line of development of methods and metaphysics above noted, takes the decisive position as the introducer of an ethical naturalism which is found in altered form even with his opponents, such as *Herbert of Cherbury* and *Cumberland.* In these antitheses the problems of the philosophy of the Enlightenment are in process of preparation.

The series of great natural scientists who exercised an immediate influence also upon philosophical questions was opened by Johann **Kepler** (1561–1630) of Weil, a town in Württemberg, who died in Regensburg after a life spent in struggle with need and anxiety. Among his works (ed. by Frisch, Frankfurt, 1858–71, 8 vols.), the most important are *Mysterium Cosmographicum, Harmonice Mundi, Astronomia Nova seu Physica Cœlestis Tradita Commentariis de Motibus Stellæ Martis.* Cf. Chr. Sigwart, *Kleine Schriften,* I. 182 ff.; R. Eucken, *Philos. Monatsh.,* 1878, pp. 30 ff. — In immediate attachment to him stands **Galileo Galilei** (born 1564 at Pisa, died 1642 at Arcetri). His works were

published in 15 vols. (Florence, 1842–56) with a biographical supplementary
volume by Arrago. Vols. 11–14 contain the *Fisico-Mathematica;* among which
we notice *Il Saggiatore* (1623) and the dialogue on the Ptolemaic and the
Copernican systems (1632). Cf. H. Martin, *Galileo, les droits de la science
et la méthode des sciences physiques* (Paris, 1668) ; P. Natorp, *Gal. als Philosoph.* (*Philos. Monatsh.*, 1882, pp. 193 ff.). Isaac **Newton** (1642–1727) comes
into consideration chiefly on account of his *Philosophiæ Naturalis Principia
Mathematica* (1687 ; 2d ed. by Cotes, 1713 ; German by Wolfers, 1872) and
his *Optics* (1704). — Of his contemporaries we notice the chemist, Robert **Boyle**
(1626–1691 ; *Chemista Scepticus; Origo Formarum et Qualitatum; De Ipsa
Natura*), and the Netherlander, Christian **Huyghens** (1629–1695 ; *De Causa
Gravitatis; De Lumine*).
        Cf. W. Whewell, *History of the Inductive Sciences* (Lond. 1837 ; German by
Littrow, Leips. 1839 ff.) ; E. F. Apelt, *Die Epochen der Geschichte der Mensch-
heit* (Jena, 1845) ; E. Dühring, *Kritische Geschichte der Principien der
Mechanik* (Leips. 1872) ; A. Lange, *Gesch. des Materialismus*, 2d ed., Iserlohn,
1873 [Eng. tr. *History of Materialism* by E. C. Thomas, Lond., 4th ed., 1892] ;
K. Lasswitz, *Gesch. der Atomistik*, 2 vols. (Hamburg and Leips. 1890).

Francis **Bacon,** Baron of *Verulam,* Viscount of St. Albans, was born in
1561, studied in Cambridge, had a brilliant career under the reigns of Elizabeth
and James I., until, as the result of political opposition, he was proceeded
against, convicted of venality, and deposed from the position of Lord High
Chancellor. He died 1626. The latest edition of his works is that by Spedding
and Heath (Lond. 1857 ff.). Aside from the *Essays (Sermones Fideles)* the
main writings are *De Dignitate et Augmentis Scientiarum* (1623 ; originally
published under the title, *The Two Books of Francis Bacon on the Proficience
and Advancement of Learning, Divine and Human,* 1605) and *Novum Organon
Scientiarum* (1620 ; originally under the title, *Cogitata et Visa,* 1612).[1] Cf.
Ch. de Rémusat, *Bacon, Sa vie, son temps, sa philosophie et son influence
jusqu'à nos jours* (Paris, 1854) ; H. Heussler, *Fr. B. und seine geschichtliche
Stellung* (Breslau, 1889) ; [*Bacon,* by J. Nichol, in Blackwood's series, Edin.
1888 : Ed. of the *Novum Organum* by Fowler, Oxford, 1878].

René **Descartes** (Cartesius), born 1596, in Touraine, and educated in the
Jesuit school at La Flèche, was originally destined for a soldier and took part in
the campaigns of 1618–1621 in the service of various leaders, but then betook
himself for the first time to Paris, and later, withdrew for many years, at different places in the Netherlands, into a scientific solitude, which he kept in the
most diligent and careful manner. After controversies in which his doctrine
had become involved at the universities in that country had rendered this place
of residence disagreeable, he accepted, in 1649, an invitation of Queen Christine
of Sweden to Stockholm, where he died the following year. His works have
been collected in Latin in the Amsterdam editions (1650, etc.), and in French
by V. Cousin (11 vols., Paris, 1824 ff.) ; the important writings have been translated into German by Kuno Fischer (Mannheim, 1863) [Eng. tr. of the *Method,
Meditations* and *Selections from the Principles* by J. Veitch, Edin. and Lond.,
1st ed., 1850–52, 10th ed., 1890 ; of the *Meditations* by Lowndes, Lond. 1878,
also in *Jour. Spec. Phil.*, Vol. IV., 1870, by W. R. Walker ; and of the *Rules for
the Direction of the Mind,* with selections from the *Med.'s, The World, The
Passions of the Soul,* etc., by H. A. P. Torrey, N.Y. 1892]. The main works
are *Le Monde ou Traité de la Lumière* (posthumously printed, 1654) ; *Essays,*
1637, among them the *Discours de la Méthode* and the *Dioptrics; Meditationes
de Prima Philosophia,* 1641, supplemented by the objections of various *savants*
and Descartes' replies ; *Principia Philosophiæ,* 1644 ; *Passions de l'Âme,* 1650.
Cf. F. Bouillier, *Histoire de la Philosophie Cartésienne* (Paris, 1854) ; X. Schmid-

---

[1] It is well known that very recently much noise has been made over the
discovery that Lord Bacon wrote Shakspere's works also, in his leisure hours.
To fuse two great literary phenomena into one may have something alluring in
it, but in any case a mistake has been made in the person. For it would be
much more probable that Shakspere had incidentally composed the Baconian
philosophy. [The Germans seem to take this "noise" much more seriously
than Shakspere's countrymen. — Tr.]

schwarzenberg, *R. D. und seine Reform der Philosophie* (Nördlingen, 1859);
G. Glogau in *Zeitschr. f. Philos.*, 1878, pp. 209 ff. ; P. Natorp, *D.'s Erkenntnisstheorie* (Marburg, 1882). [*Descartes* by J. P. Mahaffy in Blackwood's series,
Edin. and Phila., 1881 ; W. Wallace, Art. *Descartes* in *Enc. Brit.*; H. Sidgwick
in *Mind*, Vol. VII.; Rhodes in *Jour. Spec. Phil.*, XVII.

Between these two leaders of modern philosophy stands Thomas **Hobbes**,
born 1588, educated at Oxford, who was early drawn over to France by his
studies, and frequently afterwards returned thither, was personally acquainted
with Bacon, Gassendi, Campanella, and the Cartesian circle, and died 1679.
Complete edition of his works, English and Latin by Molesworth, Lond. 1839 ff.
His first treatise, *Elements of Law, Natural and Political* (1639), was published by his friends in 1650, in two parts, *Human Nature* and *De Corpore
Politico*. He published previously *Elementa Philosophiæ de Cive*, 1642 and 1647,
and further *Leviathan* or *The Matter, Form, and Authority of Government*, 1651.
A comprehensive statement is given in the *Elementa Philosophiæ*, I., *De Cor-
pore*, II., *De Homine*, 1668 (both previously in English in 1655 and 1658. Cf.
F. Tönnies in *Vierteljahrschr. f. w. Philos.*, 1879 ff. [*Hobbes*, by G. C. Robert-
son in Blackwood's series, Edin. and Phil. 1886, also Art. *Hobbes*, in *Enc.
Brit.* by same author.] F. Tönnies. *Hobbes* (Stuttgart, 1896).

Of the **Cartesian School** (cf. Bouillier, *op. cit.*) are to be noted the *Jansenists* of Port-Royal, from whose circles came the *Logique ou l'art de penser* (1662),
ed. by Anton **Arnauld** (1612–1694), and Pierre **Nicole** (1625–1695) ; also the
Mystics, Blaise **Pascal** (1623–1662 ; *Penseés sur la Religion* ; cf. the monographs
by J. G. Dreydorff, Leips. 1870 and 1875), and Pierre **Poiret** (1646–1719 ; *De
Eruditione Triplici, Solida Superficiaria et Falsa.*

The development to **Occasionalism** proceeds gradually in Louis **de la Forge**
(*Traité de l'Esprit Humain.* 1666), **Clauberg**(1622–1665 ; *De Conjunctione Corpo-
ris et Animæ in Homine*, **Cordemoy** (*Le Discernement du Corps et de l'Ame*,
1666), but finds its complete development independently of these thinkers in
Arnold **Geulincx** (1625–1669 ; a university teacher in Loewen and Leyden).
His main works are the *Ethics* (1665 ; 2d ed. with notes, 1675); *Logic*, 1662,
and *Methodus*, 1663. New ed. of his works by J. P. N. Land (3 vols., The
Hague, 1891–3). Cf. E. Pfleiderer, *A. G. als Hauptvertreter der occ. Metaphysik
und Ethik* (Tübingen, 1882) ; V. van der Hæghen, *G. Etude sur sa Vie, sa
Philosophie et ses Ouvrages* (Lüttich, 1886).

From the **Oratorium** founded by Cardinal Berulle, a friend of Descartes, to
which **Gibieuf** also belonged (*De Libertate Dei et Creaturæ*, Paris, 1630), went
forth Nicole **Malebranche** (1638–1715). His main work, *De la Recherche de la
Vérité*, appeared 1675, the *Entretiens sur la Métaphysique et sur la Religion* in
1688. Coll. works by J. Simon (Paris, 1871).

Baruch (Benedict de) **Spinoza**, born in 1632 at Amsterdam in the community of Portuguese Jews, and later expelled from this community on account
of his opinions, lived in noble simplicity and solitude at various places in Holland, and died at The Hague 1677. He had published an exposition of the
Cartesian philosophy with an independent metaphysical appendix (1663) and
the *Tractatus Theologico-politicus* (anonymously in 1670). After his death
appeared in his *Opera Posthuma* (1677), his main work, *Ethica More Geometrico
Demonstrata*, the *Tractatus Politicus*, and the fragment *De Intellectus Emendatione*. His correspondence and his recently discovered youthful work, *Tractatus
(brevis) de Deo et Homine ejusque Felicitate*, also come into consideration.
On the latter cf. Chr. Sigwart (Tübingen, 1870). The best edition of his works
is that by Van Vloten and Land (2 vols., Amsterdam, 1882 f.). Cf. T. Camerer,
Die Lehre Sp.'s (Stuttgart, 1877). [*Spinoza*, by J. Caird, Edin. 1888 ; *Spinoza*
by Martineau, Lond. 1883 ; also in *Types of Ethical Theory*, Oxford, 1886 ; F.
Pollock, *Spinoza, His Life and Phil.*, Lond. 1880 ; Seth, Art. *Spinoza*, in *Enc.
Brit.*; Arts. in *Jour. Spec. Phil.*, Vols. 11 and 16, by Morris and Dewey ; Eng.
tr. of prin. works by Elwes, Bohn Lib., 1884, of the *Ethics* by White, Lond. 1883,
and of *Selections* by Fullerton, N.Y. 1892.]

Of philosophical writers in Germany who attached themselves to the train of
the movement among the two civilised peoples of the West are to be mentioned
Joachim **Jung** (1587–1657 ; *Logica Hamburgiensis*, 1638); cf. G. E. Guhrauer.

J. J. und sein Zeitalter (Stuttg. and Tüb. 1859); the Jena mathematician, Erhard Weigel, the teacher of Leibniz and Puffendorf; Walther von **Tschirn-hausen** (1651–1708 ; *Medicina Mentis sive Artis Inveniendi Præcepta Generalia*, Amsterdam, 1687), and Samuel **Puffendorf** (1632–1694; under the pseudonym Severinus a Monzambano, *De Statu Rei publicæ Germanicæ*, 1667, German by H. Bresslau, Berlin, 1870 ; *De Jure Naturæ et Gentium*, London, 1672).

Leibniz belongs in this period, not only in point of time, but also as regards the origination and the motives of his metaphysics, while with other interests of his incredibly many-sided nature, he ranges on into the age of the Enlightenment ; cf. on this, Part V. Here, therefore, we have to consider principally his methodological and metaphysical writings : *De Principio Individui*, 1663 ; *De Arte Combinatoria*, 1666 ; *Nova Methodus pro Maximis et Minimis*, 1684 ; *De Scientia Universali seu Calculo Philosophico*, 1684 (cf. A. Trendelenburg, *Hist. Beiträge zur Philos.*, III. 1 ff.); *De Primæ Philosophiæ Emendatione*, 1694 ; *Système Nouveau de la Nature*, 1695, with the three *Éclaircissements* connected with it, 1696 ; also the *Monadologie*, 1714, the *Principes de la Nature et de la Grace*, 1714, and a great part of his extended correspondence. Among the editions of his philosophical writings the excellent edition by J. E. Erdmann (Berlin, 1840) has now been surpassed by that of C. J. Gerhardt (7 vols., Berlin, 1875–91). — On the system as a whole cf. L. Feuerbach, *Darstellung, Entwicklung und Kritik der Leibnizischen Philos.* (Ansbach, 1837), A. Nourisson, *La Philos. de L.* (Paris, 1860); E. Wendt, *Die Entwicklung der L.'schen Monadenlehre bis 1695* (Berlin, 1886). [E. Dillmann, *Eine neue Darst. der L.'schen Monadenlehre*, Leips. 1891. See also the lit. on p. 444.]

On the historical and systematic *relation of the systems* to one another : H. C. W. Sigwart, *Ueber den Zusammenhang des Spinozismus mit der cartes. Philos.* (Tüb. 1816) and *Die Leibniz'sche Lehre von der prästabilirten Harmonie in ihrem Zusammenhang mit früheren Philosophemen* (ib. 1822) ; C. Schaarschmidt, *Descartes und Spinoza* (Bonn, 1850) ; A. Foucher de Careil, *Leibniz, Descartes et Spinoza* (Paris, 1863) ; E. Pfleiderer, *L. und Geulincx* (Tüb. 1884); E. Zeller, *Sitz.-Ber. d. Berliner Akad*, 1884, pp. 673 ff. ; F. Tönnies, *Leibniz und Hobbes* in *Philos. Monatsh;* 1887, pp. 357 ff. ; L. Stein, *Leibniz und Spinoza* (Berlin, 1890). [E. Caird, Art *Cartesianism*, in *Enc. Brit.*, reprinted in Vol. 2 of his *Essays*, Lond. and N.Y. 1892 ; Saisset's *Modern Pantheism.*]

To the founders of the philosophy of law (cf. C. v. Kaltenborn, *Die Vorläufer des Hugo Grotius*, Leips. 1848; and R. v. Mohl, *Gesch. und Litteratur der Staatswissenschaften*, Erlangen, 1855–58) belong Nicolo **Macchiavelli** (1469–1527 ; *Il Principe, Discorsi sulla prima decade di Tito Livio ;* [Works, tr. by C. E. Detmold, Boston, 1883.] **Thomas More** (1480–1535 ; *De Optimo Rei publicæ Statu sive de Nova Insula Utopia*, 1516); Jean **Bodin** (1530–1597); *Six Livres de la République*, 1577 ; an extract from the *Heptaplomeres* has been given by Guhrauer, Berlin, 1841) ; Albericus **Gentilis** (1551–1611 ; *De Jure Belli*, 1588) ; Johannes **Althus** (1557–1638 ; *Politica*, Gröningen, 1610, cf. O. Gierke, *Unters. z. deutsch. Staats- u. Rechtsgesch.*, Breslau, 1880) ; Hugo **de Groot** (1583–1645 ; *De Jure Belli et Pacis*, 1645 ; cf. H. Luden, *H. G.*, Berlin, 1806).

Of the **Protestants** who treat of the philosophy of law may be named, besides Melancthon, J. Oldendorf (*Elementaris Introductio*, 1539), Nic. Hemming (*De Lege Naturæ*, 1562), Ben Winkler (*Principia Juris*, 1615) ; of the **Catholics** besides Suarez, Rob. Bellarmin (1542–1621 ; *De Potestate Pontificis in Temporalibus*) and Mariana (1537–1624 ; *De Rege et Regis Institutione*).

Natural religion and natural morals in the seventeenth century found in England their main supporters in **Herbert of Cherbury** (1581–1648 ; *Tractatus de Veritate*, 1624 ; *De Religione Gentilium Errorumque apud eos Causis*, 1663 ; on him Ch. de Rémusat, Paris, 1873), and Richard **Cumberland** (*De Legibus Naturæ Disquisitio Philosophica*, Lond. 1672). Among the Platonists or **Neo-Platonists** of England at the same time are prominent Ralph **Cudworth** (1617–1688 ; *The Intellectual System of the Universe*, Lond. 1678, Latin, Jena, 1733) and Henry **More** (1614–1687 ; *Encheiridion Metaphysicum.* His correspondence with Descartes is printed in the latter's works, Vol. X. Cousin's ed.). [*Phil. of Cudworth*, by C. E. Lowrey, with bibliog., N.Y. 1884 ; Tulloch's *Rational Theol. and Christian Phil. in Eng. in 17th Cent.*] Theophilus Gale and his son, Thomas Gale, may be added to the authors above.

§ 30. The Problem of Method.

All beginnings of modern philosophy have in common an impul-sive opposition against "Scholasticism," and at the same time a naïve lack of understanding for the common attitude of dependence upon some one of its traditions, which they nevertheless all occupy. This fundamental oppositional character brings with it the conse-quence, that in all cases where it is not merely wants of the feelings, or fanciful views that are set over against the old doctrines, reflec-tion on *new methods* of knowledge stands in the foreground. Out of the insight into the unfruitfulness of the "syllogism," which could merely set forth in proof or refutation that which was already known, or apply the same to a particular case, arises the demand for an *ars inveniendi*, a *method of investigation*, a sure way to the *discovery of the new.*

1. If now nothing was to be accomplished with the help of rhetoric, the nearest expedient was to attack the matter by the reverse method, proceeding from the particular, from the facts. This had been commended by Vives and Sanchez, and practised by Telesio and Campanella. But they had neither gained full confi-dence in experience nor known afterwards how to make any right beginning with their facts. In both lines *Bacon* believed that he could point out new paths for science, and in this spirit he set up his "New Organon" as over against the Aristotelian.

Every-day perception — he confesses, admitting the well-known sceptical arguments — offers, indeed, no sure basis for a true knowl-edge of Nature; in order to become an experience that can be used by science it must first be purified from all the erroneous additions which have grown together with it in our involuntary way of regard-ing things. These perversions or falsifications of pure experience Bacon calls *idols*, and presents his doctrine of these fallacious images in analogy with the doctrine of the fallacious conclusions in the old dialectic.[1] There are first the "idols of the tribe" (*idola tribus*), the illusions that are given in connection with human nature in general, following which we are always suspecting an order and an end in things, making ourselves the measure of the outer world, blindly retaining a mode of thought which has once been excited by impressions, and the like; then the "idols of the cave" (*idola specus*), by reason of which every individual by his natural disposi-tion, and his situation in life, finds himself shut into his cave;[2]

---

[1] *Nov. Org.* I. 39 ff.

[2] Bacon's strongly rhetorical language, rich in imagery, aims by this term (cf. *De Augm.* V. ch. 4) to recall Plato's well-known parable of the Cave (*Rep.*

then the "idols of the market" (*idola fori*), the errors which are everywhere brought about by intercourse among men, especially by language, and by adherence to the word which we substitute for the idea; finally, the "idols of the theatre" (*idola theatri*), the illusory phantoms of theories which we credulously receive from human history and repeat without subjecting them to any judgment of our own. In this connection Bacon finds opportunity to direct a most violent polemic against the word-wisdom of Scholasticism, against the rule of authority, against the anthropomorphism of earlier philosophy, and to demand a personal examination of things themselves, an unprejudiced reception of reality. Nevertheless he does not get beyond this demand; for the statements as to how the *mera experientia* is to be gained and separated from the enveloping husks of the idols are extremely meagre, and while Bacon teaches that one must not limit himself to accidental perceptions, but must set about his observation methodically, and supplement it by *experiment*[1] which he thinks out and makes for himself, this also is but a general designation of the task, and a theoretical insight into the essential nature of experiment is still wanting.

Quite similar is the case with the method of *Induction*, which Bacon proclaimed as the only correct mode of elaborating facts. With its aid we are to proceed to general cognitions (axioms), in order that we may ultimately from these explain other phenomena. In this activity the human mind, among whose constitutional errors is over-hasty generalisation, is to be restrained as much as possible; it is to ascend quite gradually the scale of the more general, up to the most general. Healthy and valuable as these prescriptions are, we are the more surprised to find that with Bacon their more detailed carrying out is completed in conceptions and modes of view which are entirely scholastic.[2]

All knowledge of Nature has for its end to understand the causes of things. Causes, however, are — according to the old Aristotelian scheme — formal, material, efficient, or final. Of these only the "formal" causes come into consideration; for all that takes place has its grounds in the "*Forms*," in the "natures" of things. Hence when Bacon's Induction searches for the "Form" of phenomena, *e.g.* for the Form of heat, Form is here understood quite in the sense of Scotism as the abiding essence or nature of phenomena. The Form of that which is given in perception is composed out of

---

514), which is the more unfortunate as, in the Platonic passage, it is precisely the general limited nature of knowledge by the senses that is dealt with.

[1] *Nov. Org.* I. 82.

[2] Cf. the circumstantial exposition in the second book of the *Nov. Org*

simpler "Forms" and their "differences," and these it is important
to discover. To this end as many cases as possible in which the
phenomenon in question appears, are brought together into a *tabula
præsentiæ*, and in like manner, those in which the phenomenon is
lacking are brought together into a *tabula absentiæ;* to these is
added, in the third place, a *tabula graduum*, in which the varying
intensity with which the phenomenon appears is compared with the
varying intensity of other phenomena.   The problem is then to be
solved by a progressive process of exclusion (*exclusio*).   The Form
of heat, for example, is to be that which is everywhere present
where heat is found, which is nowhere where heat is lacking, and
which is present in greater degree where there is more heat, and
in lesser degree where there is less heat.[1] What Bacon presents
accordingly as Induction is certainly no simple enumeration, but
an involved process of abstraction, which rests upon the metaphysical assumptions of the scholastic Formalism[2] (cf. § 27, 3); the
presage of the new is still quite embedded in the old habits of
thought.

2. It is accordingly comprehensible that Bacon was not the man
to bring to the study of Nature itself methodical or material
furtherance : but this derogates nothing from his philosophical
importance,[3] which consists just in this, that he demanded the general application of a principle, to which he yet was unable to give
any useful or fruitful form in the case of the most immediate
object for its use : namely, the knowledge of the corporeal world.
He had understood that the new science must turn from the endless
discussion of conceptions back to things themselves, that it can
build only upon direct perception, and that it must rise from this
only cautiously and gradually to the more abstract,[4] and he had
understood no less clearly that in the case of this Induction, the
point at issue was nothing other than the discovery of the simple

---

[1] In which case it turns out that the Form of heat is motion, and, indeed, a
motion which is expansive, and thus divided by inhibition and communicated
to the smaller parts of the body [*motus expansivus, cohibitus et nitens per partes
minores*].

[2] Cf. Chr. Sigwart, *Logik*, II. § 93, 3.

[3] Cf. Chr. Sigwart in the *Preuss. Jahrb.*, 1863, 93 ff.

[4] The *pedagogical* consequences of the Baconian doctrine as contrasted with
Humanism, with which, in general, the movement of natural science came in
conflict in this respect, were drawn principally by Amos *Comenius* (1592–1671).
His *Didactica Magna* presents the course of instruction as a graded ascent from
the concrete and perceptive to the more abstract ; his *Orbis Pictus* aims to give
for the school a perceptional basis for instruction about things ; his *Janua Lin-
guarum Reserrata*, finally, aims to have the learning of foreign languages
arranged so as to be taught only as it is requisite as a means for acquiring
knowledge about things.   The pedagogical views of Rattich are similar (1571–
1635).

elements of reality, from the "nature" of which, in their regular relation and connection, the whole compass of what we perceive is to be explained. Induction, he thought, will find the Forms by which Nature must be interpreted. But while in his cosmology he did not get far beyond an adherence to the traditional atomism, and even shut himself up against the great achievement of the Copernican theory, he demanded that his *empirical principle* should be applied also to *knowledge of man.* Not only the bodily existence in its normal and abnormal vital processes, but also the movement of ideas and of activities of the will, especially also the social and political system, — all these should be examined as to their moving forces ("Forms") by the method of natural science, and explained without prejudice. The *anthropological and social naturalism* which Bacon announces in the encyclopædic remarks of his work *De Augmentis Scientiarum,* contains examples of programmes[1] for many branches of knowledge, and proceeds everywhere from the fundamental purpose to understand man and all the activities of his life as a product of the same simple elements of reality which also lie at the basis of external Nature.

Still another element comes to light in this anthropological interest. To understand man is not, for Bacon, an end in itself, any more than it is such to understand Nature. His entire thought is rather subordinated to a practical end, and this he conceives in the grandest form. All human knowledge has ultimately for its sole task to procure for man dominion over the world by his knowledge of the world. *Knowledge is power,* and is the only lasting power. While therefore magic with fantastic arts sought to make itself master of the working forces of Nature, this blind endeavour became clarified with Bacon to the insight that man can owe his mastery over things only to a sober investigation of their true essence. For him, therefore, the *interpretatio naturæ* is only the means of *subjecting nature to the human mind,* and his great work for the "Renovation of the Sciences"— *Instauratio Magna, "Temporis Partus Maximus"* — bears also the title *De Regno Hominis.*

In this, Bacon expressed what was moving the heart of thousands at his time, under the impress of great events. With that series of discoveries beyond the seas, where through mistakes, adventures, and crimes, man had at last for the first time taken complete possession of his planet, with inventions such as those of the mariner's compass, of gunpowder, and of the art of printing,[2] a mighty

---

[1] If we could therefore regard as accomplished all that Bacon sets before him in prospect, we might find with him the entire natural science of to-day.

[2] Cf. O. Peschel, *Gesch. des Zeitalters der Entdeckungen,* 2d ed., Leips. 1879

change had been introduced within a short time into the greater as well as the lesser life of man. A new epoch of civilisation seemed to be opened, and an exotic excitement seized upon men's fancy. Unheard-of things should succeed; nothing was to be impossible any longer. The telescope disclosed the mysteries of the heavens, and the powers of the earth began to obey the investigator. Science would be the guide of the human mind in its victorious journey through Nature. By her inventions, human life should be completely transformed. What hopes in this respect set free the fancy for its flights we see from Bacon's Utopian fragment of the *Nova Atlantis*, and also from Campanella's *Civitas Solis*. The English Chancellor, however, held that the task of the knowledge of Nature was ultimately to make of invention, which had hitherto been for the most part a matter of chance, a consciously exercised art. To be sure, he gave life to this thought only in the fantastic picture of Solomon's house, in his Utopia; he guarded himself from seriously carrying it out; but this meaning which he attributed to the *ars inveniendi* made him an opponent of purely theoretical and "contemplative" knowledge; just from this point of view did he combat Aristotle and the unfruitfulness of monastic science. In his hand philosophy was in danger of falling from the rule of a religious end under that of technical interests.

But the issue proved again that the golden fruits of knowledge ripen only where they are not sought. In his haste for utility Bacon missed his goal, and the intellectual creations which have enabled natural science to become the basis of our external civilisation proceeded from the superior thinkers, who, with pure disinterested thought, and without any eagerness to improve the world, desired to understand the order of Nature which they admired.

3. His tendency toward the practical end of invention blinded Bacon to the theoretical value of *mathematics*. This value had at first come to consciousness in the fantastic forms which praised the number-harmony of the universe in Neo-Platonic exuberance (cf. § 29, 5), imitating the Pythagorean methods. The great investigators of Nature set out from a like admiration for the beauty and order of the universe; but the new in their teachings consists in just this, that they no longer seek this mathematical significance of the cosmical order in symbolic number-speculations, but aim to understand and prove it *from facts*. Modern investigation of Nature was born as *empirical Pythagoreanism*. This problem had been seen already by Leonardo da Vinci[1] — to have been the first to solve it

---

[1] Cf. with regard to him as a philosopher, K. Prantl, *Sitz.-Ber. der München- chener Akad.*, 1885, 1 ff.

is the glory of *Kepler.* The psychological motive of his research was the philosophical conviction of the mathematical order of the universe, and he verified his conviction by discovering the laws of planetary motion by means of a grand induction.

In this procedure it became evident, on the one hand, that the true task of induction in natural science consists in finding out that *mathematical relation* which remains the same in the entire series of the phenomena determined by measurement, and, on the other hand, that the object, in connection with which this task can be performed by research, is none other than *motion.* The divine arithmetic and geometry which Kepler sought in the universe was found in the *laws of occurrence and change (Geschehens).* Proceeding from this principle, with a more distinct methodical consciousness, *Galileo* created *mechanics as the mathematical theory of motion.* It is extremely instructive to compare the thoughts which the latter presents in the *Saggiatore* with Bacon's interpretation of Nature. Both aim to analyse into their elements the phenomena given in perception, in order to explain phenomena from the combination of these elements. But where Bacon's Induction seeks the "Forms," Galileo's *method of resolution* (analysis) searches out the simplest processes of motion capable of mathematical determination; and while interpretation with the former consists in pointing out how the natures co-operate to form an empirical structure, the latter shows in his *method of composition* (synthesis) that the mathematical theory under the presupposition of the simple elements of motion leads to the same results which experience exhibits.[1] From this standpoint experiment also acquires quite another significance : it is not merely a shrewd question put to Nature, but is the intelligent and intentional interference by which simple forms of occurrence are isolated in order to subject them to measurement. Thus, all that Bacon had merely presaged receives with Galileo a definite significance usable for the investigation of Nature, by means of the mathematical principle and its application to motion ; and in accordance with these principles of mechanics Newton was able by his hypothesis of gravitation to give the mathematical theory for the explanation of Kepler's laws.

With this, the victory of the principle of Democritus and Plato, that the sole object which true knowledge of Nature can deal with is what is capable of quantitative determination, was sealed in a completely new form ; but this time the principle was applied not to the Being, but to the Becoming or change in Nature. Scientific

---

[1] This methodical standpoint Hobbes makes entirely his own (cf. *De Corp.*, ch. 6), and indeed in expressly rationalistic antithesis to the empiricism of Bacon.

insight reaches as far as the mathematical theory of motion extends. Exactly this standpoint of the Galilean physics is taken in theoretical philosophy by *Hobbes*.[1] Geometry is the only certain discipline; all knowledge of Nature is rooted in it. We can know only such objects as we can construct, so that we derive all further consequences from this our own operation. Hence knowledge of all things, in so far as it is accessible for us, consists in tracing back what is perceived to motion of bodies in space. Science has to reason from phenomena to causes, and from these latter in turn to their effects : but phenomena are, in their essence, motions; causes are the simple elements of motion, and effects are again motions. Thus arises the apparently materialistic proposition : philosophy is the doctrine of the motion of bodies ! This is the extreme consequence of the separation of philosophy from theology, which began with the English Franciscans.

The essential result for philosophy in these methodical beginnings of natural research is, therefore, twofold : empiricism was corrected by mathematics, and the shapeless Pythagoreanism of the humanistic tradition was made by empiricism definite mathematical theory. These lines meet and are bound together in Galileo.

4. In mathematical theory, accordingly, was found that *rational* factor which Giordano Bruno had demanded in his treatment of the Copernican doctrine for a critical elaboration of sense perception.[2] Rational science is mathematics. Proceeding from this conviction, *Descartes* undertook his reform of philosophy. Educated in the Scholasticism of the Jesuits, he had attained the personal conviction [3] that satisfaction for an earnest craving for truth was to be found neither in metaphysical theories nor in the learned polymathy of the empirical disciplines, but in mathematics alone; and by following the pattern of mathematics, — himself, as is well known, a creative mathematician, — he thought to transform all the rest of human knowledge : his philosophy aims to be a universal mathematics. In the generalisation of the Galilean principle requisite for this purpose, some of the factors which made the principle fruitful for the special tasks of natural research fell away, so that Descartes' teaching is not usually counted as an advance in the history of physics; but the power of his influence upon the philosophical development, in which he was the ruling mind for the seventeenth century and beyond, was all the greater.

To those methodical thoughts which are common to Bacon and

---

[1] Cf. the beginning of *De Corpore.*
[2] G. Bruno, *Dell' Inf. Univ. e Mond.* 1 in. (L. 307 f.).
[3] Cf. the fine exposition in the *Discours de la Méthode.*

Galileo, Descartes added a postulate of the greatest importance: he demanded that the method of induction or resolution should lead to a *single principle of highest and absolute certainty,* from which afterwards, by the method of composition, the whole compass of experience must find its explanation. This demand was entirely original, and had its root in the felt need for a systematic, connected whole of all human knowledge; it rested ultimately upon his surfeit of the traditional reception of historically collected knowledge, and upon his longing for a new philosophical creation from one mould. Descartes will, then, by an inductive enumeration and a critical sifting of all ideas, press forward to a single, certain point, in order from this point to deduce all further truths. The first task of philosophy is *analytic,* the second *synthetic.*

The classical carrying out of this thought is presented in the *Meditations.* The philosopher portrays his struggle after truth in a dramatic dialogue with himself. Proceeding from the principle " de omnibus dubitandum," the whole circuit of ideas is reviewed on all sides, and in the process we meet the whole apparatus of sceptical arguments. We experience the change of opinions and the deceptions of the senses too often, says Descartes, to permit of our trusting them. In the face of the variety of impressions which the same object makes under different circumstances, it is not possible to decide which of these impressions, and, indeed, whether any one of them, contains the true essence of the thing; and the liveliness and sureness with which we can dream in our actual experience must excite in us the scruple which can never be completely set aside, as to whether we are not perhaps dreaming even when we believe that we are awake and perceiving. Meanwhile, at the basis of all the combinations which the imagination can produce lie the simple elementary acts of consciousness, and in connection with these we meet with truths of which we are undeniably obliged to say that we cannot help recognising them, as, for example, the simple propositions of arithmetic $2 \times 2 = 4$, and the like. But how if now we were so constituted that from our very nature we must necessarily err? how if some demon had created us, whose pleasure it was to give us a Reason that would necessarily deceive while it supposed itself to be teaching the truth? Against such a delusion we should be defenceless, and this thought must make us mistrustful even with reference to the most evident utterances of reason.

After fundamental doubt has been thus pressed even to the farthest extreme, it proves that the doubt breaks off its own point. that it itself presents a fact of completely unassailable certainty:

in order to doubt, in order to dream, in order to be deceived, I must be. Doubt itself proves that I, as a thinking *conscious being* (*res cogitans*), exist. The proposition *cogito sum* is true as often as I think or pronounce it. And, indeed, the certainty of Being is contained in none of my activities except that of consciousness. That I go to walk I can imagine in my dream:[1] that I am conscious cannot be merely my imagination, for imagination is itself a kind of consciousness.[2] The *certainty of the Being or existence of consciousness* is the one fundamental truth which Descartes finds by the analytic method.

Rescue from doubt consists therefore in the *Augustinian argument of the Reality of the conscious nature or essence* (cf. § 22, 1). But its application with Descartes[3] is not the same as with Augustine himself and with the great number of those on whom his doctrine was influential just in the transition period. For Augustine, the self-certainty of the soul was valued as the surest of all experiences, as the fundamental fact of inner perception by means of which the latter obtains for the theory of knowledge a preponderance over outer perception. Thus — not to recall again Charron's moralising interpretation — Campanella particularly had employed the Augustinian principle when, not unlike the great Church Father, he gave to the elements of this experience of self the meaning of metaphysical prime elements (cf. § 29, 3). In a completely analogous manner — not to speak of Locke[4] — *Tschirnhausen*, in a supposed adherence to Descartes, had later regarded self-knowledge as the *experientia evidentissima*,[5] which is therefore to serve as the *a posteriori* beginning of philosophy (cf. below, No. 7), so that from it all further knowledge can be constructed *a priori;* for in self-knowledge is contained the threefold truth, that we are effected by some things well and by others ill, that we understand some and not others, and that in the process of ideation we occupy a passive attitude with reference to

---

[1] Descartes' reply to Gassendi's objection (V. 2) ; cf. *Princ. Phil.* I. 9.

[2] The ordinary translation of *cogitare, cogitatio* by "think" (*Denken*) is liable to occasion misunderstanding, since *Denken* in German [and the same is true of *think*, in English, at least in philosophical terminology] signifies a particular kind of theoretical consciousness. Descartes himself elucidates the meaning of *cogitare* (*Med.* III. ; *Princ. Phil.* I. 9), by enumeration : he understands by it to doubt, affirm, deny, understand, will, abhor, imagine, feel a sensation, etc. For that which is common to all these functions we have in German scarcely any word but " Bewusstsein " [consciousness]. The same is also true with regard to Spinoza's use of the term ; cf. his *Princ. Phil. Cart.* I., Prop. IV., Schol., and also *Eth.* II., Ax. III., and elsewhere.

[3] Who besides, at the outset, seems not to have known the historical origin of this argument. Cf. *Obj.* IV., and *Resp.*

[4] Cf. below, §§ 33 f.

[5] Tschirnhausen, *Med. Ment.* (1695), pp. 290–94.

the outer world, — three points of attachment for the three rational sciences, ethics, logic, and physics.

5. With *Descartes*, on the contrary, the proposition *cogito sum* has not so much the meaning of an experience, as rather that of the first fundamental rational *truth*. Nor is its evidence that of an inference,[1] but that of immediate *intuitive certainty*. The analytic method seeks here, as with Galileo, the *simple, self-intelligible elements*, out of which all else is to be explained; but while the physicist discovers the perceptional elementary form of motion, which is to make comprehensible all that takes place in the corporeal world, the metaphysician is hunting for the *elementary truths of consciousness*. In this consists the *rationalism* of Descartes.

This rationalism expresses itself in the fact that the superiority of self-consciousness is found in its complete *clearness* and *distinctness*, and in the fact that Descartes propounded as his principle for the synthetic method the maxim, *Everything must be true which is as clear and distinct as self-consciousness, i.e.* which presents itself before the mind's vision as surely and underivably as the mind's own existence. " Clear " is defined by Descartes [2] as that which is intuitively present and manifest to the mind, " distinct " as that which is entirely clear in itself and precisely determined. And those mental presentations — or ideas,[3] as he calls them after the manner of later Scholasticism — which are in this sense clear and distinct, whose evidence is not to be deduced from any others, but is grounded solely in themselves, he calls *innate ideas.*[4] With this expression he indeed incidentally connects also the psycho-genetic thought that these ideas are imprinted upon the human soul by God, but for the most part he desires to give only the epistemological significance of *immediate, rational evidence.*

These two meanings are peculiarly mingled in Descartes' *proofs for the existence of God*, which form an integrant constituent of his theory of knowledge, in so far as this "idea" is the first for which, in the synthetic procedure of his method a clearness and distinctness or intuitive evidence of the " natural light," equal to that of self-consciousness, is claimed. The new (so-called Cartesian) proof which he introduces in this connection,[5] has a multitude of scholastic

---

[1] *Resp. ad Obj.* II.   [2] *Princ. Phil.* I. 45.

[3] [German *Idee*. I follow the ordinary English usage in spelling the word as used by Descartes without a capital.]

[4] Cf. E. Grimm, *D.'s Lehre von den angeborenen Ideen* (Jena, 1873), and also P. Natorp, *D.'s Erkenntnisstheorie* (Marburg, 1882). That *innatus* is better translated by *eingeboren* than by the usual *angeboren* has been remarked by R. Eucken, *Geschichte und Kritik der Grundbegriffe der Gegenwart*, p. 73.

[5] *Med.* III.

assumptions.   He argues that the individual self-consciousness
knows itself to be finite, and therefore imperfect (according to the
old identification of determinations expressing value with ontological
gradations), and that this knowledge can be derived only from the
conception of an absolutely perfect being (*ens perfectissimum*).   This
latter conception which we find within us must have a cause which,
nevertheless, is not to be found within our own selves, nor in any
other finite things.   For the principle of causality requires that at
least as much Reality be contained in the cause as there is in the
effect.   This — in the scholastic sense — realistic principle is now
applied, in analogy to Anselm's argument, to the relation of the
idea in the mind (*esse in intellectu* or *esse objective*) to the Real
(*esse in re* or *esse formaliter*), in order to give the inference that we
should not have the idea of a most perfect being if the idea had not
been produced in us by such a being himself.   This anthropologico-
metaphysical proof has then with Descartes the significance that
by it that former sceptical hypothetical phantom of a deceiving
demon is again destroyed.   For since the perfection of God involves
his veracity, and it is impossible that he should so have created us
that we should necessarily err, *confidence in the lumen naturale*, that
is, in the immediate evidence of rational knowledge, is *restored*, and
thus definitively grounded.   Thus modern rationalism is introduced
by Descartes by the circuitous route of Scholasticism.   For this
proof gives the charter for acknowledging with complete certainty
as true all propositions which manifest themselves in clear and distinct light before the reason.   Here belong, firstly, all truths of
mathematics, but here belongs also the *ontological* proof for the
existence of God.   For with the same necessity of thought — thus
Descartes takes up Anselm's argument [1] — with which the geometrical propositions with regard to a triangle follow from the definition
of the triangle, it follows from the mere definition of the most Real
being that the attribute of existence belongs to him.   The possibility
of thinking God suffices to prove his existence.

In this way it follows from the criterion of clearness and distinctness, that of finite things also, and especially of bodies, so much can
be known as is clearly and distinctly perceived.   But this is for
Descartes the *mathematical* element, and is limited to the *quantitative
determinations*, while all the sensuous-qualitative elements in perception are regarded by the philosopher as unclear and confused.   On this
account metaphysics and the theory of knowledge terminate for him,
too, in a *mathematical physics*.   He designates [2] the sensuous appre-

---

[1] *Med.* V.   [2] *Med.* VI.

hension of the qualitative, "imagination" (*imaginatio*). The apprehension of that which can be mathematically constructed he terms, on
the other hand, "intellectual" knowledge (*intellectio*), and strongly as
he knows how to prize the help which experience gives in the former,
a really scientific insight rests, in his opinion, only upon the latter.

The distinction between distinct and confused presentations
(which goes back to Duns Scotus and farther) serves Descartes
also to solve the *problem of error,* which results for him out of his
principle of the *veracitas dei,* because it does not seem possible to
see how, in accordance with that principle, perfect deity could so
arrange human nature as to allow it to err at all.   Here Descartes
helps himself [1] by a peculiarly limited *doctrine of freedom,* which
might be consistent with either Thomistic determinism or Scotist
indeterminism.   It is assumed, that is, that only clear and distinct
presentations exercise so cogent and compelling a power upon the
mind that it cannot avoid recognising them, while with reference to
the unclear and confused presentations it retains the boundless and
groundless activity of the *liberum arbitrium indifferentiæ* (its farthest-
reaching power, which in the Scotist fashion is set in analogy with
the freedom of God).   Thus error arises when affirmation and negation follow arbitrarily (without rational ground) in the case of
unclear and indistinct material for judgment.[2]   The demand which
follows from this of withholding judgment in all cases where a sufficiently clear and distinct insight is not present recalls too distinctly
the ancient ἐποχή ("suspense") to permit us to overlook the relationship of this theory of error, with the doctrines of the Sceptics
and Stoics as to the συγκατάθεσις (cf. pp. 167, 208).[3]   In fact, Descartes
recognised distinctly the will-factor in judgment (agreeing here,
too, with the epistemology of Augustine and Duns Scotus), and
Spinoza followed him in this, so far as to designate affirmation or
denial as a necessary characteristic of every idea, and thus to teach
that man cannot think without at the same time willing.[4]

6. Descartes' mathematical reform of philosophy had a peculiar
fate.   Its metaphysical results began a rich and fruitful development; its tendency as regards method, however, soon became sub-

---

[1] *Med.* IV.

[2] Error appears accordingly as an act of free will parallel to the act of sin,
and thus as guilt; it is the guilt or fault of self-deception.   This thought was
carried out particularly by Malebranche (*Entret.* III. f.).

[3] This relationship extends consistently to Descartes' ethics also.   From the
clear and distinct knowledge of reason follows necessarily right willing and act-
ing; from the obscure and confused impulses of the sensibility result practically
sin and theoretically error, by abuse of freedom.   The ethical ideal is the
Socratic-Stoic ideal of the rule of reason over the sensibility.

[4] *Eth.* II., Prop. 49.

jected to a misunderstanding which exactly reversed its meaning. The philosopher himself desired to see the analytical method employed in a great proportion of instances, even in the case of particular problems, and thought of the synthetic method as a progress in discovery from one intuitive truth to another. His disciples, however, confounded the creatively free intellectual activity, which Descartes had in mind, with that rigidly demonstrative system of exposition which they found in *Euclid's text-book of geometry.* The monistic tendency of the Cartesian methodology, the fact that it set up a highest principle from which all other certainty should follow, favoured this exchange, and out of the new method of investigation there came into being again an *ars demonstrandi.* The ideal of philosophy appeared to be the task of developing from its fundamental principle all its knowledge as a system of as rigidly logical consistency as that with which Euclid's text-book deduces geometry with all its propositions from axioms and definitions.

A request of this sort had been answered by Descartes with a tentative sketch, though with express reference to the doubtfulness of this transfer;[1] but the allurement to find the significance of *mathematics* for philosophical method in the circumstance, that it is the *ideal of demonstrative science,* seems only to have been strengthened thereby. At least, it was in this direction that the influence of the Cartesian philosophy proved strongest for the following period. In all the change of epistemological investigations until far into the eighteenth century this conception of mathematics was a firmly established axiom for all parties. Indeed, it became even a lever for scepticism and mysticism, under the direct influence of Descartes, in the case of men like *Pascal.* Since no other human science, so the latter argued, neither metaphysics nor the empirical disciplines, can attain mathematical evidence; man must be modest in his efforts after rational knowledge, and must the more follow the impulse of his heart toward presageful faith, and the feeling of tact which belongs to a noble conduct of life. The Mystic *Poiret* (influenced by Boehme), also, and the orthodox sceptic *Huet,*[2] turned away from Cartesianism because it could not pause in its programme of universal mathematics.

Positive beginnings toward a transformation of the Cartesian method into the *Euclidean line of proof* are found in the Port-Royal

---

[1] *Resp. ad Obj.* II.

[2] Pierre Daniel *Huet* (1630–1721), the learned Bishop of Avranches, wrote *Censura Philosophiæ Cartesianæ* (1689), and *Traité de la Faiblesse de l'Ésprit Humain* (1723). His Autobiography (1718) is also instructive on the point mentioned above. Cf. on him Ch. Bartholmèss (Paris, 1850).

logic and in the logical treatises of Geulincx; but in the system of *Spinoza* this methodical schematism stands before us complete and perfect as from one mould.   He first gave an exposition of the Cartesian philosophy *"more geometrico,"* by developing the content of the system step by step in propositions, after first setting up definitions and axioms.   Each of these propositions was proved from the definitions, axioms, and preceding propositions; while corollaries and scholia giving freer elucidations were added to certain of the propositions.   Into this same rigid, unwieldy form Spinoza pressed his own philosophy also in the *Ethics,* and believed that it was thus as surely demonstrated as the Euclidean system of geometry.   This presupposed not only the flawless correctness of the demonstrative process, but also an unambiguous evidence and an unassailable validity of the definitions and axioms.   A look at the beginning of the *Ethics* (and not only of the first, but also of the following books) suffices to convince one of the *naïveté* with which Spinoza brings forward the complicated and condensed constructions of scholastic thought as self-evident conceptions and principles, and thereby anticipates implicitly his whole metaphysical system.

This *geometrical method* has, however, in Spinoza's thought — and in this consists its psycho-genetic justification — at the same time its material as well as formal significance.   The fundamental religious conviction that all things necessarily proceed from the unitary essence of God seemed to him to require a method of philosophical knowledge, which in the same manner should derive from the idea of God the ideas of all things.   In the true philosophy the order of ideas ought to be the same as the real order of things.[1]   But from this it follows of itself that the real process of the procedure of things forth from God must be thought after the analogy of the logical procedure of the consequent from its ground or reason, and thus the character of the method which Spinoza fixed upon for the problem of philosophy involved in advance the metaphysical character of its solution; cf. § 31.

7.   Little as men dared, in the immediately following period, to make the content of the Spinozistic philosophy their own, its methodical form exercised, nevertheless, an impressive influence: and the more the geometrical method became settled in the philosophy of the schools, the more the *syllogistic procedure* entered again with it, since all knowledge was to be deduced from the highest truths by

---

[1] The view that true knowledge as genetic definition must repeat the process by which its object arises was carried out especially by *Tschirnhausen,* who did not shrink from the paradox that a complete definition of laughter must be able to produce laughter itself !   (*Med. Ment.* 67 f.)

regular inferences. Especially did the mathematically schooled Cartesians in Germany take up the geometrical method along this line : this was done by *Jung* and *Weigel*, and the academic impulse to the preparation of text-books found in this method a form with which it could have the utmost sympathy. In the eighteenth century Christian *Wolff* (cf. Part V.) pursued this line in the most comprehensive manner with his Latin text-books, and for the systematisation of a firmly established and clearly thought out material there could be in fact no better form. This was shown when *Puffendorf* undertook to deduce the entire system of Natural Right by the geometrical method, as a logical necessity from the single principle of the need of society.

When this view was in process of coming into existence *Leibniz* came into sympathy with it under the especial influence of Erhard Weigel, and was at the beginning one of its most consistent supporters. He not only made the jest of giving this unwonted garb to a political brochure,[1] but was seriously of the opinion that philosophical controversies would find their end for the first time when a philosophy could once make its appearance in as clear and certain a form as that of a mathematical calculation.[2]

Leibniz pursued this thought very energetically. The stimulus of Hobbes, who also — though with quite another purpose, cf. § 31, 2 — declared thinking to be a reckoning with the conceptional signs of things, may have been added ; the Art of Lull and the pains which Giordano Bruno had taken with its improvement were well known to him. In Cartesian circles, also, the thought of transforming the mathematical method to a regular art of invention had been much discussed : besides Joachim Jung, the Altorf Professor *Joh. Christopher Sturm*,[3] had also exercised an influence upon Leibniz in this respect. Finally, the thought of expressing the fundamental metaphysical conceptions, and likewise the logical operations of their combination after the manner of the mathematical sign-language by definite characters, seemed to offer the possibility of writing a philosophical investigation in general formulæ, and by this means raising it beyond the capability of being expressed in a definite language — an effort toward a universally scientific language, a "*Lingua Adamica*," which likewise appeared at the time

---

[1] In the pseudonymous *Specimen demonstrationum politicarum pro rege Polonorum eligendo* (1669), he proved by "geometrical method" in sixty propositions and demonstrations that the Count Palatine of Neuburg must be chosen king of the Poles.

[2] *De Scientia Universali seu Calculo Philosophico* (1684).

[3] The author of a *Compendium Universalium seu Metaphysicæ Euclideæ.*

of Leibniz in numerous supporters.[1]   So, too, Leibniz busied himself
to an extraordinary degree with the thought of a *characteristica universalis*, and a method of philosophical calculus.[2]

The essential outcome of these strange endeavours was, that an
attempt was necessarily made to establish those highest truths,
from the logical combination of which all knowledge was to be
deduced. So Leibniz, like Galileo and Descartes, must proceed to
search out that which, as *immediately and intuitively certain*, forces
itself upon the mind as *self-evident*, and by its combinations grounds
all derived knowledge. In the course of these reflections Leibniz
stumbled upon the discovery [3] (which Aristotle had made before
him), that there are two completely different kinds of this intuitive
knowledge: universal truths self-evident to reason, and facts of
experience. The one class has timeless validity; the other, validity
for a single instance: *vérités éternelles* and *vérités de fait*. Both have
in common that they are intuitively certain, *i.e.* are certain in themselves and not by deduction from anything else; they are called,
therefore, *primæ veritates*, or, also, *primæ possibilitates*, because in
them the possibility of all that is derivative has its ground. For
the "possibility" of a conception is known either by a "causal
definition" which derives the same from the first possibilities, that
is, *a priori;* or by the immediate experience of its actual existence,
that is, a *posteriori*.

These two kinds of "primitive truths" — the rational and the
empirical, as we see — Leibniz attached in a very interesting manner
to the two Cartesian marks of intuitive self-evidence, *clearness* and
distinctness. To this end he shifts to a slight extent the meaning
of both expressions.[4] That idea is clear which is surely distinguished from all others and so is adequate for the recognition of its
object; that idea is distinct which is clear even to its particular
constituent parts and to the knowledge of their combination.
According to this, the *a priori*, "geometrical" or "metaphysical"
eternal truths are clear *and* distinct; while on the other hand the
a posteriori, or the truths relating to facts, are clear, indeed, but not
distinct. Hence the former are perfectly transparent, conjoined
with the conviction of the *impossiblity of the opposite*, while in the
case of the latter the opposite is thinkable. In the case of the
former the intuitive certainty rests upon the *Principle of Contradic-*

---

[1] Such attempts had been projected by J. J. Becker (1661), G. Dalgarn (1661),
Athanasius Kircher (1663), and J. Wilkins (1668).
[2] Cf. A. Trendelenburg, *Historische Beiträge zu Philosophie*, Vols. II., III.
[3] *Meditationes de Cognitione Veritate et Ideis* (1684).
[4] Ib. at the beginning, Erd's. ed., p. 79.

tion; in the case of the latter the possibility guaranteed by the actual fact needs still an explanation in accordance with the *Principle of Sufficient Reason.*

At the beginning, Leibniz intended this distinction only with reference to the imperfection of the human understanding. In the case of rational truths we see into the impossibility of the opposite; with empirical truths this is not the case, and we must content ourselves with establishing their actuality : [1] but the latter also, in the *natura rerum* and for the divine understanding, are so grounded that the opposite is impossible, although it remains thinkable for us. If Leibniz compared this distinction with that of commensurable and incommensurable magnitudes, he meant at the beginning that incommensurability lies only in man's limited knowing capacity. But in the course of his development this antithesis became for him an absolute one; it gained metaphysical significance. Leibniz now distinguished *realiter* between an *unconditional necessity*, which involves the logical impossibility of the opposite, and a *conditional* necessity, which has "only" the character of a matter of fact. He divided the principles of things into those of which the opposite is unthinkable, and those of which the opposite is thinkable : he distinguished metaphysically, also, between *necessary* and *contingent truths.* This, however, cohered with metaphysical motives, which arose from an after-working of the Scotist theory of the contingency of the finite, and overthrew the geometrical method.

§ 31. Substance and Causality.

The real [as contrasted with formal] result of the new methods was in metaphysics, as in natural science, a transformation of the fundamental ideas of the nature of things, and of the mode of their connection in the processes of Nature : the conceptions of substance and causality acquired a new content. But this change could not proceed so radically in metaphysics as in natural science. In this latter more limited realm, after the Galilean principle had once been found, it was possible in a certain measure to begin *ab ovo* and produce a completely new theory : in the more general philosophical doctrines the power and authority of tradition were much too great to make it possible or permissible that it should be completely set aside.

This distinction asserted itself already in connection with the delicate *relation sustained to religious conceptions.* Natural science

---

[1] The Aristotelian distinction of διότι and ὅτι.

could isolate itself absolutely from theology, and maintain toward it an attitude of complete indifference: metaphysics, by its conception of the deity and by its theory of the mental or spiritual world, was brought again and again into hostile or friendly contact with the religious sphere of ideas.   A Galileo declared that the investigations of physics, whatever their result might be, had not the least thing to do with the teaching of the Bible,[1] and a Newton was not prevented by his mathematical natural philosophy from burying himself with the most ardent piety in the mysteries of the Apocalypse.   But the metaphysicians, however indifferent their thought as regards religion, and however strictly they might prosecute their science in the purely theoretical spirit, were still always obliged to consider that they had to do with objects concerning which the Church doctrine was fixed.   This gave modern philosophy a somewhat delicate position: mediæval philosophy had brought to the objects of Church dogma an essentially religious interest of its own as well; modern philosophy regarded them, if at all, from the theoretical standpoint only.   Hence those felt themselves most secure who, like Bacon and Hobbes, restricted philosophy also entirely to natural research, declined to enter upon a metaphysics proper, and were willing to let dogma speak the only words with regard to the deity and the super-sensible destiny of man.   Bacon did this with large words behind which it is difficult to recognise his true disposition;[2] Hobbes rather let it be seen that his naturalistic opinion, like the Epicurean, saw in ideas as to the supernatural a superstition resting upon a defective knowledge of Nature, — a superstition which by the regulation of the state becomes the binding authority of religion.[3]   Much more difficult, however, was the position of those philosophers who held fast to the metaphysical conception of the deity in their very explanation of Nature; Descartes' whole literary activity is filled with an anxious caution directed toward avoiding every offence to religion, while Leibniz could attempt to carry through in a much more positive manner the conformity of his metaphysics to religion; and on the other hand the example of Spinoza showed how dangerous it was if philosophy openly brought to the front the difference between its conception of God and the dogmatic conception.

1. The main difficulty of the case inhered in the circumstance that the new methodical principle of *mechanics* excluded all tracing of

---

[1] Cf. the letter to the Grand Duchess Christine, *Op.* II. 26 ff.

[2] *De Augm. Scient.* IX., where the supernatural and incomprehensible is set forth as the characteristic and serviceable quality of faith.

[3] *Leviathan*, I. 6 ; cf. the drastic expression, ib. IV. 32.

corporeal phenomena back to spiritual forces. Nature was despiritu-
alised; science would see in it nothing but the movements of smallest
bodies, of which one is the cause of the other. No room remained
for the operation of supernatural powers. So first of all, at one
stroke, magic, astronomy, and alchemy, in which the Neo-Platonic
ghosts and spirits had held sway, became for science a standpoint of
the past. Leonardo had already demanded that the phenomena of the
external world should be explained by *natural causes* only ; the great
systems of the seventeenth century without exception recognise only
such, and a Cartesian, Balthasar Bekker, wrote a book[1] to show that
in accordance with the principles of modern science, all appearances of ghosts, conjurations, and magic arts must be reckoned as
injurious errors, — a word of admonition which was very much in
place in view of the luxuriant superstition of the Renaissance.

But with the spirits, *teleology,* also, was obliged to give place.
The explanation of natural phenomena by their purposiveness
always came ultimately in some way or other to the thought of a
spiritual creation or ordering of things, and so was contradictory
to the principle of mechanics. At this point the victory of the
system of Democritus over the natural philosophy of Plato and
Aristotle was most palpable ; this, too, was emphasised most forcibly
by the new philosophy. *Bacon* counted the teleological mode of
regarding Nature as one of the idols, and, indeed, as one of the
dangerous idols of the tribe, — the fundamental errors which become
a source of illusion to man through his very nature : he taught that
philosophy has to do only with formal or efficient causes, and expressed his restriction of philosophy to physics and his rejection of
metaphysics precisely by saying that the explanation of Nature is
physics if it concerns *causæ efficientes,* metaphysics if it concerns
causæ finales.[2] In the case of Hobbes, who was the disciple of
Bacon and Galileo, the same view is self-explaining. But *Descartes,*
also, desires to see all final causes kept at a distance from the
explanation of Nature — he declares it audacious to desire to know
the purposes of God.[3] Much more open, and keenest by far, is the
polemic of *Spinoza*[4] against the anthropomorphism of teleology.
In view of his idea of God and God's relation to the world, it is
absurd to speak of ends of the deity, and especially of such as have
reference to men ; where all follows with eternal necessity from the
essential nature of the deity, there is no room for an activity according to ends. The English Neo-Platonists, such as Cudworth and

---

[1] Balthasar *Bekker* (1634–1698), *De Betoverte Wereld* (1690).
[2] *De Augm.* III. 4.   [3] *Med.* IV.
[4] Cf. principally *Eth.* I. Append.

Henry More, combated this fundamental mechanico-antiteleological feature of the new metaphysics with all the eloquence of the old arguments, but without success. The teleological conviction was obliged to renounce definitively the claim of affording scientific explanation of particular phenomena, and only in the metaphysical conception of the whole did Leibniz (cf. below, No. 8), and similarly a part of the English students of Nature, find ultimately a satisfactory adjustment between the opposing principles.

With the exclusion of the spiritual from the explanation of Nature, still a third element of the old view of the world fell away, viz. the thought of the difference in kind and in value of the spheres of Nature, as it had been embodied most distinctly in the Neo-Platonic graded realm of things, following the ancient Pythagorean precedent. In this respect the fantastic natural philosophy of the Renaissance had already done a forcible work of preparation. The Stoic doctrine of the omnipresence of all substances at every point of the universe had been revived by Nicolaus Cusanus; but it was in connection with the victory of the Copernican system, as we see in Bruno, that the idea of the *homogeneity of all parts of the universe* first completely forced its way to recognition. The sublunary world could no longer be contrasted as the realm of imperfection, with the more spiritual spheres of the stellar heaven; matter and motion are alike in both. It was from this thought that Kepler and Galileo proceeded, and it became complete when Newton recognised the identity of force in the fall of the apple and the revolution of the stars. For modern science, the old distinction in essence and in value between heaven and earth exists no longer. The *universe is one in nature throughout.* This same view, moreover, presented itself in opposition to the Aristotelian and Thomistic development system of Matters and Forms. It did away with the whole army of lower and higher forces — the much combated *qualitates occultæ;* it recognised the mechanical principle of motion as the only ground of explanation for all phenomena, and therefore, removed also the *distinction in principle between the animate and the inanimate.* Though here Neo-Platonism had co-operated toward overcoming this antithesis by its view of the animation of the entire universe, the reverse task now arose for the Galilean mechanics, namely, that of *explaining mechanically the phenomena of life also.* The discovery of the mechanism of the circulation of the blood by Harvey [1] (1626) gave to this tendency a

---

[1] In which he had been anticipated by Michael Servetus (burned 1553 in Geneva by Calvin's instrumentality).

vigorous impulse; Descartes expressed it in principle in his statement that the bodies of animals are to be regarded scientifically as most complex automata, and their vital activities as mechanical processes. Hobbes and Spinoza carried out this thought more exactly; a zealous study of reflex motions began in the medical schools of France and the Netherlands, and the conception of the soul as vital force became completely disintegrated. Only the Platonists and the adherents of the vitalism of Paracelsus and Boehme, such as Van Helmont, held fast to this conception in the old manner.

2. This *mechanistic despiritualisation* of Nature corresponded completely to that *dualistic theory of the world,* which from epistemological motives had been in course of preparation in terministic Nominalism, — the theory of a *total difference between the inner and the outer world.* To the knowledge of their qualitative difference was now added that of their real and causal separateness. The world of bodies appeared not only quite different in kind from that of mind, but also as entirely sundered from it in its existence and in the course of its motions. The doctrine of the *intellectuality of the sense qualities,* revived in the philosophy of the Renaissance by the Humanists, had contributed an extraordinary amount toward sharpening the above antithesis. The doctrine that colours, tones, smells, tastes, and qualities of pressure, heat, and touch are not real qualities of things, but only signs of such in the mind, had passed over from the Sceptical and Epicurean literature into most of the doctrines of modern philosophy with a repetition of the ancient illustrations. Vives, Montaigne, Sanchez, and Campanella were at one in this; Galileo, Hobbes, and Descartes revived the teaching of Democritus, that to these qualitative differences of perception nothing but quantitative differences correspond in the *natura rerum,* and this in such a way that the former are the inner modes of mentally representing the latter. Descartes regarded sense qualities as obscure and confused ideas, while the conception of the quantitative determinations of the outer world, on account of its mathematical character, was for him the only clear and distinct idea of them.

According to Descartes, therefore, not only the sensuous feelings, but also the contents of sensation, belong not to the spatial, but to the psychical world only, and represent in this sphere the geometrical structures of which they are the signs. In our examination of an individual object we can,[1] to be sure, gain a knowledge of this

---

[1] Cf. *Med.* VI. which allows perhaps the plainest view of the very close relation which Descartes' physical research had to experience.

true mathematical essence of bodies only by the aid of perceptions, and in these perceptions the true mathematical essence is always alloyed with the qualitative elements of the "imagination." But just in this consists the task of physical research, to dissolve out this real essence of bodies from the subjective modes of our mental representation by means of reflection upon the clear and distinct elements of perception.   John *Locke*, who later adopted and made popular this view of Descartes, designated[1] those qualities which belong to bodies in themselves as *primary*, and called those *secondary*, on the other hand, which belong to a body only by virtue of its action upon our senses.[2]   Descartes allowed as primary qualities only shape, size, position, and motion, so that for him the physical body coincided with the mathematical (cf. below, No. 4).   In order to maintain a distinction between the two, Henry More,[3] on the contrary, demanded that impenetrability, regarded as the property of filling space, should also be reckoned to the essential nature of bodies, and Locke,[4] in accordance with this view, took up "solidity" into the class of primary qualities.

With *Hobbes*[5] these thoughts become modified more in accordance with the terministic conception.   He regards space (as *phantasma rei existentis*) and time (as *phantasma motus*) as also modes of mental representation, and it is just because we can therefore construct these ourselves that mathematical theory has the advantage of being the sole rational science.   But instead of drawing phenomenalistic conclusions from this premise, he argues that philosophy can treat only of bodies, and must leave everything spiritual to revelation. Scientific thought consequently consists, for him, only in the immanent combination of *signs*.   These are partly involuntary in perceptions, partly arbitrary in words (similarly Occam, cf. § 27, 4).   It is only by means of the latter that general conceptions and propositions become possible.   Our thinking is hence a *reckoning* with verbal signs.   It has its truth in itself and stands as something completely heterogeneous by the side of the outer world to which it relates.

3. All these suggestions become compressed in the system of Descartes to form the doctrine of the *dualism of substances*.   The analytic method was intended to discover the simple elements of reality which were self-explanatory and not susceptible of farther

---

[1] *Essay, Human Understanding*, II. 8, § 23 f.
[2] As *tertiary* qualities, Locke added further the "powers" for the operation of one body upon others.
[3] Desc. *Œuv.* (C.), X. pp. 181 ff.
[4] *Essay*, II. 4.
[5] *Human Nature*, chs. 2–5 ; *Leviathan*, chs. 4 ff.

deduction.   Descartes discovered that all that can be experienced is
a species either of spatial or of conscious Being or existence.   *Spatiality*, or the quality of filling space, and *consciousness* ("extension"
and "thought" according to the usual translation of *extensio* and *cogitatio*) are the ultimate, simple, original *attributes* of reality.   All
that is is either spatial or conscious.   For these two prime predicates are related disjunctively.   What is spatial is not conscious;
what is conscious is not spatial.   The self-certainty of mind is only
that of the personality as a conscious being.   Bodies are real in so
far as they have in themselves the quantitative determinations of
spatial existence and change, of extension and motion,   All things
are either bodies or minds; substances are either spatial or conscious : *res extensæ and res cogitantes.*

The world falls thus into two completely different and completely
separated realms : that of bodies and that of minds.   But in the
background of this dualism there stands in the thought of Descartes
the conception of the *deity* as the *ens perfectissimum* or *perfect substance.*   Bodies and minds are *finite things;* God is *infinite Being.*[1]
The *Meditations* leave no doubt as to the fact that Descartes accepted the conception of God quite in accordance with the interpretation of *scholastic Realism.*   The mind in its own Being, which
it recognises as a limited and imperfect one, apprehends with the
same intuitive certainty the Reality of the perfect, infinite Being
also (cf. above, § 30, 5).   To the ontological argument is added the
relation of God and the world in the form brought forward by
Nicolaus Cusanus, namely, that of the antithesis of the infinite and
the finite.   But the above-mentioned relationship with the Realism
of the Middle Ages appears most distinctly in the development of
metaphysics that succeeded Descartes : for the *pantheistic consequences* of this presupposition, which had been carefully held back
in the scholastic period, were now spoken out with complete clearness and sureness.   And if we find in the doctrines of Descartes'
successors a strong similarity with those which in the Middle Ages
could lead but a more or less repressed existence, this is intelligible
even without the assumption of a direct historical dependence,
merely by the pragmatic connection and the logical necessity of the
conclusions.

4. The common metaphysical name of "substance," applied to
God in the infinite sense, and to minds and bodies in a finite sense,
could not permanently cover the problems which were hidden be-

---

[1] So likewise Malebranche said (*Rech.* III. 2, 9 a. E.) that God could properly
be called only *Celui qui est*, he is *l'être sans restriction, tout être infini est
universel.*

neath it. The conception of substance had come into a state of flux, and needed further re-shaping. It had almost lost touch with the idea of "thing," the category of inherence; for just the combination of a multiplicity of determinations into the idea of a unitary concrete entity, which is essential to this category, was completely lacking in Descartes' conception of finite substances, since these were held to be characterised by *one* fundamental quality, spatiality or consciousness. All else that was found in substances must therefore be regarded as a modification of its fundamental quality, of its *attribute.* All qualities and states of bodies are *modes* of their spatiality or extension: all qualities and states of mind are *modes* of consciousness (*modi cogitandi*).

It is involved in this that all particular substances belonging to either class, all bodies on the one hand and all minds on the other, are alike in their essence, their constitutive attribute. But from this it is only a step farther to the idea in which this likeness is thought as metaphysical identity. All bodies are spatial, all minds are conscious; individual bodies are distinguished from one another only by different modes of spatiality (form, size, situation, motion); individual minds are distinguished from one another only by different modes of consciousness (ideas, judgments, activities of will). Individual bodies are modes of spatiality, individual minds are modes of consciousness. In this way the attribute obtains metaphysical preponderance over individual substances, which now appear as its modifications; the *res extensæ* become *modi extensionis;* the *res cogitantes, modi cogitationis.*

Descartes himself drew this conclusion only in the domain of natural philosophy, to which in general he restricted the carrying out of his metaphysical doctrine in its principles. Here, however, the general conception of modification took on, of itself, a definite significance, and one capable of apprehension by perception or imagination, viz. that of limitation (*determinatio*). Bodies are *parts of space*, limitations of the universal space-filling quality or extension.[1] Hence for Descartes the conception of body coincides with that of a limited spatial magnitude. A body is, as regards its true essence, a portion of space. The elements of the corporeal world are the "*corpuscles*,"[2]

---

[1] Cf. *Princ. Phil.* II. 9 f., where, at the same time, it appears quite clearly that this relation of the individual body to universal space is made equivalent to that of individual and species.

[2] For the corpuscular theory, Descartes found many suggestions in Bacon, Hobbes, Basso, Sennert, and others. The variety in the development of this theory, which rests upon the dialectic between the mathematical and the physical momenta, has more interest for natural science than for philosophy. An excellent exposition is found in Lasswitz, *Geschichte der Atomistik.*

i.e. the firm spatial particles which *realiter* are no longer divisible ; as mathematical structures, however, they are infinitely divisible ; that is, there are no atoms. From these presuppositions follow, likewise, for Descartes, the impossibility of empty space, and the infinitude of the corporeal world.

For the mental world the analogous claim was pronounced by *Malebranche.* In connection with the epistemological motives (cf. below, No. 8) which made it seem to him that no knowledge of things is possible except in God, he came [1] to the conception of the *raison universelle*, which, as being alike in all individual minds, cannot belong to the modes of the finite mind, but is rather that of which finite minds are themselves modifications, and can, just on this account, be none other than an attribute of God. God is in so far the "place of minds" or spirits, just as space is the place of bodies. Here, also, as the expression proves, the relation which obtains in conceptions between the universal and the particular underlies the thought, and following the analogy of the Cartesian conception of space and body this relation is thought in perceptional or picturate terms as *participation.* [2] All human insight is a participation in the infinite Reason, all ideas of finite things are but determinations of the idea of God, all desires directed toward the particular object are but participations in that love toward God as the ground of its essence and life, which necessarily dwells in the finite mind. To be sure, Malebranche came into a very critical situation by thus making the finite mind disappear completely in the universal divine mind, as its modification. For how, in accordance with this, should he explain the self-subsistence and self-activity which it seemed were quite notoriously present in those inclinations and volitions of man which opposed God ? In this difficulty nothing availed but the word "freedom," in using which Malebranche was indeed obliged to confess that freedom was an impenetrable mystery. [3]

5. In this course of thought pursued by Malebranche appears clearly the inevitable logical consistency with which the attributes, which were regarded by Descartes as the common essence belonging to either of the two classes of finite substances, could ultimately be thought only as the *attributes of the infinite substance or deity.* But precisely in this point consists the fundamental motive of *Spinozism*, which developed along this line out of Cartesianism directly and at the outset, and at the same time developed to the farthest

---

[1] *Rech. de la Vér.* III. 2, 6 ; *Entret.* I. 10.
[2] Recall the Platonic μέθεξις !   [3] Cf. above, p. 394, note 2.

consequence.   Spinozism likewise holds as firmly to the qualitative
as to the causal dualism of spatiality and consciousness.   The spatial and the spiritual worlds are entirely heterogeneous and absolutely independent of each other.   But the whole endless series of
bodies, with their divisions, forms, and motions, are only the modes
of extension, just as the endless series of minds with their ideas
and volitions are only the modes of consciousness.   Hence these
finite "things" are no longer entitled to the name of "substance."
That only can be called substance, whose attributes are extension
and consciousness themselves, viz. the infinite existence or Being,
the *deity*.   But its essence, in turn, cannot be exhausted in these
two attributes which are accessible to human experience; the *ens
realissimum* involves within itself the actuality of the *infinite number of all possible attributes*.

The ultimate ground of this position also lies in the scholastic-
realistic conception of the most real being.   Spinoza's definition of
substance or *the deity*, as the essence (*essentia*) which involves its
own existence, is only the condensed expression of the ontological
proof for the existence of God: the "*aseïtas*" is preserved in the
term "*causa sui*"; substance as that "*quod in se est et per se concipitur*" is again but another transcription of the same thought.
Proceeding from these definitions, the proof for the oneness and
infinitude of substance[1] followed as a matter of course.

That, however, we have here to do with an entirely realistic
course of thought becomes clearly manifest from Spinoza's doctrine
of the nature of substance itself and of its relation to the attributes.
For the Spinozistic system says absolutely nothing of substance or
of the deity farther than the formal determinations contained in the
conception of the *ens realissimum*, of absolute Being.   Every predicate expressing any content is, on the contrary, expressly denied:
and in particular Spinoza is especially careful to refuse[2] to the divine
essence the modifications of consciousness, such as intellectual cognition [*intellectus, Erkenntniss*] and will.   Just as little of course
does he recognise the modifications of extension as being predicates
of the divine essence, though he had no polemical inducement to
express this especially.   God himself is therefore neither mind
nor body; of him it can only be said, that he is.   It is evident that
the old *principle of negative theology* is here present with a changed
form of expression.   Knowledge of all finite things and states leads
to two highest universal conceptions: space-filling quality or extension, and consciousness.   To both of these a higher metaphysical

---

[1] *Eth.* I. Props. 1–14.   [2] Ib. I. 31.

dignity is ascribed than to finite things; they are the attributes, and the things are their modes. But if the process of abstraction now rises from these two determinations, the last which contain any content, to the most general, to the *ens generalissimum,* then all definite content falls away from the conception of this being, and only the empty Form of substance is left. For Spinoza, also, the deity is all and thus — nothing. His doctrine of God lies quite along the path of Mysticism.[1]

But if God is thus the general essence of finite things, he does not exist otherwise than in them and with them. This applies first of all to the attributes. God is not distinct from them, and they are not distinct from him, just as the dimensions of space are not distinct from space itself. Hence Spinoza can say also that God consists of countless attributes, or *Deus* sive *omnia ejus attributa.*[2] And the same relation is afterwards repeated between the attributes and the modes. Every attribute, because it expresses the infinite essence of God in a definite manner, is again infinite in its own way; but it does not exist otherwise than with and in its countless modifications. God then exists only in things as their universal essence, and they only in him as the modes of his reality. In this sense Spinoza adopts from Nicolaus Cusanus and Giordano Bruno the expressions *natura naturans* and *natura naturata.* God is Nature: as the universal world-essence, he is the *natura naturans;* as sumtotal of the individual things in which this essence exists modified, he is the *natura naturata.* If in this connection the *natura naturans* is called occasionally also the efficient cause of things, this creative force must not be thought as something distinct from its workings; this cause exists nowhere but in its workings. This is Spinoza's complete and unreserved *pantheism.*

Finally this relation is repeated yet again in the distinction which Spinoza establishes between the infinite and the finite modes.[3] If each of the countless finite things is a mode of God, the infinite connection or coherence which exists between them must also be regarded as a mode, and, indeed, as an *infinite mode.* Spinoza affirms three of these.[4] The deity as the universal world-thing appears in individual things, which are finite modes; to them corresponds as

---

[1] To this corresponds also his *theory of cognition* with its three stages, which sets "*intuition,*" as the immediate apprehension of the eternal logical resulting of all things from God, as knowledge *sub specie æternitatis,* above perception and the activity of the intellect.

[2] Which, however, is in nowise to be interpreted as if the attributes were self-subsistent prime realities and "God" only the collective name for them (as K. Thomas supposed, *Sp. als Metaphysiker,* Königsberg, 1840). Such a crassly nominalistic cap-stone would press the whole system out of joint.

[3] *Eth.* I. 23 and 30 ff.   [4] *Ep.* 64 (*Op.* II. 219).

infinite mode the universe. In the attribute of extension the finite modes are the particular space-forms; the infinite mode is infinite space, or matter [1] itself in its motion and rest. For the attribute of consciousness, the *intellectus infinitus* [2] stands beside the particular functions of ideation and will. Here Spinoza reminds us immediately of the realistic pantheism of David of Dinant (cf. § 27, 1). His metaphysics is the last word of mediæval Realism. [3]

6. With these motives relating to the problem of the qualitative difference of substances modern philosophy struggled out of its dualistic presuppositions to a monistic adjustment; but at the same time, still more powerful motives became mingled in the process, — motives which grew out of the real and causal separation of the spatial and the conscious worlds. At first, indeed, it was the principles of mechanics themselves which demanded the attempt to isolate completely the course of events in each of the two spheres of finite substances.

This succeeded in the corporeal world in a relatively simple manner. In this domain, the *idea of cause had acquired a completely new significance* through Galileo. According to the scholastic conception (which even in Descartes' *Meditations,* in a decisive passage, was still presented with axiomatic validity) causes were *substances* or things, while effects, on the other hand, were either their activities or were other substances and things which were held to come about only by such activities : this was the Platonic-Aristotelian conception of the αἰτία. Galileo, on the contrary, went back to the idea of the older Greek thinkers (cf. § 5), who applied the causal relation only to the *states* — that meant now to the *motions* of substances — not to the Being of the substances themselves. Causes are motions, and effects are motions. The relation of *impact* and *counter-impact,* of the *passing over of motion from one corpuscle to another,* [4] is the original *fundamental form of the causal relation,* the form which is clear to perception or imagination (*anschaulich*), is intelligible in

---

[1] This equivalence holds good with Spinoza as well as with Descartes.

[2] This *intellectus infinitus* appears again in the ethical part of the Spinozistic system as *amor intellectualis quo deus se ipsum amat.* In both cases Malebranche's "*raison universelle*" amounts to the same thing.

[3] Geulincx also, in a manner similar to that of Spinoza and Malebranche, regards finite bodies and minds as only "limitations," "*præcisiones*" of the universal infinite body and the divine mind. Cf. *Met.* p. 56. If we think away limitation from ourselves, he says, ib. 237 ff., there is left — God.

[4] Hence for Descartes the mechanical principle excluded possibility of action at a distance, just as it excluded empty space. This forced him to the artificial hypotheses of the *vortex theory,* by which he aimed to give a physical ground for the Copernican view of the world (popular exposition by Fontenelle, *Entretiens sur la Pluralité des Mondes,* 1686). The grounds on which this doctrine was displaced by the Newtonian theory of gravitation are no longer philosophical, but purely physical in their nature.

itself, and explains all others. And the question as to the nature of this fundamental relation was answered by the *principle of mathematical equality*, which, in turn, passed over into that of *metaphysical identity*. So much motion in the cause, so much in the effect also. Descartes formulated this as the *law of the conservation of motion* in Nature. The sum of motion in Nature remains always the same: what a body loses in motion it gives to another. As regards the amount of motion, there is in Nature nothing new, especially no impulse from the spiritual world.[1] Even for the kingdom of organisms this principle was carried through, at least as a postulate, though as yet with very weak grounds. Animals, also, are machines whose motions are evoked and determined by the mechanism of the nervous system. Descartes thought of this mechanism more precisely (and with him Hobbes and Spinoza) as a motion of finest (gaseous) substances, the so-called *spiritus animales*,[2] and sought the point of transition from the sensory to the motor nervous system in man, in a part of the brain which has no correlative, *i.e.* is a single and not a paired organ, the pineal gland or *conarium*.

The other part of the task proved much more difficult: namely, that of understanding the mental life without any relation to the corporeal world. Easy and clear to perception as was the action of one body upon another, it did not yield a mode of representing an incorporeal connection between different minds, that could be used scientifically. Spinoza, for example, expressed the general metaphysical postulate very energetically, when he promised in entering upon the third book of the Ethics, that he would treat the actions and desires of man as if lines, surfaces, and bodies were the subject of discussion; for the important thing is neither to asperse them nor to deride them, but to understand them. But the solution of this problem was limited in advance to investigating the causal connection between the *activities of consciousness in the individual mind*: dualism demanded a psychology free from all physiological constituents. It is all the more characteristic of the predominance of the spirit of natural science in the seventeenth century, that it attained this psychology demanded by the theory, only in the most limited degree. And even the beginnings toward this are ruled by the endeavour to apply the methodical principle of mechanics, which

---

[1] Hence Hobbes excluded from physics the Aristotelian and Thomistic conception of the unmoved mover, while Descartes, who in this point also proceeded more metaphysically, made motion to have been communicated to matter at the beginning by God.

[2] An inheritance from the physiological psychology of the Greeks, in particular from that of the Peripatetics.

was celebrating its triumphs in the theory of outer experience, to the comprehension of the inner world also.

For just as the investigation of Nature from Galileo to Newton directed its energies toward finding out the simple fundamental form of corporeal motion, to which all complex structures of outer experience could be reduced, so Descartes desired to establish the fundamental forms of psychical motion, out of which the multiplicity of inner experiences would become explicable. In the theoretical domain this seemed attained by establishing the immediately evident truths (the innate ideas); in the practical field there grew out of this demand the new problem of a *statics and a mechanics of the movements of feeling* (*Gemüthsbewegungen*). In this spirit Descartes and Spinoza produced their natural history of the *emotions* (*Affecte*) and *passions*,[1] the latter author by combining the thoughts of the former with those of Hobbes. Thus *Descartes* derives the whole host of particular passions, as species and sub-species, from the six fundamental forms of wonder (*admiratio*), love, and hate, desire (*désir*), pleasure and pain [or joy and sadness, *Lust und Unlust*] (*lœtitia — tristitia*); thus *Spinoza* develops his system of the emotions out of desire, pleasure, and pain (*appetitus, lœtitia, tristitia*) by pointing out the ideational processes in connection with which these emotions have become transferred from their original object, the self-preservation of the individual, to other "ideas."

A peculiar side-attitude is taken in this regard by the two English thinkers. For *Bacon* and *Hobbes*, a mechanical conception of the mental is the more natural in proportion as they endeavour to draw the mental more closely into the circle of the physical. Both, that is, regard the empirical psychical life, and therefore, also, the sphere of consciousness which in Descartes' system was to have nothing to do with the corporeal world, as something which essentially belongs thereto; on the other hand, there is set over against the whole world of perception rather a something spiritual [spiritual in the religious sense, *Geistliches*] than a something mental or intellectual [*Geistiges*]. Ideas and volitions as they are known by experience are held to be at bottom activities of the body also, and if besides these we speak yet of an immortal soul (*spiraculum*), of a spiritual world and of the divine mind or spirit, this should fall to the province of theology. But according to this view the natural science theory cannot be characterised much otherwise than as an

---

[1] Descartes, *Les Passions de l'Âme;* Spinoza, *Eth.* III., and *Tract. Brev.* II. 5 ff. Cf. below, No. 7.

anthropological materialism; for it aims to understand the entire series of empirical psychical activities as a mechanical process connected with the bodily functions. This problem was propounded by Bacon; Hobbes attempted to solve it, and in doing so became the father of the so-called *associational psychology.* With the same outspoken *sensualism* as *Campanella,* of whose deductions his own frequently remind us, — especially with regard to the mechanism of ideas, — he seeks to show that *sense-impressions* give the only elements of consciousness, and that by their combination and transformation memory and thought also come about. In the practical domain the impulse toward self-preservation and the feelings of pleasure and pain which arise in connection with impressions are then characterised analogously as the elements out of which all other feelings and activities of will arise. Hobbes, too, projected thus a "natural history" of the emotions and passions, and this was not without influence upon that of Spinoza, whose theory of the emotions is always looking towards the other attribute [*i.e.* extension].

From these presuppositions of method the *denial of the freedom of the will* in the sense of indeterminism followed with inexorable consistency for *Hobbes* and for *Spinoza.* Both attempted — and Spinoza did it in the baldest form that can be conceived — to exhibit the strict necessity which prevails even in the course of the process of motivation: they are types of *determinism.* For Spinoza, therefore, there is no freedom in the *psychological* sense. Freedom can mean only, on the one hand, metaphysically, the absolute Being of the deity determined by nothing but itself, and, on the other hand, ethically, the ideal of the overcoming of the passions through reason.

7. In this it became already evident that in the presence of the facts of psychology, that absolute separation between the corporeal and the mental world which metaphysics demanded was not to be maintained. But Descartes himself met quite the same experience. The nature of the mind itself might, indeed, explain the clear and distinct ideas and the forms of the rational will which resulted from these, but it could not explain the obscure and confused ideas, and the emotions and passions connected with them. These present themselves rather as a *disturbance of the mind*[1] (*perturbationes animi*), and since this perturbation which gives occasion for the

---

[1] This is the interest, not only ethical, but also theoretical, which induced Descartes to treat states psychologically so different as emotions and passions, from the same point of view and in one line. Cf. for the following *Passions de l'Ame,* **I.,** and *Meds.* V. and VI.

abuse of freedom (cf. above, § 30, 5) cannot be due to God, its origin must be sought ultimately in an *influence exercised by the body*. In the disturbances of the feeling there is, therefore, for Descartes an indubitable fact, which cannot be explained from the fundamental metaphysical principles of his system. Here, therefore, the philosopher sees himself forced to recognise an *exceptional relation*, and he adjusts this for himself in a way that had been foreshadowed by the anthropology of the *Victorines* (cf. § 24, 2). The nature (*natura*) of man, he teaches, consists in the *inner union of two heterogeneous substances*, a mind and a body, and this marvellous (*i.e.* metaphysically incomprehensible) union has been so arranged by God's will that in this single case the conscious and the spatial substances act upon each other. Animals remain, for Descartes, bodies; their "sensations" are only nervous movements, out of which stimulations of the motor system arise in accordance with the reflex mechanism. In the human body, however, the mental substance is present at the same time, and in consequence of this co-existence the storm of the animal spirits in the pineal gland excites a disturbance in the mental substance also, which manifests itself in the latter as an unclear and indistinct idea, *i.e.* as sense-perception, as emotion, or as passion.[1]

With the disciples, the systematic impulse was greater than with the master. They found in this *influxus physicus* between mind and body the vulnerable point in the Cartesian philosophy, and exerted themselves to set aside the exception which the philosopher had been obliged to assert in the anthropological facts. This, however, did not go on without effecting a new, and in a certain sense regressive, alteration in the conception of *causality*, in that the metaphysical *moment* once more gained preponderance over the mechanical. The immanent causal processes of the spatial and of the conscious worlds were regarded as intelligible in themselves; but the transcendent causal process from one of these worlds into the other formed a problem. No difficulty was found in the idea that one motion transformed itself into another or that one function of

---

[1] On this Descartes then builds his Ethics. In such perturbations the mind occupies a passive attitude, and it is its task to free itself from these in clear and distinct knowledge. *Spinoza* carried out this intellectualistic morals in an extremely grand and impressive manner (*Eth.* IV. and V.). The antithesis of an active and passive attitude of the finite mind is indeed gained from the standpoint of his metaphysics only artificially (*Eth.* III., Def. 2): but he carried through with compelling consistency the thought, that the overcoming of the passions follows from a knowledge of them, from the insight into the necessary divine system of all things; he taught that human nature must perfect itself in the blessedness of the *active emotions* which consist only in the activity of the pure impulse toward knowledge (*Eth.* V. 15 ff.), and thus set up an ideal of life which reaches the height of the Greek θεωρία.

consciousness — for example, a thought — should pass over into another: but it seemed impossible to understand how sensation should come out of motion, or motion out of will. Physical and logical causality seemed to offer no difficulty; so much the greater was that presented by *psycho-physical causality*. In the case of the latter the consciousness dawned that the relation of *equality or identity* between cause and effect, by means of which mechanical and logical dependence seemed intelligible, does not exist. Hence an inquiry must here be made for the principle by which the two elements of the causal relation, cause and effect, which do not in themselves belong together, are connected with each other.[1] Where this principle was to be sought could not be a matter of doubt for the disciples of Descartes : God, who produced the union of the two substances in man's nature, has also so arranged them that the functions of the one substance are followed by the corresponding functions of the other. But on this account these functions in their causal relation to one another are not properly, and in their own nature, efficient causes, but only *occasions* in connection with which the consequences determined *by divine contrivance* appear in the other substance, — not *causæ efficientes*, but *causæ occasionales*. The true "cause" for the causal connection between stimuli and sensations, and between purposes and bodily movements, is *God*.

Such considerations are multiplied in the whole development of the Cartesian school. Clauberg brings them into use for the theory of perceptions, Cordemoy for that of purposive motion; their full development is attained in the "Ethics" of *Geulincx*. Yet in the latter author doubt is not entirely excluded as to whether God's causality in this connection is regarded as a special intervention in each individual case, or as a general and permanent arrangement. In some passages, indeed, the former is the case,[2] but the spirit of the doctrine, taken as a whole, doubtless involves the latter. Geulincx expresses himself most clearly in the illustration of the clocks :[3] as two clocks which have been made alike by the same artificer continue to move in perfect harmony, " *absque ulla causalitate qua alterum hoc in altero causat, sed propter meram dependentiam, qua utrumque ab eadem arte et simili industria constitutum est,*" so the

---

[1] That the fundamental difficulty in *all* causal relations was in this actually stumbled upon, first became clear at a later time through Hume. Cf. § 34.

[2] For example, in the analogy of the child in the cradle, *Eth.* 123. It seems, besides, that the first edition of the *Ethics* (1665), in fact, introduced more the *deus ex machina*, while the annotations added in the second edition (1675) present throughout the profounder view.

[3] *Eth.*, p. 124, note 19.

corresponding functions of mind and body follow each other in accordance with the world-order once determined by God.[1]

8. This *anthropological* rationale of *Occasionalism* fits from the beginning into a more general metaphysical course of thought. The Cartesian system already contained the premises for the inference that in the case of all that takes place in finite substances, the efficient principle derives, not from these substances themselves, but from the deity. Thinking in minds takes place by means of the inborn ideas which God has given them; to the corporeal world he has communicated a *quantum* of motion which changes only in its distribution among the individual corpuscles, but in the case of the individual body it is, so to speak, only temporarily concealed. Minds can create new ideas as little as bodies can create new motion ; the sole cause is God.

The Cartesians had all the more occasion to emphasise the *sole causality of God,* as their doctrine encountered violent contradiction in the orthodoxy of both Confessions, and became involved in the theological controversies of the time. Friend and foe had quickly recognised the relationship of Cartesianism with the doctrine of Augustine ;[2] and while on this account the Jansenists and the Fathers of the Oratory, who lived in the Augustinian-Scotist atmosphere, were friendly to the new philosophy, the orthodox Peripatetics, and especially the Jesuits, made war upon it all the more violently. Thus the *old opposition* between *Augustianism and Thomism* came out in the controversy over Cartesianism. The consequence was that the Cartesians brought into the foreground as far as possible those elements in which their doctrine was allied to the Augustinian. So *Louis de la Forge*[3] attempted to prove the complete identity of Cartesianism with the doctrine of the Church Father, and emphasised especially the fact that according to both thinkers the sole ground of all that takes place in bodies as well as minds is God. Just this was later designated by *Malebranche*[4] as the sure mark of a Christian philosophy, while the most dangerous

---

[1] If, therefore, Leibniz, when he later claimed for his " pre-established harmony " (*Éclairc.* 2 and 3) this same analogy in frequent use at that time, characterised the Cartesian conception by an immediate dependence of the two clocks upon one another, and the Occasionalistic by a constantly renewed regulation of the clocks on the part of the clock-maker, this was applicable at most to some passages in the first edition of the *Ethics* of Geulincx.

[2] Kinship and opposition apply also to still other points. Descartes and the priests of the Oratory (Gibieuf, Malebranche) are at one against Thomism in the Augustinian and Scotist doctrine of the boundless freedom of the deity ; they maintain again that the good is good because God so willed it, not *per se* (cf. § 26, 2, 3), etc.

[3] *Trait. de l'Espr. Hum.*, Préf.   [4] *Recherche,* VI. 2, 3.

error of heathen philosophy consists in the assumption of metaphysical self-subsistence and capacity for spontaneous action on the part of finite things.

With *Geulincx*, likewise, all finite things are deprived of the causal *moment* or element of substantiality. In this he proceeds from the principle[1] that one can himself do that only of which he knows how it is done. From this it follows in the anthropological field, that the mind cannot be the cause of the bodily movements — no one knows how he sets to work even but to raise his arm; it follows farther in the cosmological field, that bodies which have no ideas whatever cannot operate at all, and finally, for the theory of knowledge, that the cause of perceptions is to be sought not in the finite mind — for this does not know how it comes to perceive — nor in bodies; therefore it is to be sought only in God. He produces in us a world of ideas which in its wealth of qualities is much richer and more beautiful than the actual corporeal world itself.[2]

The epistemological *motif* finds finally with *Malebranche*[3] a still more profound apprehension. Cartesian dualism makes a direct knowledge of the body by mind absolutely impossible : such a knowledge is excluded not only because no *influxus physicus* is possible between the two, but also because, in view of the total heterogeneity of the two substances, it is not possible to see how even an idea of the one is thinkable in the other. In this respect, also, mediation is possible only through the deity, and Malebranche takes refuge in the Neo-Platonic world of Ideas in God. Man does not know bodies; he knows their Ideas in God. This *intelligible corporeal world in God* is, on the one hand, the archetype of the actual corporeal world created by God, and on the other hand, the archetype of those ideas which God has communicated to us of this actual corporeal world. Our knowledge is like the actual bodies, just as two magnitudes which are equal to a third are equal also to each other. In this sense Malebranche understood that philosophy teaches that we *behold all things in God.*

9. Quite different was the solution which *Spinoza* gave to the Occasionalistic problems. The explanation of any mode of the one attribute by a mode of the other was excluded by the conception of

---

[1] *Eth.*, p. 113 ; *Met.*, p. 26.

[2] The remnant of self-activity in finite beings that remains in the system of Geulincx consists in the immanent mental activity of man. Cf. *Eth.* 121 f. The " autology," or *inspectio sui*, is, therefore, not only the epistemological starting-point of the system, but also its ethical conclusion. Man has nothing to do in the outer world. *Ubi nihil vales, ibi nihil velis.* The highest virtue is a modest contentment, submission to God's will — humility, *despectio sui.*

[3] *Rech.* III. 2.

the attribute as he had defined it (see above, No. 5) ; it held of the attribute as of substance,[1] *in se est et per se concipitur.* Accordingly there could be no question of the dependence of the spatial upon consciousness, or *vice versa;* the appearance of such a dependence which presents itself in the anthropological facts needed, therefore, another explanation, and as a matter of course this was to be sought by the aid of his conception of God.   If, however, the doctrine that God is the sole cause of all that takes place is for this reason found also with Spinoza, his agreement with the Occasionalists exists only in the motive and the word, but not in the meaning or spirit of the doctrine.   For according to Geulincx and Malebranche, God is the creator; according to Spinoza, he is the universal essence or nature of things; according to the former, God creates the world by his will; according to the latter, the world *follows necessarily* from the nature of God [or is the *necessary consequence* of the nature of God]. In spite of the likeness in the word *causa,* therefore, the causal relation is really thought here in a sense entirely different from that which it has there.   With Spinoza it means not, "God creates the world," but, "he is the world."

Spinoza always expresses his conception of real dependence, of causality, by the word " follow " (*sequi, consequi*) and by the addition, "as from the definition of a triangle the equality of the sum of its angles to two right angles follows."   The dependence of the world upon God is, therefore, thought as a *mathematical consequence.*[2] This conception of the causal relation has thus completely stripped off the empirical mark of "producing " or " creating " which played so important a part with the Occasionalists, and replaces the perceptional idea of active operation with the *logico-mathematical relation of ground and consequent* [*or reason and consequent; Grund und Folge*].   Spinozism is a consistent identification of the relation of cause and effect with that of ground and consequent.   The causality of the deity is, therefore, not in time, but is *eternal,* that is, timeless ; and true knowledge is a consideration of things *sub quadam œternitatis specie.*   This conception of the relation of dependence resulted of itself from the conception of the deity as the universal essence or nature : from this nature all its modifications follow *timelessly,* just as all propositions of geometry follow from the nature of space. The geometrical method knows no other causality than that of the "eternal consequence "; for rationalism, only that form of dependence which is peculiar to thought itself, namely, the logical proced-

---

[1] *Eth.* I., Prop. 10.
[2] Cf. Schopenhauer, *Ueber die vierfache Wurzel des Satzes vom zureichende Grunde,* ch. 6.   [*Fourfold Root,* etc., Bohn Lib.]

ure of the consequent from its antecedent reason, passes as in itself intelligible, and on this account as the schema also for events or cosmic processes : [1] real dependence also should be conceived neither mechanically nor teleologically, but only logico-mathematically.

But now, as in geometry, all follows indeed from the nature of space, and yet each particular relation is fixed by other particular determinations, so, too, in the Spinozistic metaphysics the necessary procedure of things forth from God consists in the determination of every individual finite entity by other finite things. The sum of finite things and the modes of each attribute form a chain of strict determination, a chain without beginning and without end. The necessity of the divine nature rules in all ; but no mode is nearer to the deity, or farther from the deity, than is any other. In this the thought of Nicolaus Cusanus of the incommensurability of the finite with the infinite asserts itself — no series of stages of emanation leads from God down to the world : everything finite is determined again by the finite, but in all God is the sole ground of their essence or nature.

If this is the case, the unity of essence must appear also in the relation of the attributes, however strictly these may be separated qualitatively and causally. It is still the same divine essence which exists here in the form of extension, and there in the form of consciousness. The two attributes are then necessarily so related to each other that to every mode of the one a definite mode of the other corresponds. This *correspondence* or *parallelism* of the attributes solves the enigma of the connection of the two worlds : ideas are determined only by ideas, and motions only by motions ; but it is the like cosmic content of the divine essence which forms the connection of the one class, and also that of the other ; the same content is in the attribute of consciousness as in the attribute of extension. This relation is presented by Spinoza in accordance with the scholastic conceptions of the *esse in intellectu* and the *esse in re*. The same that exists in the attribute of consciousness as object (*objective*), as the content of our ideas, exists in the attribute of extension as something actual, independent of any idea or mental representation (*formaliter*).[2]

---

[1] Spinoza's pantheism has therefore the closest resemblance to the scholastic mystical *Realism* of Scotus Erigena (cf. § 23, 1), only that in the latter's system it is still more the case that the logical relation of the general to the particular forms the only schema ; from this resulted, in his case, the emanistic character which is lacking in Spinoza.

[2] But neither of these two modes of existence is more original than the other, or forms a prototype for the other : both express equally the nature of God (*exprimere*). Hence an idealistic interpretation of Spinoza is as incorrect as a materialistic, although both might be developed out of his system.

Spinoza's conception, then, is this: every finite thing as a mode of the divine essence, *e.g.* man, exists in like measure in both attributes, as mind and as body: and each of its particular functions belongs also in like measure to both attributes, as idea and as motion.   As idea, it is determined by the connection of ideas, as motion by that of motions; but in both, the content is the same by virtue of the correspondence of the attributes.   *The human mind is the idea (Idee) of the human body*, both as a whole and in detail.[1]

10. The conclusion of this movement of thought which had passed through so many divarifications was reached in the metaphysical system of *Leibniz*, — a system which is equalled by none in the entire history of philosophy in all-sidedness of motives and in power of adjustment and combination.   It owes this importance not only to the extensive learning and the harmonising mind of its author, but especially to the circumstance that he was at home in the ideas of ancient and mediæval philosophy with as deep and fine an understanding of their significance as he had for the conceptions formed by the modern study of Nature.[2]   Only the inventor of the differential calculus, who had as much understanding for Plato and Aristotle as for Descartes and Spinoza, who knew and appreciated Thomas and Duns Scotus as well as Bacon and Hobbes, — only he could become the creator of the " pre-established harmony."

The reconciliation of the mechanical and the teleological views of the world, and with this the *uniting of the scientific and the religious interests* of his time, was the leading motive in the thought of Leibniz.   He wished to see the mechanical explanation of Nature, the formulation of which in its scientific conceptions he himself essentially furthered, carried through to its full extent, and at the same time he cast about for thoughts by the aid of which the purposeful living character of the universe might nevertheless remain comprehensible.   The attempt must therefore be made — an attempt for which there were already intimations in the doctrine of Descartes — to see whether the whole mechanical course of events could not be ultimately traced back to efficient causes, whose purposeful nature should afford an import and meaning to their working taken as a whole.   The whole philosophical development of Leibniz has the aim to substitute for the corpuscles, " entelechies," and to win back for the indifferent God of the geometrical method the rights of the Platonic αἰτία.   The ultimate goal of his philosophy is to under-

---

[1] The difficulties which arose in this connection from self-consciousness, and those also from the postulate of the countless attributes, Spinoza did not solve: cf. the correspondence with Tschirnhausen, *Op.* II. 219 f.

[2] Cf. *Syst. Nouv.* 10.

stand the mechanism of the cosmic processes as the *means* and *phenomenal form* by which the living content or import of the world realises itself.   For this reason he could no longer think "cause" as only "Being," could no longer think God merely as *ens perfectissimum,* could no longer think "substance" as characterised merely by an attribute of unchangeable existence, and could no longer think its states merely as modifications, determinations, or specifications of such a fundamental quality: cosmic processes or change became again for him *active working (Wirken)*; substances took on the meaning of *forces,*[1] and the philosophical conception of God also had, for its essential characteristic, creative force.   This was Leibniz' fundamental thought, that this creative force evinces itself in the mechanical system of motions.

Leibniz attained this *dynamical* standpoint first in his theory of motion, and in a way which of itself required that the same standpoint should be carried over into metaphysics.[2]   The mechanical problem of inertia and the process begun by Galileo of resolving motion into infinitely small impulses, which together formed the starting-point for the authoritative investigations in natural science by Huyghens and Newton, led Leibniz to the principle of the infinitesimal calculus, to his conception of the "*vis viva,*" and especially, to the insight that the essential nature of bodies, in which the ground of motion is to be sought, consists not in extension, nor yet in their mass (impenetrability), but in their capacity to do work, — in force.   But if *substance* is *force,* it is *super-spatial* and *immaterial.*   On this account Leibniz finds himself compelled to think even corporeal substance as immaterial force.   Bodies are, in their essential nature, force; their spatial form, their property of filling space and their motion are effects of this force.   The substance of bodies is *meta*physical.[3]   In connection with Leibniz' doctrine of knowledge this purports that rational, clear, and distinct cognition apprehends bodies as force, while sensuous, obscure, and confused cognition apprehends them as spatial structures.   Hence, for Leibniz, space is neither identical with bodies (as in Descartes), nor the presupposition for them (as with Newton), but a force-product of substances, a *phœnomenon bene fundatum,* an order of co-existence, —

---

[1] La substance est un être capable d'action.   *Princ. de la Nat. et de la Grâce.*
1.   Cf. *Syst. Nouv.* 2 f., "Force primitive."

[2] *Syst. Nouv.* 3.

[3] With this the co-ordination of the two attributes, *extensio* and *cogitatio*, was again abolished; the world of consciousness is the truly actual, the world of extension is phenomenon.   Leibniz sets the intelligible world of substances over against the phenomena of the senses or material world in a completely Platonic fashion (*Nouv. Ess.* IV. 3).   Cf. § 33 f.

not an absolute reality, but an *ens mentale*.[1] And the same holds true, *mutatis mutandis*, of time.   From this it follows further, that the laws of mechanics which refer to these spatial manifestations of bodies are not rational, not "geometrical" truths, but truths which relate to matters of fact, and are contingent.   They could be thought otherwise [*i.e.* the opposite is not inconceivable].   Their ground is not logical necessity, but — purposiveness or appropriateness.   They are *lois de convenance;* and have their roots in the *choix de la sagesse*.[2]   God chose them because the purpose of the world would be best fulfilled in the form determined by them.   If bodies are machines, they are such in the sense that machines are purposively constructed works.[3]

11. Thus again in Leibniz, but in a maturer form than in Neo-Platonism, *life* becomes the principle for explaining Nature; his doctrine is *vitalism*.   But life is variety, and at the same time unity.   The mechanical theory led Leibniz to the conception of infinitely many individual forces, metaphysical points,[4] as likewise to the idea of their continuous connection.   He had originally leaned toward the atomic theory of Democritus and the nominalistic metaphysics; the Occasionalist movement, and above all, the system of Spinoza, made him familiar with the thought of the All-unity; and he found the solution, as Nicolaus Cusanus and Giordano Bruno had found it before, in the principle of the *identity of the part with the whole*.   Each force is the world-force, the cosmic force, but in a peculiar phase; every substance is the world-substance, but in particular form.   Hence Leibniz gives to the conception of *substance* just this meaning: it is *unity in plurality*.[5]   This means that every substance in every state "represents" the multitude of other substances, and to the nature of "representing" belongs always the unifying of a manifold.[6]

With these thoughts are united, in the system of Leibniz, the

---

[1] Cf. chiefly the correspondence with des Bosses.
[2] *Princ.* 11.   [3] Ib. 3.
[4] *Syst. Nouv.* 11.   [5] *Monad.* 13–16.
[6] Leibniz is here served a very good turn (cf. *op. cit.*) by the ambiguity in the word "*représentation*" (which applies also to the German "*vorstellen*" [and to the English "representation"]), in accordance with which the word means, on the one hand, to supply the place of or serve as a symbol of, and on the other hand, the function of consciousness.   That every substance "represents" the rest means, therefore, on the one hand, that all is contained in all (Leibniz cites the ancient σύμπνοια πάντα and also the *omnia ubique* of the Renaissance), and on the other hand, that each substance "perceives" all the rest.   The deeper sense and justification of this ambiguity lies in the fact that we cannot form any clear and distinct idea whatever of the unifying of a manifold, except after the pattern of that kind of connection which we experience within ourselves in the function of consciousness ("synthesis" in Kant's phraseology).

postulates which had been current in the metaphysical movement
since Descartes; namely, that of the isolation of substances with
reference to one another, and that of the correspondence of their
functions having its origin in the common world-ground.   Both *motifs*
are most perfectly brought out in the *Monadology*.   Leibniz calls his
force-substance *monad*, — an expression which might have come to
him along various lines of Renaissance tradition.   Each monad is
with reference to the rest a perfectly independent being, which can
neither experience nor exercise influence.   The monads "have no
windows," and this "windowlessness" is to a certain extent the
expression of their "metaphysical impenetrability."[1]   But this
quality of being completely closed to outward influence receives
first of all a positive expression from Leibniz in his declaration
that the monad is a *purely internal principle:*[2] substance is hence a
force of *immanent activity:* the monad is *not physical, but psychical*
in its nature.   Its states are representations (*Vorstellungen*), and
the principle of its activity is desire (*appétition*), the "tendency" to
pass over from one representation to another.[3]

Each monad is nevertheless, on the other hand, a "mirror of the
world"; it contains the whole universe as a representation within
itself; in this consists the living unity of all things.   But each is
also an *individual*, distinct from all others.   For there are no two
substances in the world alike.[4]   If now the monads are not distinguished by the content which they represent, — for this is the same
with all,[5] — their difference can be sought only in their mode of
representing this content, and Leibniz declares that the difference
between the monads consists only in the *different degree of clearness
and distinctness* with which they "represent" the universe.   Descartes'
epistemological criterion thus becomes a metaphysical predicate by
reason of the fact that Leibniz, like Duns Scotus (cf. p. 331), conceives of the antithesis of distinct and confused as an antithesis in
the force of representation or in *intensity*.   Hence the monad is regarded as active in so far as it represents clearly and distinctly, as
passive in so far as it represents obscurely and confusedly:[6] hence,
also, its impulse (*appétition*) is directed toward passing from obscure

---

[1] *Monad.* 7.   Cf. *Syst. Nouv.* 14, 17.
[2] *Monad.* 11.   [3] Ib. 15–19.
[4] Leibniz expressed this as the *principium identitatis indiscernibilium*
(*Monad.* 9).
[5] Here, to be sure, Leibniz overlooked the fact that no real content is reached
in this system of mutual representation of substances.   The monad *a* represents
the monads *b, c, d, . . . x.*   But what is the monad *b* ?   It is in turn the representation of the monads *a, c, d, . . . x.*   The same is true for *c*, and so on *in
infinitum.*
[6] *Monad.* 49.

to clear representations, and the "clearing up" of its own content is the goal of its life. To this above-mentioned intensity of the representations Leibniz applies the mechanical principle of infinitely small impulses : he calls these infinitely small constituent parts of the representative life of the monads *petites perceptions*,[1] and needs this hypothesis to explain the fact, that according to his doctrine the monad evidently has very many more representations than it is conscious of (cf. below, § 33). In the language of to-day the *petites perceptions* would be *unconscious mental states* (*Vorstellungen*).

Of such differences in degree of clearness and distinctness there are infinitely many, and in accordance with the law of continuity — *natura non facit saltum* — the monads form an uninterrupted graded series, a *great system of development*, which rises from the "simple" monads to souls and minds.[2] The lowest monads, which represent only obscurely and confusedly, *i.e.* unconsciously, are therefore only passive; they form *matter*. The highest monad, which represents the universe with perfect clearness and distinctness, — just for this reason there is but one such, — and is accordingly pure activity, is called the *central monad* — God. Inasmuch as each of these monads lives out its own nature, they all harmonise completely with each other at every moment[3] by virtue of the sameness of their content, and from this arises the appearance of the action of one substance upon others. This relation is the *harmonie préétablie des substances* — a doctrine in which the principle of *correspondence*, introduced by Geulincx and Spinoza for the relation of the two attributes, appears extended to the totality of all substances. Here as there, however, the principle as carried out involves the uninterrupted determination in the activity of all substances, the strict necessity of all that takes place, and excludes all chance and all freedom in the sense of uncaused action. Leibniz also rescues the conception of freedom for finite substances only in the ethical meaning of a control of reason over the senses and passions.[4]

The pre-established harmony — this relationship of substances in their Being and life — needs, however, a *unity* as the ground of its explanations, and this can be sought only in the central monad. God, who created the finite substances, gave to each its own content

---

[1] *Ib.* 21.

[2] *Princ.* 4. In this connection the "soul" is conceived of as the central monad of an organism, in that it represents most distinctly the monads constituting this, and accordingly only with a lesser degree of distinctness the rest of the universe. *Monad.* 61 ff.

[3] *Syst. Nouv.* 14.

[4] *Eo magis est libertas quo magis agitur ex ratione*, etc. Leibniz, *De Libert.* (*Op.*, Erd. ed., 669).

in a particular grade of representative intensity, and thereby so arranged all the monads that they should harmonise throughout. And in this necessary process in which their life unfolds, they realise the end of the creative Universal Spirit in the whole mechanical determination of the series of their representations. This relation of mechanism to teleology makes its way finally, also, into the epistemological principles of Leibniz. The deity and the other monads sustain the same relation to each other as the infinite and finite substances sustain in the system of Descartes. But for the rationalistic conception of things, only the infinite is a necessity of thought, while the finite, on the contrary, is something " contingent," in the sense that it might also be thought otherwise, that the opposite contains no contradiction (cf. above, § 30, 7). Thus the antithesis of eternal and necessary truths takes on metaphysical significance : only *God's Being* is an *eternal truth;* he exists, according to the principle of contradiction, with logical or *absolute necessity.* Finite things, however, are *contingent;* they exist only in accordance with the principle of sufficient reason, by virtue of their determination by another; the world and all that belongs to it has only conditioned, *hypothetical necessity.* This *contingency of the world,* Leibniz, in agreement with Duns Scotus,[1] traces back to the *will of God.* The world might have been otherwise; that it is as it is, it owes to the choice which God made between the many *possibilities.*[2]

Thus in Leibniz all threads of the old and the new metaphysics run together. With the aid of the conceptions formed in the school of mechanics he formulated the presages of the philosophy of the Renaissance into a systematic structure, where the ideas of Greece found their home in the midst of the knowledge acquired by modern investigation.

§ 32. Natural Right.

The Philosophy of Right of the Renaissance was also dependent, on the one hand, upon the stimulus of Humanism, and on the other, upon the needs of modern life. The former element is shown not only in the dependence upon ancient literature, but also in the revival of the ancient conception of the state, and in the attachment to its traditions; the latter make their appearance as a theoretical generalisation of those interests, in connection with which the

---

[1] The relations of Leibniz to the greatest of the Scholastics are to be recognized not only in this point, but also in many others ; though as yet they have unfortunately not found the consideration or treatment that they deserve.

[2] Cf., however, in addition, below, § 35.

secular states during this period took on the form of autonomous
life.

1. All these motives show themselves first in *Macchiavelli.* In
his admiration of Rome, the Italian *national feeling* speaks immediately, and it was from the study of ancient history that he gained
his theory of the *modern state*, at least as regards its negative side.
He demanded the complete independence of the state from the
Church, and carried Dante's Ghibelline doctrine of the state to its
farthest consequence. He combats the temporal sovereignty of the
Papacy as the permanent obstacle to an Italian national state, and
so that separation between the spiritual and the secular, which is
common to all the beginnings of modern thought, is completed for
the practical field in his system, as it had been before with Occam
and Marsilius of Padua (cf. p. 328). The consequence of this,
however, as with the Nominalists just mentioned, was that the state
was conceived not teleologically, but in purely *naturalistic* fashion
as a product of needs and interests. From this fact is explained
the singleness of aim and regardlessness with which Macchiavelli
carried out his theory of the acquisition and preservation of princely
power, and with which he treated politics solely from the point of
view of the warfare of interests.

The relation of church and state, moreover, excited an especial
interest in the sixteenth and seventeenth centuries, because it played
a part that was always important and often decisive in the conflicts
and shiftings of confessional oppositions. Here an interesting
exchange of conceptions came about. The Protestant view of the
world, which in accordance with its first principle changed the
mediæval distinction in value between the spiritual and the secular,
and removed the ban of the "profane" from the secular spheres
of life, saw in the state also a divine order; and the *Reformation
Philosophy of Right*, under the lead of *Melancthon*, limited the right
of the state more by the right of the invisible, than by the claims
of the visible Church; indeed, the divine mission of the magistrates
afforded a valuable support for the Protestant State-church. Much
less could the *Catholic Church* feel itself under obligation to the
modern state; and although it thereby departed from Thomism, it
allowed itself to be pleased by such theories as those of Bellarmin
and Mariana, in which the state was conceived of as a work of
human composition or as a compact. For with this theory the state
lost its higher authority, and to a certain extent its metaphysical
root; it appeared capable of abolition; the human will which had
created it might dissolve it again, and even its supreme head was
deprived of his absolute inviolability. While the Protestants re-

garded the state as an immediate divine order, for the Catholics, as being a human arrangement, it needed the sanction of the Church and ought not to be regarded as valid where this was lacking; but it should retain this sanction only when it placed itself at the service of the Church. So Campanella taught that the Spanish Empire (*monarchia*) had as its task to place the treasures of foreign parts of the world at the disposal of the Church for her contest with the heretics.

2. But in time these oppositions in the philosophy of rights yielded to *confessional indifferentism*, which had attained the mastery in theoretical science also, and since the state was regarded as essentially an order of earthly things, the relation of man to God fell outside its sphere of action. Philosophy demanded for the citizen the right which she claimed for herself, the right of a free, individual attitude toward the religious authorities of the time, and became thereby the champion of *toleration*. The state has not to trouble itself about the religious opinion of individuals, the right of the citizen is independent of his adherence to this or that confession: this demand was the necessary result of the confessional controversies of the sixteenth and seventeenth centuries, which had heaved and tossed so passionately to and fro. In this view unbelieving indifference, and positive conviction which had to defend itself against political authority of the opposite creed, came to an agreement.

In this spirit Macchiavelli had already written against the sole authority of the Roman Church; but it was by Thomas *More* that the principle of toleration was first proclaimed in its completeness. The inhabitants of his happy island belong to the most varied confessions, which all live peacefully side by side without any political importance being attributed to the variety of their religious views. They have even united upon a common worship, which each party interprets in its own sense, and supplements by special forms of worship. So, too, Jean *Bodin*, in his *Heptaplomeres*, makes highly educated typical representatives, not only of the Christian confessions, but also of Judaism, Mohammedanism, and Heathendom, find a form of worshipping God, which is equally satisfactory to all. Finally, in a more abstract manner, Hugo *Grotius* completely separated divine and human right in the sharp distinctness with which he presented the principles of the philosophical science of rights, basing divine right upon revelation and human right upon reason; demanding at the same time, however, an equally sharp and thoroughgoing separation of the spheres of life to which they apply.

But the classical "Doomsday Book" for the toleration movement was *Spinoza's Theologico-political Tractate*, which went to the root of the much-treated matter. Utilising many thoughts and examples from the older Jewish literature influenced by Averroism, this work demonstrated that religion, and especially the religious documents, have neither the province nor the design of teaching theoretical truths, and that the essence of religion consists not in the recognition of particular dogmas, but in the disposition and the will and action determined by it. From this it follows incontestably that the state has still less ground or right to trouble itself about the assent of its citizens to particular dogmas, and that it should rather by virtue of its real authority restrain every attempt toward a constraining of the conscience, which may proceed from any of the ecclesiastically organised forms of religious life. The mystically profound religious nature of Spinoza alienated him from the dogmatic government of the churches and from belief in the literal statements of their historical documents. He asserted the principle that religious books, like all other phenomena of literature, must be historically explained as to their theoretical import, that is, must be understood from the point of view of the intellectual condition of their authors, and that this *historical criticism* takes away from those former theoretical views their binding and normative significance for a later time.

3. With the political and churchly political interests became associated the *social*. No one gave them a more eloquent expression than Thomas *More*. After a thrilling portrayal of the misery of the masses the first book of the *Utopia* comes to the conclusion that society would do better if instead of the Draconian justice with which she punishes the violation of her laws, she should stop the sources of crime. The author maintains that the greater part of the guilt for the wrong-doing of the individual is due to the perverted arrangement of the whole. This latter consists in the *inequality of property* brought about by the use of money, for this inequality gives occasion to all the aberrations of passion, of envy, and of hatred. The ideal picture of the perfect state of society upon the island of Utopia, which More sketches in contrast to the present condition, is in its main features an imitation of the ideal state of Plato. This humanistic revival is, however, distinguished from its prototype in a manner characteristic for modern socialism, by its *abolition of class-distinctions*, which seemed necessary to the ancient thinker in consequence of his reflection upon the actually given difference in the intellectual and moral status of individuals. In an abstraction that was a prototype for the succeeding development More proceeded

from the thought of the equality of all citizens before the *law*, and changed into an equality of *claim* or *title* for all citizens those forms of community which Plato had demanded of the ruling classes as a renunciation of the natural impulses toward an individual sphere of interests.   With Plato the preferred classes were to renounce all private property in order to devote themselves entirely to the general weal : with More the abolition of private property is demanded as the surest means for doing away with crime, and is based upon the equality of title which all have to the common possession.   But at the same time the English Chancellor still holds fast to the ideal model of the ancient philosopher, in so far as to treat this entire equality in the division of material interests, as the indispensable basis for making it possible to all citizens to enjoy in like measure the ideal goods of society, science, and art.   A normal working day of six hours for all members of society will be enough, he thinks, to satisfy all external needs of the community : the remaining time should remain free for every one for nobler employment.   With these characteristics the programme for all the higher forms of modern socialism grows in the thought of More out of the Platonic project.

But the spirit of the Renaissance was animated by much more worldly interests.   Stimulated by the magic of discoveries, dazzled by the glitter of inventions, it set itself the task of transforming by its new insights the whole outer condition of human society as related to the natural conditions of life, and saw before itself an *ideal of comfort* for human life, which should develop from a complete and systematic use of the knowledge and control of Nature made possible by science.   All social injuries will be healed by raising human society, by means of the scientific advancement of external civilisation, beyond all the cares and all the need which now vex it.   A few inventions like the compass, the art of printing, and gunpowder, says Bacon, have sufficed to give human life new motion, greater dimensions, mightier development.   What transformations stand before us when invention once becomes an intelligently exercised art !   The social problem is thus transferred to an *improvement of the material condition of society*.

In Bacon's *New Atlantis*[1] a happy island-people in carefully guarded seclusion is brought before us, which by skilful regulations receives information of the progress in civilisation made by all other peoples, and at the same time, by the systematic prosecution of research, discovery, and invention, raises to the highest

---

[1] The title of this Utopia and much else in it is a reminiscence of Plato's fragment, *Critias* (113 f.).

point the control of Nature for the practical interests of human life. All kinds of possible and impossible inventions are related in fantastic prophecy,[1] and the whole activity of the " House of Solomon " is directed toward improving the material state of society, while the portrayal of the political relations is only superficial and unimportant.

In Campanella's *State of the Sun*, on the other hand, in which the after-effects of More's *Utopia* are very noticeable, we come to a complete project of the *socialistic future state*, which is even pedantically ordered down to all of its minor relations. This state does not shrink in any direction from the most extreme violence to the freedom of the individual's life. From the mathematically delineated plan of the imperial city to the division of hours for daily work and enjoyment, the determination of professions, the pairing of the men and women, the astrologically predetermined hour for sexual unions, — all takes place here from an arrangement by the state for the welfare of the whole, and an extended, carefully worked out system of bureaucracy (in which there is an admixture of metaphysical motives)[2] is built up upon the graded knowledge of the citizens. The more any one knows, the more power he ought to have in the state, in order to rule and improve by his knowledge the course of Nature. The points of view in this improvement look essentially toward external civilisation in Campanella's system also. With him, indeed, four hours of daily labour should suffice on the average to assure the good cheer of society, and upon this prosperity all should have a like claim.

4. In spite of all that is fantastic and whimsical,[3] the thought nevertheless asserts itself in Campanella's *State of the Sun*, still more than in More's *Utopia*, that the state should be an artificial product of human insight for the removal of social injuries. Neither writer desired to set up a mere creation of fancy, any more than did Plato ; they believe in the possibility of realising "the best political constitution " by rational reflection upon an order of social relations

---

[1] In addition to the microscope and the telescope, the microphone and telephone are not wanting ; there are giant explosive materials, flying-machines, all sorts of engines with air and water power, and even "some kinds " of perpetual motion ! But the author lays special value upon the fact that by better culture of plants and animals, by unsuspected chemical discoveries, by baths and air-cures, diseases are to be banished and life prolonged ; experiments on animals are also introduced in the interest of medicine.

[2] Beneath the supreme ruler, — Sol or Metaphysicus, — who must embody all knowledge within himself, stand first of all three princes, whose spheres of activity correspond to the three "primalities " of Being, Power, Wisdom and Love (cf. § 29, 3), etc.

[3] Fantastic is especially the strong element of astrological and magical superstition ; whimsical, his monkish rude treatment of the sexual relations.

that shall be in accordance with Nature. In this, to be sure, they encountered much opposition. *Cardanus* combated Utopias on principle, and in their stead commended to science the task of comprehending the necessity with which the actual states of history develop in their special definite nature, out of the character, the relations of life, and the experiences of peoples; he would have them regarded as natural products like organisms, and would apply to their conditions the medical categories of health and disease. In a larger way, and free from the Pythagorean astrology in which the mathematician Cardanus indulged, but with a strongly constructive fancy, the practical statesman *Bodin* attempted to understand the manifold character of historical reality as manifested in political life.

But the tendency of the time was much more toward seeking a right founded in Nature for all times and relations alike, and to be recognised by reason alone: although a man like *Albericus Gentilis* desired to reduce the principles of private right to physical laws by analogies of childlike crudeness. A firmer and more fruitful ground was gained when *human nature*, instead of general "Nature," was taken as a starting-point. This was done by Hugo *Grotius*. Like Thomas Aquinas, he found the fundamental principle of natural right in the *social need*, and found the method for its development in logical deduction. That which reason recognises as agreeing with man's social nature and following therefrom — in this consists the *jus naturale*[1] — that cannot be changed by any historical mutation. The thought of such an absolute right, which exists only by its foundation in reason, and which exists independently of the political power and rather as the ultimate ground of this power, was brought home to Grotius by the analogy of international law with which his investigation was primarily concerned. On the other hand, however, by virtue of this material principle, private right became the authoritative presupposition for political right also. The satisfaction of individual interests, protection of life and property, appeared as the essential end to be subserved by the ordering of rights. Formally and methodically, on the contrary, this philosophical system of rights was entirely deductive; it aimed only to draw the logical consequences of the principle of society. In like manner *Hobbes* also regarded the *corpus politicum* as a machine capable of being deduced from the conception of its end by pure intellectual activity, and the philosophical doctrine of rights as a perfect demonstrable science. At the same time this field seemed

---

[1] *De Jure Bell. et Pac.* I. 1, 10.

adapted in a pre-eminent degree to the application of the geometrical method, and *Puffendorf* introduced the whole apparatus of this method by combining Grotius and Hobbes, and developing the whole system synthetically from the thought that the individual's instinct toward self-preservation could be rationally and successfully fulfilled only by satisfying his social need.   In this form natural right persisted as the ideal of a "geometrical" science until far on into the eighteenth century (Thomasius, Wolff, indeed, even to Fichte and Schelling), and survived the general decline of the Cartesian principle.

5. Looking now at the contents rather than at the form, we find that the ultimate ground of public life and of social coherence was placed in the *interests of individuals:* the mechanics of the state found in the character of the impulses of the individual man that self-intelligible and simple element,[1] out of which the complex structures of life viewed as a subject of law and rights (*Rechtslebens*) might be explained in accordance with the Galilean principle.   With this the doctrine of the state also went back to the Epicurean theory of social atomism [2] (cf. pp. 174 f.), and the synthetic principle by which the origin of the state was to be understood was the *contract.*   From Occam and Marsilius down to Rousseau, Kant, and Fichte, this contract theory was dominant in political philosophy.   Grotius and Hobbes devoted themselves to carrying it out in the most careful manner.   To the political contract by which the individuals unite themselves to a community of interests, is attached the contract of sovereignty or subjection, by means of which the individuals hand over their rights and authority to the magistracy.   This proved to be a general frame in which the most varied political theories fitted.   While Grotius, and likewise Spinoza, found the interests of the citizens to be best guaranteed by an aristocratic republican constitution, *Hobbes* could deduce from the same presupposition his theory of a *purely secular absolutism*, according to which the political power should be inviolably united in one personality, the universal will in the individual will of the sovereign.

In closest connection with the contract theory appears the development of the conception of *sovereignty.*   The source of all power, according to this theory, is the popular will, from which the political contract and the contract of submission have proceeded; the proper bearer of the sovereignty is the people.   Meanwhile the con-

---

[1] The term "*conatus*" applies in this sense to both domains, the physical and the psychical, with Hobbes and Spinoza.

[2] As in the theoretical domain, so also in the practical, the principle of Democritus and Epicurus obtains with great efforts a late victory.

tract and the transfer of right and power completed thereby, are regarded by some writers as irrevocable, and by others as capable of recall.   So Bodin, in spite of his doctrine of popular sovereignty, maintains the unlimited character and unconditional authority of the royal power, the inviolability of the ruler and the unjustifiability of all opposition against him; with *Hobbes* the sovereignty of the people is still more completely absorbed into that of the monarch, whose will here stands quite in the sense of the *l'état c'est moi* as the sole source of rights in the positive political life. In opposition to this view, and decidedly more consistent in view of their presupposition, the "*monarchomachischen* [opposed to an absolute monarchy] theories," whose chief representative besides Buchanan (1506–1582) and Languet (1518–1581) was Althus of Lower Saxony, maintained that the governmental contract becomes liable to dissolution as soon as the sovereign ceases to rule rightly, *i.e.* in the interest and according to the will of the people. If the contract is broken on one side, it is no longer binding for the other party; in this situation the sovereignty returns again to its original bearers. If man has made the state with a purpose and under reflection, then he abolishes it again when it becomes evident that it has failed to fulfil its purpose. Thus the Renaissance is already providing in advance the *theory of revolution.*[1]

All these theories, however, received their especial colouring from motives growing out of the particular relations of *church and state,* — a colouring which depended upon the question whether the unrestricted power of the ruler was felt as dangerous or as beneficial in consequence of his relation to the Confessions. The most radical standpoint in real politics was taken by *Hobbes* by virtue of his religious indifferentism : religion is a private opinion, and only that opinion which the sovereign professes has political standing or value. No other religion or Confession can be tolerated in public life. Hobbes gave the philosophical theory for the historical *cujus regio illius religio.* And *Spinoza* attached himself to him in this. He stood for freedom of thought and against all compulsion of conscience, but for him religion was only a matter of knowledge and disposition; for the public manifestation of religious feeling in the church and in public worship, it was in the interest of order and peace that only the form fixed by the magistracy should obtain. In a more positive sense the *Protestant Philosophy of Right* declared for

---

[1] These principles were defended with special application to the English conditions of the seventeenth century, and to the right of the "Revolution" of that time by the poet John *Milton* (*Defensio pro Populo Anglicano*, 1651), and by Algernon *Sidney* (*Discourses of Government*, 1683).

the sovereignty in church and state of the kingdom existing by the grace of God; while in this school, also, as for example in the case of Althus, the sovereignty of the people was defended as over against a magistracy holding another creed. The same motive was decisive where the *Jesuits* maintained that the magistracy might be removed and that the assassination of the prince was excusable (cf. above).

6. In the case of *Hobbes* the rationale of the contract theory rested on more general motives. If the social and political life was to be comprehended from the point of view of "human nature," the English philosopher found the fundamental, all-determining characteristic of human nature in the *impulse toward self-preservation* or *egoism*, the simple, self-evident principle for explaining the entire volitional life. Here his materialistic metaphysics and sensualistic psychology (cf. § 31) made it appear that this instinct toward self-preservation, in its original essence, was directed only toward the preservation and furtherance of the sensuous existence of the individual. All other objects of the will could serve only as means to bring about that supreme end. Agreeably to this principle, also, there was no other norm of judgment for man as a natural being than that of furtherance or hindrance, of profit or of harm: the distinction of good and evil, of right and wrong, is not possible upon the standpoint of the individual, but only upon the *social* standpoint, where the common interest instead of the individual's interest forms the standard. So *egoism became the principle of all practical philosophy;* for if the individual's instinct toward self-preservation was to be restricted and corrected by the command of the state, yet this state itself was regarded as the most ingenious and perfect of all the contrivances which egoism had hit upon to attain and secure its satisfaction. The *state of nature*, in which the egoism of each stands originally opposed to the egoism of every other, is a *war of all against all:* to escape this the state was founded as a contract for the mutual warrant of self-preservation. The social need is not original: it only results necessarily as the most efficient and certain means for the satisfaction of egoism.

Spinoza adopted this doctrine, but gave it a more ideal significance by introducing it into his metaphysics. "*Suum esse conservare*" is for him also the quintessence and fundamental motive or all willing. But since every finite mode belongs equally to both attributes, its impulse toward self-preservation is directed as well toward its conscious activity, *i.e.* its *knowledge*, as toward its maintenance in the corporeal world, *i.e.* its *power*. This individual striving, interpreted along the lines of the Baconian identity of knowledge and power, forms for Spinoza the ground of explanation for the empirical life of the state, in accordance with the principle that each one's right extends as far as his power. In this process of explanation Spinoza moves mainly in the lines of Hobbes, and deviates from him only, as noticed above, in his view as to the best form of constitution. This same complication of conceptions, however, presents itself to Spinoza as affording also a starting-point for his mystico-religious ethics. For since the true *"esse"* of every finite thing is the deity, the only perfect satisfaction of the impulse toward self-preservation is to be found in "love to God." That Malebranche, who spoke so vehemently of the "atheistical Jew," taught the same in slightly different words — *"mit ein bischen anderen Worten"* — has already been mentioned (§ 31, 4).

7. Hobbes' theory of egoism — the "selfish system," as it was later termed for the most part — found vigorous opposition among his countrymen.[1] The reduction of all activities of the will, without any exception, to the impulse toward self-preservation excited both ethical revolt and the theoretical contradiction of psychological experience. The warfare against Hobbes was undertaken primarily by the *Neo-Platonist school of Cambridge*, whose chief literary representatives were Ralph *Cudworth* and Henry *More*. In this controversy the antithesis of φύσις and θέσις developed after the ancient prototype. For Hobbes, right and moral order arose from social institution; for his opponents they were original and immediately certain demands of Nature. Both parties opposed the *lex naturalis* to the theological dogmatic grounding of practical philosophy : but for Hobbes natural law was the demonstrable consequence of intelligent egoism; for the "Platonists" it was an immediate certainty, innate in the human mind.

Cumberland proceeded against Hobbes in the same line. He would have man's social nature regarded as being as original as his egoism: the "benevolent" *altruistic* inclinations, whose actual existence is not to be doubted, are objects of direct self-perception which have an original independence of their own ; the social need is not the refined product of a shrewd self-seeking, but — as Hugo Grotius had conceived of it — a primary, constitutive characteristic of human nature. While egoism is directed toward one's own private weal, the altruistic motives are directed toward the universal weal, without which private weal is not possible. This connection between the welfare of the individual and that of the

---

[1] Cf. J. Tulloch, *Rational Theology and Christian Philosophy in England in the 17th Cent.* (Lond. 1872).

public, which in Hobbes appeared as due to the shrewd insight of man, is regarded by Cumberland as a provision of God, whose commandment is hence considered to be the authoritative principle for obeying those demands which express themselves in the benevolent inclinations.

To the side of this *natural morality of reason,* which was thus defended against orthodoxy on the one hand and sensualism on the other, came the *natural religion of reason,* which had been set up by *Herbert of Cherbury* in opposition to these same two positions. Religion also shall be based neither upon historical revelation nor upon human institution; it belongs to the inborn possession of the human mind. The *consensus gentium* — so argues Herbert in the manner of the ancient Stoics — proves that belief in the deity is a necessary constituent of the human world of ideas, a *demand of reason ;* but on this account that only which corresponds to those demands of the reason can stand as true content of religion, as contrasted with the dogmas of religions.

Thus the questions of practical philosophy which appear in English literature in the very lively discussion excited by Hobbes, gradually became transferred to the *psychological* realm. What is the origin of right, morals, and religion in the human mind? — so runs the problem. With this, however, the movements of the philosophy of the Enlightenment are introduced.

PART V.

THE PHILOSOPHY OF THE ENLIGHTENMENT.

In addition to the literature cited on p. 348, cf.

Leslie Stephen, *History of English Thought in the 18th Cent.* Lond. 1876.

J. Mackintosh, *On the Progress of Ethical Philosophy during the 17th and 18th Centuries.* Edin. 1872.

Ph. Damiron, *Mémoires pour servir à l'Histoire de la Philosophie au 18me Siècle.* 3 vols., Paris 1858–64.

E. Zeller, *Geschichte der deutschen Philosophie seit Leibniz.* München, 1873.

Also H. Hettner, *Litteraturgeschichte des 18. Jahr.* 3 parts.

THE natural rhythm of intellectual life brought with it the result that in the modern as in the Greek philosophy a first cosmologico-metaphysical period was followed by a period of an essentially anthropological character, and that thus once more the newly awakened, purely theoretical efforts of philosophy must yield to a practical conception of philosophy as *"world-wisdom."* In fact, all features of the *Greek sophistic* movement are found again with ripened fulness of thought, with broadened variety, with deepened content, and, therefore, also, with added energy in their antitheses in the *Philosophy of the Enlightenment*, which coincides approximately in time with the *eighteenth century*. In the place of Athens now appears the whole breadth of the intellectual movement among European civilised peoples, and scientific tradition counts now as many thousands of years as it then counted centuries; but the tendency as a whole and the objects of thought, the points of view and the results of the philosophising, show an instructive similarity and kinship in these two periods so widely separated in time and so different in the civilisations which formed their background. There prevails in both the same turning of thought toward the subject's inner nature, the same turning away from metaphysical subtlety with doubt and disgust, the same preference for an empirical genetic consideration of the human psychical life, the same inquiry as to the possibility and the limits of scientific knowledge, and the same passionate interest in the discussion of the problems of life and society. No less characteristic, lastly, for both periods is the penetration of philosophy into the broad circles of general culture and the fusion of the scientific with the literary movement.

But the basis for the Enlightenment of the eighteenth century was given in the general features of a *secular view of life*, as they had been worked out during the Renaissance by the fresh movements in art, religion, politics, and natural research. While these had found their metaphysical formulation in the seventeenth century, the question now came again into the foreground, how man should conceive, in the setting of the new *Weltanschauung*, his own nature and his own position: and in the presence of the value set upon this question, the interest in the various metaphysical conceptions in which the new *Weltanschauung* had been embodied, retreated more and more decidedly into the background. Men contented themselves with the general outlines of metaphysical theories, in order to employ themselves the more thoroughly with the questions of human life; and all the doctrines of the Enlightenment which offer such a vehement polemic against speculation are, in truth, working from the beginning with a *metaphysics of the "sound common sense"* which at last raised its voice so high, and which ultimately only assumed as self-evident truth that which had fallen to it from the achievements of the labour of preceding centuries.

The beginnings of the philosophy of the Enlightenment are to be sought in *England*, where, in connection with the well-ordered conditions which followed the close of the period of the revolution, a powerful upward movement of literary life claimed philosophy also in the interests of general culture. From England this literature was transplanted to *France*. Here, however, the opposition of the ideals which it brought with it to the social and political status, worked in such a way that not only was the presentation of the thoughts more excited and vehement from the outset, but the thoughts themselves also take on a sharper point, and turn their negative energy more powerfully against the existing conditions in Church and state. At first from France, and then from the direct influence of England,[1] also, *Germany* received the ideas of the Enlightenment, for which it had already received an independent preparation in a more theoretical manner: and here these ideas found their last deepening, and a purification and ennobling as well,

---

[1] Cf. G. Zart, *Der Einfluss der englischen Philosophen auf die deutsche Philos. des 18. Jahrh.* (Berlin, 1881).

as they came to an end in the German *poetry* with which the *Renaissance of classical Humanism* was completed.

John *Locke* became the leader of the *English* Enlightenment by finding a popular form of empirico-psychological exposition for the general outlines of the Cartesian conception of the world. While the metaphysical tendency of the system brought forth an idealistic after-shoot in *Berkeley*, the anthropologico-genetic mode of consideration extended quickly and victoriously to all problems of philosophy. Here the opposition between the *sensualistic associational psychology* and the nativistic theories of various origin continued to have a decisive influence upon the course of development. It controlled the vigorous movement in *moral philosophy*, and the development of *deism* and *natural religion*, which was connected with it; and it found its sharpest formulation in the epistemological field, where the most consistent and deepest of English thinkers, David *Hume*, developed empiricism to *positivism*, and thereby called forth the opposition of the *Scottish* school.

The pioneer of the *French* Enlightenment was Pierre *Bayle*, whose *Dictionnaire* turned the views of the cultivated world completely in the direction of religious scepticism; and it was along this line chiefly that the English literature was then taken up in Paris. *Voltaire* was the great writer, who not only gave this movement its most eloquent expression, but also presented the positive elements of the Enlightenment in the most emphatic manner. But the development pressed with much greater weight toward the negative side. In the common thinking of the *Encyclopædists* became completed step by step the change from empiricism to sensualism, from naturalism to materialism, from deism to atheism, from enthusiastic to egoistic morals. In opposition to such an *Enlightenment of the intellect*, whose lines all converge in the positivism of *Condillac*, there appeared in *Rousseau* a *feeling-philosophy* of elemental power, leading to the intellectual shaping of the *Revolution*.

Germany was won for the Enlightenment movement by the Leibnizian philosophy and the great success which Wolff achieved, in his activity as a teacher, in developing and transforming it, but here, in consequence of the lack of a unifying public interest, the tendency toward *individual culture* was predominant. For the ends of this individual culture, the ideas of the " philosophical century " were elaborated in psychological and epistemological as well as in the moral, political, and religious fields with great multiplicity, but without any new creation of principles until fresh life and higher points of view were brought by the *poetical movement* and the great personalities of its bearers, Lessing and Herder, to the dry intelligence with which a boastful *popular philosophy* had extended itself, especially in connection with the Berlin Academy.[1] This circumstance kept the German philosophy of the eighteenth century from losing itself in theoretico-sceptical self-disintegration like the English, or from being shattered in practical politics like the French: by contact with a great literature teeming with ideas a new great epoch of philosophy was here prepared.

John **Locke**, born 1632, at Wrington near Bristol, was educated at Oxford, and became involved in the changeful fortunes of the statesman Lord Shaftesbury. He returned home from exile in Holland with William of Orange in 1688, filled several high political offices under the new government which he also often publicly defended, and died while living in the country at leisure, in 1704. His philosophical work bears the title *An Essay concerning Human Understanding* (1690); besides this are to be mentioned *Some Thoughts on Education* (1693), *The Reasonableness of Christianity* (1695), and, among his posthumous works, *Of the Conduct of the Understanding*. Cf. Fox Bourne, *The Life of J. L.* (Lond. and N.Y. 1876); Th. Fowler, *J. L.* (Lond. 1880); [*Locke*, by A. C. Fraser, Blackwood series, Edin. and Phila. 1890, and article *Locke* in *Enc. Brit.*; T. H. Green in his *Int. to Hume*; J. Dewey, *Leibniz's New Essays*, Chicago, 1888; Edition of his works by Low, 1771, also ed. Lond. 1853; Philos. wks. in Bohn Lib. Crit. ed. of the *Essay* by Fraser, 1894].

George **Berkeley** was born in Killerin, Ireland, in 1685, took part as a clergyman in missionary and colonisation attempts in America, became Bishop of Cloyne 1734, and died 1753. His *Theory of Vision* (1709) was a preparation for his *Treatise on the Principles of Human Knowledge* (1710). This main work was later followed by the *Three Dialogues between Hylas and Philonous*, and by *Alciphron or the Minute Philosopher*. Edition of his works by Fraser, 4 vols., Lond. 1871; the same writer has also given a good exposition of his thought as a whole (Blackwood series, Edin. and Lond. 1881). Cf. Collyns Simon, *Universal Immaterialism*, Lond. 1862.

The **Associational Psychology** found its chief supporters in Peter **Brown** (died 1735 Bishop of Cork; *The Procedure, Extent, and Limits of Human Understanding*, 1719), David **Hartley** (1704-1757; *De Motus Sensus et Idearum Generatione*, 1746; *Observations on Man, his Frame, his Duty, and his Expectations*, 1749), Edward **Search**, pseudonym for Abraham **Tucker** (1705-1774; *Light of Nature*, 7 vols., Lond. 1768-1777), Joseph **Priestley** (1733-1804; *Hartley's Theory of the Human Mind on the Principle of the Association of Ideas*, 1775; *Disquisitions relating to Matter and Spirit*, 1777), John Horne **Tooke** (1736-1812; Ἔπεὰ πτερόεντα or *The Diversions of Parley*, 1798; cf. Stephen, *Memoirs of J. H. T.*, Lond. 1813), Erasmus **Darwin** (1731-1802; *Zoonomia or the Laws of Organic Life*, 1794-1796), finally, Thomas **Brown** (1778-1820; *Inquiry into the Relation of Cause and Effect*, 1804; posthumously, the *Lectures on the Philosophy of the Human Mind*, 1820, delivered in Edinburg). Cf. Br. Schoenlank, *Hartley u. Priestley als Begründer des Associationismus* (Halle,1882); L. Ferri, *Sulla Dottrina Psichologica dell' Associazione, Saggio Storico e Critico* (Rome, 1878) [Fr. tr. Paris, 1883. Cf. also *Hartley and James Mill* by G. S. Bower, Lond. 1881. For bibliography for the writers mentioned in this and the following paragraphs consult Porter's appendix to Eng. tr. Ueberweg's *Hist. Phil.*].

Of the opponents to this movement who Platonise in the older manner, Richard **Price** (1723-1791) became known especially by his controversy with Priestley: —

Priestley, *The Doctrine of Philosophical Necessity* (1777); Price, *Letters on Materialism and Philosophical Necessity;* Priestley, *Free Discussions of the Doctrines of Materialism* (1778).

---

[1] Cf. Ch. Bartholmèss, *Histoire Philosophique de l'Académie de Prusse,* Paris, 1859.

Among the **English moral philosophers, Shaftesbury** (Anthony Ashley Cooper, 1671–1713) takes a most important place. His writings were collected under the title, *Characteristics of Men, Manners, Opinions and Times* (1711). Cf. G. v. Gizycki, *Die Philosophie Sh.'s* (Leips. and Heidelberg, 1876). — After him various groups diverge. The intellectualistic tendency is represented by Samuel **Clarke** (1675–1729; *A Demonstration of the Being and Attributes of God*, 1705 ; *Philosophical Inquiry concerning Human Liberty*, 1715 ; cf. his correspondence with Leibniz) and William **Wollaston** (1659–1724 ; *The Religion of Nature Delineated*, 1722). — The morality based on feeling was represented by Francis **Hutcheson** (1694–1747 ; *Inquiry into the Original of our Ideas of Beauty and Virtue*, 1725 ; *A System of Moral Philosophy*, 1755 ; cf. Th. Fowler, *Shaftesbury and Hutcheson*, Lond. 1882) ; Henry **Home**, pseud. for Lord Kames (1696–1782 ; *Essays on the Principles of Morality and Natural Religion*, 1751 ; *Elements of Criticism*, 1762) ; Edmund **Burke** (1730–1797 ; *Philosophical Inquiry into the Origin of our Ideas of the Sublime and Beautiful*, 1756) ; Adam **Ferguson** (1724–1816 ; *Institutions of Moral Philosophy*, 1769), and in a certain sense also, Adam **Smith** (1723–1790 ; *Theory of Moral Sentiments*, 1759) ; the principle of authority was defended by Joseph **Butler** (1692–1752 ; *Sermons upon Human Nature*, 1726) [*Butler*, in Blackwood series by W. L. Collins, 1881], and William **Paley** (1743–1805 ; *Principles of Moral and Political Philosophy*, 1785). The ethics of the associational psychology was developed chiefly by Jeremy **Bentham** (1748–1832 ; *Introduction to the Principles of Morals and Legislation*, 1789 ; *Traité de Législation Civile et Pénale*, brought together by E. Dumont, 1801 ; *Deontology*, ed. by J. Bowring, 1834 ; works in 11 vols., Edin. 1843). — In a peculiar isolated position appears Bernhard de **Mandeville** (1670–1733 ; *The Fable of the Bees, or Private Vices made Public Benefits*, 1706, later with illustrative dialogues, 1728 ; *Inquiry into the Origin of Moral Virtue*, 1732 ; *Free Thoughts on Religion, Church, Government*, 1720). On him cf. P. Sakmann (Freiburg, 1898).

The literature of **Deism** coincides, for the most part, with the above-named literature of moral philosophy ; but in addition to those named the following writers are also prominent : John **Toland** (1670–1722 ; *Christianity not Mysterious*, 1696 ; *Letters to Serena*, 1704 ; *Adeisidæmon*, 1709 ; *Pantheisticon*, 1710) ; Anthony **Collins** (1676–1729 ; *A Discourse of Free Thinking*, 1713) ; Matthew **Tindal** (1656–1733 ; *Christianity as Old as the Creation*, 1730) ; Thomas **Chubb** (1679–1747 ; *A Discourse concerning Reason with Regard to Religion*, 1730) ; Thomas **Morgan** (died 1743 ; *The Moral Philosopher*, 3 parts, 1737 ff.) ; finally, Lord **Bolingbroke** (1672–1751) ; works ed. by Mollet in 5 vols., 1753 f. ; cf. F. v. Raumer, *Abhandl. der Berl. Akad.* 1840). — Cf. V. Lechler, *Geschichte des englischen Deismus* (Stuttgart and Tüb. 1841).

England's greatest philosopher is David **Hume**, born, 1711, in Edinburg, and educated there. After he had spent some time as merchant, he lived for several years in France, occupied in study, and composed his work of genius, the *Treatise on Human Nature* (printed 1739 f.). The failure of this book induced him to work it over and publish it under the title *Inquiry concerning Human Understanding*, as a second volume of his more successful *Essays, Moral, Political and Literary* (1748), and to add *An Inquiry concerning the Principles of Morals* (1751), and also *The Natural History of Religion* (1755). As librarian of the Advocates' Library in Edinburg he found opportunity to write his *History of England*. After a stay in Paris, where he received great honour and came into connection with Rousseau among others, he was for some time Under-Secretary of State in the Foreign Office, but finally returned to Edinburg, where he died, 1776. The *Dialogues concerning Natural Religion* and some smaller treatises appeared posthumously. Ed. of his works by Green and Grose in 4 vols. (Lond. 1875). His autobiography was published by his friend, Adam Smith (1777). Cf. J. H. Burton, *Life and Correspondence of D. H.* (Edin. 1846–50) ; E. Feuerlein in the *Zeitschr. "Der Gedanke"* (Berlin, 1863 f.) ; E. Pfleiderer, *Empirismus und Skepsis in D. H.'s Philosophie* (Berlin, 1874) ; T. Huxley, *D. H.* (Lond. 1879) ; Fr. Jodl, *Leben u. Philosophie D. H.'s* (Halle, 1872) ; A. Meinong, *Hume-Studien* (Vienna, 1877, 1882) ; G. v. Gizycki, *Die Ethik D. H.'s* (Breslau, 1878). [W. Knight, Blackwood series, 1886 ; esp. Int. by T. H. Green in his ed. of the works. Selby-Bigge eds. of the *Treatise* (1888) and the *Enquiry* (with *Introd.* 1894), Clar. Press, are excellent.

The **Scottish** School was founded by Thomas **Reid** (1710–1796, Professor at Glasgow ; *Inquiry into the Human Mind on the Principles of Common Sense,* 1764 ; *Essays on the Intellectual Powers of Man,* 1785 ; *Essays on the Active Powers of Man,* 1788, complete ed. by W. Hamilton, Edin. 1827). [Selections ed. by E. H. Sneath, N.Y. 1892, contains bibliog. Cf. A. Seth, *Scottish Philosophy,* Edin. and Lond. 1885, and art. *Reid* in *Enc. Brit.*] Besides James **Oswald** (died 1793, *Appeal to Common Sense in Behalf of Religion,* 1766) and James **Beattie** (died 1805, *Essay on the Nature and Immutability of Truth,* 1770), the school had its chief academical and literary representative in Dugald **Stewart** (1753–1828, Professor in Edinburg ; *Elements of the Philosophy of the Human Mind,* 3 parts, 1792–1827 ; ed. of his works by W. Hamilton, 10 vols., Edin. 1854 ff.).

Pierre **Bayle**, the type of sceptical polyhistory, born 1647 at Carlat, led a life disquieted by twice changing his Confession, was finally a professor in Sédan and Rotterdam, and died 1706. His influential life work is embodied in his *Dictionnaire Historique et Critique* (1695 and 1697). Cf. L. Feuerbach, *P. Bayle nach seinen für die Geschichte der Philosophie und Menschheit interessantesten Momenten,* Ansbach, 1833.

Of the works of **Voltaire** (François Arouet le Jeune, 1694–1778 ; the main events of his literary life are his flight to London, his stay with the Marquise du Châtelet iι Cirey, his visit with Frederick the Great in Potsdam, and his rest in old age at the country seat Ferney, near Geneva), the following are principally to be considered here : *Lettres sur les Anglais* (1784), *Métaphysique de Newton* (1740), *Éléments de la Philosophie de Newton mis à la Portée de tout le Monde* (1741), *Examen important de Mylord Bolingbroke* (1736), *Candide ou sur l' Optimisme* (1757), *Dictionnaire Philosophique* (1764), *Le Philosophe Ignorant* (1767), *Réponse au Système de la Nature* (1777), the poem *Les Systèmes,* etc. Cf. E. Bersot, *La Philosophie de V.* (Paris, 1848); D. F. Strauss, *V.* (Leips. 1870); J. Morley, *V.* (Lond. and N.Y. 1872).

More sceptical in metaphysical aspects appear natural scientists and mathematicians such as **Maupertuis** (1698–1759; active in connection with the Berlin Academy ; *Essai de Philosophie Morale,* 1750 ; *Essai de Cosmologie,* 1751 ; controversial writings between him and the Wolffian, S. König, collected Leips. 1758), or **d'Alembert** (*Mélanges de Littérature, d' Histoire et de Philosophie,* 1752); others proceed more naturalistically, such as **Buffon** (1708–1788 ; *Histoire Naturelle Générale et Particulière,* 1749 ff.) and Jean Battiste **Robinet** (1735–1820 ; *De la Nature,* 1761 ; *Considérations Philosophiques de la Gradation Naturelle des Formes d'Être* 1767).

Sensualism appears in connection with materialism in Julien Offrai de **Lamettrie** (1709–1751 ; *Histoire Naturelle de l' Âme,* 1745 ; *L' Homme Machine,* 1748 ; *L' Art de Jouir,* 1751 ; *Œuvres,* Berlin, 1751 ; on him F. A. Lange, *Gesch. des Mater.,* I. 326 ff. [Eng. tr. *Hist. of Mater.,* Vol. II. 49 ff.] ; Nérée Quépat, Paris, 1873); it appears solely as psychological theory with Charles **Bonnet** (1720–1793 ; *Essai de Psychologie,* 1755 ; *Essai Analytique sur les Facultés de l' Âme,* 1759 ; *Considérations sur les Corps Organisés,* 1762 ; *Contemplation de la Nature,* 1764 ; *Palingénesies Philosophiques,* 1769), and with a positivistic pointing in Etienne Bonnot de **Condillac** (1715–1780 ; *Essai sur l' Origine de la Connaissance Humaine,* 1746 ; *Traité des Systèmes,* 1749 ; *Traité des Sensations,* 1754 ; *Logique,* 1780 ; *Langue des Calculs* in the complete edition, Paris, 1798 ; cf. F. Réthoré, *C. ou l'Empirisme et le Rationalisme,* Paris, 1864). The last representatives of these theories are, on the one hand, Pierre Jean George **Cabanis** (1757–1808 ; *Les Rapports du Physique et du Moral de l' Homme,* 1802 ; *Œuvres,* Paris, 1821–25), on the other side, Antoine Louis Claude **Destutt de Tracy** (1754–1836; *Élements d' Idéologie,* in 4 parts, 1801–15, together 1826). — Cf. Fr. Picavet, *Les Idéologues* (Paris, 1891).

The literary concentration of the Enlightenment movement in France was the **Encyclopædia** (*Encyclopédie ou Dictionnaire Raisonné des Sciences, des Arts et des Métiers,* 28 vols., 1752–1772, supplement and index, 7 vols., extending to 1780). Besides d'Alembert, who wrote the introduction, the editor and intellectual head of the circle from which it proceeded was Denis **Diderot** (1713–1784 ; *Pensées Philosophiques,* 1746 ; *Pensées sur l' Interprétation de la Nature,* 1754 ; of the posthumous publications the *Promenade d'un Sceptique,* the *Entretien* *d'Alembert et de Diderot*, and the *Rêve d'Alembert* are to be emphasised; worthy of mention also is the *Essai de Peinture; Œuvres Complètes*, Paris, 1875, 20 vols.; cf. K. Rosenkranz, *D., sein Leben und seine Werke*, Leips. 1866; J. Morley, *D. and the Encyclopœdists*, Lond. 1878). Further collaborators upon the Encyclopædia (aside from Voltaire and Rousseau, who became separated from the work at an early date) were **Turgot** (article *Existence*), Daubenton, Jaucourt, Duclos, Grimm, Holbach, etc. From the same circle (*"Les Philosophes"*) proceeded later the **Système de la Nature** (pseud. author, Mirabeau, 1770), which is in the main to be attributed to Dietrich von **Holbach** (1723–1789, from the Palatinate ; *Le bon Sens ou Idées Naturelles opposées aux Idées Surnaturelles*, 1772 ; *Éléments de la Morale Universelle*, 1776, etc.). [On the *Système de la Nature* cf. Lange, *Hist. of Mat.*, II. 92 ff.] With him co-operated **Grimm** (1723–1807 ; *Correspondance Littéraire*, 1812), the mathematician Lagrange, the Abbé Galiani, Naigeon, and others ; the concluding chapter, "Abrégé du Code de la Nature." is perhaps from Diderot's pen ; **Helvétius** wrote a very popular exposition, " Vrai Sens du Système de la Nature," 1771. The same writer (Claude Adrien Helvétius, 1715–1771) gave the sharpest expression to the morals of the sensualistic associational psychology in his much read book, *De l'Esprit* (1758 ; cf. also his posthumous work, *De l'Homme de ses Facultés et de son Éducation*, 1772).

The theory of English constitutionalism was adopted in France by **Montesquieu** (1689–1755 ; *Lettres Persanes*, 1721 ; *De l'Esprit des Lois*, 1748). Social problems were treated on the one side by the so-called **Physiocrats** such as **Quesnay** (*Tableaux Économiques*, 1758) ; **Turgot** (*Reflexions sur la Formation et la Distribution des Richesses*, 1774, opposed by Galiani, *Dialogues sur le Commerce des Blés*) and others, on the other side by the **Communists** such as **Morelly** (*Code de la Nature*, 1755), and **Mably**, the brother of Condillac (*De la Législation ou Principes des Lois*, 1776.

The most notable figure of the French Enlightenment was Jean Jacques **Rousseau** (born, 1712, in Geneva, died, 1778, in Ermenonville after an adventurous life, which toward the end was troubled by melancholy and hallucinations of persecution). His main writings — aside from the autobiographical *Confessions* [tr., Lond. 1876] — are *Discours sur les Sciences et les Arts* (1750), *Discours sur l'Origine et les Fondemens de l'Inégalité parmi les Hommes* (1773), *La Nouvelle Héloïse* (1761), *Émile ou sur l'Éducation* (1762) [abr. tr., Boston, 1885], *Du Contrat Social* (1762). Cf. F. Brockerhoff, *R., sein Leben und seine Werke* (Leips. 1863 and 1874) ; E. Feuerlein in " *Der Gedanke* " (Berlin, 1866) ; L. Moreau, *J. J. R. et le Siècle Philosophique* (Paris, 1870) ; J. Morley, *J. J. R.* (Lond. 1873) ; R. Fester, *R. und die deutsche Geschichtsphilosophie* (Stuttgart, 1890) ; [E. Caird, *R.* in *Essays*, Vol. I.].

The philosophical **theory of the Revolution** was developed chiefly by Charles François de **St.-Lambert** (1716–1803 ; *Principes des Mœurs chez toutes les Nations ou Catéchisme Universel*, 1798), Const. Fr. Chassebœuf Comte de **Volney** (1757–1820 ; *Les Ruines*, 1791 ; *La Loi Naturelle ou Principes Physiques de la Morale, déduits de l'Organisation de l'Homme et de l'Univers ou Catéchisme du Citoyen Français*, 1793), Marie Jean Ant. Nic. de **Condorcet** (1743–1794 ; *Esquisse d'un Tableau Historique du Progrès de l'Esprit Humain*, 1795), Dominique **Garat** (1749–1833 ; cf. *Conte Rendu des Séances des Écoles Normales*, II. 1–40). Cf. L. Ferraz, *La Philosophie de la Révolution* (Paris, 1890).

Gottfried Wilhelm **Leibniz**, the many-sided founder of **German** philosophy, was born, 1646, in Leipsic, studied there and at Jena, received his degree in Altorf, and was then, through his acquaintance with Boyneburg, drawn into the diplomatic service of the Elector of Mayence. In this service, pursuing political and scientific plans of his own, he travelled as a member of an embassy to Paris and London, with an incidental visit to Spinoza in The Hague, and then entered the service of the court of Hanover and Brunswick as librarian and court historian. In all these positions he was active in his public and diplomatic capacity in the interests of the German national spirit and of peace between the Confessions. Later he lived at the court of the first Prussian Queen Sophie Charlotte, a Hanoverian princess, in Charlottenberg and Berlin, where the Academy was founded under his direction ; afterwards he lived for some time in Vienna, to consult archives. Here he gave the stimulus for the foundation of an academy, a project which was later carried out, and the St. Petersburg Academy was also due to his influence. He died, 1716, at Hanover. The manifold nature of his activity, and the way in which his life was split up, is shown also in the fact that his scientific views are, for the most part, deposited only in fragmentary essays, and in an incredibly extensive correspondence. The best edition of his philosophical writings is the most recent by C. J. Gerhardt, 7 vols. (Berlin, 1875–90). The metaphysical treatises have been cited above (p. 382). For his influence upon the philosophy of the Enlightenment, the following come chiefly into consideration, aside from the correspondence with Bayle and Clarke: *Essais de Théodicée sur la Bonté de Dieu, la Liberté de l' Homme et l' Origine du Mal* (Amsterdam, 1710), and the *Nouveaux Essais sur l'Entendement Humain*, first published in 1765, by Raspe. Cf. G. E. Guhrauer, *G. W. Frhr. v. L.* (Breslau, 1842) ; E. Pfleiderer, *L. als Patriot, Staatsmann und Bildungsträger* (Leips. 1870); art. *L.* in *Ersch und Gruber's Enc.*, by W. Windelband ; L. Feuerbach, *Darstellung, Entwicklung und Kritik der L.'schen Phil.* (Ansbach, 1844) ; E. Nourisson, *La Philosophie de L.* (Paris, 1860) ; L. Grote, *L. und seine Zeit* (Hanover, 1869) ; O. Caspari, *L.'s Philosophie* (Leips. 1870) ; J. T. Merz, *L.* (Lond. 1884); [J. Dewey, *Leibniz's New Essays*, Chicago, 1888 ; art. *Leibniz* in *Enc. Brit.*, by Sorley ; Eng. tr. of *Imp. Phil. Works*, by G. M. Duncan, New Haven, 1890 ; of the *New Essays*, by A. G. Langley, Lond. and N.Y. 1893].

Among the most influential " Enlighteners" in Germany was Leibniz's contemporary and fellow-countryman, Christian **Thomasius** (1655–1728 ; *Einleitung zur Vernunftlehre, Ausführung der Vernunftlehre*, both in 1691 ; *Einl. zur Sittenlehre*, 1692 ; *Ausführung d. Sittenlehre*, 1696 ; *Fundamenta Juris Naturæ et Gentium ex Sensu Communi Deducta*, 1705 ; cf. A. Luden, *C. Th.*, Berlin, 1805).

The centre of scientific life in Germany during the eighteenth century was formed by the teaching and school of Christian **Wolff.** He was born, 1679, in Breslau, studied at Jena, was Privat-docent at Leipsic, and taught in Halle until he was driven away in 1723 at the instigation of his orthodox opponents ; he then became Professor at Marburg. In 1740 Frederick the Great called him back to Halle with great honour, and he was active there until his death in 1754. He treated the entire compass of philosophy in Latin and German textbooks ; the latter all bear the title *Vernünftige Gedanken* [" Rational Thoughts," treating psychology, metaphysics, physics, physiology, botany, astronomy, ethics, politics, etc.] ; in detail: *von den Kräften des menschlichen Verstandes*, 1712 ; *von Gott, der Welt und der Seele des Menschen, auch allen Dingen überhaupt*, 1719 ; *von der Menschen Thun und Lassen*, 1720 ; *vom gesellschaftlichen Leben der Menschen*, 1721 ; *von den Wirkungen der Natur*, 1723 ; *von den Absichten der natürlichen Dinge*, 1724 ; *von den Theilen der Menschen, Thiere und Pflanzen*, 1725. The Latin works, *Philosophia Rationalis sive Logica*, 1718 ; *Philosophia Prima sive Ontologia*, 1728 ; *Cosmologia*, 1731 ; *Psychologia Empirica*, 1732 ; *Rationalis*, 1734 ; *Theologia Naturalis*, 1736 ; *Philosophia Practica Universalis*, 1738 ; *Jus Naturæ*, 1740 ff. ; *Jus Gentium*, 1749 ; *Philosophia Moralis*, posthumously pub., 1756. — Cf. K. G. Ludovici, *Ausführlicher Entwurf einer vollständigen Historie der Wolff'schen Philosophie* (Leips. 1736 ff.). Also W. L. G. v. Eberstein, *Versuch einer Geschichte der Logik und Metaphysik bei den Deutschen von Leibniz an* (Halle, 1799).

Among the **Wolffians** may be named, perhaps, G. B. **Bilfinger** (1693–1750, *Dilucidationes Philosophicæ de Deo, Anima Humana, Mundo*, etc., 1725) ; M. **Knutzen** (died 1751 ; *Systema Causarum Efficientium*, 1746 ; cf. B. Erdmann, *M. Kn. und seine Zeit*, Leips. 1876) ; J. Chr. **Gottsched** (1700–1766 ; *Erste Gründe der gesammten Weltweissheit*, 1734) ; Alex. **Baumgarten** (1714–1762 ; *Metaphysica*, 1739 ; *Æsthetica*, 1750–58).

As representatives of the geometrical method appear M. G. **Hansch** (1683–1752 ; *Ars Inveniendi*, 1727) and G. **Ploucquet** (1716–1790 ; cf. A. F. Böck, *Sammlung von Schriften, welche dem logischen Calcül des Hernn P. betreffen*, Frankfort and Leips. 1766) ; as opponents of the same, Pierre **Crousaz** (1663–1748 ; *Logik*, 1712 and 1724 ; *Lehre vom Schönen*, 1712), Andreas **Rüdiger** (1671–1731 ; *De Sensu Veri et Falsi*, 1709 ; *Philosophia Synthetica*, 1707) and Chr. A. **Crusius** (1712–1775 ; *Entwurf der nothwendigen Vernunftwahrheiten*, 1745 ; *Weg zur Gewissheit und Zuverlässigkeit der menschlichen Erkenntniss*, 1747.) An eclectic intermediate position is taken by J. Fr. **Budde** (1667–1729 ;

Institutiones Philosophiæ Eclecticæ, 1705) and by the historians of philosophy, J. J. **Brucker** and D. **Tiedmann**, and also by Joh. **Lossius** (*Die physichen Ursachen des Wahren*, 1775) and A. **Platner** (1744–1818; *Philosophische Aphorismen*, 1776 and 1782).

Of more independent importance are J. H. **Lambert** (born, 1728, at Mülhausen, died, 1777, in Berlin; *Kosmologische Briefe*, 1761; *Neues Organon*, 1764; *Architektonik*, 1771) and Nic. **Tetens** (1736–1805; *Philosophische Versuche über die Menschliche Natur und ihre Entwicklung*, 1776 f.; cf. Fr. Harms, *Ueber die Psychologie des N. T.*, Berlin, 1887). Both stand in literary connection with **Kant** (cf. Part VI. ch. 1), whose pre-critical writings belong likewise in this setting; these are principally *Allgemeine Naturgeschichte und Theorie des Himmels*, 1755; *Principiorum Primorum Cognitionis Metaphysicæ Nova Dilucidatio*, 1755; *Monadologia Physica*, 1756; *Die falsche Spitzfindigkeit der vier syllogistischen Figuren*, 1762; *Der einzig mögliche Beweisgrund zu einer Demonstration des Daseins Gottes*, 1763; *Versuch. den Begriff der negativen Grössen in die Weltweisheit einzuführen*, 1763; *Ueber die Deutlichkeit der Grundsätze der natürlichen Theologie und Moral*, 1764; *Beobachtungen über das Gefühl des Schönen und Erhabenen*, 1764; *Träume eines Geistersehers, erläutert durch Träume der Metaphysik*, 1766; *De Mundi Sensibilis atque Intelligibilis Forma et Principiis*, 1770. Cf. R. Zimmerman, *Lambert der Vorgänger Kant's*, 1879. [On Lambert and Tetens, cf. A. Riehl, *Der philosophische Kriticismus*, Leips. 1876. For the pre-critical writings of Kant, E. Caird, *The Critical Philosophy of Immanuel Kant*, Glasgow, Lond., and N.Y. 1889, Fischer's *Kant;* Cohen, *Die systematischen Begriffe in Kant's vorkritischen Schriften*, and the works cited in first par., p. 536.]

Deism found a vigorous and instructive support in Germany among numerous Wolffians, though nothing new in principle was added. Characteristic of this was the translation of the Bible by Lorens **Schmidt**. The standpoint of historical criticism of the biblical writings was maintained by Salomon **Semler** (1725–1791). The sharpest consequences of the deistic criticism were drawn by Samuel **Reimarus** (1699–1768; *Abhandlungen von den vornehmsten Wahrheiten der natürlichen Religion*, 1754; *Betrachtung über die Triebe der Thiere*, 1760, especially his *Schutzschrift für die vernünftigen Verehrer Gottes*, 1767 [not pub.], from which Lessing edited the "Wolfenbüttler Fragmente," and, in more recent time, Dav. Fr. Strauss edited an extract, Leips. 1862). Joh. Chr. Edelmann was a Spinozistic free-thinker (1698–1767). Cf. K. Mönckeberg, *Reimarus und Edelmann* (Hamburg, 1867).

The movement of the so-called **Pietism**, allied to Mysticism, which was begun by **Spener** (1635–1705), and carried forward with organising energy by Aug. Herm. **Francke** (1663–1727), had only an indirect influence upon philosophy during this period; at a still farther distance stand the more isolated members of mystic sects such as Gottfried Arnold (1666–1714) and Conrad Dippel (1673–1734).

Empirical psychology was represented among the Germans in the eighteenth century by numerous names, comprehensive collections, text-books, and special investigations. There are Casimir von Creuz (1724–1770), Joh. Gottl. Krüger (*Versuch einer experimentalen Seelenlehre*, 1756), J. J. Hentsch (*Versuch über die Folge der Veränderung der Seele*, 1726), J. Fr. Weiss (*De Natura Animi et Potissimum Cordis Humani*, 1761), Fr. v. Irwing (*Erfahrungen und Untersuchungen über den Menschen*, 1777 ff.) *et al.* The "*Magazin zur Erfahrungsseelenlehre*," edited by **Moritz** (1785–1793), formed a place for collecting contributions to this favourite science. Further literature in K. Fortlage, *System der Psychologie*, I. 42 f.

A theory of art upon the basis of empirical psychology is found in Baumgarten's pupil, G. Fr. Meier (1718–1777), and especially in Joh. Georg **Sulzer** (1720–1779; *Theorie der angenehmen Empfindungen*, 1762; *Vermischte Schriften*, 1773 ff.; *Allgemeine Theorie der schönen Künste*, 1771–1774, a lexicon of æsthetics).

Of the **Popular Philosophers** may be mentioned Moses **Mendelssohn** (1729–1786; *Briefe über die Empfindungen*, 1755; *Ueber die Evidenz in den Metaphysischen Wissenschaften*, 1764; *Phædon*, 1767; *Morgenstunden*, 1785; *Werke*, ed. by Brasch, Leips. 1881), the book-dealer Fr. **Nicolai** (1733–1811), who published successively the *Bibliothek der schönen Wissenschaften*, the

Briefe die neueste deutsche Literatur betreffend, the *Allgemeine deutsche Bibliothek,* and the *Neue Allgemeine deutsche Bibliothek ;* further J. Aug. **Eberhard**
(1738–1809), Joh. Bernh. **Basedow** (1723–1790), Thomas **Abbt** (1738–1766),
Joh. Jac. **Engel** (1741–1802 ; editor of the *Philosoph für die Welt*), J. J. H.
Feder (1740–1821), Chr. **Meiners** (1747–1810), Chr. **Garve** (1742–1798).

A highly interesting position personally is occupied by **Frederick the Great,**
the Philosopher of Sanssouci. On him, cf. Ed. Zeller, *Fr. d. Gr. als. Philosoph*
(Berlin, 1886).

Of **Lessing's** writings those of chief importance for the history of philosophy
are the *Hamburger Dramaturgie,* the *Erziehung des menschen Geschlechts,*
the *Wolfenbüttler Fragmente,* and the theological controversial writings. Cf.
Rob. Zimmerman, *Leibniz und Lessing (Studien und Kritiken,* I. 126 ff.) ;
E. Zirngiebl, *Der Jacobi-Mendelssohn'sche Streit über Lessing's Spinozismus*
(Munich, 1861) ; C. Hebler, *Lessing-Studien* (Berl., 1862) ; W. Dilthey (*Preuss.
Jahrb.* 1879). [Eng. tr. of the *Ham. Dram.* and *Education of Human Race*
in Bohn Lib.; of *Laoccoon,* by Phillimore, Lond. 1875 ; cf. Sime, *Lessing,* Lond.
1873, 1879.]

Among **Herder's** writings belong in this period, *Ueber den Ursprung der
Sprache,* 1772 ; *Auch eine Philosophie der Geschichte der Menschheit,* 1774 ;
Vom Erkennen und Empfinden der menschlichen Seele, 1778 ; *Ideen zur
Philosophie der Geschichte der Menschheit,* 1784 ff. [Eng. tr., Lond. 1800] ;
Gott, Gespräche über Spinoza's System, 1787 ; *Briefe zur Beförderung der
Humanität,* 1793 ff. (on his later philosophical literary activity, cf. below, Part
VI. ch. 2). Cf. R. Haym, *H. nach seinem Leben und seinen Werken* (Berlin,
1877–85) ; E. Melzer, *H. als Geschichtsphilosoph* (Neisse, 1872) ; M. Kronen-
berg, *H.'s Philosophie* (Heidl. 1889) [art. *Herder* in *Enc. Brit.* by J. Sully].

Cf. also J. Witte, *Die Philosophie unserer Dichterheroen* (Bonn, 1880).

CHAPTER I.

THE THEORETICAL QUESTIONS.

"THE proper study of mankind is man." This word of Pope's is characteristic of the whole philosophy of the Enlightenment, not only in the practical sense that this philosophy finds the ultimate end of all scientific investigation to be always man's "happiness," but also, in the theoretical point of view, in so far as this philosophy, as a whole, aims to base all knowledge upon the observation of the actual processes of the psychical life. After Locke had set up the principle,[1] that prior to all metaphysical considerations and controversies the general question must be decided of how far human insight reaches, and that this in turn is possible only by exact exhibition of the sources from which knowledge derives, and of the course of development by which it is brought about, — from that time *epistemology*, the theory of knowledge, was brought into the front rank of philosophical interests, and at the same time *empirical psychology* was recognised as the authoritative and decisive court of last resort for epistemology. The legitimate reach of human ideas should be judged by the way in which they arise. Thus experiential psychology with all the tacit assumptions which are customary in it becomes at once the basis of the whole philosophical view of the world, and the favourite science of the age, and is at the same time the instrument of mediation between science and general literature. As in this latter field, the predominant characteristic among both Englishmen and Germans was that of depicting minds and reflecting or viewing one's self in the literary looking-glass, so philosophy should draw only the image of man and of the activities of his consciousness. Societies for the "observation of man" were founded, all sorts of dilettante accounts of remarkable experiences were garnered in large "magazines," and the government of the French Republic in its official system of instruction,[2] replaced "philosophy" by the sounding title, "Analyse de l'entendement humain."

---

[1] Introduction to the *Essay*. Cf. M. Drobisch, *Locke, Der Vorläufer Kant's* (*Zeitschr. f. exacte Philosophie*, 1861).
[2] Cf. the highly amusing *Séances des Ecoles Normal*, first year.

While accordingly among the theoretical questions of the Enlightenment philosophy, those as to the origin, development, and knowing power of human ideas stood uppermost, these were from the beginning placed beneath the presupposition of popular metaphysics, viz. that of *naïve realism*. There, "without," is a world of things, of bodies or of who knows what else, — and here is a mind which is to know them. How do the ideas, which reproduce within the mind that world of things, get into it? This way of stating the problem of knowledge, which is like that of the ancient Greeks, controls the theoretical philosophy of the eighteenth century completely, and attains in it both most perfect formulation and decisive disintegration. Just in this respect the *Cartesian metaphysics with its dualism of conscious and corporeal substances* takes a controlling position through the entire age of the Enlightenment, and the popular empirical mode of expression in which it was presented by *Locke*, made this author the leader of the new movement. The methodical and metaphysical considerations which had reached a great development, and one full of character in Descartes' important disciples, were now translated into the language of empirical psychology, and so arranged for the comprehension of the ordinary mind.

In connection with this, however, the *terminism* which was inherent in all modern philosophy, and which had been fostered especially in England (Hobbes), forced its way victoriously to the surface; the qualitative separation of the content and forms of consciousness from the "outer world," to which alone they were nevertheless held to relate, was carried farther and deeper, step by step, until it at last reached its extreme consequence in *Hume's* positivism. To the scientific dissolution which metaphysics thus experienced, corresponded in turn a popularly practical and pretentiously modest turning away from all speculation of more than ordinary refinement, or an all the more express profession of adherence to the truths of sound common sense.

Whatever metaphysical interest remained vigorous in the Enlightenment literature attached itself to the religious consciousness and to those endeavours which hoped to attain out of the strife of religious Confessions to a universal and rational conviction. In the *deism* which extended over Europe from the English *free-thinking* movement, the positive views of the world and of life of the Enlightenment period became concentrated, and while these convictions at the outset developed out of the connection with the natural science metaphysics of the preceding century, and in consequence of this devoted an especially lively interest to the problems of *teleology*, they became shifted with time more and more from the metaphysical to the moral, from the theoretical to the practical domain.

§ 33. Innate Ideas.

With regard to the question as to the origin of ideas the philosophy of the Enlightenment found already in the field the sharply pronounced antithesis of *Sensualism* and *Rationalism*.

1. The first of these had been defended by Hobbes on the theoretical as also upon the practical domain, inasmuch as he held man, in so far as he is an object of scientific knowledge, to be an entirely sensuous being, bound to the sensations and impulses of the body. All ideas, in his view, have their origin in the activity of the senses, and the mechanism of association was held to explain the arising of all other psychical structures from these beginnings. Such doctrines seemed to bring in question the super-sensuous dignity of man, and that not only in the eyes of the orthodox opponents of Hobbes ; the same motive determined the Neo-Platonists also to lively opposition. Cudworth especially had distinguished himself in this respect; in his combating of atheism [1] he had Hobbes in mind as one of his main opponents, and in opposition to the doctrine that all human ideas arise from the operation of the outer world upon the mind, he appeals especially to mathematical conceptions. The corporeal phenomena never completely correspond to these; the most we can say is that they resemble them.[2] In treating the conception of God, on the other hand, he lays claim to the argument of the *consensus gentium*, and carries it out [3] in most extensive manner to show that this idea is innate. In like manner, Herbert of Cherbury had already grounded all the main doctrines of natural religion and morals by the aid of the Stoic and Ciceronian doctrine of the *communes notitiæ*.

The doctrine of innate ideas was conceived in a somewhat different sense by Descartes [4] and his disciples. Here the psychological question as to the origin of ideas was less in mind, although this question, too, at a decisive passage in the *Meditations* (*Med.* III.) received the answer that the innateness of the idea of God was to be conceived of as a sign which the creator had imprinted upon his creature; but on the whole the great metaphysician had laid more weight upon the point that the criterion of innateness consists in *immediate evidence* or certainty. Hence he had finally extended the designation (almost stripped of the psychological meaning be-

---

[1] In the *Systema Intellectuale*, especially at the close, V. 5, 28 ff.
[2] Ib. V. 1, 108 ff. (p. 905 ff. Mosh.).
[3] The whole fourth chapter is devoted to this task.
[4] Cf. E. Grimm, *Descartes' Lehre von den angeborenen Ideen*, Jena, 1873.

longing to it at the outset) of the Latin *ideæ innatæ* to all that *lumine naturali clare et distincte percipitur.* Direct assent had been adduced by Herbert of Cherbury also as the characteristic mark of innate ideas.[1]

2. *Locke's* polemical attitude toward the maintenance of innate ideas has, indeed, an epistemological purpose, but is really determined only by the *psycho-genetic* point of view. He asks primarily only whether the soul at its birth brings complete knowledge into the world with it, and finds this question deserving of a negative answer.[2] In consequence of this the development of the thesis "No innate principles in the mind" in the first book of Locke's Essay is directed less against Descartes than against the English Neo-Platonists.[3] It combats first of all the *consensus gentium,* by an appeal to the experience of the nursery and of ethnology; it finds that neither theoretical nor practical principles are universally known or acknowledged. Nor does it except from this demonstration (with an express turn against Herbert) even the idea of God, since this is not only very different among different men, but is even entirely lacking with some. Nor does Locke allow the evasion suggested by Henry More,[4] that innate ideas might be contained in the soul not actually, but implicitly: this could only mean, according to Locke, that the soul is capable of forming and approving them, — a mark which would then hold for all ideas. The immediate assent, finally, which was held to characterise that which is innate, does not apply in the case of the most general abstract truths, just where it is wanted; and where this immediate assent is found it rests upon the fact that the meaning of the words and of their connection has been already apprehended at an earlier time.[5]

Thus the soul is again stripped of all its original possessions: at birth it is like an unwritten sheet (cf. p. 203), — white paper void of all characters.[6] In order to prove this positively, Locke then pledges himself to show that all our "ideas"[7] arise from experience. Here he distinguishes simple and complex ideas in the assumption that the latter arise out of the former: for the simple ideas, how-

---

[1] *De Veritate* (1656), p. 76.

[2] In which, moreover, Descartes completely agreed with him, for it was Descartes' opinion also that it was not to be assumed that the mind of the child pursues metaphysics in its mother's womb. *Op.* (C.) VIII. 269.

[3] Cf. (and also for the following) G. Geil, *Die Abhängigkeit Locke's von Descartes* (Strassburg, 1887).

[4] H. More, *Antidot. adv. Ath.* I. 3 and 7, and Locke, I. 2, 22. Cf. Geil, *op. cit.,* p. 49.

[5] Locke, I. 2, 23 f.   [6] Ib. II. 1, 2.

[7] The term "idea" had lost its Platonic sense already in later Scholasticism and taken on the more general meaning of any mental modification whatever (*Vorstellung*).

ever, he announces two different sources: *sensation* and *reflection*, *outer* and *inner perception*. Under sensation he understands the ideas of the corporeal world, brought about by the medium of the bodily senses; under reflection, on the other hand, the knowledge of the activities of the soul itself called out by the above process. Psycho-genetically, therefore, these two kinds of perception are so related that sensation is the occasion and the presupposition for reflection,—as regards their matter or content the relation is, that all content of ideas arises from sensation, while reflection, on the contrary, contains the consciousness of the functions performed in connection with this content.

3. To these functions, however, belonged also all those by means of which the combination of the elements of consciousness into complex ideas takes place, *i.e.* all processes of thought. And here Locke left the relation of the intellectual activities to their original sensuous contents in a popular indefiniteness which gave occasion to the most various re-shapings of his teaching soon after. For, on the one hand, those activities appear as the *"faculties"* of the mind, which in reflection becomes conscious of these its own modes of functioning (as for example, the capacity of having ideas itself,[1] *"perception,"* is treated as the most original fact of reflection, to understand which every one is sent to his own experience); on the other hand, the mind, even in these relating activities, such as recollecting, distinguishing, comparing, connecting, etc., is regarded throughout as passive and bound to the content of the sensation. Hence it was possible for the most various views to develop out of Locke's doctrine, according to the *varying degree of self-activity* which was ascribed to the mind in its process of connecting its ideas.

Of particular interest in this connection, by reason of the problems of epistemology and metaphysics derived from the Middle Ages, was the development of the *abstract ideas* out of the data of sensation. Like the greater part of English philosophers, Locke was an adherent of *Nominalism*, which professed to see in general concepts nothing but internal, intellectual structures. In explaining these general ideas, however, Locke made more account of the co-operation of "signs," and in particular of *language*. Signs or words, when attached more or less arbitrarily to particular parts of ideas, make it possible to lay special stress upon these parts and bring them out from their original complexes, and thereby render possible the farther functions by which such isolated and fixed contents of

---

[1] *Essay*, II. 9, 1 f.

consciousness are put into logical relations to one another.[1] Hence
for Locke, as formerly for the Epicureans, and then for the Ter-
minists, logic was coincident with the science of signs, *semiotics*.[2]
By this means room was gained for a demonstrative science of conceptions and for all abstract operations of the knowing mind, quite
in the spirit of Occam, in spite of the sensualistic basis upon which
all content of ideas was held to rest.   None of these determinations
were philosophically new, nor has their exposition in Locke any
originality or independent power of thought: it is, however, smooth
and simple, of agreeable transparency and easy to understand; it
despises all scholastic form and learned terminology, glides skilfully
over and away from all deeper problems, and thus made its author
one of the most extensively read and influential writers in the history
of philosophy.

4. Strongly as Locke had emphasised the independent existence
of inner experience by the side of the outer (as followed from his
metaphysical attachment to Descartes, on which see below, § 34, 1),
he yet made the dependence of reflection upon sensation, as regards
origin and content, so strong that it proved the decisive factor in
the development of his doctrine.   This transformation to complete
sensualism proceeded along different paths.

In the epistemological and metaphysical development of Nominalism this transformation led with Locke's English successors to
extreme consequences.   Berkeley[3] not only declared the doctrine of
the Reality of abstract conceptions to be the most extraordinary of
all errors in metaphysics, but also — like the extreme Nominalists
of the Middle Ages — denied the existence of abstract ideas within
the mind itself.   The illusory appearance of such ideas arises from
the use of words as general terms; but in truth, even in connection
with such a word, we always think merely the sensuous idea, or the
group of sensuous ideas, which at the beginning gave rise to that
term.   Every attempt to think the abstract alone shatters upon the
sensuous idea, which always remains as the sole content of intellectual
activity.   For even the remembered ideas and partial ideas which
can be separated out, have no other content than the original sense-

---

[1] The development of these logical relations between the ideational contents
which have been singled out and fixed by means of the verbal signs, appears
with Locke, under the name of the *lumen naturale*.   Descartes had understood
by this as well intuitive as also demonstrative knowledge, and had set all this
natural knowing activity over against revelation ; Locke, who treats the intuitive
with terministic reserve (cf. § 34, 1), restricts the signification of the "light of
nature" to the logical operations and to the consciousness of the principles
which obtain in these, according to the nature of the thinking faculty.

[2] *Essay*, IV. 21, 4.

[3] *Princ. of Human Knowledge*, 5 ff.

impressions, because an idea can never copy anything else than another idea. Abstract ideas, therefore, are a fiction of the schools; in the actual activity of thought none but sensuous particular ideas exist, and some of these can stand for or represent others similar to them, on account of being designated by the same term.

David *Hume* adopted this doctrine in its full extent, and on the ground of this substituted for Locke's distinction of outer and inner perception another antithesis with altered terminology, viz. that of the original and the copied. A content of consciousness is either original or the copy of an original, — either an *"impression"* or an *"idea."* All ideas, therefore, are copies of impressions, and there is no idea that has come into existence otherwise than by being a copy of an impression, or that has any other content than that which it has received from its corresponding impression. It appeared, therefore, to be the task of philosophy to seek out the original for even the apparently most abstract conceptions in some impression, and thereby to estimate the value for knowledge which the abstract conception has. To be sure, Hume understood by impressions by no means merely the elements of outer experience; he meant also those of inner experience. It was, therefore, according to Locke's mode of expression, the simple ideas of sensation and reflection which he declared to be impressions, and the wide vision of a great thinker prevented him from falling into a shortsighted sensualism.

5. A development of another sort, which yet led to a related goal, took place in connection with the aid of *physiological psychology.* Locke had only thought of sensation as dependent upon the activity of the bodily senses, but had regarded the elaboration of sensation in the functions underlying reflection as a work of the mind; and though he avoided the question as to immaterial substance, he had throughout treated the intellectual activities in the narrower sense as something incorporeal and independent of the body. That this should be otherwise regarded, that thinkers should begin to consider the physical organism as the bearer or agent not only of the simple ideas, but also of their combination, was easily possible in view of the indecisive ambiguity of the Lockian doctrines, but was still more called out by one-sided conclusions drawn from *Cartesian* and *Spinozistic theories.*

Descartes, namely, had treated the whole psychical life of the animal as a mechanical process of the nervous system, while he had ascribed the human psychical life to the immaterial substance, the *res cogitans.* The more evident the completely sensuous nature of human ideation now seemed in consequence of Locke's investigation, the nearer lay the question whether it was possible to maintain the position, that the same processes which in the animal seemed capable of being understood as nervous processes, should be traced back in the case of man to the activity of an immaterial psychical substance. — From another side, Spinoza's parallelism of the attributes worked in the same direction (cf. above, § 31, 9). According to this view a process in the bodily life *corresponds* to every process of the psychical life, without either process being the cause of the other, or one process being the original and the other the derived. (Such, at least, was the thought of the philosopher himself.) This had now been conceived of at first by its opponents as materialism, as if Spinoza meant that the fundamental process was the bodily, and the psychical process only its accompanying phenomenon. But among its adherents also, both physicians and natural scientists, such as the influential *Boerhave* of Leyden, a mode of thought inclining strongly toward materialism soon substituted itself for the master's doctrine. This took place in connection with the experiences of experimental physiology which, following Descartes' stimulus, employed itself largely with a study of reflex movements.

It is interesting that the consequences of these combinations of thought appeared in literary form first in Germany. Here as early as 1697 a physician named *Pancratius Wolff* taught in his *Cogitationes Medico-legales* that thoughts are mechanical activities of the human body, especially of the brain, and in the year 1713 appeared the anonymous *Correspondence concerning the Nature of the Soul* (*Briefwechsel vom Wesen der Seele*),[1] in which, screened by pious refutations, the doctrines of Bacon, Descartes, and Hobbes are carried out to an anthropological materialism. A distinction of degree only is recognised between the psychical life of the animal and that of man; ideas and activities of the will are without exception regarded as functions of excited nerve-fibres, and practice and education are given as the means by which the higher position of man is reached and maintained.

In England the procedure was more cautious. In a way similar to that in which Locke had carried out the Baconian programme, men now studied primarily the internal mechanism of the psychical activities, and the development of the higher out of the elementary states according to purely psychological laws: such was the work of Peter Brown in the epistemological field, and that of others upon the domain of the activities of the will. In the same manner proceeded

---

[1] Of which Lange gives an account, *Gesch. des Mat.*, I. 319 ff. (2d ed. [Eng. tr., *History of Materialism*, II. 37 ff.]).

David *Hartley* also, who brought into common use the expression *association* [1] (which had already been used before this) for the combinations and relations which arise between the elements.   He wished to conceive these relations, which he analysed with all the care of a natural scientist, solely as psychical processes, and held fast to their complete incomparableness with material processes, even with the most delicate forms of corporeal motion.   But he was also a physician, and the connection of the mental life with the states of the body was so clear to him that he made the *constant correspondence* of the two and the mutual relationship of the psychical functions and the nervous excitations, which, at that time, were termed "*vibrations*," [2] the main subject-matter of his psychology of association. In this work he held fast to the qualitative difference between the two parallel series of phenomena and left the metaphysical question, as to the substance lying at their basis, undecided : but with reference to *causality* he fell insensibly into materialism, in that he conceived of the mechanism of the nervous states as ultimately the primary event, and that of the psychical activities as only the phenomenon accompanying this event.   To simple nervous excitations correspond simple sensations or desires ; to complex, complex.   This scientific theory, to be sure, involved him in serious contradictions with his pious faith, and the "Observations" show how earnestly and fruitlessly he struggled between the two.   Quite the same is true of *Priestley*, who even made the farther concession to materialism of letting fall the heterogeneity between the psychical and bodily processes, and desiring to replace psychology completely by nerve physiology.   On this account he also abandoned entirely the standpoint of inner experience defended by the Scots, but at the same time desired to unite with his system the warmly supported conviction of a teleological deism.

Anthropological materialism was worked out in its baldest form by the Frenchman, *Lamettrie*.   Convinced by medical observations upon himself and others of the complete dependence of the mind upon the body, he studied the mechanism of life in animals and men, following Boerhave's suggestions, and Descartes' conception of the former seemed to him completely applicable to the latter also.   The distinction between the two, which is only one of degree, permits for human psychical activities also no other explanation than that they are mechanical functions of the brain.   On this account it is

---

[1] In the later, especially the Scottish literature, and in particular with Thomas *Brown*, the expression "association" is often replaced by *suggestion*.

[2] Instead of this term Erasmus Darwin introduced the expression, "motions of the sensorium."

an encroachment of metaphysics to ascribe to the "mind" a substantiality of its own in addition to that of matter. The conception of matter as that of a body which is in itself dead and needs mind or spirit as its moving principle, is an arbitrary and false abstraction: experience shows that matter moves itself and lives. It is just Descartes' mechanics which has proved this, says Lamettrie, and therefore the inevitable consequence of this mechanics is materialism. And that all psychical life is only one of the functions of the body, is evident from the fact that not a single content is found in the mental life which is not due to the excitation of some one of the senses. If we think of a man as the Church Father Arnobius proposed, — so writes Lamettrie,[1] to establish his sensualism which had developed from Locke, — who from his birth on had been excluded from all connection with his kind, and restricted to the experience of a few senses, we should find in him no other ideational contents than those brought to him through just these senses.

6. Less important in principle, but all the more widely extended in the literary world, were the other re-shapings which Locke's doctrine experienced in France. *Voltaire*, who domesticated it among his countrymen by his *Lettres sur les Anglais*, gave it a completely sensualistic stamp, and even showed himself — though with sceptical reserve — not disinclined to entrust to the Creator the power of providing the I, which is a corporeal body, with the capacity of thinking also. This sceptical sensualism became the fundamental note of the French Enlightenment.[2] *Condillac*, who at the beginning had only expounded Locke's doctrine and defended it against other systems, professed his adherence to this sceptical sensualism in his influential *Traité des Sensations*. Whatever the mind may be, the content of its conscious activities is derived solely from sense-perception. Condillac develops the theory of associational psychology in connection with the fiction of a statue, which, equipped only with capacity of sensation, receives one after another the excitations of the different senses which are added to it, and by this means gradually unfolds an intellectual life like that of man. Here the fundamental idea is that the mere co-existence of different sensations in the same consciousness brings with it *of itself the sensation of their relation to each other and to the*

---

[1] At the close of the *Histoire Naturelle de l'Âme*. Cf. also above, p. 225, note 1.

[2] The same mode of thought asserts itself also in the beginnings of æsthetic criticism in the form of the principle that the essence of all art consists in the "imitation of beautiful Nature." The type of this conception was *E. Batteux* (1713–1780) with his treatise, *Les Beaux Arts réduits à un même Principe* (1746).

object or the self. In accordance with this principle the process is depicted by which all the manifold psychical activities become unfolded out of perception : in the theoretical series, by virtue of the differences in intensity and in repetition of sensations, there grow successively attention, recognising recollection, distinction, comparison, judgment, inference, imagination, and expectation of the future; and finally with the help of signs, especially those of language, arise abstraction and the grasping of general principles. But in addition to sensation, perception has also the feeling-element of pleasure and pain, and out of this, in connection with the movement of ideas, develop desire, love and hate, hope, fear,[1] and — as the result of all such changes of the practical consciousness — finally, the moral will. So knowledge and morality grow upon the soil of the sensibility.

This systematic construction had great success. The systematic impulse, which was repressed in the metaphysical field (cf. § 34, 7), threw itself with all the greater energy upon this *"analysis of the human mind"* as a substitute; and as Condillac himself had already woven many acute observations into his exposition of the development process, so a whole throng of adherents found opportunity to take part in the completion of this structure by slight changes and shiftings of the phases, by innovations in nomenclature and by more or less valuable deductions. The Government of the Revolution recognised as philosophy only this study of the empirical development of intelligence, and Destutt de *Tracy* gave it later the name *" Ideology."*[2] So it came about that at the beginning of our century philosophers were in France usually called ideologists.

7. With reference to the nature of the mind in which these transformations of sensation (*sentir*) were held to take place, a great part of the ideologists remained by Condillac's positivistic reserve; others went on from Voltaire's problematical to Lamettrie's assertive materialism, — at first, in Hartley's fashion emphasising the thoroughgoing dependence of combinations of ideas upon nervous processes, then with express maintenance of the materiality of the psychical activities. This development is most clearly to be seen in the case of *Diderot*. He set out from the position of Shaftesbury and Locke, but the sensualistic literature became more potent from step to step

---

[1] In the development of the practical series of conscious acts, the influence of Descartes' and Spinoza's theory of the emotions and passions asserted itself with Condillac and his disciples, as also in part among the English associational psychologists.

[2] It is not impossible that this nomenclature in case of de Tracy was intended to be the counterpart to Fichte's " Wissenschaftslehre," — Science of Knowledge (cf. below, Part VI. ch. 2).

in the Editor of the Encyclopædia; he followed up the hypotheses of hylozoism [1] (cf. below, § 34, 9), and finally took part in the composition of the *Système de la Nature*. This work set forth the human psychical activities within the framework of its metaphysics as the fine invisible motions of the nerves, and treated their genetic process just as Lamettrie had done. Among the later ideologists *Cabanis* is prominent in this respect by the newness of his physiological point of view; he takes account of the progress of natural science in so far as to seek the conditions of the nerves, to which man's psychical states (*le moral*) must be referred, no longer merely in mechanical motions, but in *chemical* changes. Ideation is the secretion of the brain, just as other secretions are produced by other organs.

In opposition to this, another line of ideology held fast to Locke's principle that all content of ideas may indeed be due to the senses, but that in the functions directed toward combining such content the peculiar character of the mind's nature shows itself. The leader of this line of thought was *Bonnet*. He, too, in a manner similar to that of Condillac, adopts the mode of consideration commended by Lamettrie, adverting to Arnobius, but he is much too well-schooled as an investigator of Nature to fail to see that sensation can never be resolved into elements of motion, that its relation to physical states is synthetic, but not analytic. Hence he sees in the mechanism of the nervous system only the *causa occasionalis* for the spontaneous *reaction of the mind*, and the substantiality of the mind seems to him to be proved by the *unity of consciousness*. He connects with this theory all sorts of fantastic hypotheses.[2] Religious ideas speak in his assumption of the immaterial mind-substance, but sensualism admits an activity of this substance only in connection with the body; for this reason, in order to explain immortality and the uninterrupted activity of the mind, Bonnet helps himself by the hypothesis of an æthereal body which is joined essentially with the soul and takes on a coarser material external organism, according to its dwelling-place in each particular case.

This union of sensualism with the maintenance of self-subsistent substantiality and capacity of reaction on the part of the mind passed over to Bonnet's countryman, *Rousseau*, who combated with its aid the psychological theories of the Encyclopædists. He found that this characteristic quality of the mind, the unity of its function, evinces itself in *feeling* (*sentiment*), and opposed this original natu-

---

[1] The decisive transition-writing is *d'Alembert's Dream.*
[2] In the *Palingénésies Philosophiques.*

ralness of its essence to the cold and indifferent mechanism of ideas, which would debase the mind to an unconditional dependence upon the outer world. The *feeling of individuality* rebelled with him against a doctrine according to which there is nothing in man's consciousness but the play, as if upon an indifferent stage, of a mass of foreign contents accidentally coming together, which unite and then separate again. He wished to bring out the thought that it is not the case that the mental life merely takes place within us, but that it is rather true that we are ourselves present as actively determining personalities. This conviction dictated Rousseau's opposition to the intellectualistic Enlightenment, which in the sensualism of Condillac and of the Encyclopædists wished to regard man's inner life as only a mechanical product of sensational elements excited from without: to psychological atomism Rousseau opposes the principle of the Monadology.

In the same manner, and perhaps not without influence from Rousseau in his arguments, *St. Martin* raised his voice against the prevailing system of Condillac; he even came out of his mystical retreat to protest in the sessions of the *Ecoles Normales* [1] against the superficiality of sensualism. The ideologists, he says, talk a great deal about human nature; but instead of observing it they devote their energies to put it together (*composer*).

8. The *Scottish philosophers* are the psychological opponents of sensualism in all its forms. The common ground on which this contrast developed is that of psychology regarded as philosophy. For *Reid*, also, and his disciples seek the task of philosophy in the investigation of man and his mental capacities; indeed, they fixed still more energetically and one-sidedly than the various schools of their opponents the methodical point of view that all philosophy must be empirical psychology. But this view of the human physical activity and its development is diametrically opposed to that of the sensualists. The latter hold the simple, the former the complex, the latter the individual ideas, the former the judgments, the latter the sensuous, the former the internal, the latter the particular, the former the general, to be the original content of the mind's activity. Reid acknowledges that Berkeley's idealism and Hume's scepticism are as correct consequences from Locke's principle as is Hartley's materialism; but just the absurdity of these consequences refutes the principle.

In opposition to this, Reid will now apply the Baconian method of induction to the facts of inner perception in order to attain by an

---

analysis of these to the *original truths,* which are given from the
beginning in connection with the nature of the human mind, and
which assert themselves in the development of its activities as
determining *principles.* Thus, putting aside all help of physiology,
the fundamental science psychology shall be perfected as a kind of
natural science of inner observation. In the solution of this task,
Reid himself, and after him especially Dugald *Stewart,* develop a
considerable breadth and comprehensiveness of vision in the apprehension of the inner processes and a great acuteness in the analysis
of their essential content : a multitude of valuable observations on
the genetic processes of the mental life is contained in their extensive investigations. And yet these investigations lack in fruitful-
ness of ideas as well as in energetically comprehensive cogency.
For they everywhere confuse the demonstration of that which can
be discovered as universally valid content in the psychical functions, with the assumption that this is also genetically the original
and determining : and since this philosophy has no other principle
than that of psychological fact, it regards without criticism all that
can in this manner be demonstrated to be actual content of mental
activity, as *self-evident truth.* The sum-total of these principles is
designated as *common sense,* and as such is held to form the supreme
rule for all philosophical knowledge.

9. In the philosophy of the German Enlightenment all these
tendencies mingle with the after-workings of the Cartesian and
Leibnizian rationalism. The twofold tendency in the method of
this latter system had taken on a fixed systematic form through
the agency of Christian *Wolff.* According to him, all subjects
should be regarded both from the point of view of the eternal
truths and from that of the contingent truths : for every province
of reality there is a knowledge through conceptions and another
through facts, an *a priori* science proceeding from the intellect and
an *a posteriori* science arising from perception. These two sciences
were to combine in the result in such a way that, for example, empirical psychology must show the actual existence in fact of all
those activities which, in rational psychology, were deduced from
the metaphysical conception of the soul, and from the "faculties"
resulting from this conception. On the other hand, following Leibniz's precedent, the distinction in value of the two modes of knowledge was so far retained as to regard only the intellectual knowledge
as clear and distinct insight, while empirical (or, as they said at
that time, historical) knowledge was regarded as a more or less
obscure and confused idea of things.

Psychologically, the two kinds of knowledge were divided, in accordance with the Cartesian model, into the *ideæ innatæ* and the *ideæ adventitiæ.* Yet Wolff himself, agreeably to the metaphysical direction of his thought, laid less weight upon the genetic element. But the opposite was the case with his adherents and opponents, who were already standing under the influence of the French and English theories. The general course of the development was that the importance which Leibniz and Wolff had conceded to empiricism was increased more and more by the penetration of the Lockian principles. The psychological method gained the preponderance over the metaphysico-ontological step by step, and within the psy‐chological method increasing concessions were made to sensualism, of such a nature that ultimately not only earnest men of science like Rüdiger and Lossius, but especially a great part of the "popu‐lar philosophers" supported completely the doctrine that all human ideas arise from sense-perception. The motley and irregular series of stages in which this process completed itself has only a literary-historical interest,[1] because no new arguments came to light in con‐nection with it.

Only one of these men used the psychologico-epistemological dualism which prevailed in the German philosophy of the Enlight‐enment, to make an original and fruitful turn. Heinrich *Lambert,* who was fully abreast of the natural science of his time, had grown into intelligent sympathy with the mathematico-logical method as completely as he had into an insight into the worth of experience: and in the phenomenology of his *New Organon,* in attempting to fix the limits for the psychological significance of these two elements of knowledge, he disposed the mixture of the *a priori* and *a posteriori* constituents requisite for knowing reality, in a way that led to the *distinction of form and content in ideas.* The content-elements of thought, he taught, can be given only by per‐ception: but their mode of connection, the form of relation which is thought between them, is not given from without, but is a proper activity of the mind. This distinction could be read out of Locke's ambiguous exposition:[2] but no one had conceived it so sharply and precisely from this point of view as Lambert. And this point of view was of great importance for the genetic consideration of the ideas of the human mind. It followed from it, that it was neither possible to derive the content from the mere form, nor the form of knowledge from the content. The first refuted the logical rational

---

[1] Cf. W. Windelband, *Gesch. d. neueren Philosophie,* I. §§ 53–55.
[2] Cf. the demonstration in G. Hartenstein, *Locke's Lehre von der mensch‐lichen Erkenntniss in Vergleichung mit Leibniz' Kritik derselben* (Leips 1861. *Abhandl. d sächs. Ges. d. Wissensch.*).

ism with which Wolff would spin all ontology and metaphysics out from the most general principles of logic, and ultimately from the one principle of contradiction; the other took the basis away from sensualism, which thought that with the contents of perception the knowledge also of their relations was immediately given. Out of this grew for the "improvement of metaphysics" the task of dissolving out these relating forms from the total mass of experience, and of making clear their relation to content. But Lambert sought in vain for a single unifying principle for this purpose,[1] and his "*Architektonik*" finally contented itself with making a collection of them not based on any internal principle.

10. While all these theories as to the origin of human ideas were flying about in the literary market, the reconciling word upon the problem of innate ideas had been long spoken, but was waiting in a manuscript in the Hanoverian library for the powerful effect which its publication was to produce. *Leibniz*, in his *Nouveaux Essais*, had provided the Lockian ideology with a critical commentary in detail, and had embodied within it the deepest thoughts of his philosophy and the finest conclusions of his Monadology.

Among the arguments with which Locke combated the doctrine that ideas were innate, had been that with which he maintained that there could be nothing in the mind of which the mind knew nothing. This principle had also been pronounced by him[2] in the form that the soul thinks not always. By this principle the Cartesian definition of the soul as a *res cogitans* was brought into question: for the essential characteristic of a substance cannot be denied it at any moment. In this sense the question had been often discussed between the schools. Leibniz, however, was pointed by his Monadology to a peculiar intermediate position. Since, in his view, the soul, like every monad, is a "representing" power, it must have perceptions at every moment: but since all monads, even those which constitute matter, are souls, these perceptions cannot possibly all be clear and distinct. The solution of the problem lies, therefore, again in the conception of *unconscious representations* or *petites perceptions* (cf. above, § 31). The soul (as every monad) always has ideas or representations, but not always conscious, not always clear and distinct ideas; its life consists in the development of the unconscious to conscious, of the obscure and confused to clear and distinct ideas or representations.

In this aspect Leibniz now introduced an extremely significant

---

[1] This is best seen in his interesting correspondence with Kant, printed in the works of the latter.

[2] *Essay* II. 1, 10 f.

conception into psychology and epistemology. He distinguished between the states in which the soul merely *has* ideas, and those in which it is *conscious* of them. The former he designated as perception, the latter as *apperception*.[1] He understood, therefore, by apperception the process by which unconscious, obscure, and confused representations are raised into clear and distinct consciousness, and thereby recognised by the soul as its own and *appropriated by self-consciousness.* The genetic process of the psychical life consists in the *changing of unconscious into conscious representations* or ideas, in taking up perceptions into the clearness and distinctness of self-consciousness. In the light of the Monadology Leibniz's methodological view of the empirical or contingent truths (cf. § 30, 7) took on a peculiar colouring. The fact that the monads have no windows makes it impossible to conceive of perception metaphysically as a working of things upon the soul:[2] the ideas of sense, or sense-presentations, must rather be thought as activities which the soul, by virtue of the pre-established harmony, develops in an obscure and confused manner (as *petites perceptions*), and the transformation which takes place in them can be regarded only as a process of making them distinct and of clearing them up, — as a taking up into self-consciousness, as *apperception.*

Sensibility and *understanding*, the distinction between which with Leibniz coincides with that of different degrees of clearness and distinctness, have, therefore, in his view, the same content, only that the former has in obscure and confused representation what the latter possesses as clear and distinct. Nothing comes into the soul from without; that which it consciously represents has been already unconsciously contained within it: and on the other hand, the soul cannot bring forth anything in its conscious ideas which has not been within it from the beginning. Hence Leibniz must decide that in a certain sense, that is, unconsciously, all ideas are innate; and that in another sense, that is, consciously, no idea is innate in the human soul. He designates this relation, which had been previously sketched in the principles of the Monadology, by the name *virtual innateness of ideas.*

This thought, which is at once treated as the controlling point of view at the opening of the *New Essays*, is carried out especially with reference to the universal or eternal truths. This was indeed the burning question: here the one party (the Neo-Platonists, and in part the Cartesians) maintained that these were innate "actu-

---

[1] *Princ. de la Nat. et de la Grâce,* 4, where the relationship with the Lockian reflection comes out strongly ; *Nouv. Ess.* II. 9, 4.

[2] *N. E.* IV. 4, 5.

ally," as fully formed (*fertige*) truths; the others (Hobbes, and in part Locke) would explain them from the co-operation of sensational elements. Leibniz, however, carries out the thought that such principles are contained already in perception, as *petites percep-tions*, that is, as the *involuntary forms of relating thought*, but that after this unconscious employment of them they are apperceived, that is, raised to clear and distinct consciousness and so recognised in connection with experience. The form of the soul's activity which is afterwards brought to clearness and distinctness of intellectual apprehension as a universal principle, an eternal truth, inheres already in the sensuous representation, though unclear and confused. Hence while Locke had appropriated for his own use the scholastic principle *nihil est in intellectu quod non fuerit in sensu*, Leibniz adds thereto *nisi intellectus ipse*.[1]

11. When the *Nouveaux Essais* were printed in 1765, they excited great attention. Lessing was translating them. That the life of the soul transcends all that is clear and distinctly conscious, and is rooted in obscurely presaged depths, was an insight of the highest value for the literature which was just struggling out of the intellectual dryness of the Enlightenment, and out of insipid correctness to an unfolding full of genius, — and an insight all the more valuable as coming from the same thinker that Germany honoured as the father and hero of its Enlightenment. In this direction Leibniz worked especially upon *Herder:* we see it not only in his æsthetic views,[2] but still more in his prize essay "On the Knowing and Feeling of the Human Soul."

Under the preponderance of the methodological point of view, the Leibnizo-Wolffian school had strained the opposition between rational and empirical knowledge as far as possible, and had treated understanding and sensibility as two separate faculties. The Berlin Academy had wished to see the mutual relation of these two separated powers, and the share which each has in human knowledge, investigated: Herder played the true Leibniz — as the latter had developed himself in the *Nouveaux Essais* — against the prevailing system of the schools when he emphasised in his treatise the living unity of man's psychical life, and showed that sensibility and understanding are not two different sources of knowledge, but only the different stages of one and the same living activity with which the monad comprehends the universe within itself. All the ideas with which the soul raises itself in its development, step by step, from the consciousness of its immediate environment to the knowledge of

---

[1] *Nouv. Ess.* II. 1, 2.   [2] Cf. principally the fourth *Kritische Wäldchen*.

the harmony of the universe, are innate within the soul as internal powers. This deeper unity of sensibility and understanding, Herder called *feeling;* and in this also in his inquiry as to the "Origin of Language," he found the function which embraces all senses like a unity, and by means of which the psycho-physical mechanism of producing and hearing sounds (*Tönens* and *Hörens*) is raised to become the expression of thought.

12. More important still was another effect of the work of Leibniz. It was no less a thinker than *Kant* who undertook to build up the doctrine of the *Nouveaux Essais* into a system of epistemology (cf. § 34, 12). The Königsberg philosopher was stimulated by that work to one of the most important turns in his development, and completed it in his *Inaugural Dissertation.*[1] He had already grown out of the Wolffian school-metaphysics and had been long employed with the examination of the empirical theories, and yet could not satisfy himself with them.[2] On the contrary, he was proceeding in the direction of establishing metaphysics upon a new basis, and was following Lambert's attempts to make a beginning at the work in connection with the distinction of form and content in knowledge. Now Leibniz showed with reference to the "eternal truths" that they inhered already as involuntary relating forms within sense experience itself, to be raised and brought to clear and distinct consciousness by the reflection of the understanding. This principle of virtual innateness is the nerve of Kant's *Inaugural Dissertation :* the metaphysical truths lie in the soul as laws of its activity,[3] to enter into active function on occasion of experience, and then to become object and content of the knowledge of the understanding.

Kant now applies this point of view in a new and fruitful manner to sensuous knowledge. From methodical reasons he opposed this to intellectual knowledge much more sharply even than the Wolffians : but on this account the question for him was, whether there are perhaps in the world of the senses just such original form-relations as had been pointed out in the intellectual world by Leibniz and recognised by Kant himself (cf. § 8, and the whole Sectio IV. of the treatise *De mundi sensibilis et intelligibilis forma et principiis*) : and thus he discovered the "pure Forms of the sensibility" — *space and time.* They are not innate in the ordinary sense, but acquired, yet not abstracted from the data of sensibility, but *ab ipsa mentis*

---

[1] The dependence of this essay upon the *Nouveaux Essais* has been shown by W. Windelband, *Vierteljahrschr. f. wissensch. Philos.*, I., 1876, pp. 234 ff.

[2] This is best proved by the essay which apparently stands farthest removed from metaphysics, *The Dreams of a Ghost Seer.* Cf. also Part VI. ch. 1.

[3] *De Mundi Sens. et Int.*, § 6 : *dantur per ipsam naturam intellectus.* Cf. § 8, also the corollary to § 3.

actione secundum perpetuas leges sensa sua coordinante [from the very action of the mind co-ordinating its sensations according to perpetual laws], and like the intellectual Forms they are recognised by attending to the mind's activity on occasion of experience, — the business of mathematics.

Another formulation was given to the principle of virtual innateness by *Tetens.* He wrote his essays on human nature and its development under the impression received from Kant's *Inaugural Dissertation.* He, too, declares that the "acts of thought" are the first original relation-thoughts (*Verhältnissgedanken*) : we learn them by applying them when we think; and thus they prove themselves to be the *natural laws of thought.* The universal principles which lie at the basis of all philosophical knowledge are, accordingly, "subjective necessities" in which the essential nature of the thinking soul itself comes to consciousness.

§ 34. Knowledge of the Outer World.

The background of all these theories is their epistemological purpose. This, however, assumes from the beginning a somewhat narrower place under the presupposition of the naïve realism which became attached to the Cartesian metaphysics. The principle of the *cogito ergo sum* made the self-knowledge of the mind's nature appear as the original certainty, as that which was self-evident and immediately free from doubt; but the greater the difference in kind which was conceived to exist between the world of consciousness and that of space and bodies, the greater the difficulties that presented themselves with reference to the possibility of knowing this latter world. This fact was taught at once by the metaphysical development immediately after Descartes (cf. § 31), and the same was now repeated in the most various forms in connection with the translation of these same thoughts into the language of empirical psychology and sensualism.

There is thus in the epistemology of modern philosophy from its beginning a *superiority attributed to inner experience*, by virtue of which *knowledge of the outer world becomes problematical.* In this an after-working of the *Terminism*, with which the Middle Ages had ended, asserts itself throughout the whole extent of modern thought as a determining mode of view: the heterogeneity of the outer and inner worlds gives the mind a proud feeling of a substantial quality peculiar to itself as contrasted with things, but at the same time a certain degree of uncertainty and doubtfulness in orienting itself in this world which is to it strange and foreign. In this way the very statement of the fundamental problem in the philosophy of the Enlightenment shows itself to be an echo of that deepening of the mind within itself, that placing of consciousness upon an independent basis over against the outer world, with which the ancient philosophy ended its course. In this was rooted the power of the Augustinian spirit over modern philosophy.

1. The preponderance of the inner experience asserts itself very strongly also with *Locke*, although in principle he placed sensation and reflection upon an equality psychologically, and in his genetic theory even made the latter dependent upon the former. But in assigning the epistemological values this relation is at once reversed in the spirit of the Cartesian principles. For the dualism of finite substances which the great French metaphysician had propounded is quietly introduced by Locke in conjunction with the dualism of the sources of experience : sensation is designed to furnish knowledge of the corporeal outer world, reflection to give knowledge of the activities of the mind itself : and in this consideration it is naturally found that the latter is much more suited to its task than the former. Our knowledge of our own states is *intuitive* and the most certain of all ; and with a knowledge of our states we are at the same time perfectly and undoubtedly sure of our own existence also. Locke presents this doctrine of the certainty of knowledge of self with an almost verbal adherence to Descartes.[1] With reference to our knowledge of the corporeal world, on the other hand, his attitude is much more reserved. Such a knowledge is possible only through sensation ; and although it still deserves the name knowledge, it yet lacks complete certainty and adequacy. Primarily, it is only the presence of the idea in the mind that is intuitively certain ; that a thing corresponds to the idea is not intuitively certain, and demonstration can at most teach that there is a thing there, but can predicate nothing concerning this thing.

To be sure, Locke is not at all in agreement with himself on this point. In connection with his theory of the ideas of sensation, he adopts the doctrine of the intellectual nature of the sense qualities quite in the form worked out by Descartes (cf. § 31, 2), designates them happily by the distinction of primary and secondary qualities, adds, as tertiary qualities, such powers as express the relation of one body to another, declares primary qualities to be those which really belong to bodies in themselves, and reckons, also, impenetrability in this class, in addition to those assigned to it by Descartes. As compared with the doctrine of Hobbes, this is in its essence a

---

[1] *Essay* IV. 9, 3.

decided relapse into the mode of thought of Democritus and Epicurus, as is shown, also, in the fact that Locke follows the theory of images in tracing stimulations to the affection of the nerves by minute particles streaming out from objects.[1] On the whole, therefore, the fundamental Cartesian basis of mathematical knowledge of Nature is here reaffirmed and even more widely extended.

But Locke's decision in connection with his analysis of the idea of substance has an entirely different purport. Like Occam, he distinguishes from intuitive knowledge and knowledge given by sensation, demonstrative knowledge: this has to do, not with the relation of ideas to the outer world, but with the relation of ideas to one another. In its value as knowledge it stands after the intuitive, but superior to the sensitive.[2] *Demonstrative thinking* is then conceived of entirely *terministically*, something as in the case of Hobbes, as a reckoning with concept signs. The necessity attaching to the demonstration holds only within the world of ideas; it concerns, as one class, general or abstract ideas to which no proper reality corresponds in *natura rerum*. If ideas are once present, judgments may be formed concerning the relations which exist between them, quite apart from any reference to the things themselves; and it is with such judgments alone that demonstrative knowledge has to do. Such "complex" ideas are *thought-things*, which, after they have been fixed by definition, can enter into the union with others determined in each case by the respective contents, without thereby acquiring any relation to the outside world. Among these modes of union, that which is expressed by the *idea of substance* (the category of inherence) is conspicuous in an especial manner. For all other contents and relations can be thought only as belonging to some substance. This relation, therefore, has Reality, —the idea of substance is, according to Locke's expression, ectypal, — but only in the sense that we are forced to assume a real substrate for the modes given in particular ideas, without being able to make any assertion as to what this substrate itself is. Substance is the supporter, itself unknown, of known qualities, which we have occasion to assume belong together.

This view that substances are unknowable does not, indeed, hinder Locke from taking in hand at another passage,[3] in an entirely Cartesian fashion, a division of all substances into "cogitative and incogitative." On the other hand, he applies the view to his treat-

---

[1] *Essay*, II. 8, 7 ff.   Cf. also B. Rüttenauer, *Zur Vorgeschichte des Idealismus und Kriticismus* (Freiburg, 1882), and Geil, *op. cit.*, pp. 66 ff.
[2] Ib. IV. 2.
[3] Ib. II. 23, 29; IV. 10, 9.

ment of the *cogito ergo sum.* This principle he carries over entirely from the metaphysical realm into that of empirical psychology. Self-certainty is for him that of the "internal sense"; intuition in this case refers only to our states and activities, not to our essence ; it shows us, indeed, immediately and without doubt, *that* we are, but not *what* we are. The question as to the substance of the soul (and accordingly the question also as to its relation to the body) is as incapable of an answer as the question as to the "what" of any substance whatever.

Nevertheless, Locke holds it to be possible to gain a *demonstrative certainty of the existence of God.* For this purpose he adopts the first of the Cartesian proofs (cf. § 30, 5) in a somewhat modified form, and adds the ordinary cosmological argument. An infinite, eternal, and perfect being must be thought, an ultimate cause of finite substances of which man intuitively knows himself to be one.

So manifold and full of contradictions are the *motifs* which cross in Locke's doctrine of knowledge. The exposition, apparently so easy and transparent, to which he diluted Cartesianism, glides over and away from the eddies which come up out of the dark depths of its historical presuppositions. But as the ambiguous, indeterminate nature of his psychology unfolded itself in the antithesis in the following developments, so, too, this epistemological metaphysics offered points of departure for the most varied transformations.

2. The very first of these shows an audacious energy of one-sidedness in contrast with the indecisiveness of Locke. *Berkeley* brought the ascendency of inner experience to complete dominance by putting an end to the wavering position which Locke had taken upon the question as to the knowledge of bodies. This he did with the aid of his extreme Nominalism and with a return to the doctrines of Hobbes. *He demolished the conception of corporeal substance.* According to the distinction of primary and secondary qualities, it was held that a part of that complex of ideas which perception presents us as a body should be separated out, and another part retained as alone real; but this distinction, as Hobbes had already taught (cf. § 31, 2), is in the nature of the case erroneous. The "mathematical" qualities of bodies are as truly ideas within us as the sense qualities, and Berkeley had demonstrated exactly this point with analogous arguments in his *Theory of Vision.* He attacks the warrant of the distinction of Descartes (and of Democritus). But while, according to this view, all qualities of bodies without exception are ideas in us, Locke has retained as their real supporter a superfluous unknowable "substance"; in a similar way others speak of matter as the substrate of sensible qualities.

But in all these cases, says Berkeley, it is demanded of us to regard an abstraction as the only actual reality. Abstract ideas, however, do not exist, — they do not exist even in the mind, to say nothing of existing in *natura rerum.* Locke was then quite right in saying that no one could know this "substance": no one can even think it; it is a fiction of the schools. For the naïve consciousness, for "common sense," whose cause Berkeley professes to maintain against the artificial subtlety of philosophers, bodies are just exactly what is perceived, no more and no less; it is only the philosophers who seek for something else behind what is perceived, — something mysterious, abstract, of which they themselves cannot say what it is. For the unperverted mind, body is what one sees, touches, tastes, smells, and hears: its *esse* is *percipi.*

Body is then nothing but a *complex of ideas.* If we abstract from a cherry all the qualities which can be perceived through any of the senses, what is left? Nothing. The *idealism* which sees in a body nothing farther than a bundle of ideas is the view of the common man; it should be that of philosophers also. Bodies possess no other reality than that of *being perceived.* It is false to suppose that there is in addition to this a substance inherent within them, which "appears" in their qualities. They are nothing but the sum of these qualities.

In reply to the question that lies close at hand, in what the difference consists between the "real" or actual body and that which is only imagined or dreamed of, if all bodies are only perceived, Berkeley answers with a *spiritualistic metaphysics.* The ideas which constitute the existence of the outer world are activities of spirits. Of the two Cartesian worlds only one has substantial existence; only the *res cogitantes* are real substances, the *res extensæ* are their ideas. But to finite spirits the ideas are *given,* and the origin of all ideas is to be sought only in the infinite Spirit, in *God.* The reality of bodies consists, therefore, in this, that their ideas are communicated by God to finite spirits, and the order of succession in which God habitually does this we call *laws of Nature.* Hence Bishop Berkeley finds no metaphysical difficulty in supposing that God under certain circumstances departs from the usual order for some especial end, and in this case man speaks of miracles. On the other hand, a body is unreal which is presented only in the individual mind according to the mechanism of memory or imagination, and without being at the same time communicated to the mind by God. And finally, since the actual corporeal world is thus changed into a system of ideas willed by God, the purposiveness which its arrangement and the order of its changes exhibit gives rise to no further problem.

The parallelism between this inference from Locke and that which Malebranche had drawn from Descartes is unmistakable; and Malebranche and Berkeley are also at one in holding that God alone is the active force in the world, and that no individual thing is efficiently operative (cf. § 31, 8). It is extremely interesting to see how the extreme Realism of the Frenchman and the extreme Nominalism of the Englishman amount to the same thing. The grounds on which the views are based could not be more different: the result is the same. For what still separated the two could be easily removed out of the way. This was proved by a contemporary and countryman of Berkeley's, Arthur *Collier* (1680–1732) in his interesting treatise *Clavis Universalis.*[1] Malebranche,[2] indeed, as a Cartesian, had not directly demurred to the reality of the corporeal world, but had held that we could understand the knowledge of this world by man, only on the hypothesis that the ideas of bodies in God are the common original, in accordance with which God produces, on the one hand, the actual bodies, and, on the other, the ideas of these bodies in finite minds. Collier showed now that in this theory the reality of the corporeal world played a completely superfluous rôle: since no actual relation between the corporeal world and human ideas is assumed, the value of human ideas for knowledge remains quite the same if we posit only an ideal corporeal world in God, and regard this as the real object of human knowledge.

The idealism, which proceeded in this way from the *cogito ergo sum* along several paths, was attended by still another paradox as a by-product, which is occasionally mentioned in the literature of the eighteenth century without any definite name or form. Each individual mind has certain, intuitive knowledge only of itself and of its states, nor does it know anything of other minds except through ideas, which refer primarily to bodies and by an argument from analogy are interpreted to indicate minds. If, however, the whole corporeal world is only an idea in the mind, every individual is ultimately certain only of his own existence; the reality of all else, all other minds not excluded, is problematical and cannot be demonstrated. This doctrine was at that time designated as *Egoism,* now it is usually called *Solipsism.* It is a metaphysical

---

[1] The alternative title of the book reads, *A New Inquiry after Truth, being a Demonstration of the Non-Existence or Impossibility of an External World* (Lond. 1123). It was edited together with Berkeley's treatise in the German " *Collection of the Principal Writings which deny the Reality of their own Body (! !) and of the whole Corporeal World,*" by Eschenbach (Rostock, 1756).

[2] Whose doctrine had become known in England by the agency especially of John *Norris* (*Essai d'un Theorie du Monde Idéal,* Lond. 1704).

sport which must be left to the taste of the individual; for the solipsist refutes himself by beginning to prove his doctrine to others.

Thus, following in the train of the *Meditations*, in which Descartes recognised self-consciousness as the rescuing rock in the sea of doubt, the result was finally reached which Kant later characterised as a scandal to philosophy; namely, that a proof was demanded for the reality of the outer world, and none adequate could be found. The French materialists declared that Berkeley's doctrine was an insane delusion, but was irrefutable.

3. The transformation of Locke's doctrine by Berkeley leads farther in a direct line to *Hume's* theory of knowledge. To the nominalistic denial of abstract ideas the penetrative and profound Scot attached his distinction of all intellectual functions into impressions, and ideas which are copies of impressions; and coincident with his distinction is that of intuitive and demonstrative knowledge. Each kind of knowledge has its own kind of certainty. Intuitive knowledge consists simply in the affirmation of actually present impressions. What impressions I have, I can declare with absolute certainty. I can make no mistake in this, in so far as I keep within the bounds of simply stating that I have a perception possessing this or that simple or complex content, without adding any conceptions which would put any interpretation upon this content.

As among the most important of these impressions which have immediate intuitive certainty Hume reckons the relations in space and time of the contents of sensation, — the fixing of the co-existence or succession of elementary impressions. The spatial order in which the contents of perception present themselves is undoubtedly given immediately with the contents themselves, and we likewise possess a sure impression as to whether the different contents are perceived at the same time or in succession. *Contiguity* in space and time is therefore intuitively given together with the impressions, and of these *facts* the human mind possesses a knowledge which is perfectly certain and in nowise to be questioned. Only, in characterising Hume's doctrine, it must not be forgotten that this absolutely certain matter-of-fact quality, which belongs to impressions, is solely that of their presence as mental states. In this meaning and restriction intuitive knowledge embraces not only the facts of inner experience, but also those of outer experience, but at the price of recognising that the latter are properly only species of the former, — a knowledge, that is, of mental states.

Contiguity in space and time is, however, but the most elementary form of association between perceptions ; besides this Hume reckons two other laws, those of resemblance (or contrast, respectively) and causality. As regards the former of these two forms of relation, we have a clear and distinct impression of the likeness or unlikeness of sensations, and of the different degrees of these ; it consists in the knowledge of the degree of resemblance in our own (sensitive) action, and belongs therefore to the impressions of the inner sense, which Locke called reflection. On this is based, consequently, a demonstrative knowledge of complete certainty ; it concerns the forms of that comparison between magnitudes which we perform upon the given contents of our ideas, and is nothing but an analysis of the regularity with which this takes place. This demonstrative science is mathematics ; it develops the laws of equality and proportion with reference to numbers and space, and Hume is inclined to concede a still higher epistemological value to arithmetic than to geometry.[1]

4. But *mathematics is also the sole demonstrative science;* and is that just because it relates to nothing else than the possible relations between contents of ideas, and asserts nothing whatever as to any relation of these to a real world. In this way the terministic principle of Hobbes (cf. § 30, 3) is in complete control with Hume, but the latter proceeds still more consistently with his limitation of this theory to pure mathematics. For Hume declares that no assertion respecting the external world is capable of demonstration ; all our knowledge is limited to the ascertaining and verifying of impressions, and to the relations of these mental states to each other.

Hence it seems to Hume an unauthorised trenching of thought beyond its own territory, when the resemblance between ideas is interpreted as meaning metaphysical identity ; this is the case in every employment of the conception of *substance.* Whence is this conception ? It is not perceived, it is not found as a content either in particular sensations or in their relations ; substance is the unknown, indescribable support of the known contents of ideas. Whence this idea for which no impression is to be found in the whole circuit of sensations as its necessary original ? Its origin is to be sought in reflection. It is the copy of a frequertly repeated conjunction of ideas. By the repeated being together of impressions, by the *custom* of the like ideational process there arises by virtue of the law of *association of ideas* the necessity of the idea of their co-existence, and the *feeling* of this associative necessity of the

---

[1] *Treat.* I. 2, 1 ; I. 3, 1.

ideational process is thought as a real belonging together of the elements of association, *i.e.* as substance.

The thought-form of inherence is thus psychologically explained, and at the same time epistemologically rejected; nothing corresponds to it further than the feeling of a likeness in the ideational conjunction; and since we can never know anything of existence except by immediate sense-perception, the Reality of the idea of substance is incapable of proof. It is clear that Hume thus makes Berkeley's doctrine his own, so far as it concerns corporeal things. But Berkeley had but half done his work upon the idea of substance. He found that bodies are only complexes of sensations; that their being is identical with their being perceived; that there is no sense or meaning in hypostatising their belonging together, as an unknown substance: but he let the psychical substances, spirits, the *res cogitantes*, stand; he regarded them as the supports or agents in which all these ideational activities inhere. Hume's argument applies to this latter class also. What Berkeley showed of the cherry is true also of the " self." Inner perception, also (such was the form which it had actually taken on already with Locke; cf. above, No. 1), shows only activities, states, qualities. Take these away, and nothing remains of Descartes' *res cogitans* either: only the " custom " of constant conjunction of ideas in imagination is at the basis of the conception of a "mind"; the self is only a " bundle of perceptions."[1]

The same consideration holds also, *mutatis mutandis,* for *causality,* that form under which the necessary connection between contents of ideas is usually thought: but this is neither intuitively nor demonstratively certain. The relation of cause and effect is not perceived; all that we can perceive by the senses is the relation in time, according to which one regularly follows the other. If, now, thought interprets this sequence into a consequence, this *post hoc* into a *propter hoc*,[2] this too has no basis in the content of the ideas causally related to each other. From a " cause " it is not possible to deduce logically its " effect "; the idea of an effect does not contain within it that of its cause. It is not possible to understand the causal relation analytically.[3] Its explanation is, according to

---

[1] *Treat.* I., Part IV. The objectionable consequences which resulted from this for religious metaphysics perhaps occasioned Hume, when working over his *Treatise* into the *Essays,* to let drop this which cut most deeply of all his investigations.

[2] In this respect Hume had a forerunner in his countryman Joseph *Glanvil* (1636–1680), who combated the mechanical natural philosophy from the standpoint of orthodox scepticism in his *Scepsis Scientifica,* 1665.

[3] The same thought lay already at the basis of the Occasionalistic metaphysics (cf. § 31, 7); for the essential reason for its taking refuge in mediation by the will of God was the *logical incomprehensibility* of the causal relation.

Hume, to be gained by means of association of ideas.   Through the repetition of the same succession of ideas, and the custom of finding them follow each other, an inner necessity or compulsion arises of imagining and expecting the second after the first ; and the feeling of this inner necessity with which one idea calls up another is interpreted as a real objective necessity, as if the object corresponding to the first idea forced that corresponding to the other to a real existence in *natura rerum.*   The impression in this case [of which the idea of cause and effect is a copy] is the necessary relation between the ideational *activities* [activities of the "imagination"], and from this arises, in the idea of causality, the idea of a necessary relation between the ideational *contents* [*i.e.* that A causes B ; whereas the case really is that the *idea* of A causes the *idea* of B, *i.e.* recalls it by the law of association].

[In view of the extreme condensation of the above statement, a fuller outline of Hume's discussion of causality may be useful.   As found in the *Treatise* it is briefly as follows : All knowledge as to matters of fact (" probability "), if it goes beyond the bare present sensation, depends on causation.   This contains three essential elements, — contiguity, succession, and necessary connection.   We can explain the first two (*i.e.* can find the impression from which they come), but no impression of sensation can be found for the third and most important.   To aid in the search for its origin we examine the principle both in its general form and in its particular application, asking (1), why we say that whatever begins to exist must have a cause, and (2), why we conclude that a particular cause must necessarily have a particular effect.

(1) Examination of the first gives the negative result that the principle is not intuitively or demonstratively certain (the opposite is not inconceivable), *hence it is not derived purely a priori, i.e.* by analysing relations between ideas ; therefore it must be from experience. — (2) *But how from experience?* Taking for convenience the second question stated above, the particular instead of the general, it is evident (*a*) that the *senses* cannot tell that a particular effect will follow a given cause ; they are limited to the present.   Nor (*b*) can such knowledge as to future events be gained by *reasoning* on experience, as this would involve knowing that instances of which we have had no experience must resemble those of which we had experience (would assume the uniformity of Nature).   (*c*) Therefore the principle apparently must come from the only remaining faculty, *imagination.*   This seems at first impossible, in view of the strong *belief* which attaches to these ideas (*e.g.* that fire will burn), in contradistinction from ordinary ideas of fancy.   The question as thus shifted now becomes :   (3) *How explain the fact that we believe* that a particular effect will follow a given cause ?   The only difference between the ideas of the senses and memory (in which we believe) and those of fancy (in which we do not) is that of the feeling joined with them.   The ideas of memory are more strong and

---

The same was also recognised by Kant in his "*Attempt to introduce the Conception of Negative Quantities into Philosophy* " (cf. the general remark at the close) in a manner essentially in agreement with Hume.   And finally, *Thomas Brown* (*On Cause and Effect*), who also is not disinclined to Occasionalism (cf. *op. cit.,* pp. 108 ff.), in a very interesting way deduces psychologically, and at the same time rejects epistemologically (ib. 184 ff.), the demand for an " explaining " or " understanding " of the actual succession of facts in time.   Perception shows causes and effects roughly.   The explanation of the process consists, then, in its analysis into particular, simple and elementary causal relations.   By this means the illusion arises as if these latter must be yet again made analytically comprehensible.

lively. Hence the problem is, What makes the idea (*e.g.* that fire will burn) so "lively" that I believe in it ? and the solution is, that as I find this belief arising not from a single instance, but only from the *constant conjunction* of the two impressions, the liveliness must be due to *custom, i.e.* to the habitual association of the ideas. " All probable reasoning is nothing but a species of sensation."

This same doctrine explains the origin of the idea of necessary connection. For this does not arise from one instance, but from several. Repetition discovers nothing new, nor does it produce anything new in the objects, but it does produce something in the *mind, viz.* a determination to pass from one object to its usual attendant. The idea of necessity must arise from some impression. There is no external impression that can give rise to it, hence it must be an impression of reflection, and the only one available is that propensity which custom produces to pass from an object to the idea of its usual attendant. *Necessity is something that exists in the mind*, not in objects. This is confirmed by comparative psychology (animals infer from experience through custom), by the theory of probabilities, and (in the *Inquiry*) by the freedom of the will, since belief may be reached in all these without necessarily holding to any objective necessary connection. — *Tr.*]

In this way, Hume's theory of knowledge disintegrates the two fundamental conceptions about which the metaphysical movement of the seventeenth century had revolved. Substance and causality are relations between ideas, and cannot be proved or substantiated either by experience or by logical thought: they rest upon the fictitious substitution of impressions derived from reflection, for those of sensation. But with this, the ground is completely taken from under the feet of the ordinary metaphysics, and in its place appears only epistemology. The metaphysics of things gives place to a *metaphysics of knowledge*.

6. Hume's contemporaries characterised this result of his investigations — especially out of regard for its consequences with respect to religious metaphysics (cf. § 35, 6) — as *Scepticism:* yet it is essentially different from those doctrines to which this name historically belongs. The settling of facts by sense-experience is, for Hume, intuitive certainty ; mathematical relations pass for demonstrative certainty : but, as for all alleged assertions by means of conceptions ["by abstract reasoning"] with reference to a reality other than that belonging to ideas ["concerning matter of fact and existence"], Hume cries, "Into the fire with it !" There is no knowledge of what things are and how they work : we can say only what we perceive by sensation, what arrangement in space and time and what relations of resemblance we experience between them. This doctrine is absolutely consistent and *honest empiricism:* it demands that if the only source of knowledge is perception, nothing further shall be mingled with this than what it actually contains. With this, all theory, all examination of cause, all doctrine of the "true Being" behind "phenomena" is excluded.[1] If we characterise

---

[1] Berkeley is, therefore, correctly understood only from the point of view of

this standpoint as *Positivism,* in accordance with the terminology of our century, we may say that its systematic basis was established by Hume.

But England's deepest thinker gave to this radical theory of knowledge a characteristic supplement. The associations of ideas which lie at the basis of the conceptions of substance and causality are, indeed, attended by neither intuitive nor demonstrative certainty; instead of this, however, they are accompanied by a *conviction which has its roots in feeling,* a natural *belief,* which, unperverted by any theoretical reflections, asserts itself victoriously in man's practical procedures, and is completely adequate for the attainable ends of life and for the knowledge relating to these.   On this rests the *experience* of daily life.   To question this never came into Hume's mind : he only wishes to prevent this from playing the rôle of *an experimental science,* for which it is inadequate.   With the entire earnestness of philosophical depth he unites an open vision for the needs of practical life.

7. For the reception of this positivism the intellectual temper was less favourable in England than in *France.*   Here the renunciation of any attempt at a metaphysics of things lay already prepared in the fundamental sceptical tendency which had made its appearance so repeatedly from the Cartesian philosophy ; and the prevalence of this temper had been especially furthered by *Bayle,* whose criticism was, indeed, in principle directed chiefly against the rational grounding of religious truths ; but at the same time applied to all knowledge reaching beyond the sensuous, and therefore to all metaphysics.   Besides this, there was in the French literature a freer tendency that belongs to men of the world, which had likewise been furthered by Bayle, and at the same time by the influence of Englishmen, — a tendency which would strip off the fetters of the system of the schools, and demanded the immediate reality of life instead of abstract conceptions.   Thus *Bacon's* doctrine, with its limitation of science to physical and anthropological experience, became more efficacious in France than in his own home.   The " point de système " meets us here at every step ; no one any longer wishes to know anything of the " causes premières," and this Baconian platform with all its encyclopædic and programmatic extension was laid down by *d'Alembert* as the philosophical basis of the *Encyclopædia.*[1]

Hume : his idealism is half positivism. He lays especial weight upon the point that behind the ideas of bodies we are not still to seek for something abstract, something existent in itself. If this principle be extended to minds, we have Hume's doctrine ; for with the fall of Berkeley's spiritualistic metaphysics, the order of phenomena willed by God, to which he had reduced causality, falls also.

[1] In the *Discours Préliminaire.*

In Germany the Wolffian system was opposed with the *"point de système"* by men like Crousaz and Maupertuis on grounds of taste, and, in fact, the pedantry of this text-book philosophy offered many points of attack.   In contrast with this the German *Popular Philosophy* prided itself upon its absence of system ; as developed by Mendelssohn it would refrain from all subtleties as to that which cannot be experienced, and employ itself the more with that which is useful for men.   And, lastly, we find a fine example of harmony with this temper in *Kant's Dreams of a Ghost-Seer*, where he lashes the architects of various artificial worlds of thought with sharp irony, and pours out copious scorn upon metaphysical endeavour with a gallows-humour which touches his own inclination in a most sensitive point.   Among the German poets Wieland is in this same spirit the witty anti-metaphysician.

8. A very peculiar turn was taken by positivism, finally, in the later doctrine of *Condillac*.   In him converge the lines of the French and the English Enlightenment, and he finds a positivistic synthesis of sensualism and rationalism, which may be regarded as the most perfect expression of modern terminism.   His *Logic* [1] and his post-humous *Langue des Calculs* developed this doctrine.   It is built up essentially upon a theory of " *signs* " (*signes*). [2]   Human ideas are all of them sensations, or transformations of such, and for these no especial powers of the soul are needed. [3]   All knowledge consists in the consciousness of the relations of ideas, and the fundamental relation is that of equality.   The business of thinking is only to bring out the relations of equality between ideas. [4]   This is done by analysing the complexes of ideas into their constituent elements and then putting them together again : *décomposition des phénomènes* and *composition des idées*.   The isolation of the constituent elements which is requisite for this can, however, be effected only with the aid of signs or language.   All language is a method for the analysis of phenomena, and every such method is a "language." The different kinds of signs give different " dialects " of the human language : as such Condillac distinguishes five,— the fingers (gestures), sound-language, numbers, letters, and the signs of the infinitesimal calculus.   Logic, as the universal grammar of all these

---

[1] A text-book for " Polish professors."

[2] After the *Langue des Calculs* became known, the Institute of Paris and the Berlin Academy gave out, almost at the same time, the theory of signs as the subject for their prizes.   At both places a great number of elaborations were presented, mostly of very inferior value.

[3] This Condillac maintains against Locke, and indeed already in his *Traité des Sensations*, and his school do the same against the Scots.

[4] In these determinations lie suggestions from Hobbes as well as from Hume.

languages, determines, therefore, mathematics also, and indeed the higher as well as the elementary, as special cases.

All science thus contains only *transformations.* The thing to be done is always to make out that the unknown, which one is seeking, is really something already known; that is, to find the *equation* which shall put the unknown x equal to a composition of ideas : it is just for this end that the structures of perception must be previously decomposed. It is evident that this is but a new generalising mode of expression for Galileo's doctrine of the method of resolution and composition; but it rises here upon a purely sensualistic basis; it denies the constructive element which Hobbes had so sharply emphasised and makes of thinking a reckoning with only given quantities. In doing this it rejects all thought of a relation of these data to metaphysical reality, and sees in scientific knowledge only a structure built up of equations between contents of ideas in accordance with the principle *le même est le même.* The human world of ideas is completely isolated within itself, and truth consists only in the equations that can be expressed within this world by "signs."

9. Indifferent as this *Ideology* professed to be metaphysically, its sensualistic basis, nevertheless, involved a materialistic metaphysics. Even though nothing was to be said as to the reality corresponding to sensations, there still remained in the background the popular idea that sensations are produced by bodies. On this account the cautious restraint that belonged to these positivistic consequences of sensualism needed only to be neglected to convert the anthropological materialism, which had developed in the psychological theories, into a metaphysical and dogmatic materialism. And so Lamettrie spoke out with coquettish recklessness what many others did not dare to confess to themselves, to say nothing of confessing or defending it openly.

But other lines of thought in natural science, independently of ideology, were also driving toward materialism. *Lamettrie* had very rightly seen that the principle of the mechanical explanation of Nature would ultimately tolerate nothing in addition to matter moved by its own forces : long before *Laplace* gave the well-known answer that he did not need the "hypothesis of the deity" French natural philosophy had attained this standpoint. That the world of gravitation lives in itself was Newton's opinion also; but he believed that the first impulse for its motions must be sought in an action of God. *Kant* went a step farther when he cried in his *Natural History of the Heavens,* "Give me matter, and I will build you a world." He pledged himself to explain the whole universe of the fixed stars after the analogy of the planetary system,[1] and traced the origination of the individual heavenly bodies out of a fiery-fluid primitive condition solely to the opposed working of the two fundamental forces of matter, attraction and repulsion. But Kant was convinced that the explanation which is sufficient for solar systems shatters when applied to the blade of grass and the caterpillar; the *organism* seems to him to be a miracle (*Wunder*) in the world of mechanics.

The French philosophy of Nature sought to overcome this obstacle also, and to put the problem of organisation out of the world. Among the countless atom-complexes, it taught, there are also those which possess the capacity of preserving and propagating themselves. *Buffon*, who pronounced and carried through with full energy this frequently expressed thought, gave to such atom-complexes the name *organic molecules*, and by assuming this conception all organic life might be regarded in principle as an activity of such molecules, which develops according to mechanical laws, in contact with the external world.[2] This had been already done by Spinoza, of whose theory of Nature Buffon frequently reminds us; the latter, also, speaks of God and "Nature" as synonyms. This *naturalism* found in mechanics, accordingly, the common principle for all corporeal occurrence. But if now ideology taught that ideas and their transformations should be regarded as functions of organisms, if it no longer was regarded as impossible, but more and more seemed probable, that the thing which thinks is the same that is extended and moves, if Hartley and Priestley in England and Lamettrie in France showed that a change in consciousness is a function of the nervous system, — it was but a step from this to teach that ideas with all their transformations form only a special case of the mechanical activity of matter, only a particular kind of its forms of motion. While Voltaire had expressed the opinion that motion and sensation might perhaps be attributes of the same unknown substance, this *hylozoism* changed suddenly into decided *materialism* as soon as the dependence of the psychical upon the physical was given the new interpretation of a likeness in kind between the two, and it is often only by soft and fine shades of expression that the one is

---

[1] The suggestion for this brilliant astro-physical hypothesis, to which Lambert also came very near in his *Kosmologischen Briefen*, and which was developed later in a similar manner by Laplace, was due perhaps to a remark by Buffon. Cf. O. Liebmann, *Zur Analysis der Wirklichkeit*, 2d ed., p. 376.

[2] This principle of Buffon was further developed later by *Lamarck* (*Philosophie Zoologique*, Paris, 1809), who attempted to explain the transformation of organisms from the lower to the higher forms by a mechanical influence of the outer world, by adaptation to the environment.

converted into the other. This transition is presented in the writings of *Robinet.* He gives a metaphysical flight to the philosophy of Nature. Finding support in the development system of the Leibnizian Monadology, he regards the graded scale of things as an infinite multiplicity of forms of existence, in which the two factors of corporeality and psychical function are mixed in all the different relations possible, so that the more the nature of a particular thing unfolds in the one direction, the less is its activity in the other. This holds true, also, according to Robinet, in the case of the vital movements of individual creatures ; the force which they use mentally is lost physically, and conversely. Regarded as a whole, however, the psychical life appears as a special form which the fundamental material activity of things is able to assume, to be later translated back again into its original form. Robinet thus regards ideas and activities of the will as mechanical transformations of the nervous activity which can be changed back again into that. Nothing takes place psychically which was not predisposed in the physical form ; and the body, accordingly, receives in psychical impulses only the reaction of its own motion.

In the *Système de la Nature* materialism appears at last undisguised as a purely dogmatic metaphysics. It introduces itself with the Epicurean motive of wishing to free man from fear of the supersensuous. It shall be shown that the supersensuous is only the invisible form of activity of the sensuous. No one has ever been able to think out anything of a supersensuous character that was not a faded after-image of the material. He who talks of idea and will, of soul and God, thinks of nervous activity, of his body and the world over again in an abstract form. For the rest, this "Bible of Materialism" presents no new doctrines or arguments in its painfully instructive and systematically tedious exposition : yet a certain weight in its conception taken as a whole, a greatness of stroke in drawing the lines of its *Weltanschauung,* a harsh earnestness of presentation, is not to be mistaken. This is no longer a piquant play of thoughts, but a heavy armed attack upon all belief in the immaterial world.

10. In spite of psycho-genetic opposition, the problem of knowledge as conceived by the supporters of "innate ideas" was not all too unlike the view which obtained with the sensualists. The dualistic presupposition assumed by both classes made it difficult for the latter to understand the conformity which the ideas called out in the mind by bodies bear to the bodies themselves. But it seemed almost more difficult still to understand that the mind should cognise a world independent of it, by means of the development of the

thought-forms which are grounded in its own nature. And yet exactly this is an assumption so deeply rooted in human thought, that it passes for the most part as self-evident and a matter of course, not only for the naïve consciousness, but also for philo- sophical reflection. It was the mission of the Terminism, whose after-workings were active in modern philosophy, to shake this fun- damental dogmatic conviction, and push forward for consideration the question as to the ground of that conformity between necessity of thought, on the one hand, and reality on the other. Even Des- cartes had found it necessary to support the knowing power of the *lumen naturale* by the *veracitas dei*, and thereby had shown the only way which the metaphysical solution of the problem could take.

To be sure, where that philosophical impulse was lacking which directs its θαυμάζειν — its wonder — upon just that which is appar- ently self-evident and a matter of course, the difficulty just men- tioned weighed less heavily. This was the case with *Wolff*, in spite of all his power of logical clearness and systematic care, and with the *Scots*, in spite of all their fineness of psychological analysis. The former proceeds to deduce, *more geometrico*, an extensive ontol- ogy, and a metaphysics with its parts relating to God, to the world, and to the soul, all from the most general formal laws of logic, — from the principle of contradiction and that of sufficient reason (and this second principle is even to be reduced to the first). Wolff, indeed, stands so completely within the bounds of this logical schematism that the question never seems to occur to him at all, whether his whole undertaking — namely, that of spinning "a sci- ence of all that is possible, in so far as it is possible" out of logical propositions — is authorised in the nature of the case. This problem was concealed for him the more as he confirmed every rational science by an empirical science [*e.g.* Rational by Empirical Psychol- ogy, etc.], — an agreement, indeed, which was possible only because his *a priori* construction of metaphysical disciplines borrowed from experience step by step, though the loan was unnoticed. Neverthe- less, this system, which was blessed with so many disciples, had the great didactic value of setting up and naturalising strictness in thought, clearness of conceptions, and thoroughness in proof, as the supreme rules for science, and the pedantry which unavoidably stole in with these found a sufficient counterpoise in other intellectual forces.

The *Scottish* philosophy contented itself with seeking out the principles of sound common sense. Every sensation is the sign — Reid too, thinks as terministically as this — of the presence of an object; thinking guarantees the reality of the subject; whatever actually comes into being must have a cause, etc. Such principles are absolutely certain; to deny them or even to doubt them is absurd. This is especially true, also, of the principle that what the understanding recognises clearly and distinctly is necessarily so. In this is formulated the general principle of a philosophical attitude which is called *dogmatism* (after Kant), unconditional confidence in the agreement of thought with reality. The above examples of the particular principles show how eclectically this common sense sought to gather its fundamental truths from the different systems of philosophy. In this respect the "gesunde Menschenverstand" [sound common sense] of the German popular philosophers was entirely in accord with it. Mendelssohn, like Reid, was of the opinion that all extremes in philosophy were errors, and that the truth lay in the mean position : every radical view has a germ of truth which has been forced artificially to a one-sided and diseased development. A sound, healthy thinking (Nicolai, especially, lays weight on this predicate) does justice to all the different motives and so finds as its philosophy — the opinion of the average man.

11. In the mind of *Leibniz* the problem was solved by the hypothesis of the pre-established harmony. The monad knows the world because it is the world : the content which it represents is from the beginning the universe, and the law of the monad's activity is the law of the world. On account of its "having no windows" it has no experience at all in the proper sense : nevertheless the possibility of knowing the world is so established in its very essence that all its states must be regarded as just such a knowledge. There is, accordingly, no difference between intellect and sensibility, either as regards the objects to which they refer, or as regards the way in which consciousness relates itself to these objects : the only difference is that sensibility cognises the indistinct phenomenal form, while intellect cognises the true essence of things. From a scientific point of view, therefore, knowledge by the senses was treated partly as the imperfect, preliminary stage, partly as the indistinct anti-type for the intellect's insight : the "historical" sciences were regarded either as preparations for the philosophical, or as lower appendages.

From this relation a peculiar consequence resulted. The sensuous mode of representation, too, has a certain peculiar perfection of its own, which differs from the clearness and distinctness of intellectual knowledge in apprehending the phenomenal form of its object without any consciousness of grounds or reasons : and in this perfection, characteristic of sensuous knowledge, Leibniz[1] had set the *feeling of*

---

[1] Cf. esp. *Princ. de la Nat. et de la Grâce,* 17.

the beautiful. When, now, one of Wolff's disciples, *Alexander Baum-garten*, in whom the architectonic impulse toward systematisation was developed to a particularly high degree, wished to place by the side of logic as the science of the perfect use of the intellect, a corresponding science of the perfection of sensation, an *æsthetics*, this discipline took on the form of a *science of the beautiful.*[1] Thus æsthetics,[2] as a branch of philosophical knowledge, grew up, not out of interest in its subject-matter, but with a decided depreciation of it ; and as a "step-sister" [lit. *posthumous: nachgeborene Schwester*] of logic she was treated by the latter with very little understanding for her own peculiar nature, and with a cool intellectual pedantry. Moreover, this last-named rationalist, who followed Leibniz in regarding the actual world as the best, and therefore, as the most beautiful among all possible worlds, could set up no other principle for the theory of art than the sensualistic one of imitating Nature, and developed this principle essentially into a tedious poetics. But in spite of this, it remains Baumgarten's great service to have treated the beautiful again, and for the first time in modern philosophy, in a systematic way from the general conceptions of philosophy, and by so doing to have founded a discipline that was destined to play so important a part in the further development of philosophy, especially in that of Germany.

12. The Leibnizo-Wolffian conception of the relation between sense and understanding, and especially the *geometrical method* introduced for rational knowledge, encountered numerous opponents in the German philosophy of the eighteenth century, whose opposition proceeded not only from the incitements of English and French sensualism and empiricism, but from independent investigations as to the methodical and epistemological *relation between mathematics and philosophy.*

In this latter line *Rüdiger*, and, stimulated by him, *Crusius*, contended most successfully against the Wolffian doctrine. In opposition to Wolff's definition of philosophy as the science of the possible, Rüdiger asserted that its task is to know the *actual*. Mathematics, and, therefore, also a philosophy which imitates the methods of mathematics, have to do only with the possible, with the contradictionless agreement of ideas with one another; a true philosophy needs the real relation of its conceptions to the actual, and such a

---

[1] Cf. H. Lotze, *Gesch. der Aesthetik in Deutschland* (Munich, 1868).
[2] The name "æsthetics" was then adopted at a later time by Kant, after some resistance at first, for the designation of the philosophical doctrine of the beautiful and of art, and from him passed over to Schiller, and through the latter's writings into general use.

relation is to be gained only by perception. *Crusius* made this point of view his own; and although he thought in a less sensualistic manner than his predecessor, he yet criticised in a quite similar manner from that point of view the effort of the geometrical method to know reality by employing only logical forms. He rejected the ontological proof for the existence of God, since out of conceptions alone existence can never be inferred; existence (as Kant expressed it) cannot be dug out of ideas. In the same line, also, was the exact distinguishing between the real relation of causes and effects and the logical relation of ground and consequent, which Crusius urged in his treatment of the principle of ground or reason. For his own part he used this difference between real and ideal grounds to oppose the Leibnizo-Wolffian determinism, and especially to set up the Scotist conception of the unrestricted free will of the Creator, in opposition to the Thomist conception of the relation between the divine will and the divine intellect, which the rationalists maintained. The turning away from natural religion, which lay in all these inferences, made the stricter Protestant orthodoxy favourably disposed toward the doctrine of Crusius.

The investigation as to the fundamental difference in method between philosophy and mathematics, that cut deepest and was most important in results, was that undertaken by *Kant,* whose writings very early refer to Crusius. But in his prize treatise *On the Clearness of the Principles of Natural Theology and Morals* he brings a decisive statement. The two sciences are related as opposite in every respect. Philosophy is an analytic science of *conceptions,* mathematics a synthetic science of *magnitudes:* the former *receives* its conceptions, the latter *constructs* its magnitudes; the former *seeks* definitions, the latter *sets out from* definitions; the former needs experience, the latter does not; the former rests upon the activity of the *understanding,* the latter upon that of the *sensibility.* Philosophy, therefore, in order to know the real, must proceed *zetetically:* it must not try to imitate the constructive method of mathematics.

With this fundamental insight into the sensuous character of the cognitive foundations of mathematics, Kant exploded the system of the geometrical method. For, according to his view, sensibility and understanding can no longer be distinguished as lower and higher grades of clearness and distinctness in knowledge. Mathematics proves that sensuous knowledge can be very clear and distinct, and many a system of metaphysics proves that intellectual knowledge may be very obscure and confused. The old distinction must therefore be exchanged for another, and Kant attempts a substitute by defining sensibility as the faculty of *receptivity*, understanding as that of *spontaneity*. He does this in his *Inaugural Dissertation*, and upon this builds a new system of epistemology,[1] leaning upon the psychological principle of virtual innateness (cf. § 33, 12).

The main outlines of the system are the following: the Forms of the sensibility are space and time; those of the understanding are the most general conceptions. Out of reflection upon the one class arises mathematics; upon the other class, metaphysics; — both *a priori* sciences of unconditional certainty. But Forms of (receptive) sensibility give only the necessary knowledge of the *appearance* of things in the human mind (*mundus sensibilis phœnomenon*); the Forms of the understanding, on the contrary, give adequate knowledge of the true essential nature of things (*mundus intelligibilis noumenon*). That these Forms of the understanding are able to do this is due to the fact, that the understanding, as well as things themselves, has its origin in the divine mind; that we, therefore, by means of it, see things to a certain extent "in God."[2]

§ 35. Natural Religion.

The epistemological motives which ruled the eighteenth century were not in general favourable to metaphysics: if, in spite of this, they brought their sceptical and positivistic tendency to complete expression in but few instances, this was due to the religious interest which expected from philosophy a decision as to its problems. The religious unrest and wars from which Germany, France, and England had suffered, and the quarreling over dogmas which had been connected with them, had been followed already in the seventeenth century by a feeling of surfeit and disgust for the distinctions in creeds: the "wretched century of strife," as Herder called it, longed for peace. In England the temper of the *Latitudinarians* extended itself, and on the continent *efforts toward union* were taken up again and again in spite of frequent failure. Bossuet and Spinola on one side, and *Leibniz* on the other, worked long in this direction: the latter projected a *systema theologicum*, which should contain the fundamental doctrines of Christianity common to all three Confessions, and when the negotiations with the Catholics no longer

---

[1] The system of the *Inaugural Dissertation* is only one stage in Kant's development; he gave it up again forthwith; hence it belongs in his pre-critical time and in this period.

[2] This doctrine, presented with an appeal to Malebranche (Sectio IV.), is accordingly just the system of the pre-established harmony between knowledge and reality which Kant later rejected so energetically (Letter to M. Herz, Feb. 21, 1772).

offered any hope, he attempted, at least, to employ his relations to the courts of Hanover and Berlin to bring about a union between the Lutherans and the Reformed body, — this, too, indeed without any immediate result.

Locke, on the other hand, in his three *Letters concerning Toleration*, brought together the thoughts of the *toleration movement* into the theory of the "free church in the free state," — into the demand that the modern state, raised above all Church tutelage, should tolerate and protect every religious belief as personal opinion, and every religious society as a free association, in so far as it does not threaten to disturb political order.

But the more the union was thwarted by the resistance of theologians, the more nourishment came to the life of the *Mystic sects*, whose supra-confessional tendencies were in harmony with the efforts toward union, and which spread in the eighteenth century with a multitude of interesting manifestations. The *Pietism* founded by Spener and Francke kept nearest to the Church life, and was therefore most successful. This, nevertheless, allows a certain indifference toward dogmatic faith to appear, but in compensation lays all the more weight upon the increase of personal piety and upon the purity and religious colouring of conduct.

1. In connection with all these movements stands the tendency of the Enlightenment philosophy toward *establishing the universal, "true" Christianity by means of philosophy.* True Christianity is in this sense identified with the *religion of reason*, or *natural religion*, and is to be dissolved out from the different forms of positive, historical Christianity. At first, such a universal Christianity was still allowed the character of a revealed religion, but the complete agreement of this revelation with reason was maintained. This was the position taken by Locke and Leibniz, and also by the latter's disciple, Wolff. They conceive the relation between natural and revealed religion quite in accordance with the example of Albert and Thomas (cf. p. 321): revelation is above reason, but in harmony with reason; it is the necessary supplement to natural knowledge. That is revealed which the reason cannot find out of itself, but can understand as in harmony with itself after the revelation has taken place.

Proceeding from this idea, the *Socinians* had already taken a step further. They, too, recognised very vigorously the necessity of revelation; but they emphasised, on the other hand, that nothing can be revealed that does not prove accessible to rational knowledge. Hence only what is rational in the religious documents is to be regarded as revealed truth; *i.e.* reason decides what shall be held to be revelation. From this standpoint the Socinians separated the Trinity and the Incarnation from the content of revelation, and in general transferred revelation from the realm of theoretical truths to an entirely different field. They comprehend religion under the characteristic of *law*, and this constitutes their peculiar position. What God reveals to man is not a metaphysics, but a *law*. This he did in Moses, and so in Christ he gave a new law. But if religion objectively is law-giving, subjectively it is fulfilling the law, — not an acceptance of theoretical doctrines, nor even merely a moral disposition, but subjection to the law revealed by God and a keeping of all its prescriptions. This alone has been made by God the condition of eternal blessedness — a juridical conception of religion, which, with its resort to the principle of the boundless authority of what is determined by divine power, seems to contain strongly Scotist elements.

2. If, however, the criterion of revelation is ultimately to lie solely in the rationality of the same, the completely consistent result of this theory is, that historical revelation should be set aside as superfluous, and natural religion alone retained. This was done by the English *Deists;* and *Toland* is their leader in so far as he first undertook to strip Christianity, *i.e.* the universal religion of reason, of all mysteries, and reduce it, as regards the knowledge which it contains, to the truths of the "natural light," *i.e.* to a philosophical theory of the world. But the content which the Enlightenment philosophy sought to give to this, its religion of Nature, had two sources, — theoretical and practical reason. As regards the first, Deism contains a metaphysics based upon natural philosophy; in the second aspect it involves a theory of the world from the point of view of moral philosophy. In this way the natural religion of the Enlightenment was involved in the movement of theoretical, and also in that of practical problems: these its two elements stood in close connection, but found each a particular development, so that they could diverge and become mutually isolated. The relation between these two constituents was as determining in its influence for the history of natural religion as was the common relation which they sustained to the positive religions.

The complete union of the two elements is found in the most important thinker of this movement, *Shaftesbury.* The centre of his doctrine and of his own nature is formed by what he himself called *enthusiasm*, — enthusiasm for all that is true, good, and beautiful, the elevation of the soul above itself to more universal values, the living out of the whole peculiar power of the individual by the devotion to something higher. Nor is religion anything else: a life of increased and enhanced personality, a knowing one's self to be one with the great connected all of reality. But this noble pas· sion, like every other, grows from admiration and strong emotion to love. The source of religion is, therefore, objectively as well as subjectively, the harmony and beauty and perfection of the universe; the unavoidable impression received from this perfection awakens enthusiasm. With a warm heart Shaftsbury portrays the order of things, the purposiveness of their inter-play, the beauty of their formation, the harmony of their life, and shows that there is nothing in itself evil — nothing which entirely misses its mark. Whatever appears an evil in one system of individuals, proves itself in another, or in a higher connection, to be still a good, as a necessary member in the purposeful structure of the whole. All imperfection of the particular vanishes in the perfection of the universe; every discord is lost in the harmony of the world.

This *universal optimism,* whose theodicy is in its conceptions completely Neo-Platonic in character, knows therefore but one proof for the existence of God, the *physico-theological.* Nature bears everywhere the marks of the artist, who has unfolded the loveliness of his own nature in the charm of phenomena with the highest intelligence and sensitiveness. Beauty is the fundamental conception of this *Weltanschauung.* Its admiration of the universe is essentially æsthetic, and the taste of the cultivated man is, for Shaftsbury, the basis of both religious and moral feeling. For this reason his teleology also is the tasteful one of artistic apprehension; like Giordano Bruno he seeks the purposiveness of the universe in the harmonious beauty of each of its individual structures. All that is petty and utilitarian in teleological thought is here stripped off, and a wave of poetic world-glorification that carries all before it goes through Shaftesbury's writings. It was on this account that they worked so powerfully upon the German poets, upon Herder,[1] and upon Schiller.[2]

3. Few, indeed, of the philosophers of the Enlightenment stand upon this height. Voltaire and Diderot[3] allowed themselves at first to be swept along to such an enthusiastic view of the world. Maupertuis and Robinet had also something of the universalistic tendency; in Germany, Reimarus in his reflections concerning the mechanical instincts of animals, shows at least a sensibility for the artistically delicate detailed work of Nature and for the internal

---

[1] Herder, *Vom Erkennen und Empfinden.*
[2] Schiller, *Philisophische Briefe* (Julius).
[3] Particularly in the *Pensées Philosophiques.*

end which she realises in her organic structures. But the great mass of the philosophical writers of the eighteenth century is so controlled by the anthropological interest and the practical aims of philosophy that it investigates rather the *uses* which the arrangement of the universe and the activities of its parts yield for the *wants of man;* and if those of higher temper have in view principally the furthering and perfecting of the moral nature, they still do not despise the point of view of usefulness and every-day "happiness."

Thus æsthetic teleology is cut off by the Stoic doctrine of utility, and the technical analogy, with which men like Leibniz, Newton, and Clarke had thought of the subordination of mechanism to teleology, could not but be favourable to this utilitarian conception. For the purposiveness of machines consists just in yielding an advantage, just in the fact that their product is something else, something in addition to their own working. And this analogy was quite welcome also to the "Enlighteners," who frequently praised the harmony of their philosophy with natural science; they employed this mode of view as against the conception of miracle found in positive religion. Reimarus, too, held that only bunglers need to assist their machines afterwards, and that it is unworthy of perfect intelligence to come into such a position. But if it was asked what the end of the world-machine is, the answer of the Enlightenment was, the *happiness of man,* or perhaps at most, that of created beings in general. This trade in the small wares of usefulness (*Nützlich-keitskrämerei*) was carried out in the most tasteless manner in the German Enlightenment. Wolff's empirical teleology (*Designs of Natural Things*) excites one's mirth by the petty points of view which he assigns to the creative intelligence, and the *Popular Philosophers* vied with each other in portraying in broad and pleasing pictures the neat and comfortable way in which this universe is fitted up for the *homo sapiens,* and how well one may live in it if he bears himself well.

A nobler thought, even at that time, was that of *Kant,* when in his *Natural History of the Heavens* he adopted the Leibnizo-Newtonian conception, but left behind all that talk about the use of the world for man, and directed his look toward the perfection which displays itself in the infinite multiplicity of the heavenly bodies, and in the harmony of their systematic constitution; and with him, by the side of the happiness of creatures, appears always their ethical perfecting and elevation. But he, too, esteems the *physico-theological*[1] *proof* for the existence of God as that which is the most

---

[1] This term points back into the seventeenth century, and seems to have

impressive for man, though he grants strict cogency as little to this as to the cosmological and ontological. The popular philosophy, on the contrary, had its favourite just in this proof, and it forms a general characteristic of natural religion.

4. The presupposition of this course of thought was the conviction that the world is really so perfect and purposive as to support the proof in question. Believing souls brought this conviction with them, and the literature of the eighteenth century proves that it was assumed without question in wide circles as a valid premise of the argument; sceptical minds demanded that this also should be demonstrated, and so roused the problems of *theodicy*. In most cases the Enlightenment philosophy resorted here to the same (ancient) arguments which Shaftesbury brought into the field, but the sceptical-orthodox method, of pointing to the limited nature of human knowledge and to the darkness in the ways of Providence, was not despised.

A new turn was given to theodicy by *Leibniz*. He had been brought by Bayle's incisive criticism to the necessity of adding experimental proof to his system of Monadology by showing the perfection of the universe. Setting in motion to this end the highest conceptions of his metaphysics, he attempted to show that the actual presence of evil in the world does not make out a case against its having originated from an all-good and all-powerful creative activity. Physical evil, he maintains, is a necessary consequence of moral evil in the ethical world order; it is the natural punishment of sin. Moral evil, however, has its ground in the finiteness and limitation of creatures, and this latter is *metaphysical evil*. As a finite thing the monad has obscure and confused sensuous representations or ideas, and from these follow necessarily the obscure and confused sensuous impulses, which are the motives to sin. The problem of theodicy is thus reduced to the question, Why did God create or permit metaphysical evil ?

The answer to this question is very simple. Finiteness belongs to the conception of a created being; limitation is the essential nature of all creatures. It is a logical necessity that a world can exist only out of finite beings which reciprocally limit each other and are determined by their creator himself. But finite beings are imperfect. A world that should consist of nothing but perfect beings is a contradiction in terms. And since it is also an "eternal," that is, a conceptional or rational truth, that out of metaphysical evil follows first moral and further physical evil, that out of finiteness follows sin, and out of sin sorrow, it is then a logical necessity that a world without evil is unthinkable.   However much, therefore, the goodness of God might desire to avoid evil, the divine wisdom, the "*région des vérités éternelles*," makes a world without evil an impossibility.   Metaphysical truths are independent of the divine will; the latter in its creative activity is bound to them.

But, on the other hand, the goodness, which belongs to the conception of God as truly as does his wisdom, is a guarantee that the evils are as few as possible.   The world is contingent, *i.e.* it may be thought as being other than it is.   There is an infinite number of possible worlds, none of them entirely without evil, but some affected with much more numerous and heavy evils than others. If now from among all these possible worlds, which God's wisdom spread out before him, he created this actual world, it can only have been the choice of the best that guided him in so doing; he has made real the one which contains the least and the fewest evils. The contingency of the world consists in the fact that it exists, not with metaphysical necessity, but through a choice exercised among many possibilities; and since this choice proceeds from the all-good will of God, it is unthinkable that the world is any other than the best.   Theodicy cannot proceed to deny the evil in the world, for evil belongs to the very idea of the world; but it can prove that this world contains as little evil as is in any way possible in accordance with metaphysical law.   God's goodness would gladly have produced a world without evil, but his wisdom permitted him only the *best among possible worlds.*

Hence arises the common expression, *optimism*.   Whether this experimental proof of the physico-theological view of the world succeeds, may be left undecided.   The eighteenth century conceived of the matter as though it was the essential aim of Leibniz to prove that the world is the most perfect that can be thought; that he did this only under the presupposition of the metaphysical necessity of evil, was, in characteristic fashion, scarcely noted in the literature of that time, which itself was through and through "optimistic" in its thought.   In a historical aspect the most noteworthy thing in this theodicy is the peculiar mixture of Thomist and Scotist metaphysics.   The world is such as it is only because God has so willed it; by virtue of his omnipotence he might have chosen another; but in the choice of the possibilities before him the divine will is bound to the divine intellect as the "eternal truths."   Above all reality hovers the fate prescribed by logic.

5. In the forms hitherto developed the teachers of natural religion believed that they could attain along the physico-theological path to the conception of the deity as creative intelligence, and for this phase of the development the name *Deism* is customarily employed. The conception of God as personality, which survived in this procedure as the last remnant from positive religion, offered a hold for the moral side also of natural religion, and in turn found in that its support. But where only the theoretical element was pursued, natural religion found itself involved in the course of development taken by naturalistic metaphysics, and found in this finally its downfall. Toland already gave a completely *pantheistic* turn to the admiration of Nature, which for him constituted the essential content of religious feeling, and with the hylozoism which developed among the French natural scientists (cf. § 34, 9) the transcendence of God, as well as his personality, was at an end; and when then the complete dominance of the mechanical explanation of Nature was proclaimed, when the organic world also was recognised as in principle the product of the universal mechanism of Nature, the physico-theological proof lost its power over the mind. In addition to this the premises of the argument were questioned. The Lisbon earthquake (1755) which shocked all Europe made many waver in their ideas of the perfection and adaptedness of the world's arrangement; the indifference with which Nature destroys human life and all its content of ends and worth seemed to speak much more for a blind necessity in all that takes place than for a teleological disposition of the world-process. Voltaire, in whom this revolution in point of view became complete, began in *Candide* to make sport of the "best of possible worlds," and the element of natural philosophy in natural religion crumbled to pieces.

The *Système de la Nature* drew the last consequences with its atheism and materialism. All adaptation, all order of Nature, is only a phenomenon in the human mind. Nature itself knows only the necessity of atomic motion, and in it there are *no worth-determinations*, which are dependent upon ends or norms of value. Nature's conformity to law is active with the same rigour in those things which appear to us aimless or unpurposive, irregular or anomalous, as in the things which we judge with reference to their agreement with our designs or customs, and approve as purposeful. The wise man should make this *indifference of Nature* his own; he should see through the relativity of all conceptions of ends; there is no real norm or order. This principle was applied by Diderot to æsthetics. The *correctness of Nature* is accordingly the only thing that art should display, the only thing that it should grasp and give back;

beauty is one of those valuations which have no objective validity. Materialism knows only an *art void of ideals*, only the indifferent copy of any reality whatever.

6. While the foundations of Deism based on natural philosophy were thus crumbling from within, its epistemological basis began also to waver; for all attacks upon the possibility of a metaphysics struck also at that of a natural religion, which indeed in its contents exhibited but a survival of religious metaphysics. In this respect the *Baconian* system was the most dangerous foe of the deistic doctrine. It allowed religion to stand only as revelation and combated the possibility of knowing its doctrines by the aid of reason, or even of merely bringing them into accord with reason. No one supported this standpoint more energetically than Pierre *Bayle*. He worked systematically to show that all dogmatic doctrines were contrary to reason; he laid bare their contradictions with penetrating keenness; he sought to prove that they were absurd for the natural reason. But he uncovered, also, the weak points in Deism; he denied the cogency of the philosophical arguments for the existence of God and the immortality of the soul, and took special occasion in connection with the problems of theodicy to prove the inadequacy of the "natural light": even in controversy with Leibniz he was not worsted. Religion is, therefore, possible for him only as positive revelation in contradiction with philosophical knowledge. He defends with all keenness the twofold truth. And therefore, although perhaps for himself he might have credit for a faith contrary to reason, — his writings and especially the articles of his much read *Dictionnaire* were not less dangerous to the theoretical doctrines of positive religion than to those of Deism.

Finally *Hume*, also, on epistemological grounds dissolved the union which the other English empiricists and nominalists, and indeed, even the materialists, like Hartley and Priestley, sought to maintain with natural religion. If there is no metaphysics of things at all, philosophical religion falls also. Hume, indeed (as Cleanthes in the dialogue), acknowledges in the spirit of his practical probabilism that the world on the whole makes the incontestable impression of purposiveness and rational order, and finds, therefore, that that belief, on which all our experience rests, is applicable also to the (physico-theological) assumption of a unity in creation and in the direction of the whole. But from the standpoint of science (as Philo) he cannot regard this belief as capable of being established by reason. In particular he asserts, in accordance with the principles of the theory of probability, that it is quite explicable, even on the hypothesis of a purely mechanical theory, that amid

the countless combinations of atoms, one which was durable, purposive, and well ordered should at last come about and become fixed.
So the case remains with a problematical decision. Natural religion
is a reasonable mode of view for the practical man, but it should
not profess to be a scientific doctrine.

7. The more the metaphysical factor in Deism retreated for these
or other reasons, the more the " true Christianity," which Deism
professed to be, became restricted to a *moral conviction.* This had
been already prepared by Herbert of Cherbury, who stood farther
removed from natural philosophy, and had been quite definitely
expressed by Spinoza.   According to this view the essence of
religion consists in moral action, and the religious life has for its
true content, deliberation upon duty, and the seriousness of a conduct of life determined by this.   This in itself alone gave but very
pale and vanishing lines for a *Weltanschauung.*   There remained an
indefinite idea of an all-good God, who created man for happiness,
who should be worshipped by a virtuous life, and who will exercise
an equalising justice in an eternal life, so that such virtue will
receive the reward which is lacking to it here.   No one will fail to
notice the pure, noble thought which lived in this moralising Deism,
or the high value which belongs to it historically, because in opposition to the one-sidedness and strife of confessional zeal it brought
the ideals of toleration and philanthropy, respect for the purely
human appreciation of the ethical disposition, and modesty in personal opinion, to a position of honour in literature and social life.
But, on the other hand, it is also true that there has never been a
more meagre form of religious life than this.   Its religion has no
taste of earth, and with the mysteries which the Enlightenment
would not tolerate, understanding for the depths of religious life
was lost also.   There is nothing more of anxiety for the soul's salvation, of the struggle for redemption, of the ardent feeling of deliverance.   Deism, therefore, failed in vital religious power; it was an
artificial product of cultured society, and when the German Enlighteners wrote books to preach the deistic morals to children,
they only proved how little they understood of real religion.

Among the great mass of the supporters of this standpoint in
the *"popular philosophy"* all possible degrees of uncertainty prevail
as to how far those moral remnants of the religious view of the
world are still capable of a theoretical grounding, and how far they
are to be regarded as merely constituents of the ethical consciousness. Full clearness on this point rules in *Voltaire's* later thought.
Here he has been so far seized upon by Bayle's scepticism as to
acknowledge no longer any metaphysical authorisation: the deity

and immortality are now for him only valid as *postulates of the moral feeling;* faith in them is regarded as only the condition for moral action. If this belief should perish, the motives for honest conduct, and thus the foundations of social order, would, he thinks, perish with it: *si Dieu n'existait pas, il faudrait l'inventer.*

8. Different as are these individual forms in which natural religion developed, they all agree on one point, — in their depreciatory criticism of positive religions. Only that is regarded as true in these religions, in which they all agree with each other and with natural religion; all that is taught beyond this, with an appeal to a special revelation, the deists turn from the door, and it was precisely in this respect that they called themselves *free thinkers.* The claims made by the revelational doctrine encountered, therefore, an especially vigorous contradiction. Collins refuted the proof from prophecy, Woolston the proof from miracles,— both by seeking to give for the corresponding accounts in the religious documents a natural explanation so far as possible. This attempt, which aimed not to involve in doubt the credibility of the biblical narratives, but to explain them by purely natural causes, frequently in a very fantastic fashion and excluding all that is mysterious and supernatural, has been characterised and employed in Germany especially as *rationalistic* interpretation. It was here, too, that *Reimarus*, in his *Schutzschrift*, proceeded in the sharpest manner against the possibility of revelation, which he declared to be superfluous, unthinkable, and untrue. Others directed their criticism against individual doctrines of dogmatics. Diderot attacked the moral attributes in the Christian conception of God, and Voltaire exercised his wit in unsparing derision of the dogmas and ceremonies of all religions and Confessions.

But in his case also there was at bottom the earnest thought, that all these additions of the positive religions were so many obscurations and corruptions of the true religion, for which, like the other deists, he felt called to contend. They were filled with the conviction that natural religion is an inheritance of all men, a conviction set within the nature of man himself, and that it was, therefore, the original state of the religious life. From this point of view all positive religions appear as depraved forms which have entered in the course of history, and a progress in the history of religion consists, therefore, in every case in nothing but a return to the primitive, pure, and uncorrupted religion. Hence according to *Tindal* the true Christianity, which coincides with Deism, is as old as creation. Jesus did not bring a revelation, he only rehabilitated the true worship of God in the face of the decay of the

ancient religions; but the Christian churches have again corrupted
his work, and free-thinking desires to return to him. So, too, *Lessing*
distinguished between Christianity and the religion of Christ.

If now it was asked, what were the causes that brought about
this distortion of true religion, the Enlighteners were entirely
devoid of any historical comprehension for these : what they held
to be false seemed to them possible only through voluntary invention. They were so strongly convinced of the evidence that their
Deism was the only true system, that all other teachings seemed to
them explicable only by lying and deceit, and that the proclaimers
of these seemed to have acted only in their own interests. It is
then the general doctrine of the deists that the historical basis of
positive religions is invention and deceit. Even Shaftesbury knew
no other way of explaining how enthusiasm, which constitutes true
religion, could be distorted to the fanaticism of superstition. The
hatred of priests felt by the Enlighteners was most sharply expressed on this point also in the *Schutzschrift* of Reimarus.

9. Such incapacity to do justice to the historical nature of positive religions agreed well with the universal lack in historical sense
and understanding which was peculiar to the whole philosophy of
the Enlightenment. This had its ground in the fact that modern
thought had made its growth, hand in hand with natural science,
in investigating that which is either timelessly or always valid.
Only in a few instances was this ban broken through.

This was done first and with clearest consciousness by David
Hume. While he found that religion cannot be based upon demonstrative rational knowledge, he showed also that the question as
to the origin of religion in the human mind must be completely
separated from the speculative investigation. This new question
he treated solely in accordance with psychological principles, as a
" Natural History of Religion." He shows how in the primitive
apprehension of Nature and in the feelings of fear and hope, of
terror and of blessing, which are associated with it, and in the comparison of the course of Nature with the vicissitudes of human life,
there lay the incitements to the formation of ideas of higher beings,
and to worship designed to appease or to flatter. The natural,
primitive form of religion is, therefore, polytheism, which thinks
and treats these higher powers in a completely anthropomorphic
manner. But the manifold forms assumed by myth fuse in accordance with the laws of the association of ideas; myths pass over into
each other, and ultimately the whole body of religious ideas becomes
condensed into the belief in a single divine being, to whom the purposeful order of the universe is due. — a faith, to be sure, which

cannot preserve itself in a pure form, but is associated in various ways with its original presuppositions. The history of religion is the gradual transformation of polytheism into monotheism, and its result coincides with that teleological view of the world which Hume had developed as the view of the intelligent man, not, indeed, capable of scientific proof, but bound up with the natural feeling of belief.

This mode of apprehending the subject from the point of view of psychology and the history of civilisation was reinforced by that from the point of view of philology and the history of literature, which found expression in the *historical biblical criticism* founded by Salomon *Semler*. This began to carry out the thought formulated by Spinoza,[1] that the biblical books must be treated just as other writings as regards their theoretical contents, their origin, and their history; that they must be understood from the point of view of their time and the character of their authors. Semler directed particular attention to the point that the different parties of the early Christians find expression in the books of the New Testament. While it may be that the hypotheses to which he came in this respect have been left behind by later science, it is nevertheless true that a scientific way out of the radicalism into which the deistic movement had run was here shown, and Semler therefore raised his voice against the spokesmen of the Enlightenment.

Lessing took part in these questions from still another side. He was certainly not the man to make his conviction bend to a tenet; he saw through and rejected, as few others, the limitation which will find its sole truth in that which has been transmitted historically; but he guarded himself well from playing the judge, who now, after thousands of years, shall decide as to the genuineness of the three rings. But it is not merely this that separates him from the great mass of the Enlighteners; he is himself a deep, religious nature, and, like Herder,[2] sees in religion a living relation of man to God, and God to man. Hence *religion is not possible without revelation*, and the history of religions is the series of the revelations of God, is the *education of the human race* by God. Lessing assumes the well-planned succession of these revelations to be such,

---

[1] In what degree Spinoza's writings were known to the religious Enlighteners in Germany appears, among other things, from the interesting fact that Lorenz Schmidt, the leader of the Wertheim translation of the Bible, is the anonymous editor of a book in which, under the mask of a "Refutation of the Doctrine of Spinoza by the Famous Philosopher Christian Wolff," an excellent translation of Spinoza's *Ethics* is offered, and finally only a few paragraphs from Wolff's German writings are appended (printed Frankfort and Leips. 1744).

[2] Cf. Herder's treatise on the *Aelteste Urkunde des Menschengeschlechts.*

that the deeper meaning of each is unfolded more clearly and distinctly in that which follows. So even the New Testament, the second elementary book, over which the more advanced scholar now "stamps and glows," gives us a premonition of an *eternal gospel.* In carrying out this thought of Origen's,[1] Lessing indicates in but a tentative manner indefinite lines which lie in the direction of a mystico-speculative interpretation of dogmas.

[1] *Education of the Human Race,* § 72 ff.

CHAPTER II.

PRACTICAL QUESTIONS.

THE natural religion of the eighteenth century sought in morals the support which a metaphysics of the natural-science sort could not permanently afford it. This was possible by reason of the fact, that in the meantime this branch also of philosophical investigation had won its complete independence of positive religion. And in fact, this freeing process, which had already begun in the train of the religiously indifferent metaphysics of the seventeenth century, had completed itself in a relatively speedy and simple manner. But the peculiar character of the new age asserted itself here also, in the very early transfer of the point of interest in these investigations to the *psychological* domain; and here philosophy encountered the literary inclination of the age, which was directed toward a profounder employment of man with himself, toward an overhauling of his feelings and an analysing of his motives, and toward the "sentimental" fostering of personal relations. The individual revelling in his own inner life, *the monad enjoying self,* is the characteristic phenomenon of the age of the Enlightenment. The individualism of the Renaissance, which in the seventeenth century had been repressed by external forces, now broke forth again with a more inward power from the stiff dignity of ceremonious, formal life: bounds were to be broken through, externalities cast away, and the pure, natural life of man brought out.

But the more important the individual thus became to himself, and the more many-sided his view in weighing questions regarding the import of his true happiness, the more morality, society, and the state became to him a problem. How comes the *individual* — so runs the fundamental practical question of the Enlightenment philosophy — to a life connected with others, which extends in influence and authority beyond the individual himself? Through all the animated discussions of these problems goes, as a tacit assumption, the view that the individual in his natural (as it was always conceived) determinate character is the original datum, is that which is self-

500

intelligible, and that all the relations which go beyond the individual are to be explained from him as a starting-point. In so far the naturalistic metaphysics of the seventeenth century — thought here more after the analogy of atomism, there more after that of the Monadology — forms the background for the morals of the eighteenth.

The constantly progressing process in which these presuppositions became more clear and distinct brought with it the result, that the *principles of ethics* found a valuable clearing up in the discussions of this period. For inasmuch as the ethical life was regarded as something added to the natural essence of the individual, as something that must first be explained, it was necessary, on the one hand, to establish by an exact discrimination what the thing to be explained really is, and on the other hand, to investigate on what the worth and validity of the ethical life rests: and the more morality appeared to be something foreign to the natural essence of the individual, the more the question as to the motives which induce man to follow ethical commands asserted itself, side by side with the question as to the ground of the validity of those commands. And so three main questions appeared, at the beginning much involved, and then becoming complicated anew: what is the content of morality? on what rests the validity of the moral laws? what brings man to moral action? The *principles of morals* are set forth according to the three points of view of the *criterion*, the *sanction*, and the *motive*. This analysis and explanation, however, showed that the various answers to these separate questions were capable of being combined with each other in the most various ways: so the clearing and separating process above named results precisely from the motley variety and changing hues exhibited by the doctrines of moral philosophy in the eighteenth century. *Shaftesbury* stands in the centre of the movement as the mind that stimulates in all directions and controls in many lines; while, on the other hand, the movement reaches no definite conclusion in this period, on account of the differences in the statements of the question (cf. § 39).

A typical feature of the fundamental individualistic tendency of this ethics was the repeatedly renewed consideration of the *relation of virtue and happiness:* the final outcome, expressed more or less sharply, was that the satisfaction of the individual's impulses was raised to be the standard of value for the ethical functions. The system of practical philosophy built up upon this principle is *Utilitarianism*, the varied development of which forms the centre in the complicated courses of these reflections.

But out of this arose the much more burning question, as regards the political and social order, — the question, namely, as to the *value for happiness of the social union,* of public institutions and their historical development. That which exists and has come into being historically has lost once more its immediate validity and naïve valuation: it should justify itself before the critical consciousness, and prove its right to existence by the advantages which it yields for the happiness of individuals. From this point of view was developed the political and social philosophy of the eighteenth century; upon this standpoint this philosophy assumed its critical attitude toward historical reality, and in accordance with this standard, finally, it examined the results of the historical progress of human civilisation. The worth of *civilisation* itself and the *relation of Nature and history* became thus a problem which received its most impressive formulation from *Rousseau,* and which, in opposition to the movements excited by him, and in conjunction with the convulsions of the Revolution, gave form to the beginnings of the *Philosophy of History.*

§ 36. The Principles of Morals.

Fr. Schleiermacher, *Grundlinien einer Kritik der bisherigen Sittenlehre* (1803), W. W. III. Vol. 1.

H. Sidgwick, *The Methods of Ethics* (4th ed., Lond. and N.Y. 1890).

[J. Martineau, *Types of Ethical Theory*, Vol. II.]

[W. L. Courtney, *Constructive Ethics* (Lond. 1886).]

THE most fruitful incitements to the discussion of ethical problems proceeded in both positive and negative directions from *Hobbes.* The "selfish system" propounded by him extended its influence throughout the entire eighteenth century. It was carried out into all of its consequences, and was an ever-powerful stimulus to draw out opposing theories, which just for this reason were also dependent upon it. In a certain sense this is true of Cumberland, who indeed defended the validity of ethical laws as eternal truths in opposition to psychological relativity, and yet at the same time would have the *universal welfare* regarded as their essential and determining content.

1. The position of *Locke* with reference to these questions is still less definitely formulated than his attitude with regard to theoretical questions. No doubt the treatment of practical principles occupies almost the larger space in his attack upon "innate ideas," as is natural from the fact that his opposition is there directed against the Platonism of the Cambridge school. But the positive indications upon ethical subjects (and indeed there is nothing that goes beyond indications), which are found scattered through his

writings, do not in any important degree transcend mere psychologism.   Locke regards the moral judgment as demonstrative knowledge, because it has for its object a relation, namely, the agreement or non-agreement of a man's action with a *law* ["conformity or disagreement men's voluntary actions have to a rule, to which they are referred, and by which they are judged of"].[1]   Accordingly the *imperative* character seems essential for ethics.   The existence of such norms, however, presupposes not only a law-giver, but also his power to visit obedience to his laws with a reward, and disregard of them with punishment; for only through the expectation of these consequences, Locke holds, can a law work upon the will.

If the philosopher was certain of not deviating from the "common sense" of the average man with such principles, he was equally secure in the three instances which he adduces of the law-giving authority, — public opinion, the state, and God.   And in the highest of these instances he found again the point of attachment for the remnant of Cartesian metaphysics which his empiricism had preserved.   For identically the same will of God is known by revelation and by the "natural light" (according to Locke's philosophy of religion; cf. § 35, 1).   The law of God is the law of Nature.   But its content is, that the order of Nature fixed by God attaches injurious consequences to certain actions, and useful consequences to others, and that *therefore* the former are forbidden, the latter commanded.   Thus the moral law gains a metaphysical root without losing its utilitarian content.

2. The need of a *metaphysical basis of morals* asserted itself also in other forms, and in part in a still stronger degree, though it was common to the whole Cartesian school to regard right will as the necessary and inevitable consequences of right insight.   In this respect Cartesianism was seconded by the whole throng of Platonists, who were so hostile to it in natural philosophy — at first, Henry More[2] and Cudworth,[3] later, especially, Richard Price.[4]   They all proceeded from the thought that the moral law is given with the inmost nature of reality which has proceeded forth from God, and that it is therefore written with eternal and unchangeable letters in every reasonable being.   With much enthusiasm but with few new arguments, they defended the Stoic-Platonic doctrine in its Christian-theistic transformation.

---

[1] Cf. *Essay conc. Hum. Un.*, II. 28, 4 ff.

[2] *Encheiridion Ethicum* (1667).

[3] Whose *Treatise concerning Eternal and Immutable Morality* was first published by Chandler, in 1731.

[4] *Questions and Difficulties in Morals* (Lond. 1758).

This *intellectualism,* in connection with rationalistic metaphysics, took a direction that was widely removed from the Scotist recourse to the divine will which had been revived by Descartes and still more by Locke, and instead of this proceeded to determine the content of the moral law solely by metaphysical relations, and, accordingly, in the last instance, by logical criteria. Just in this appeared its contrast to all the psychologically influenced theories, which, in some form or other, always returned to feelings of pleasure and pain as the central nerve of ethical determinations. This is clearest in the case of *Clarke,* who professed to find the objective principle of morals in the "fitness" of an action to its determining relations, and who claimed for the knowledge of this fitness a self-evidence analogous to the knowledge of mathematical truth, and in the Cartesian spirit was convinced that the feeling of obligation, by which the will is determined to the appropriate action, develops inevitably from such an insight into the fitness of things. Ethical inferiority, accordingly, appeared quite in the ancient fashion (cf. § 7, 6) to be the result of ignorance or of erroneous opinion. *Wollaston,* stimulated by Clarke, gave to the same thought the turn, that since every action involves a (theoretical) judgment as to its underlying relations, the decision as to whether the act is right or wrong in the ethical sense depends upon the rightness (correctness) or wrongness of this judgment.

3. Pierre *Bayle* takes a peculiar position with reference to these questions: he supports a *rationalism without any metaphysical background.* In his case the interest of fixing morals upon a firm basis, as opposed to all dependence upon dogmatic doctrines, was active in the strongest and most radical manner. While in declaring metaphysical knowledge in general to be impossible he opposed the rational grounding of natural religion as well as that of positive dogma, he yet gave back with full hands to the "reason" in the practical domain what he had taken from it in the theoretical realm. Incapable of knowing the essence of things, the human reason is, according to him, completely furnished with the consciousness of its duty: powerless without, it is complete master of itself. What it lacks in science it has in conscience: a knowledge of eternal and unchangeable truth.

The ethical reason, Bayle holds therefore, remains everywhere the same, however different men, peoples, and times may be in their theoretical insight. He teaches for the first time with clear consciousness the *practical reason's complete independence of the theoretical;* but this, too, he is glad to bring to its sharpest point with reference to theology. Revelation and faith are regarded by him in the Catholic manner as essentially theoretical illumination, and just on this account they seem to him to be indifferent for morality. He admired the ethical excellence of ancient heathenism, and believed in the possibility of a morally well-ordered community of atheists. While, therefore, his theoretical scepticism might seem favourable to the Church, his moral philosophy was necessarily attacked as her most dangerous foe.

If the ethical principles were in this discussion proclaimed by Bayle also as " eternal truths," he did it in the original Cartesian sense, where interest centered not so much about the psychological question of innateness, as rather about the epistemological point of view of immediate evidence not brought about through the medium of logic. In this sense the virtual innateness of ethical truths was held of course by *Leibniz*, and it was in the spirit of both that *Voltaire*, who approached Bayle's standpoint the more in proportion as his attitude toward metaphysics became more sceptical (cf. § 35, 5), said of the ethical principles that they were innate in man just as his limbs were : he must learn to use both by experience.

4. Bayle very likely had the support of general opinion when he ascribed to the ethical convictions a worth exalted above all change and all difference of theoretical opinions; but he was successful, perhaps, just because he treated those convictions as something known to all, and did not enter upon the work of bringing their content into a system, or of expressing them as a unity. Whoever attempted this seemed hardly able to dispense with a principle taken either from metaphysics or from psychology.

Such a determination of the conceptions of morality by a principle was made possible by the metaphysics of *Leibniz*, though it was only prepared by him incidentally and by way of indications, and was first carried out by Wolff in systematic, but also in cruder forms. The Monadology regards the universe as a system of living beings, whose restless activity consists in unfolding and realising their original content. In connection with this Aristotelian conception the Spinozistic fundamental idea of the *" suum esse conservare "* (cf. § 32, 6) becomes transformed into that of a purposeful vocation or destiny, which Leibniz and his German disciples designated as *perfection*.[1] The "law of Nature," which for this ontology also is coincident with the moral law, is the striving of all beings toward perfection. Since now every process of perfecting, as such, is connected with pleasure, and every retrogression in life's development with pain, there follows from this the ancient identification of the ethically good with well-being or happiness.

---

[1] Leibniz, *Monad.* 41 ff.

Natural law, therefore, demands of man that he should do all that serves his perfection, and forbids all that threatens to bring him loss in his perfection. From this thought Wolff develops the whole system of duties, bringing to his aid especially the principle of mutual furtherance: man needs for his own perfecting other men, and works toward his own perfection in helping them toward the fulfilment of their vocation. In particular, however, it followed from these premises that man must know what truly conduces to his perfecting; for not all that is momentarily felt to be a further-ance of life proves truly and permanently a step toward perfection. Hence morality is throughout in need of ethical knowledge, — of right insight into the nature of man and things. From this point of view the *enlightenment or "clearing up" of the understanding* appears the *pre-eminent ethical task*. With Leibniz this follows immediately from the conception of the monad.[1] The monad is the more perfect, — and perfection Leibniz defines in genuine scholastic fashion as *grandeur de la réalité positive,* — the more it shows its activity in clear and distinct representations; the natural law of its develop-ment is the clearing up of its original obscure representative content (cf. § 31, 11). Wolff's circumstantial deduction takes rather the form of pointing out in experience the useful consequences of knowledge. It remains thus quite within the setting of the homely aim which the German teacher-philosopher (*Kathederphilosoph*) set before his scientific work, viz. to make philosophy usable and prac-tically efficient, by clearness of conceptions and plainness of proofs.

5. This tendency Wolff had adopted from his teacher *Thomasius,* the father of the Enlighteners, a man who was indeed wanting in the pre-eminence that characterised the mind of Leibniz, but was given all the more an understanding for the wants of his time, a capacity for agitation, and a spirit for efforts toward the public good. Intellectual movements of the Renaissance that had been checked in the seventeenth century revived again at its close. Thomasius would transplant philosophy from the lecture hall into real life, — put it into the service of the general weal; and since he understood little of natural science, his interest turned toward criticism of public institutions. Reason only should rule in the life of the whole, as well as in that of the individual: so he fought honour-ably and victoriously against superstition and narrowness, against torture and witch-trials. Enlightenment in the sense of Thomasius is hence far from having the metaphysical dignity which Leibniz gave it. It gains its value for individuals and for society first by the uses which it yields and which can be expected from it alone.

---

[1] Cf. Leibniz, *Monad.* 48 ff.

Perfection and *utility* are accordingly the two characteristics which with Wolff make *Enlightenment* an ethical principle. The former comes out more strongly in connection with the general metaphysical basis; the latter in the particular building out of the system. And in the same way this duality of criteria goes through Wolff's school and the whole popular philosophy,— only, the more superficial the doctrines become, the broader the space taken by utility. Even *Mendelssohn* gives as the reason for turning aside from all deeper and more refined subtilty, that philosophy has to treat only just so much as is necessary for man's happiness. But because this eudæmonism of the Enlightenment had from the outset no higher point of view than that of the education and welfare of the average man, it fell into another limitation, the most jejune philistinism and sensible, prosaic commonplace. This might be in place and most beneficial in effect in a certain stratum of popular literature, not high, indeed, but broad; but when such a success on the part of the Enlighteners "went to their heads," when they applied the same measuring rod to the great phenomena of society and history, when this excessive pride of the empirical understanding would allow nothing to stand except what it had known "clearly and distinctly," then the noble features of the Enlightenment became distorted to that well-intentioned lack of comprehension, as type of which *Friedrich Nicolai*, with all his restless concern for the public good, became a comic figure.[1]

6. The great mass of the German Enlighteners did not suspect how far they were wandering from the living spirit of the great Leibniz with this dry utility of abstract rules. Wolff, indeed, had already let the pre-established harmony fall metaphysically also, and so proved that the finest meaning of the Monadology had remained hidden from him. Hence he and his successors had no comprehension for the fact, that Leibniz's principle of perfection made the *unfolding of the content of the individual life* and the shaping out of its dimly felt originality, the task of the ethical life, in the same degree as his metaphysics asserted the peculiar nature of each individual being in the face of all others. This side of the matter first came into power in Germany, when the period of genius dawned in literature, and the passionate feeling of strongly individual minds sought its own theory. The form which it then found in Herder's treatises, and likewise in Schiller's *Philosophical Letters*, was, however, much more strongly determined by another doctrine

---

[1] Cf. Fichte, *Fr. Nicolai's Leben und sonderbare Meinungen* (1801), W. W. VIII. 1 ff.

than it was by Leibniz, — by a doctrine which, in spite of the difference in the conceptions in which it was carried out, had in its
ethical temper the closest relationship with that of the German
metaphysician.

Shaftesbury had given to the idea of perfection a form that was
less systematic but all the more impressive and clear to the imagination. The ancient conception of life, in accordance with which
morality coincides with the undisturbed unfolding of man's true and
natural essence, and therefore with his true fortune, was directly
congenial to him and became the living basis of his thought. Hence,
with Shaftesbury, the ethical appears as the truly human, as the
flower of man's life, as the complete development of his natural
endowments. In this is fixed at the outset Shaftesbury's attitude
toward Cumberland and Hobbes. He cannot, like the latter, regard
egoism as the sole fundamental characteristic of the natural man ;
he rather agrees with the former in recognising the altruistic inclinations as an original inborn endowment. But neither can he see
in these inclinations the sole root of morality ; to him morality is
the completion of the entire man, and therefore he seeks its principle
in symmetrical development and in the harmonious interaction of the
two systems of impulses. This theory of morals does not demand
the suppression of one's own weal in favour of that of others ; such
a suppression appears to it to be necessary only in the lower stages
of development : the fully cultivated man lives as truly for himself
as for the whole,[1] and just by unfolding his own individual character does he set himself as a perfect member in the system of the
universe. Here Shaftesbury's optimism expresses itself most fully
in his belief, that the conflict between the egoistic and the altruistic
motives, which plays so large a part in the lower strata of humanity,
must be completely adjusted in the ripe, mature man.

But for this reason the ethical ideal of life is with this thinker
an entirely *personal* one. Morality consists for him, not in the
control of general maxims, not in the subordination of the individual's will to norms or standards, but in the rich and *full living out
of an entire individuality.* It is the sovereign personality which
asserts its ethical right, and the highest manifestation in the ethical
realm is the *virtuosoship,* which allows none of the forces and none
of the lines of impulse in the individual's endowment to be stunted,

---

[1] Pope compared this relation with the double motion of the planets about the
sun and their own axes (*Essay on Man*, III. 314 ff.). Moreover, it was through
the same poet that Shaftesbury's theory of life worked on Voltaire, while
Diderot (in his work upon the *Inquiry concerning Virtue and Merit*) attached
himself directly to Shaftesbury.

but brings all the manifold relations into harmony in a perfect conduct of life, and thus brings about both the individual's happiness
and his most efficient working for the welfare of the whole. Thus
the Greek ideal of the *kalokagathia* finds a new expression in the
Weltanschauung of the Monadology (cf. § 7, 5).

7. While the moral principle has thus with Shaftesbury already
received an æsthetical colouring in its contents, this colouring appears consistently in a yet stronger degree when he deals with the
question as to the *source of knowledge* for ethical tasks. This source,
by metaphysicians and sensualists alike, was found in rational knowledge either of the nature of things or of the empirically useful : in
both cases principles resulted that were capable of demonstration
and universally valid. The morals of virtuosoship, on the contrary,
must take its individual life-ideal from the depths of the individual
nature; for it morality was grounded upon *feeling*. The ethical
judgments by which man approves those impulses which Nature has
implanted within him to further his own and others' weal, or, on the
other hand, disapproves the "unnatural" impulses that work against
those ends, — these judgments rest on man's ability to make his
own functions the object of study, *i.e.* upon "reflection" (Locke);
they are not merely, however, a knowledge of one's own states, but
are *emotions of reflection*, and as such they form within the "inner
sense" the *moral sense*.

Thus the psychological root of the ethical was transplanted from
the field of intellectual cognition to the feeling-side of the soul, and
set in the immediate vicinity of the æsthetic. The good appeared
as the beautiful in the world of will and action: it consists, like the
beautiful, in a harmonious unity of the manifold, in a perfect development of the natural endowments; it satisfies and blesses as does
the beautiful; it is, like the beautiful, the object of an original
approval fixed in man's deepest nature. This parallel ruled the
literature of the eighteenth century from Shaftesbury on: "taste"
is the fundamental faculty ethically as æsthetically. This was
perhaps most distinctly expressed by *Hutcheson,* but with a turn
which to some degree led away again from Shaftesbury's individualism. For he understood by the "moral sense" — in the purely
psychological meaning of "innateness" — an original faculty, essentially alike in all men, and with the function of judging what
is ethically to be approved. The metaphysical accessories of the
Platonists and Cartesians were gladly thrown overboard, and in
their stead he held fast the more eagerly — especially in opposition
to the "selfish system" — to the principle that man possesses a
natural feeling for the good as for the beautiful, and declared the
analysis of this feeling to be the business of philosophy.

The carrying over of this principle into the theoretical domain led in the *Scottish School* (cf. § 33, 8) to making the True parallel with the Good and the Beautiful, as the object of original approval, and thus assuming in "common sense" a kind of "logical sense." But the principle of *feeling as source of knowledge* was proclaimed in a far more pronounced manner by *Rousseau*, who based his deism upon the uncorrupted, natural feeling [1] of man, in opposition to the cool intellectual analysis with which the purely theoretical Enlightenment treated the religious life. This *feeling-philosophy* was carried out in a very indefinitely eclectic manner by the Dutch philosopher, Franz *Hemsterhuys* (of Groeningen, 1720–1790), and with quaint singularity by the talented enthusiast, *Hamann*, the "Wizard of the North." [2]

8. It was, however, in the *fusion of ethical and æsthetic investigations* that the above theory of the feelings, prepared by Shaftesbury and Hutcheson, made its influence most felt. The more the eudæmonistic morals was treated in a manner intelligible to the common mind, the more convenient it was for it to be able to invest the moral commands, as the object of a natural pleasure, with the garb of grace and attractiveness, and to be permitted to commend the good to the taste as something akin to the beautiful. The *Scottish School*, also, was not far from this mode of view, and *Ferguson* developed Shaftesbury's ideas in this manner with especial reference to the Leibnizian fundamental conception of perfection. The effect of this complication of thought for *æsthetics*, however, was that the beginnings toward a metaphysical treatment, which Shaftesbury had brought to the problems of the beautiful from the system of Plotinus, became completely overshadowed by the psychological method. The question asked was not, what the beautiful is, but how the feeling of the beautiful arises; and in the solution of this question the explanation of the æsthetic was brought into more or less close connection with ethical relations. This shows itself, too, in the case of those writers upon æsthetics who stood closer to the sensualistic psychology than did the Scots. Thus Henry *Home* conceives of the enjoyment of the beautiful as a transition from the purely sensuous pacification of desires to the moral and intellectual joys, and holds that the arts have been "invented" for that refinement of man's sensuous disposition which is requisite for his higher

---

[1] Cf. the creed of the Savoyard Vicar in *Émile*, IV. 201 ff.
[2] Johann Georg *Hamann* (of Königsberg, 1730–1788; collected writings ed. by Gildemeister, Gotha, 1857–73) combines this line of thought with a pietism not far removed from orthodoxy in his thoughtful, but illogical and unclear form of expression.

destiny.   He seeks, therefore, the realm of the beautiful in the
higher senses, hearing and especially sight, and finds as the basis,
a taste common to all men for order, regularity, and combination of
the manifold into a unity.   When he then further distinguishes
between the "intrinsic" beauty which is immediately an "object
of sense," and the beauty of "relation," these relations look essentially toward what is for the common good ethically, in the service of which beauty is thus placed.[1]   Even Edmund *Burke*, in his
effort to derive the æsthetic from elementary states of sensation
in accordance with the method of *associational psychology*, is very
strongly dependent upon the form given to the problems by contemporary moral philosophy.   His attempt to determine the *relation
of the beautiful to the sublime* — a task at which Home, also, had
laboured, though with very little success [2] — proceeds from the
antithesis of the selfish and the social impulses.   That is held to
be sublime which fills us with terror in an agreeable shudder, "a
sort of delightful horror," while we are ourselves so far away that
we feel removed from the danger of immediate pain: that is beautiful, on the contrary, which is adapted to call forth in an agreeable
manner the feelings either of sexual love or of human love in
general.

In a manner similar to that of Home, *Sulzer* placed the feeling of
the beautiful midway between that of the sensuously agreeable and
that of the good, forming thus a transition from the one to the other.
The possibility of this transfer he found in the intellectual factor
which co-operates in our apprehension of the beautiful: it appeared
to him — following the view of Leibniz (cf. § 34, 11) — as the
feeling of harmonious unity in the manifold perceived by the senses.
But just by reason of these presuppositions, the beautiful was for
him valuable and perfect only when it was able to further the
moral sense.   Art, also, is thus drawn into the service of the morals
of the Enlightenment, and the writer on æsthetics, who was so long
celebrated in Germany, shows himself but a mechanical handicrafts-
man of Philistine moralising in his conception of art and its task.
How infinitely freer and richer in *esprit* are the "Observations"
which *Kant* instituted "concerning the Feeling of the Beautiful and
the Sublime," at the time when he, too, pursued, from the psychological standpoint, and with admirable knowledge of the world, the

---

[1] For more detailed treatment, see the art. *Home* (Kames) by W. Windelband in *Ersch und Gruber's Enc.*, Vol. II. 32, 213 f.

[2] According to Home the beautiful is sublime if it is great.   The antithesis
between the qualitatively and the quantitatively pleasing seems to lie at the
basis of his unclear and wavering characterisations.

fine ramifications of the ethical and æsthetic life in individuals, families, and peoples!

Finally these thoughts gave occasion in Germany to a change in psychological theory that was rich in results. Before this it had been the custom to divide the psychical activities according to the Aristotelian example into theoretical and practical. But now the feelings, which became thus recognised in their various significance, seemed incapable of being brought either into the group of knowing, or into that of willing, without disadvantage ; it seemed rather that the feelings, as a peculiar mode of expression, in part lay at the basis, and in part followed, both of the above functions of the soul. Here, too, the suggestion came from the Leibnizian Monadology. *Sulzer*, in his Berlin lectures,[1] seems first to have pointed out that the obscure, primitive states of the monad should be separated from the developed forms of life seen in completely conscious knowing and willing, and he already found the distinguishing characteristic of these obscure states to be the conditions of pleasure and pain given with them. This was done also, in a similar way, from Leibnizian presuppositions by Jacob Friedrich *Weiss*.[2] Mendelssohn (1755) first named these states *Empfindungen* [3] [sensations], and later the same author designated the psychical power, which lies at their common basis, as the *faculty of approval (Billigungsvermögen)*.[4] But the decisive influence on terminology was exercised by *Tetens* and *Kant*. The former substituted for sensations (*Empfindungen*) the expression *feelings (Fühlungen* or *Gefühle)*,[5] and Kant used the latter almost exclusively. It was he, too, who later made the *triple division of the psychical functions into ideation, feeling, and willing (Vorstellen, Fühlen, und Wollen)* the systematic basis of his philosophy,[6] and since then this has remained authoritative. especially for psychology.

3. The counter-current, which proceeded from *Hobbes* and declared the profit or injury of the individual to be the sole possible content of the human will, maintained itself in the face of all these developments. In this theory, the criterion of ethical action was sought in a purely psychological manner in the *consequences* of such action

---

[1] 1751 f. Printed in the *Vermischten Schriften* (Berlin, 1773).

[2] J. F. Weiss, *De Natura Animi et potissimum Cordis Humani* (Stuttgart, 1761).

[3] In this Mendelssohn, with his *Letters concerning the Sensations*, refers directly to Shaftesbury.

[4] Cf. Mendelssohn, *Morgenstunden*, 1785, ch. 7 (W. I. 352).

[5] Cf. Tetens, *Versuche*, X. pp. 625 ff.

[6] In the article written between 1780 and 1790 designed at first as an introduction to the *Critique of Judgment* which has passed over into his writings under the title *Ueber Philosophie überhaupt*. Cf. Pt. VI. ch. 1.

for the *advantage of our fellow-men*. Morality exists only within the social body. The individual, if by himself and alone, knows only his own weal and woe; but in society his actions are judged from the point of view of whether they profit or injure others, and this alone is regarded as the standpoint of ethical judgment. This conception of the ethical criterion corresponded not only to the common view, but also to the felt need of finding for ethics a basis that should be destitute of metaphysics, and rest purely on empiri cal psychology. Cumberland and Locke even acceded to it in the last resort, and not only the theological moralists like Butler and Paley, but also the associational psychologists like Priestley and Hartley, attached themselves to it. The classical formula of this tendency was gradually worked out. An action is ethically the more pleasing in proportion as it produces more happiness, and in proportion as the number of men who can share this happiness becomes greater : the ethical ideal is *the greatest happiness of the greatest number.* This became the watch-word of *Utilitarianism.*

This formula, however, suggested the thought of determining *quantitatively* the ethical values for individual cases and relations. The thought of Hobbes and Locke, of grounding a knowledge of a strictly demonstrative ethics upon the utilitarian principle, seemed thereby to have found a definite form, welcome to the natural-science mode of thinking. This enticement was pursued by *Bentham,* and in this consists the peculiar element of utilitarian thought as carried out by him, — a work which he performed with a warm feeling for the public good, and which was later much referred to. The point is to find exact, definite points of view, according to which the value of every mode of action for the weal of the actor himself and of the community to which he belongs, can be determined, — partly in itself, partly in its relation to other modes of conduct; and Bentham in this table of values and their opposites, with an extensive consideration of both individual and social relations and needs, sketches a scheme of a pleasure and pain balance for reckoning the useful and injurious consequences of human activities and institutions. As with Hume (cf. below, No. 12), the reckoning of the ethically valuable falls to the province of the measuring intellect; but the factors with which it operates in this process are solely the feelings of pleasure and pain.

10. The close connection in which this utilitarianism stood historically after Hobbes with the selfish system — that is, with the assumption of the essentially egoistic character of human nature — led necessarily to the separation of the question as to the criterion of morality and the kind of knowledge by which it is apprehended,

from that as to the sanction of the moral commands and the motives for obeying them.   For the metaphysical theories, the sanction of the ethical commands lay in the eternal truths of the law of Nature : and psychologically, also, there seemed to be no further and especial motive needed for the effort toward perfection, for the living out of the personality, for the following of innate ethical inclinations; morality was self-explaining under such presuppositions.   But he who thought more pessimistically of man, he who held him to be a being determined originally and in his own nature solely by regard to his own weal or woe,—he must ask with what right an altruistic way of acting is required of such a being, and by what means such a being can be determined to obedience to this requirement.   If morality was not of itself inherent in man's nature, it must be declared how it comes into him from without.

Here, now, the principle of *authority*, already adduced by Hobbes and Locke, performed its service.   Its most palpable form was the *theological;* it was carried out with more finely wrought conceptions by *Butler*, and in a crude manner, intelligible to the common mind, by *Paley.*   Utility is for both the criterion of ethical action, and the *divine command* is for both the ground of the ethical requirements. But while Butler still seeks the knowledge of this divine will in the natural conscience — his re-interpretation of Shaftesbury's emotions of reflection, for which he himself uses also the term "reflection" — for Paley, it is rather the positive revelation of the divine will that is authoritative; and obedience to this command seems to him explicable only because the authoritative power has connected its commandment with promises of reward and threatenings of punishment. This is the sharpest separation of ethical principles, and that perhaps which corresponds most to the "common sense" of the Christian world.   The criterion of the moral is the weal of one's neighbour; the ground of our knowledge of the moral is the revealed will of God; the real ground which supplies the sanction is the will of the Supreme Being; and the ethical motive in man is the hope of the reward, and the fear of the punishment, which God has fixed for obedience and disobedience.

11. Paley thus explained the fact of ethical action by the hypothesis that man, in himself egoistic, is brought at last by the agency of the equally egoistic motives of hope and fear, and by the roundabout way of a theological motivation, to the altruistic mode of action commanded by God.   The *sensualistic psychology* substituted for the theological agency the authority of the state and the constraining forces of social life.   If the will of man is in the last resort always determinable only by his own weal and woe, his altru-

istic action is comprehensible only on the supposition that he sees in it the surest, simplest, and most intelligent means under the given relations for bringing about his own happiness. While, therefore, the theological utilitarians held that the natural egoism should be tamed by the rewards of heaven and punishments of hell, it seemed to the empiricists that the order of life arranged by the state and society was sufficient for this purpose. Man finds himself in such relations that when he rightly reflects he sees that he will find his own advantage best by subordination to existing morals and laws. The sanction of ethical demands lies, accordingly, in the legislation of the state and of public morality which is dictated by the principle of utility, and the motive of obedience consists in the fact that each one thus finds his own advantage. Thus *Mandeville, Lamettrie,* and *Helvétius* developed the " selfish system "; Lamettrie, especially, with tasteless cynicism that savoured of a desire for admiration, seeking to exhibit " hunger and love " in their lowest sensuous meaning as the fundamental motives of all human life — a wretched, because artificial, imitation of ancient Hedonism.

Morality, accordingly, appears to be only eudæmonistic shrewdness, the polished egoism of society, the refined cunning of the man who is familiar with life, and has seen that to be happy he can pursue no better path than to *act* morally, even if not to *be* moral. This view frequently finds expression in the Enlightenment philosophy as the governing principle of " the world " of that day : whether it be as the naïve, cynical confession of a writer's own disposition, as in Lord *Chesterfield's* well-known letters to his son, — or in the form of moralising reflections, as in *Labruyère's* " *Charactères*" (1680), and in *La Rochefoucauld's* " *Réflections*" (1690), where the mask is unsparingly torn off from man's ethical behaviour, and naked egoism is disclosed as the sole impelling motor everywhere, — or finally as bitter satire, as with *Swift,* where the true nature of the human beast is finally discovered by Gulliver among the Yahoos.

Hand in hand with this gloomy conception of the natural meanness of man the view goes through the age of the Enlightenment that man's education to ethical action has to appeal to just this low system of impulses, working through power and authority, with the aid of fear and hope. This shows itself characteristically even with those who claim for the mature and fully developed man, a pure morality raised above all egoism. So, for example, Shaftesbury finds positive religion with its preaching of rewards and punishments quite good enough for the education of the great mass. So, too, Prussia's philosophical king *Frederick* the Great,[1] who for himself had a consciousness of duty so strict and pure and free from all selfish considerations, and declared such to be the highest ethical good, yet thought that in the case of the education which the state gives to men it should start with their closest interests, however low these might be; for he granted to the Encyclopædists that man as a genus is never to be determined by anything else than by his own personal interests. In this respect the French Enlighteners, especially, sought to analyse the motives, by awakening which the state can win the citizens to care for the interests of the whole. *Montesquieu* showed with fine psychology how different the forms are which this relation takes under different forms of constitution. Lamettrie pointed, as Mandeville had already done, to the sense of honour or repute as the most powerful factor in the social sentiment among civilised peoples, and Helvétius carried out this thought farther.

But if the sensualistic psychology thus looked for man's ethical education from the state alone, the degree of success with which this was accomplished must serve as a standard for estimating the value of public institutions. This consequence was drawn by *Holbach,* and the most winning feature of this dry book is perhaps the honourableness and energy with which it tries to show how little the rotten conditions of the public life of that time were adapted to raise the citizen above the meanness of selfish endeavours.

12. *Hume's* moral philosophy may be regarded as the most complete embodiment of this movement, and as the most refined consideration of the motives that contend within it. It, too, stands completely upon the basis of the psychological method: man's ethical life is to be understood by a genetic investigation of his passions, feelings, and volitions. The most significant element in Hume's teaching is the separation of utilitarianism from the selfish system. The criterion of ethical approval and disapproval is, for him, too, the effect which the quality or action to be judged is adapted to produce in the form of feelings of pleasure and pain, and, like the ancients and Shaftesbury, he interprets this in the widest sense, inasmuch as he regards as objects of ethical pleasure, not only the "social virtues," such as justice, benevolence, etc., but also the "natural abilities," [2] such as prudence or sagacity, fortitude, energy, etc. But we feel this approval, even when these qualities

---

[1] Cf. especially what is adduced by E. Zeller, *F. d. G. als Philosoph,* pp. 67 ff., 105 ff., and also especially Frederick's *"Antimacchiavelli."*

[2] Here, too, the old ambiguity of *virtus* (virtue) = moral virtue, and also ability or excellence, plays a part.

are completely indifferent to our own welfare, or indeed even injurious to the same; and this cannot possibly be traced back to
egoism through the medium of mere psychological association. On
the other hand, the relation which these judgments sustain to the
complicated relations of experience forbids the assumption of their
innateness. They must rather be reduced to a simple, elementary
form, and this is *sympathy*,[1] *i.e.* primarily our capacity to *feel
with* another his weal or woe as our own, at least in a weakened
form. Such sympathetic feelings, however, are not only the
impulsive grounds of moral judgments, but also the original motives
of moral action, for the feelings are the causes of the decisions of
the will. Still, these original impulses alone are not adequate to
explain ethical judgment and action. For the more complicated
relations of life, there is need of a clarification, ordering, and comparative valuation of the factors of feeling, and this is the business
of *reason*. From the reflection of reason arise, therefore, in addition
to the natural and original values, derivative "artificial" virtues, as
the type of which Hume treats justice and the whole system of
standards of rights and law — in this, evidently, still dependent
upon Hobbes. But in the last resort these principles, also, owe
their ability to influence judgment and volition, not to rational
reflection as such, but to the feelings of sympathy to which this
appeals.

Thus the crude conception of a "moral sense" is refined by
Hume's investigation to a finely articulated system of moral psychology with its carefully differentiated conceptions, as the centre
of which we find the principle of sympathy. A farther step in
carrying out this same theory was taken in the ethical work of
Adam *Smith*. As against the externality with which ordinary
utilitarianism had placed the criterion of ethical judgment in the
pleasurable or painful consequences of the act, Hume had energetically directed attention to the fact, that ethical approval or disapproval concerns rather the *disposition* manifesting itself in the
action, in so far as this aims at the consequences in question.
Hence Smith found the essence of sympathy, not only in the
capacity of feeling these consequences with the one who experiences
them, but also in the ability to transfer one's self into the disposition or sentiment of him who acts, and to feel his motives with him.
And extending farther and farther the thought of transfer through
sympathy, the judgment which the individual pronounces upon himself in the *conscience* is then conceived as a reflex, mediated through

---

[1] Cf. *Treatise*, II. 1, 11, and II. 2, 5.

feelings of sympathy, of the judgment which he receives from others and exercises upon others.

All phenomena of the ethical life are thus rooted, according to Hume and Smith, in the *social life*, whose psychological basis is sympathy, and the founder of political economy, with his great philosophical friend, sees in the mechanism of sympathetic transfers of feeling an adjustment of individual interests similar to that which he believed himself to have discovered in the realm of the exchange of external goods, which is conducted with reference to the strait- ness of the conditions of life, in the mechanism of supply and demand in connection with the competition of labour.[1] But with these insights into the thoroughgoing dependence of the individual upon a social body, which he does not create, but in which he finds himself actually placed, the philosophy of the Enlightenment is already pointing beyond itself.

§ 37. The Problem of Civilisation.

The fundamental thought, which the philosophy of the Enlight- enment would hold as to the great institutions of human society and its historical movement, was prescribed for it in advance, partly by its dependence upon natural-science metaphysics, and partly by its own psychological tendency. This was to see in these institutions the products of the activities of individuals; and from this followed the tendency to single out those interests whose satisfaction the individual may expect from such general social connections when once these exist, and to treat them in a genetic mode of explanation as the motives and sufficient causes for the *origin* of the institutions in question, while at the same time regarding them from a critical point of view, as the standard for estimating the *value* of the same. Whatever was regarded as having been intentionally created by men should show also whether it was then really fulfilling their purposes.

1. This conception was guided into the political and juristic track primarily by *Hobbes*.   The state appeared as the work of individuals, constructed by them under the stress of need, when in a condition of war with each other and in fear for life and goods.   With its whole system of rights, it was regarded as resting upon the *compact* which the citizens entered into with each other from the above motives. The same Epicurean compact-theory, which had revived in the later Middle Ages, passed over with Nominalism into modern philosophy

---

[1] *Inquiry into the Nature and Causes of the Wealth of Nations* (Lond. 1776).

and extended its influence over the whole eighteenth century.   But the artificial construction of absolutism, which Hobbes had erected upon it, gave place more and more in consequence of political events to the doctrines of *popular sovereignty*.   This lay at the basis of the English Constitution of 1688, as well as at that of the theoretical shaping which *Locke* gave the same in his doctrine of the separation and equilibrium of the three departments of the state, the legislative, executive, and federative.   It controlled, also, as an ideal requirement, the writings of Montesquieu, who, in considering the rotten administration of law at his time, would have complete independence given to the judicial power, while he thought of the executive and federative departments (as administration within and without, respectively) as united in the one monarchical head.   It was finally carried out to a complete system of democracy in *Rousseau's Contrat Social*, in which the principle of transfer and representation was to be limited as much as possible, and the exercise of the sovereignty also to be assigned directly to the whole body of the people.   In all these transformations of the doctrine of Hobbes, the influence of the realities of historical politics is obvious, but the antithesis between Hobbes and Rousseau has also its theoretical background.   If man is regarded as by nature essentially egoistic, he must be compelled to keep the social compact by the strong arm of the state : if he is regarded as originally good and social in his feelings, as by Rousseau, it is to be expected of him that he will of himself always take part in carrying out, in the interest of the whole, the life prescribed by the compact.

It is interesting now to see that the compact-theory in the eighteenth century communicated itself also to those theories of the philosophy of right which did not have a merely psychological basis.   The *"natural right"* of this time proceeds also from the right of the individual, and seeks to derive from this the rights of individuals in their relation to each other.   Yet in carrying out this principle two different tendencies show themselves in German philosophy, leading to results that were extremely characteristic in their differences.   Leibniz had derived the conceptions of right (or law) from the most general principles of practical philosophy, following the example of the ancients.[1]   Wolff followed him in this respect also, but made it on this account the end of the political compact to secure the mutual furtherance of individuals in behalf of their mutual perfecting, enlightening, and happiness ; according

---

[1] Cf. his introduction to the *Codex Juris Gentium Diplomaticus* (1693), Works (Erd.), 118 ff.

to him, therefore, the state has to care, not merely for external safety, but also for the general welfare in the broadest extent. The consequence of this is that Wolff assigns to the state the right and duty of a thorough tutelage of the great mass of unenlightened men who are controlled by error and passion, and of intermeddling even in their private relations in the way of education. Thus Wolff gave the theory for that "paternal" despotism of the benevolent police-state under which the Germans of his time lived with very mixed feelings.

The exactly opposite result attached itself theoretically to the separation of the philosophy of right from morals, for which the way had already been prepared by *Thomasius,* with his sharp parting of the *justum* and the *honestum.* In this line the disciple of Thomasius, *Gundling* (1671–1729), maintained that *right or law was to be treated solely as the ordering of the external relations* of individuals, that it has for its end the preservation of peace without, and therefore its decrees can be enforced only as to outward relations. This limitation of the state's activity to the external protection of law evidently corresponded most fully to the dualistic spirit of the Enlightenment. If the individual has conformed to the political compact only from need and want, he will evidently be inclined to make as few concessions to the state as possible, and will be willing to sacrifice to it of his original "rights" only so much as is unconditionally requisite for the end which it is to fulfil. This was not merely the thought of the Philistine citizen, who is indeed ready to call for the police at once when anything is the matter, but privately regards the order of the laws as an enemy that must be kept from his throat as much as possible; it was also the feeling of the Enlightener of high intellectual development, who had for his rich inner life only the interest of being able to devote himself unmolested to the enjoyments of art and science. In fact, the petty spirit of the small German states, with its lack of ideals, must necessarily produce the indifference toward public life which thus found its theoretical expression. The lowest stage which the depreciation of the state reached in this respect among the cultured classes is perhaps best characterised by *William von Humboldt's* "Ideas toward an Attempt to determine the Bounds of the Operation of the State." [1] Here every higher interest of man is carefully excluded from the province of the state's authority, and the task of public government is restricted to the lower service of protecting the life and property of the citizen.

---

[1] Written 1792, published 1851 by E. Cauer.

2. If in this respect German philosophy remained quite indifferent toward the actual political condition, on the other hand there appeared in it also the general tendency of the Enlightenment to order the life of society, as that of the individual, according to the principles of philosophy.   If it is glory enough for this period to have successfully cleared away much historical lumber that had accumulated in the house-keeping of European peoples, Thomasius and Wolff, Mendelssohn and Nicolai, certainly deserve credit for their share in the work (cf. § 36, 5).   But this side of the matter came forward in an incomparably more powerful and efficient degree with the *French* Enlighteners.   It is enough here to recall *Voltaire*, who appeared as a literary power of the first rank, working unweariedly and victoriously for reason and justice.   But the contest which he carried on to a certain extent before the bar of public opinion of all Europe was taken up in detail by his fellow-countrymen, in a criticism of social institutions and by proposals for their improvement : in a broad and often passionate discussion philosophical reflection proceeds to the task of reforming the state. And here the weakness of the Enlightenment at once appears side by side with its strength.   As always, it takes the standards of its criticism for existing institutions, and of its proposals for their change, from the universal, eternal nature of man or of things; thus it loses from sight the authorisation and vital force of historical reality, and believes that it is only needed to make a *tabula rasa* of the existing conditions wherever they show themselves contrary to reason, in order to be able to build up society entire in accordance with the principles of philosophy.   In this spirit the literature of the Enlightenment, especially in France, prepared for the actual *break with history,* — the *Revolution.*   Typical in this was the procedure of Deism which, because none of the positive religions withstood its "rational" criticism, would abolish them all and put in their place the religion of Nature.

So then the French Revolution, too, attempted to decree the abstract natural state of "liberty, equality, and fraternity," the realisation of "human rights" according to Rousseau's *Social Contract.*   And numerous pens of very moderate quality hastened to justify and glorify the procedure.[1]   It is for the most part a superficial Epicureanism standing upon the basis of Condillac's positivism that acts as spokesman.   Thus *Volney* seeks, with the *Système de la Nature,* the source of all the evils of society in the

---

[1] The preference for the catechism, a form designed for education in the Church, is characteristic of this literature.

ignorance and covetousness of man, whose capacity for perfection has hitherto been restrained by religions. When all "illusions" shall be frightened away with these religions, then the newly organised society will have as its supreme rule of conduct, that "good" is only what furthers the interests of man, and the catechism for the citizen is comprehended in the rule "Conserve toi — instruis toi — modère toi — vis pour tes semblables, afin qu'ils vivent pour toi."[1] Still more materialistic is the form in which the theory of the Revolution appears with *St. Lambert*, from whom the definition that was much discussed in later literature comes : "L'homme est une masse organisée et sensible; il reçoit l'intelligence de ce qui l'environne et de ses besoins."[2] With the most superficial consideration of history, he celebrates in the Revolution the final victory of reason in history, and at the same time this Epicurean deduces that the democratic beginnings of this great event will be completed in Cæsardom! The extreme pitch of self-complacent boasting in this aspect of parliamentary dilettantism was reached by *Garat* and *Lancelin*.[3]

In contrast with these glittering generalities and declamations over the welfare of the people and the reign of reason, the earnest reality with which *Bentham* sought to make the utilitarian principle useful for legislation, appears in an extremely favourable light. This work he sought to accomplish by teaching the application of the quantitative determination of pleasure and pain values (cf. § 36, 9) to the consideration of the ends of particular statutes, with a careful regard to the existing conditions in every case.[4] Just in this he showed his insight into the fact that in the political movement the question at issue is not merely that of political rights, but above all that of *social interest*, and along just this line an enthusiastic and successful champion of the Revolution arose in *Godwin*,[5] who was not uninfluenced by Bentham. But along other lines, too,

---

[1] Volney, at the close of the *Catéchisme*, Œuvr., I. 310.

[2] St. Lambert, *Catéch. Introd.*, Œuvr., I. 53. For the characterisation of this literature it should not remain unmentioned that in St. Lambert's catechism the *Analyse de l'homme* is followed in a second book by an *Analyse de la — femme*.

[3] The organ of this movement most worthy of esteem was the *Decade Philosophique*, which saw and defended in the Revolution the triumph of the philosophy of the eighteenth century. Cf. Picavet, *Idéologues*, 86 ff.

[4] It is the more to be lamented that Bentham later in his *Deontology* attempted to give a kind of popular catechism of the utilitarian morals, which, in radical one-sidedness, in rancour and lack of understanding for other moral systems, equals the worst products of the time of the Revolution.

[5] William *Godwin* (1756–1836) published his *Inquiry concerning Political Justice and its Influence on General Virtue and Happiness* in 1793. Cf. C. Kegan Paul, *W. Godwin, his Friends and Contemporaries*, Lond. 1876, and L. Stephen, *English Thought*, II. 264 ff

the social storm is heard in the literature of the Revolution, as dull thunder still dying away in the distance. The investigations concerning the problems of *political economy*, which in France especially were chiefly promoted by the *physiocratic school*, became more and more comprehensive, and were grounded with increasing independence upon empirical principles. But while the theory of the state demanded, above all, security of possessions, there rose, from the depth of society, the *question as to the right of personal property;* and while the philosophers considered with more and more dissension the problem, how the interests of the community could be reconciled with those of the individual (cf. below), the thought forced its way to the surface that the ground of all evil with the human race lies in the striving after individual possessions, and that a social morality and a moral society will begin with the denunciation of this original sin, and not till then. Such *communistic* ideas were thrown to the world by *Mably* and *Morelly*, and a Babeuf made the first abortive conspiracy to carry out these ideas, under the Directory.

3. But the *social question* had already before this cast up its waves from its lowest depth. The contrast between the classes representing luxurious wealth and most wretched poverty, which had so great importance among the causes of the Revolution, might indeed at first be more palpable and effective; but it first acquired its full sharpness by virtue of the *antithesis between culture and non-culture*, which was linked with it by the whole development of European life, and this separating chasm was deepest and baldest in the age of the Enlightenment. The more the age plumed itself upon its "culture," the more evident it became that this was in the main a privilege of the property-owning class. In this point, too, English Deism had led the way with typical frankness. The religion of reason should be reserved for the cultivated man, just as the free, beautiful morality should be : for the ordinary man, on the other hand, *Shaftesbury* held, the promises and threatenings of positive religion must remain standing as a wheel and gallows. *Toland*, too, had presented his cosmopolitan natural worship as an *"esoteric"* doctrine, and when the later Deists began to carry these ideas among the people in popular writings, *Lord Bolingbroke*, himself a free-thinker of the most pronounced kind, declared them to be a pest of society against which the sharpest means were the best. Among the German Deists, also, men like *Semler* would have a very careful separation made between religion as a private matter and religion as a public order.

The *French* Enlightenment, as the relation of *Voltaire* to Boling-

broke shows, was from the beginning decidedly *more democratic.*
Indeed, it had the agitative tendency to play off the enlightenment of the masses against the exclusive self-seeking of the upper
ten thousand.   But with this was completed a revolution, by virtue
of which the Enlightenment necessarily turned against itself.   For
if in those strata in which it first took hold "culture" or civilisation had such consequences as appeared in the luxury of the "higher"
classes, if it had been able to do so little in the way of yielding
fruits that could be used for the needs of the masses also, its value
must appear all the more doubtful the more philosophy regarded
the "greatest happiness of the greatest number" as the proper
standard for the estimation of things and actions.

In this connection the *problem of civilisation* shaped itself out for
modern philosophy : the question whether and how far *civilisation,*
i.e. intellectual improvement (which is a historical fact), and the
change in human impulses and in the relations of human life, which
has been connected with it — whether and in how far this civilisation has served to further the moral order and man's true happiness.
The more proudly and self-complacently the average Enlightener
praised the progress of the human mind, which had reached in him
its summit of a clear and distinct rational life in theory and practice, the more burning and — uncomfortable this question became.

It is raised first, though not in a direct and square statement, by
Mandeville.   In his psychology an extreme adherent of the selfish
system, he sought to show, as against Shaftesbury, that the whole
life and charm of the social system rests solely upon the struggle
which self-seeking individuals carry on in their own interests — a
principle which worked also upon Adam Smith in his doctrine of
supply and demand.[1]   If we should think of man as stripped bare
of all egoistic impulses (this is the meaning of the *Fable of the Bees*),
and provided only with the "moral" qualities of altruism, the social
mechanism would stand still from pure absence of regard for self.
The motive power in civilisation is solely egoism, and, therefore,
we must not be surprised if civilisation displays its activity, not
by heightening the moral qualities, but only by refining and dis-
guising egoism.   And the individual's happiness is as little enhanced
by civilisation as his morality.   If it were increased, the egoism,
on which the progress of civilisation rests, would be thereby weakened.   In truth, it appears, rather, that every improvement of the
material condition, brought about by intellectual advance, calls forth
new and stronger wants in the individual, in consequence of which

---

[1] Cf. Lange, *Gesch. d. Mater.*, I. 285 [Eng. tr. I. 295].

he becomes more and more discontented; and so it turns out that the apparently so brilliant development of the whole is accomplished only at the cost of the morality and happiness of the individual.

4. In Mandeville these thoughts appear in a mild suggestion, and at the same time, in the repelling form of a cynical commendation of the egoism, whose "private vices" are "public benefits." They attained an importance for world-literature through the brilliant turn given them by *Rousseau.* With him the question concerned nothing more and nothing less than the *worth of all human history* — its worth for the morality and happiness of individuals. And he cast into the face of the Enlightenment the reproach that all growth in knowledge, and all refinement of life, had but made man more and more untrue to his true vocation and his true nature. History with its artificial structure of civilised society has deteriorated man :[1] he came forth from the hand of Nature good and pure, but his development has separated him from Nature step by step. The beginning of this "degeneration" Rousseau, in his second *Discourse,* found in the creation of property, which had for its result the division of labour, and with this the separation of the classes and, ultimately, the awakening of all evil passions : this it was that enlisted the work of the intellect permanently in the service of self-seeking.

In comparison with this unnatural condition of civilised barbarism the state of Nature appears at first as the lost paradise, and in this sense the sentimental yearning of a time intellectually and morally *blasé* found its nourishment in Rousseau's writings, above all in the *New Héloise.* The ladies of the salon were carried away with enthusiasm for the Gessnerian pastoral idyl; but on this account they mis-heard the admonition of the great Genevan.

For he did not wish to lead back to that state of Nature which had no society. He was convinced that man is provided by his creator with a capacity for being perfected (*perfectibilité*) which makes the development of his natural endowment both a duty and a natural necessity. If this development has been guided into wrong paths by the historical process which has hitherto prevailed, and, therefore, has led to demoralisation and wretchedness, *history must be begun anew;* in order to find the right way toward his development man must return from the unnatural condition of intellectual pride to the simple natural state of feeling, from the narrowness and falsehood of relations of society to his pure unstunted self. For this end, according to Rousseau, humanity as a whole needs a

---

[1] The English Deists' conception of the history of religion (cf. § 35, 8) is extended by Rousseau to all history.

political constitution, which affords the individual full freedom of
personal activity in connection with the life of the whole body, and
in accordance with the principle of equality of rights; and as individuals, humanity needs an *education*,[1] which allows the natural
endowments of the individual to unfold from his own vitality
without constraint. The optimism, which Rousseau finds in the
constitution of the natural God-descended nature of man, makes
him hope that our condition will be better, the more freely and
naturally we can develop.

5. While we thus find Rousseau in lively opposition to the historical development, and in the zealous endeavour to put in its stead
a new development "according to Nature," the last reconciling
synthesis of the ideas of the Enlightenment is the endeavour to
understand the previous course of human history itself as the
natural development of human nature; in this thought the philosophy of the eighteenth century strips off all its one-sidedness and reaches its highest consummation. The first stirring of
this is found in an isolated appearance of Italian literature, with
Vico.[2] Influenced by the Neo-Platonic metaphysics of the Renaissance, especially by Campanella, and educated by Bodin and Grotius,
he had grasped the idea of a general natural law of the development
of life, which manifests itself in the history of peoples as well as in
that of individuals, and with great learning had sought to prove
this principle of the identity of all natural development. But if in
such a conception of the naturally necessary correspondences between
the different historical systems and the fundamental biological
scheme, the thought of a purposeful inter-relation of the destinies
of nations had remained foreign to him, this had previously found

---

[1] In its details Rousseau's *Émile* frequently uses the "Thoughts," which
Locke had advanced with a much more limited purpose for the education of a
young man of higher station in society : there, too, the complete development
of the individuality was the main thing, from which the turning away from
learned one-sidedness, the direction of attention to the real and practical, the
appeal to perception and the use of individual instead of general truths in
instruction and education, followed as a matter of course. These principles,
thought out for the Englishman of superior rank, Rousseau adopts as elements
in an education which sought to develop in man, not the member of a definite
class or of a future profession, but only "the man." In this spirit his pedagogical doctrines passed over to the school of German *philanthropy*, which, under
the lead of *Basedow* (1723–1790), combined the principle of natural development with that of utility, and thought out the appropriate forms of an education
for a community by which the individual should be trained to become by the
natural way a useful member of human society.

[2] Giov. Battista *Vico* (1668–1744) became influential chiefly through his
Principj d' una scienza nuova d' intorno alla commune natura delle nazioni
(1725). Cf. K. Werner, *Giambattista V. als Philosoph und gelehrter Forscher*
(Vienna, 1879) ; R. Flint, *Vico* (Edin. and Lond. 1884); and likewise for the
following, Flint, *The Philosophy of History in Europe*, Vol I., new ed., 1893.

all the more forcible support in *Bossuet*.[1] The French prelate continues the patristic philosophy of history, which had pushed the
Redemption into the centre of the world's events. He would have
the christianising of modern nations through the empire of Charles
the Great, regarded as the concluding and decisive epoch of universal history, the whole course of which is the work of divine
providence, and the goal of which is the dominance of the one
Catholic Church. Such a theological view of the world and of
history had now, indeed, been energetically put aside by modern
philosophy, but the meagreness of the results yielded for the consideration of history by the treatment of human society from the
point of view of individual psychology is seen in the trivial lucu-
brations of *Iselin*,[2] in spite of his leaning upon Rousseau.

It was in a mind of *Herder's* universal receptiveness and fineness
of feeling that Rousseau's ideas first found in this respect, also, a
fruitful soil. But his optimism, which had matured in the atmosphere of Leibniz and Shaftesbury, did not allow him to believe in
the possibility of that aberration which the Genevan would regard
as the nature of previous history. He was rather convinced that the
natural development of man is just that which has taken place in
history. While Rousseau's conception of man's perfectibility was
treated by the Genevan's French adherents, such as St. Lambert,
and especially *Condorcet*, as the voucher for a better future, and as
an infinite perspective toward the perfecting of the race, Herder
used it — against Rousseau — as a principle of explanation for the
past, also, of the human family. *History* is nothing but the uninterrupted progress of *natural development*.

This concerned, above all, the *beginning* of history. The beginning of the life of society is to be understood, not as an arbitrary
act, whether of human reflection or of divine determination, but as a
gradually formed result of the natural connection. It has neither
been invented nor commanded, but has *become*. Characteristically
enough, these opposing views as to the origin of history, asserted
themselves earliest in theories of *language*. The individualism of
associational psychology saw in language, as is manifest particularly
in the case of Condillac,[3] an *invention* of man, — supra-naturalism,
defended in Germany by *Süssmilch*[4] saw a divine inspiration; here

---

[1] Jacques Bénigne *Bossuet* (1627–1704), the celebrated eloquent divine, wrote
the *Discours sur l'Histoire Universelle* (Paris, 1681) originally for the instruction of the Dauphin.

[2] Isaak *Iselin* of Basle (1728–1782) published in 1764 his *Philosophischen
Muthmassungen über die Geschichte des Menschheit*, 2 vols.

[3] *Logique* and *Langue des Calculs*.

[4] *Beweis, dass der Ursprung der menschlichen Sprache göttlich sei* (Berlin,
1766).

Rousseau had already spoken the word of solution when he saw in language a natural, involuntary unfolding of man's essential nature.[1]

Herder not only made this conception his own (cf. above, § 33, 11), but he extended it also consistently to all man's activities in civilisation. He proceeds, therefore, in his philosophy of history from the point of view of man's position in Nature, from that of the conditions of life which the planet affords him, and from that of his peculiar constitution, to understand from these sources the beginnings and the direction of his historical development: and in the progress of his exposition of universal history he makes, likewise, the peculiar character of each people and of its historical significance proceed from its natural endowments and relations. But at the same time the developments of the various nations do not fall apart in his treatment, as was still the case with Vico: on the contrary, they are all arranged organically as a great chain of ascending perfection. And they all form in this connected whole the ever-maturer realisation of the general constitution of human nature. As man himself is the crown of creation, so his history is the unfolding of human nature. The *Idea of Humanity* explains the complicated movement of national destinies.

In this consideration, the unhistorical mode of thinking which had characterised the Enlightenment was overcome : every form in this great course of development was valued as the natural product of its conditions, and the "voices of the peoples" united to form the harmony of the world's history, of which humanity is the theme. And out of this sprang also the task of the future, — to bring to ever richer and fuller development all the stirrings of human nature, and to realise in living unity the ripe fruits of the historical development. In the consciousness of this task of the "world-literature," far from all the pride of the meaner Enlightenment, full of the presage and anticipation of a new epoch, *Schiller* could call out, in valedictory to the "philosophical century," the joyful words : —

> " Wie schön, o Mensch, mit deinem Palmenzweige
> Stehst du an des Jahrhunderts Neige
> In edler, stolzer Männlichkeit ! " [2]

---

[1] With his arguments, though in part of another opinion, St. Martin the Mystic attacked the crude presentation of Condillac's doctrine by Garat ; cf. *Séances des Écoles Normales*, III. 61 ff.

[2] In rude paraphrase :

> How fair, O man, with victory's palm,
> Thou standest at the century's wane
> In noble pride of manliness.

PART VI.

THE GERMAN PHILOSOPHY.

To the literature cited on pp. 348 and 437, we add : —

H. M. Chalybaeus, *Historische Entwicklung der speculativen Philosophie von Kant bis Hegel*. Dresden, 1837. [Tr. Edin. and Andover, 1854.]

F. K. Biedermann, *Die deutsche Philosophie von Kant bis auf unsere Tage*. Leips. 1842 f.

K. L. Michelet, *Entwickelungsgeschichte der neuesten deutschen Philosophie*. Berlin, 1843.

C. Fortlage, *Genetische Geschichte der Philosophie seit Kant*. Leips. 1852.

O. Liebmann, *Kant und die Epigonen*. Stuttgart, 1865.

Fr. Harms, *Die Philosophie seit Kant*. Berlin, 1876.

A. S. Willm, *Histoire de la Philosophie Allemande depuis Kant jusqu'à Hegel*. Paris, 1846 ff.

H. Lotze, *Geschichte der Æsthetik in Deutschland*. Munich, 1868.

R. Flint, *Philosophy of History in Europe*, I. Edin. and Lond. 1874.

R. Fester, *Rousseau und die deutsche Geschichtsphilosophie*. Stuttgart, 1890.

[J. Royce, *The Spirit of Modern Philosophy*. Boston, 1892.]

A fortunate union of various intellectual movements produced in Germany, during the close of the preceding and at the beginning of the present century, a bloom of philosophy, which in the history of European thought can be compared only with the great development of Greek philosophy from Socrates to Aristotle. In a development, powerful alike in its intensity and extent, the German mind during the short span of four decades (1780–1820) produced a wealth of systems of philosophical *Weltanschauung*, grandly projected on all sides, such as has at no other time been compressed within so narrow a space ; and in all of these the thoughts of preceding philosophy combine to form characteristic and impressive structures. They appear in their totality as the ripe fruit of a long growth, out of which germs of a new development, as yet scarcely recognisable, are to spring.

This brilliant phenomenon had its general cause in the incomparable vigour and spirit with which the German nation at that time took up again with new strength, and carried to its completion, the movement of civilisation which began in the Renaissance and had been interrupted by external force. Germany attained the summit of its inner development at the same time that its outer history reached its lowest condition, — a process that has no equal in history. When it lay politically powerless, it created its world-conquering thinkers and poets. Its victorious power, however, lay just *in the league between philosophy and poetry*. The contemperaneousness of Kant and Goethe, and the combination of their ideas by Schiller, — these are the decisive characteristics of the time.

The history of philosophy at this point is most intimately interwoven with that of general literature, and the lines of mutual relation and stimulus run continuously back and forth. This appears characteristically in the heightened and finally decisive significance which fell in this connection to the *problems and conceptions of æsthetics*. Philosophy found thus opened before her a new world, into which she had hitherto had but occasional glimpses, and of which she now took possession as of the Promised Land. In their matter as well as their form, æsthetic principles gained the mastery, and the motives of scientific thought became interwoven with those of artistic vision to produce grand poetical creations in the sphere of abstract thought.

The ensnaring magic which literature thus exercised upon philosophy rested mainly upon its *historical universality*. With Herder and Goethe begins what we call, after them, world-literature; the conscious working out of true culture from the appropriation of all the great thought-creations of all human history. The Romantic School appears in Germany as the representative of this work. And, in analogy to this, philosophy also developed out of a wealth of historical suggestions ; it resorted with conscious deepening of thought to the ideas of antiquity and of the Renaissance, it plunged intelligently into what the Enlightenment had shown, and ended in Hegel by understanding itself as the systematically penetrating and formative comprehension of all that the human mind had hitherto thought.

But for this mighty work it needed a new conceptional basis, without which all those suggestions from general literature would have remained without effect. This philosophical power to master the ideal material of history dwelt within the *doctrine of Kant*, and this is its incomparably high historical importance. Kant, by the newness and the greatness of his points of view, prescribed to the succeeding philosophy not only its problems, but also the means for their solution. His is the mind that determines and controls on all sides. The work of his immediate successors, in which his new principle unfolded itself in all directions and finished its life historically with an assimilation of earlier systems, is best comprehended in accordance with its most important characteristic, under the name of *Idealism.*

Hence we treat the history of the German Philosophy in two chapters, of which the first embraces Kant, and the second the development of idealism. In the thought symphony of those forty years the Kantian doctrine forms the theme, and idealism its development.

CHAPTER I.

THE CRITIQUE OF REASON.

C. L. Reinhold, *Briefe über die Kantische Philosophie* (*Deutsch. Merkur* 1786 f.). Leips. 1790 ff.

V. Cousin, *Leçons sur la Philosophie de Kant.* Paris, 1842.

M. Desdouits, *La Philosophie de Kant, d'après les Trois Critiques.* Paris, 1876.

E. Caird, *The Philosophy of Kant.* Lond. 1876.

[E. Caird, *The Critical Philosophy of I. Kant,* Glasgow, Lond., and N.Y., 2 vols., 1889.]

C. Cantoni, *Em. Kant* (3 vols.). Milan, 1879–1884.

W. Wallace, *Kant.* Oxford, Edin., and Lond. 1882.

J. B. Meyer, *Kant's Psychologie.* Berlin, 1870.

THE pre-eminent position of the Königsberg philosopher rests upon the fact that he took up into himself the various motives of thought in the literature of the Enlightenment, and by their reciprocal supplementation matured a completely new conception of the problem and procedure of philosophy. He passed through the school of the Wolffian metaphysics and through an acquaintance with the German popular philosophers; he plunged into Hume's profound statement of problems, and was enthusiastic for Rousseau's gospel of Nature; the mathematical rigour of the Newtonian natural philosophy, the fineness of the psychological analysis of the origin of human ideas and volitions found in English literature, Deism from Toland and Shaftesbury to Voltaire, the honourable spirit of freedom with which the French Enlightenment urged the improvement of political and social conditions,— all these had found in the young Kant a true co-worker, full of conviction, who with a rich knowledge of the world and admirable sagacity, and also, where it was in place, with taste and wit, though far from all self-complacency and boasting, united typically within himself the best features of the Enlightenment.

But it was in connection with the difficulties of the *problem of knowledge* that he wrought out from all these foundation elements the work which gave him his peculiar significance. The more he

had originally prized metaphysics just because it claimed to give scientific certainty to moral and religious convictions, the more lasting
was its working upon him when he was forced to become convinced
by his own progressive criticism in his constant search for truth,
how little the rationalistic school system satisfied that claim which
it made.   But the more, also, was his vision sharpened for the
limitations of that philosophy which empiricism developed by the
aid of psychological method.   In studying David Hume this came
to his consciousness in such a degree that he grasped eagerly for the
aid which the *Nouveaux Essais* of Leibniz seemed to offer toward
making a metaphysical science possible.   But the epistemological
system, which he erected upon the principle of virtual innateness
extended to mathematics (cf. pp. 465 f. and 485 f.), very soon proved
its untenability, and this led him to the tedious investigations
which occupied him in the period from 1770 to 1780, and which
found their conclusion in the *Critique of Pure Reason.*

The essentially new and decisive in this was that Kant recognised the *inadequacy of the psychological method* for the solution of
philosophical problems,[1] and completely separated the questions
which surround the *origin* and the actual development of man's
rational activities, from those which relate to their *value.*   He shared
permanently with the Enlightenment the tendency to take the
starting-point of his investigations, not in our apprehension of
things, which is influenced by most various presuppositions, but
in considering the reason itself; but he found in this latter
point of view universal judgments which extend beyond all experience, whose validity can neither be made dependent upon the
exhibition of their actual formation in consciousness, nor grounded
upon any form of innateness.   It is his task to fix upon these judgments throughout the entire circuit of human rational activity, in
order from their content itself and from their relations to the
system of the rational life determined by them, to understand their
authority or the limits of their claims.

This task Kant designated as the *Critique of Reason,* and this
method as the *critical or transcendental method;* the subject-matter
to which this method was to be applied he considered to be the
investigation as to the *possibility of synthetic judgments a priori.*[2]

---

[1] Cf. the beginning of the transcendental deduction of the pure conceptions
of the understanding in the *Critique of Pure Reason,* II. 118 ff.

[2] This expression took form gradually in connection with the origination of
the *Kr. d. r. V.* through the importance which the conception of *synthesis*
acquired.   Cf. § 38.   Kant develops the above general formula in his introduction to the *Critique* in the following way : judgments are analytical when the
relation of the predicate to the subject, which is therein asserted, has its ground

This rests upon the fundamental insight that the validity of the principles of reason is entirely independent of how they rise in the empirical consciousness (whether of the individual or of the race). All philosophy is *dogmatic,* which seeks to *prove* or even merely to judge of this validity by showing the genesis of those principles out of elements of sensation, or by their innateness, whatever the metaphysical assumptions in the case may be.   The critical method, or transcendental philosophy, examines the form in which these principles actually make their appearance, in connection with the capacity which they possess of being employed *universally* and *necessarily* in experience.

From this there followed for Kant the task of a systematic investigation of reason's functions in order to fix upon their principles, and to examine the validity of these; for the critical method, which was first gained in epistemology, extended its significance of itself to the other spheres of the reason's activity.   But here the newly acquired scheme of psychological division (cf. p. 512, note 6) proved authoritative for his *analysis and treatment of philosophical problems.* As *thinking, feeling,* and *willing* were distinguished as the fundamental forms in which reason expresses itself, so the criticism of reason must keep to the division thus given; it examined separately the *principles of knowledge,* of *morality,* and of the working of things upon the reason through the medium of *feeling,* — a province independent of the other two.

Kant's doctrine is accordingly divided into a *theoretical,* a *practical,* and an *æsthetical* part, and his main works are the *three Critiques,* of the *Pure Reason,* of the *Practical Reason,* and of the *Judgment.*

Immanuel Kant, born April 22, 1724, at Königsberg, Prussia, the son of a saddler, was educated at the Pietistic Collegium Fridericianum, and attended in 1740 the University of his native city to study theology; but subjects of natural science and philosophy gradually attracted him.   After concluding his studies, he was a private teacher in various families in the vicinity of Königsberg from 1746 to 1755, habilitated in the autumn of 1755 as *Privatdocent* in

---

in the concept itself which forms the subject ("explicative judgments"); synthetical, when this is not the case, so that the addition of the predicate to the subject must have its ground in something else which is logically different from both ("ampliative judgments").   This ground is, in the case of synthetical judgments *a posteriori* ("judgments of perception," cf. *Prolegomena,* § 18, III. 215 f.), the act of perception itself; in the case of synthetical judgments *a priori,* on the contrary, *i.e.* of the universal principles employed for the interpretation of experience, it is something else; what it is is just that which is to be sought.   *A priori* is, with Kant, not a psychological, but a purely epistemological mark; it means not a chronological priority to experience, but a *universality and necessity of validity in principles of reason which really transcends all experience, and is not capable of being proved by any experience* [*i.e.* a *logical,* not a *chronological* priority].   No one who does not make this clear to himself has any hope of understanding Kant.

the philosophical faculty of Königsberg University, and was made full Professor there in 1770. The cheerful, brilliant animation and versatility of his middle years gave place with time to an earnest, rigorous conception of life and to the control of a strict consciousness of duty, which manifested itself in his unremitting labour upon his great philosophical task, in his masterful fulfilment of the duties of his academic profession, and in the inflexible rectitude of his life, which was not without a shade of the pedantic. The uniform course of his solitary and modest scholar's life was not disturbed by the brilliancy of the fame that fell upon his life's evening, and only transiently by the dark shadow, that the hatred of orthodoxy, which had obtained control under Frederick William II., threatened to cast upon his path by a prohibition upon his philosophy. He died from weakness of old age on the 12th of February, 1804.

Kant's life and personality after his earlier works has been drawn most completely by Kuno Fischer (*Gesch. d. neueren Philos.*, III. and IV., 4th ed. Heidelb. 1899); E. Arnoldt has treated of his youth and the first part of his activity as a teacher (Königsberg, 1882); [J. H. W. Stuckenberg, *Life of Kant*, Lond. 1882].

The change which was taking place in the philosopher toward the end of the seventh decade of the eighteenth century appears especially in his activity as a writer. His earlier "pre-critical" works (of which those most important philosophically have been already cited, p. 445) are distinguished by easy-flowing, graceful presentation, and present themselves as admirable occasional writings of a man of fine thought who is well versed in the world. His later works show the laboriousness of his thought and the pressure of the contending *motifs*, both in the form of the investigation with its circumstantial heaviness and artificial architectonic structure, and in the formation of his sentences, which are highly involved, and frequently interrupted by restriction. Minerva frightened away the graces ; but instead, the devout tone of a deep thought and an earnest conviction which here and there rises to powerful pathos and weighty expression hovers over his later writings.

For Kant's theoretical development, the antithesis between the Leibnizo-Wolffian metaphysics and the Newtonian natural philosophy was at the beginning of decisive importance. The former had been brought to his attention at the University by Knutzen (cf. p. 444), the latter by Teske, and in his growing alienation from the philosophical school-system, his interest for *natural science,* to which for the time he seemed to desire to devote himself entirely, co-operated strongly. His first treatise, 1747, was entitled *Thoughts upon the True Estimation of the Vis Viva,* a controverted question between Cartesian and Leibnizian physicists ; his great work upon the *General Natural History and Theory of the Heavens* was a natural science production of the first rank, and besides small articles, his promotion treatise, *De Igne* (1755), which propounded a hypothesis as to imponderables, belongs here. His activity as a teacher also showed, even on into his later period, a preference for the subjects of natural sciences, especially for physical geography and anthropology.

In theoretical philosophy Kant passed through many reversals (*mancherlei Umkippungen*) of his standpoint (cf. §§ 33 and 34). At the beginning (in the *Physical Monadology*) he had sought to adjust the opposition between Leibniz and Newton, in their doctrine of space, by the ordinary distinction of things-in-themselves (which are to be known metaphysically), and phenomena, or things as they appear (which are to be investigated physically) ; he then (in the writings after 1760) attained to the insight that a metaphysics in the sense of rationalism is impossible, that philosophy and mathematics must have diametrically opposed methods, and that philosophy as the empirical knowledge of the given cannot step beyond the circle of experience. But while he allowed himself to be comforted by Voltaire and Rousseau for this falling away of metaphysical insight, through the instrumentality of the "natural feeling" for the right and holy, he was still working with Lambert at an improvement of the method of metaphysics, and when he found this, as he hoped, by the aid of Leibniz's *Nouveaux Essais,* he constructed in bold lines the mystico-dogmatic system of his *Inaugural Dissertation.*

The progress from there on to the *System of Criticism* is obscure and controverted. Cf. concerning this development, in which the time in which he was influenced by Hume and the direction which that influence took are especially in question, the following: Fr. Michelis, *Kant vor und nach 1770* (Braunsberg, 1871); Fr. Paulsen, *Versuch einer Entwicklungsgeschichte der kantischen Erkenntnisstheorie* (Leips. 1875); A. Riehl, *Geschichte und Methode des philosophischen Kriticismus* (Leips. 1876); B. Erdmann, *Kant's Kriticismus* (Leips. 1878); W. Windelband, *Die verschiedenen Phasen der kantischen Lehre vom Ding-an-sich* (*Vierteljahrschr. f. wissensch. Philos.*, 1876). Cf. also the writings by K. Dieterich on Kant's relation to Newton and Rousseau under the title *Die kantische Philosophie in ihrer inneren Entwicklungsgeschichte,* Freiburg i. B. 1885.

From the adjustment of the various tendencies of Kant's thought proceeded the "Doomsday-book" of German philosophy, the *Critique of Pure Reason* (Riga, 1781). It received a series of changes in the second edition (1787), and these became the object of very vigorous controversies after attention had been called to them by Schelling (W., V. 196) and Jacobi (W., II. 291). Cf. concerning this, the writings cited above. H. Vaihinger, *Commentar zu K. K. d. r. V.* (Vol. I., Stuttgart, 1887 [Vol. II., 1892]), has diligently collected the literature. Separate editions of the *Kritik*, by K. Kehrbach, upon the basis of the first edition, and by B. Erdmann [and E. Adickes] upon the basis of the second edition. [Eng. tr. of the *Critique* (2d ed.), by Meiklejohn, in the Bohn Library, and by Max Müller (text of 1st ed. with supplements giving changes of 2d ed.), Lond. 1881; Paraphrase and Commentary by Mahaffy and Bernard, 2d ed., Lond. and N.Y. 1889; partial translations in J. H. Stirling's *Text-book to Kant,* and in Watson's *Selections*, Lond. and N.Y. 1888. This last contains also extracts from the ethical writings and from the *Critique of Judgment.*]

The additional main writings of Kant in his critical period are: *Prolegomena zu einer jeden künftigen Metaphysik*, 1783; *Grundlegung zur Metaphysik der Sitten*, 1785; *Metaphysische Anfangsgründe der Naturwissenschaft*, 1785; *Kritik der praktischen Vernunft*, 1788; *Kritik der Urtheilskraft*, 1790; *Die Religion innerhalb der Grenzen der blossen Vernunft,* 1793; *Zum ewigen Frieden*, 1795; *Metaphysische Anfangsgründe der Rechts- und Tugendlehre,* 1797; *Der Streit der Fakultäten*, 1798; [Eng. tr. of the *Prolegomena*, by Mahaffy and Bernard, Lond. and N.Y. 1889; of the *Prolegomena* and *Metaphysical Foundations of Natural Science*, by Bax, Bohn Library; of the ethical writings, including the first part of the *Religion within the Bounds of Pure Reason*, by T. K. Abbott, 4th ed., Lond. 1889; of the *Critique of Judgment*, by J. H. Bernard, Lond. and N.Y. 1892; of the *Philosophy of Law*, by W. Hastie, Edin. 1887; *Principles of Politics*, including the essay on *Perpetual Peace*, by W. Hastie, Edin. 1891. The contents of *Kant's Essays and Treatises,* 2 vols., Lond. 1798, is given in *Ueberweg*, II. 138 (Eng. tr.)].

Complete editions of his works have been prepared by K. Rosenkranz and F. W. Schubert (12 vols., Leips. 1833 ff.), G. Hartenstein (10 vols., Leips. 1838 f., and recently 8 vols., Leips. 1867 ff.), and J. v. Kirchmann (in the *Philos. Biblioth.*).[1] They contain, besides his smaller articles, etc., his lectures upon logic, pedagogy, etc., and his letters. A survey of all that has been written by Kant (including also the manuscript of the *Transition from Metaphysics to Physics*, which is without value for the interpretation of his critical system) is found in *Ueberweg-Heinze*, III. § 24; there, too, the voluminous literature is cited with great completeness. Of this we can give here only a choice of the best and most instructive; a survey of the more valuable literature, arranged according to its material, is offered by the article *Kant*, by W. Windelband in *Ersch und Gruber's Enc.* [The *Journal of Speculative Philosophy* contains numerous articles upon Kant. We may mention also Adamson, *The Philosophy of Kant*, Edin. 1879; art. *Kant*, in *Enc. Brit.*, by the same author; arts. in *Mind*, Vol. VI., by J. Watson, and in *Philos. Review*, 1893, by J. G. Schurmann.—E. Adickes has begun an exhaustive bibliography of the German literature in the *Philos. Review*, 1893.]

---

[1] The citations refer to the older Hartenstein edition In the case of many works the convenient editions by K. Kehrbach (*Reclam. Bib.*) make easy the transfer of the citations to the other editions.

§ 38. The Object of Knowledge.

Erh. Schmid, *Kritik der reinen Vernunft im Grundrisse.* Jena, 1786.

H. Cohen, *Kant's Theorie der Erfahrung.* Berlin, 1871.

A. Hölder, *Darstellung der kantischen Erkenntnisstheorie.* Tübingen, 1873.

A. Stadler, *Die Grundsätze der reinen Erkenntnisstheorie in der kantischen Philosophie.* Leips. 1876.

Joh. Volkelt, *I. Kant's Erkenntnisstheorie nach ihren Grundprincipien analysirt.* Leips. 1879.

E. Pfleiderer, *Kantischer Kriticismus und englische Philosophie.* Tübingen, 1881.

J. Hutchinson Stirling, *Text-Book to Kant.* Edin. and Lond. 1881.

Seb. Turbiglio, *Analisi, Storia, Critica della Ragione Pura.* Rome, 1881.

G. S. Morris, *Kant's Critique of Pure Reason*, Chicago, 1882.

Fr. Staudinger, *Noumena.* Darmstadt, 1884.

[K. Fischer's *Criticism of Kant*, trans. by Hough. Lond. 1888.]

[J. Watson, *Kant and his English Critics.* Lond. 1886.]

[H. Vaihinger, *Commentar zu Kant's Kritik d. r. Vernunft*, II. (on the *Æsthetic*). Stuttgart, 1892.]

Kant's theory of knowledge followed with tenacious consistency from the statement which modern Terminism had given to problems of knowledge (cf. pp. 466 and 482). The philosopher had grown up in the naïve realism of the Wolffian school, which without close scrutiny regarded logical necessity and reality as identical; and his liberation from the ban of this school consisted in his seeing the impossibility of determining out of "pure reason," *i.e.* through mere logical operations with conceptions, anything whatever as to the existence[1] or the causal relation[2] of real things. The metaphysicians are the architects of many a world of thought in the air;[3] but their structures have no relation to reality. Kant now sought this relation first in the conceptions given through experience, since the genetic connection of these with the reality to be known by science seemed immediately evident, but he was shaken from this "dogmatic slumber" by Hume,[4] who demonstrated that precisely the constitutive Forms of the conceptional knowledge of reality, especially the Form of causality, are not given in perception, but are

---

[1] Cf. Kant's *Sole Possible Proof for the Existence of God.*

[2] Cf. the *Essay on Negative Magnitudes*, especially the conclusion (W., I. 59 ff.).

[3] *Dreams of a Ghost Seer*, I. 3; W., III. 75.

[4] In connection with this frequently mentioned confession of Kant, it is for the most part disregarded that he characterised as "dogmatic" not only rationalism, but also the empiricism of the earlier theory of knowledge, and that the classical passage at which he uses this expression (in the preface to the *Prolegomena*, W., III. 170 f.) does not contrast Hume with Wolff, but with Locke, Reid, and Beattie only. The dogmatism from which, therefore, Kant declared that he had been freed through Hume *was that of empiricism.*

products of the mechanism of association without any demonstrable relation to the real.   Reality was not to be known from the "given" conceptions, either.   And then Kant, prompted by Leibniz, deliberated once more whether the purified conception of virtual innateness, with the aid of the "pre-established harmony" grounded in God between the monad which knows and the monad which is to be known, might not solve the mystery of the relation of thought and Being, and in his *Inaugural Dissertation* he had convinced himself that this was the solution of the problem.   But cool reflection soon showed that this pre-established harmony was a metaphysical assumption, incapable of proof and unable to support a scientific system of philosophy.   So it appeared that neither empiricism nor rationalism had solved the cardinal question, — *the relation of knowledge to its object,* in what does it consist and on what does it rest ? [1]

1.   Kant's own, long-weighed answer to this question is the *Critique of Pure Reason.*   In its final systematic form, which found an analytical explication in the *Prolegomena,* his criticism proceeds from the *fact of the actual presence of synthetic judgments a priori* in three theoretical sciences ; viz. in *mathematics,* in *pure natural science,* and in *metaphysics ;* and the design is to examine their claims to universal and necessary validity.

In this formulation of the problem the insight into the nature of reason's activity, which Kant had gained in the course of his critical development, came into play.   This activity is synthesis, *i.e.* the uniting or unifying of a manifold.[2]   This conception of *synthesis* [3] is a new element which separates the *Critique* from the *Inaugural Dissertation ;* in it Kant found the common element between the Forms of the sensibility and those of the understanding, which in his exposition of 1770 were regarded as entirely separate, in accordance with their characteristic attributes of receptivity and spontaneity respectively.[4]   It now appeared that the *synthesis of the theoretical*

---

[1] Kant's letter to Marcus Herz, Feb. 21, 1772.

[2] This frequently repeated definition makes the fundamental conception of of the critical doctrine of knowledge appear in closest proximity to the fundamental metaphysical conception of the Monadology. Cf. § 31, 11.

[3] Which is introduced in the *Transcendental Analytic* in connection with the doctrine of the categories. Sections 10 and 15 (of the first edition of the *Critique*).

[4] Hence the conception of synthesis in the present form of the *Critique of Pure Reason* comes in collision with the psychological presuppositions which passed over to the *Critique* out of the German working-over of the *Inaugural Dissertation,* which forms the *Transcendental Æsthetic* and the beginning of the *Transcendental Logic* (this was originally to have appeared immediately after 1770 under the title *Limits of the Sensibility and of the Understanding*). In the *Prolegomena* these psychological presuppositions became obliterated. Earlier, sensibility and understanding were set over against each other as receptivity and spontaneity ; but space and time, the pure Forms of the sensi-

reason completes itself in three stages : the combination of sensations into perceptions takes place in the Forms of space and time; the combination of the perceptions into experience of the natural world of reality takes place by means of concepts of the understanding; the combination of judgments of experience into metaphysical knowledge takes place by means of general principles, which Kant calls Ideas.   These three stages of the knowing activity develop, therefore, as different Forms of synthesis, of which each higher stage has the lower for its content.   The critique of reason has to investigate what the especial Forms of this synthesis are in each stage, and in what their universal and necessary validity consists.

2. As regards *mathematics*, the conception of the *Inaugural Dissertation* fits aptly, in the main, into the critique of reason.   Mathematical propositions are synthetic; they rest in the last resort upon construction in pure perception, not upon the development of conceptions.   Their necessity and universal validity, which cannot be established by any experience, is, therefore, to be explained only if an *a priori principle of perception* lies at their basis.   Kant, there-fore, shows that the general ideas of *space and time*, to which all insights of geometry and arithmetic relate, are " pure Forms of perception " or "perceptions *a priori.*"   The ideas of the one infinite space and of the one infinite time do not rest upon the combination of empirical perceptions of finite spaces and times; but with the very attributes of limit in the "beside-of-one-another " and "after-one-another" (co-existence and succession), the whole of space and the whole of time respectively are already involved in the empirical perception of particular space and time magnitudes, which can accord-ingly be presented to the mind only as parts of space in general and of time in general.   Space and time cannot be "concepts," since they relate to an object which is only a single, unique object, and which is not thought as complete, but is involved in an infinite synthesis; and further, they are related to the ideas of finite magnitudes, not as class-concepts are to their particular examples, but as the whole to the part.   If they are, accordingly, pure perceptions (*Anschauungen*), *i.e.* perceptions not founded upon empirical perceptions (*Wahrnehrnungen*), but lying at the basis of all empirical perceptions,[1] then they are, as such, necessary ; for we can indeed think

---

bility, were indeed the principles of the synthetical ordering of the sensations, and thus belonged under the general conception of synthesis, *i.e.* spontaneous unity of the manifold.   Thus the conception of synthesis burst the psychological schema of the *Inaugural Dissertation.*

[1] Here once more it must be recalled that it is but a perverted and completely erroneous conception of Kant to conceive of this " lying at the basis of " or " preceding," as referring to time.   The *nativism,* which holds space and time

everything away from them, but cannot think them away. They are the given Forms of pure perception from which we cannot escape, the *laws of relations,* in which alone we can mentally represent with synthetic unity the manifold of sensations. And further, space is the form of the outer sense, time that of the inner sense; all objects of the particular senses are perceived as spatial, all objects of self-perception as in time.

If, then, space and time are the "unchangeable Form of our sensuous receptivity," cognitions determined by these two kinds of perception without any regard to the particular empirical content, possess universal and necessary validity for the entire compass of all that we can perceive and experience. In the realm of the sensibility, — so the "Transcendental Æsthetic" teaches, — the only object of *a priori* knowledge is the *Form of the synthesis* of the manifold given through sensation, — the law of arrangement in space and time. But the universality and necessity of this knowledge is intelligible only if *space and time are nothing but the necessary Forms of man's sensuous perception.* If they possessed a reality independent of the functions of perception, the *a priori* character of mathematical knowledge would be impossible. Were space and time themselves things or real properties and relations of things, then we could know of them only through experience, and, therefore, never in a universal and necessary way. This last mode of knowledge is possible only if they are nothing but the Form under which all things in our perception must *appear.*[1] According to this principle the *a priori* and the *phenomenal* become for Kant interchangeable conceptions. *The only universal and necessary element in man's knowledge is the Form under which things appear in it.* Rationalism limits itself to the Form, and holds good even for this only at the price of the "subjectivity" of the same.

3. While Kant would thus have the spatial and chronological relations of objects of perception regarded as wholly a mode of mental representation, which does not coincide with the reality of things themselves, he distinguished this conception of their *ideality* very exactly from that "subjectivity of the qualities of sense" which was held by him, as by all philosophy after Descartes and Locke, to be self-evident.[2] And the point at issue here again is solely the ground of the phenomenality. As regards colour, taste, etc., the phenomenality had been based, since the time of Protagoras and Democritus,

---

to be inborn ideas, is un-Kantian throughout, and stands in contradiction to express declarations of the philosopher (cf., *e.g.,* above, p. 465 f.).

[1] This thought is developed with especial clearness in the *Prolegomena,* § 9.

[2] Cf. *Critique,* § 3, b. W., II. 68.

upon the difference and relativity of impressions; for the Forms of space and time, Kant deduces their phenomenality precisely from their invariability. For him, therefore, the qualities of sense offered only an individual and contingent mode of representation; while the Forms of space and time, on the other hand, present *a universal and necessary mode in which things appear.* All that perception contains, is, indeed, not the true essence of things, but an appearance or phenomenon; but the contents of sensation are "phenomena" in quite another sense than that in which the Forms of space and time are such; the former have worth only as the states of the individual subject, the latter as "objective" Forms of perception for all. Even on this ground, therefore, Kant, too, sees the task of natural science to lie in the reduction of the qualitative to the quantitative, in which alone necessity and universal validity can be found upon a mathematical basis, agreeing in this with Democritus and Galileo; but he differed from his predecessors in holding that, *philosophically considered,* even the mathematical mode of representing Nature can be regarded only as an appearance and phenomenon, though in the deeper sense of the word. Sensation gives an individual idea, mathematical theory gives a necessary, universally valid perception of the actual world; but both are merely different stages of the *phenomenal appearance,* behind which the true thing-in-itself remains unknown. Space and time hold without exception for all objects of perception, but for nothing beyond; they have "*empirical reality*" and "*transcendental ideality.*"

4. The main advance of the *Critique of Reason* beyond the *Inaugural Dissertation* consists in the fact that these same principles are extended in a completely parallel investigation to the question as to the epistemological value which belongs to the *synthetic Forms of the activity of the understanding.*[1]

Natural science needs besides its mathematical basis a number of general principles as to the connection of things. These principles, such as that every change must have its cause, are of a synthetic nature, but, at the same time, are not capable of being established by experience, though they come to consciousness through experience, are applied to experience, and find there their confirmation. Of such principles a few have indeed been incidentally propounded and treated hitherto, and it remains for the *Critique* itself to discover the "system of principles," but it is clear that without this basis the knowledge of Nature would be deprived of its necessary

---

[1] This parallelism is seen most plainly by comparing §§ 9 and 14 of the *Prolegomena.*

and universal validity. For "Nature" is not merely an aggregate of spatial and temporal Forms, of corporeal shapes and motions, but a *connected system*, which we perceive through our senses, but *think at the same time through conceptions.* Kant calls the faculty of thinking the manifold of perception in synthetic unity, the *Understanding;* and the *categories or pure conceptions of Understanding* are the *Forms of the synthesis of the Understanding*, just as space and time are the Forms of the synthesis of perception.

If now *Nature*, as object of our knowledge, were a real connected system of things, independent of the functions of our reason, we could know of it only through experience and never *a priori;* a universal and necessary knowledge of Nature is possible only if our conceptional Forms of synthesis determine Nature itself. If Nature prescribed laws to our understanding, we should have only an empirical, inadequate knowledge; *an a priori knowledge of Nature is therefore possible only if the case be reversed and our understanding prescribes laws to Nature.* But our understanding cannot determine Nature in so far as it exists as a thing-in-itself, or as a system of things-in-themselves, but *only in so far* as it appears in our thought. *A priori* knowledge of Nature is therefore possible *only if the connection which we think between perceptions is also nothing but our mode of ideation;* the conceptional relations also, in which Nature is an object of our knowledge, must be only "phenomenon."

5. In order to attain this result, the *Critique of Reason* proceeds first to assure itself of these synthetic Forms of the understanding in systematic completeness. Here it is clear from the outset that we have not to do with those analytic relations which are treated in *formal logic,* and grounded upon the principle of contradiction. For these contain only the rules for establishing relations between conceptions according to the contents already given within them. But such modes of combination as are present when we affirm the relation of cause and effect, or of substance and accident, are not contained in those analytical Forms — just this had been shown by Hume. Kant discovers here the completely new task of *transcendental logic.*[1] Side by side with the (analytic) Forms of the understanding, in accordance with which the relations of conceptions which are given as to their contents are established, appear the *synthetic Forms of understanding*, through which perceptions are made objects of conceptional knowledge. Images of sensation, co-ordinate in space and changing in time, become "objective" only by being *thought* as

---

[5] Cf. M. Steckelmacher, *Die formale Logik Kant's in ihren Beziehungen zur transscendentalen* (Breslau, 1878).

things with abiding qualities and changing states; but this relation expressed by means of the *category* inheres analytically neither in the perceptions nor in their perceptional relations as such.   In the analytic relations of formal logic thinking is dependent upon its objects, and appears ultimately with right as only a reckoning with given magnitudes.   The synthetic Forms of transcendental logic, on the contrary, let us recognise the understanding in its creative function of *producing* out of perceptions the *objects of thought itself.*

At this point, in the distinction between formal and transcendental logic, appears for the first time the fundamental antithesis between Kant and the conceptions of the Greek theory of knowledge which had prevailed up to his time.   The Greek theory assumed "the objects" as "given" independently of thought, and regarded the intellectual processes as entirely dependent upon the objects; at the most it was the mission of the intellectual processes to reproduce these objects by way of copy, or allow themselves to be guided by them.   Kant discovered that the objects of thought are none other than the products of thought itself.   This *spontaneity* of reason forms the deepest kernel of his *transcendental idealism.*

But while he thus with completely clear consciousness set a new epistemological *logic of synthesis* by the side of the analytical logic of Aristotle, which had as its essential content the relations involved in subsuming ready-made conceptions under each other (cf. § 12), he yet held that both had a common element, viz: *the science of judgment.*   In the judgment the relation thought between subject and predicate is asserted as holding objectively ; all objective thinking is judging.   Hence if the *categories* or *radical conceptions of the understanding* are to be regarded as the relating forms of the synthesis by which objects arise, there must be as many categories as there are kinds of judgments, and every category is the mode of connecting subject and predicate which is operative in its own kind of judgment.

Kant accordingly thought that he could deduce the *table of the categories* from that of the judgments.   He distinguished from the four points of view of Quantity, Quality, Relation, and Modality, three kinds of judgments for each: Universal, Particular, Singular, — Affirmative, Negative, Infinite, — Categorical, Hypothetical, Disjunctive, — Problematic, Assertoric, Apodictic; and to these were to correspond the twelve categories: Unity, Plurality, Totality, — Reality, Negation, Limitation, — Inherence and Subsistence, Causality and Dependence, Community or Reciprocity, — Possibility and Impossibility, Existence and Non-existence, Necessity and Contingency.   The artificiality of this construction, the looseness of

the relations between Forms of judgment and categories, the un-
equal value of the categories, — all this is evident, but Kant
unfortunately had so much confidence in this system that he treated
it as the architectonic frame for a great number of his later
investigations.

6. The most difficult part of the task, however, was to demonstrate in the "Transcendental Deduction of the Pure Conceptions
of the Understanding" how the categories "make the objects of
experience." The obscurity into which the profound investigation
of the philosopher necessarily came here is best brightened up by
a fortunate idea of the *Prolegomena*. Kant here distinguishes *judgments of perception*, *i.e.* those in which only the relation of sensations
in space and time for the individual consciousness is expressed, and
judgments of experience, *i.e.* those in which such a relation is
asserted as objectively valid, as given in the object; and he finds
the difference in epistemological value between them to be, that
in the judgment of experience the spatial or temporal relation is
regulated and grounded by a category, a conceptional connection,
whereas in the mere judgment of perception this is lacking. Thus,
for example, the succession of two sensations becomes objective and
universally valid when it is thought as having its ground in the
fact that one phenomenon is the cause of the other. All particular
constructions of the spatial and temporal synthesis of sensations
become objects only by being combined according to a *rule of the
understanding*. In contrast with the individual mechanism of
ideation, in which individual sensations may order themselves,
separate and unite in any way whatever, stands objective thinking, which is equally valid for all, and is bound to fixed, co-
herent, ordered wholes, in which the connections are governed by
conceptions.

This is especially true in the case of relations in time. For since
phenomena of outer sense belong to the inner sense as "determinations of our mind," all phenomena without exception stand under
the Form of the inner sense, *i.e.* of time. Kant, therefore, sought
to show that between the categories and the particular Form of
perception in time a "schematism" obtains, which first makes it
possible at all to apply the Forms of the understanding to the
images of perception, and which consists in the possession by every
individual category of a schematic similarity with a particular form of
the time relation. In empirical knowledge we use this schematism
to interpret the empirically perceived time relation by the corresponding category [*e.g.* to apprehend regular succession as causality];
transcendental philosophy, conversely, has to seek the justification

of this procedure in the fact that the category, as a rule of the understanding, gives the corresponding time relations a rational basis as object of experience.

In fact, the individual consciousness finds in itself the contrast between a movement of ideas (say of the fancy), for which it claims no validity beyond its own sphere, and, on the other hand, an *activity of experience*, in the case of which it knows itself to be bound in a way that is likewise valid for all others. Only in this dependence consists the reference of thought to an object. But if it was now recognised that the ground of the objective validity of the time (and space) relation can rest only in its determination by a rule of the understanding, it is on the other hand a fact that the consciousness of the individual knows nothing of this co-operation of the categories in experience, and that he rather accepts the result of this co-operation as the objective necessity of his apprehension of the synthesis of sensations in space and time.

The production of the object, therefore, does not go on in the individual consciousness, but lies already at the basis of this consciousness; for this production, a higher common consciousness must therefore be assumed, which comes into the empirical consciousness of the individual, not with its functions, but only with their result. This Kant termed in the *Prolegomena, consciousness in general;* in the *Critique, transcendental apperception,* or the "*I*" [or "*self*," or "*ego*"].

Experience is accordingly the system of phenomena in which the spatial and temporal synthesis of sensation is determined by the rules of the understanding. Thus "Nature as phenomenon" is the object of an *a priori* knowledge; for the categories hold for all experience, because experience is grounded only through them.

7. The universal and necessary force and validity of the categories find expression in the *Principles of the Pure Understanding*, in which the conceptional Forms unfold themselves through the medium of the schematism. But here it is at once evident that the main weight of the Kantian doctrine of the categories falls upon the third group, and thus upon those problems in which he hoped "to solve Hume's doubt." From the categories of Quantity and Quality result only the "Axiom of Perception," that all phenomena are extensive magnitudes, and the "Anticipations of Empirical Perception" according to which the object of sensation is an intensive magnitude; in the case of Modality there result only definitions of the possible, actual, and necessary, under the name of the "Postulates of Empirical Thought." On the other hand, the *Analogies of Experience* prove that in Nature substance is permanent, and that

its quantum can be neither increased nor diminished, that all changes take place according to the law of cause and effect, and that all substances are in thorough-going reciprocity or inter-action.

These, therefore, are the universally and necessarily valid principles and highest premises of all natural science, which are universally and necessarily valid without any empirical proof; they contain what Kant calls the *metaphysics of Nature.* In order that they may be employed, however, upon the Nature given through our senses, they must pass through a mathematical formulation, because Nature is the system of sensations perceived in the Forms of space and time and ordered according to the categories. This transition is effected through the empirical conception of *motion,* to which all occurrence and change in Nature is theoretically to be reduced. At least, science of Nature, in the proper sense, reaches only so far as we can employ mathematics: hence Kant excluded psychology and chemistry from natural science as being merely descriptive disciplines. The "Metaphysical Elements of Natural Science" contain, accordingly, all that can be inferred universally and necessarily concerning the laws of motion, on the ground of the categories and of mathematics. The most important point in Kant's philosophy of Nature, as thus built up, is his *dynamic theory of matter,* in which he now deduces from the general principles of the *Critique* the doctrine already laid down in the "Natural History of the Heavens," that the substance of that which is movable in space is the product of two forces which maintain an equilibrium in a varying degree, — those of attraction and repulsion.

8. But in accordance with Kant's presuppositions, the above metaphysics of Nature can be only a *metaphysics of phenomena*: and no other is possible, for the categories are Forms for relating, and as such are in themselves empty; they can refer to an object only through the medium of perceptions, which present a manifold content to be combined. This perception, however, is, in the case of us men, only the sensuous perception in the forms of space and time, and as a content for their synthetic function we have only that given in sensations. Accordingly, *the only object of human knowledge is experience, i.e.* phenomenal appearance; and the division of objects of knowledge into phenomena and noumena, which has been usual since Plato, has no sense. A knowledge of things-in-themselves through "sheer reason," and extending beyond experience, is a nonentity, a chimera.

But has, then, the conception of the thing-in-itself any rational meaning at all? and is not, together with this, the designation of all objects of our knowledge as "phenomena," also without meaning?

This question was the turning-point of Kant's reflections. Hitherto all that the naïve conception of the world regards as " object " has been resolved partly into sensations, partly into synthetic Forms of perception and of the understanding; nothing seems to remain besides the individual consciousness as truly existing, except the "consciousness in general," the transcendental apperception. But where, then, are the "things," of which Kant declared that it had never come into his mind to deny their reality ?

The *conception of the thing-in-itself* can, to be sure, no longer have a positive content in the *Critique of Reason,* as it had with Leibniz, or in Kant's *Inaugural Dissertation;* it can no longer be the object of purely rational knowledge, it can no longer be an " object " at all. But it is at least no contradiction, merely to think it. Primarily, purely hypothetically, and as something the reality of which is neither to be affirmed nor to be denied, — a mere "problem." Human knowledge is limited to objects of experience, because the perception required for the use of the categories is in our case only the receptive sensuous perception in space and time. If we suppose that there is another kind of perception, there would be for this other objects, likewise, with the help of the categories. Such objects of a non-human perception, however, remain still only phenomena, though this perception again might be assumed as one which arranges the *given* contents of sensation in any manner whatever. Nevertheless, if one should think of a *perception of a non-receptive kind,* a perception which synthetically produced not only its Forms, but also its contents, — a truly "productive imagination," — its objects would necessarily be no longer phenomena, but things-in-themselves. Such a faculty would deserve the name of an *intellect- ual perception* (or intuition), or *intuitive intellect;* it would be the unity of the two knowing faculties of sensibility and understand- ing, which in man appear separated, although by their constant reference to each other they indicate a hidden common root. The possibility of such a faculty is as little to be denied as its reality is to be affirmed; yet Kant here indicates that we should have to think a supreme spiritual Being in this way. Noumena, or *things- in-themselves,* are therefore *thinkable in the negative sense as objects of a non-sensuous perception,* of which, to be sure, our knowledge can predicate absolutely nothing, — they are thinkable as *limiting con- ceptions* of experience.

And ultimately they do not remain so completely problematical as would at first appear. For if we should deny the reality of things-in-themselves, " all would be immediately resolved into phenomena," and we should thus be venturing the assertion that nothing is real except what appears to man, or to other sensuously receptive beings. But this assertion would be a presumption completely incapable of proof. Transcendental idealism must, therefore, not deny the reality of noumena; it must only remain conscious that they cannot in any wise become objects of human knowledge. Things-in-themselves must be thought, but are not knowable. In this way Kant won back the right to designate the objects of human knowledge as "*only* phenomena."

9. With this the way was marked out for the third part of the critique of the reason, the *Transcendental Dialectic.*[1] A metaphysics of that which cannot be experienced, or, as Kant prefers to say, of the supersensuous, is impossible. This must be shown by a criticism of the historical attempts which have been made with this in view, and Kant chose, as his actual example for this, the Leibnizo-Wolffian school-metaphysics, with its treatment of rational psychology, cosmology, and theology. But at the same time, it must be shown that that which is incapable of being experienced, which cannot be known, must yet necessarily be thought; and the *transcendental illusion* must be discovered, by which even the great thinkers have at all times been seduced into regarding this, which must necessarily be thought, as an object of possible knowledge.

To attain this end Kant proceeds from the antithesis between the activity of the understanding and the sensuous perception by the aid of which alone the former produces objective knowledge. The thinking, which is determined by the categories, puts the data of the sensibility into relation with one another in such a way, that every phenomenon is *conditioned* by other phenomena : but in this process the understanding, in order to think the individual phenomenon completely, must needs *grasp the totality of the conditions* by which this particular phenomenon is determined in its connections with the whole experience. But, in view of the endlessness of the world of phenomena in its relation to space and time, this demand cannot be fulfilled. For the categories are principles of relation between phenomena; they cognise the conditionality or conditional character of each phenomenon only *by means of other phenomena*, and demand for these again insight into their conditional nature as determined by others, and so on to infinity.[2] Out of this relation

---

[1] As regards the subject matter, the Transcendental Æsthetic, Analytic, and Dialetic, as the Introduction shows, form the three main co-ordinate parts of the *Critique ;* the formal schematism of the division which Kant imitated from the arrangement of logical text-books usual at that time, is, on the contrary, entirely irrelevant. The "Doctrine of Method" is in fact only a supplement extremely rich in fine observations.

[2] Cf. the similar thoughts in Nicolaus Cusanus and Spinoza, though there metaphysically applied ; above, pp. 347 and 419.

between understanding and sensibility result for human knowledge *necessary and yet insoluble problems;* these Kant calls Ideas, and the faculty requisite for this highest synthesis of the cognitions of the understanding he designates as *Reason* in the narrower sense.

If now the reason will represent to itself as solved, a problem thus set, the sought totality of conditions must be thought as some thing *unconditioned*, which, indeed, contains in itself the conditions for the infinite series of phenomena, but which is itself no longer conditioned. This conclusion of an infinite series, which for the knowledge of the understanding is in itself a contradiction, must nevertheless be thought, if the task of the understanding, which aims at totality in connection with the infinite material of the data of the senses, is to be regarded as performed. The Ideas are hence ideas or mental representations of the unconditioned, which must necessarily be thought without ever becoming object of knowledge, and the transcendental illusion into which metaphysics falls consists in regarding them as given, whereas they are only *imposed* or *set as a task* (*aufgegeben*). In truth they are not constitutive principles through which, as through the categories, objects of knowledge are produced, but only *regulative principles,* by which the understanding is constrained to seek for farther and farther connecting links in the realm of the conditioned of experience.

Of such Ideas Kant finds three ; the unconditioned for the totality of all phenomena of the inner sense, of all data of the outer sense, of all the conditioned in general, is thought respectively as the *soul, the world, and God.*

10. The criticism of rational psychology in the "Paralogisms of Pure Reason" takes the form of pointing out in the usual proofs for the substantiality of the *soul,* the *quaternio terminorum* of a confusion of the logical subject with the real substrate; it shows that the scientific conception of substance is bound to our perception of that which persists in space, and that it is therefore applicable only in the field of the external sense, and maintains that the Idea of the soul as an unconditioned real unity of all phenomena of the inner sense, is indeed as little capable of proof as it is of refutation, but is at the same time the heuristic principle for investigating the inter-connections of the psychical life.

In a similar way, the section on the "Ideal of the Reason" treats the Idea of *God.* Carrying out with greater precision his earlier treatise on the same subject, Kant destroys the cogency of the arguments brought forward for the existence of God. He combats the right of the *ontological* proof to infer existence from the conception alone; he shows that the *cosmological* proof involves a *petitio principii* when it seeks the "first cause" of all that is "contingent" in an "absolutely necessary" being; he proves that the teleological or *physico-theological* argument at the best — granted the beauty, harmony, and purposiveness or adaptation of the universe — leads to the ancient conception of a wise and good "Architect of the world." But he emphasises that the denial of God's existence is a claim which steps beyond the bounds of our experiential knowledge, and is as incapable of proof as the opposite, and that rather the belief in a living, Real unity of all reality constitutes the only powerful motive for empirical investigation of individual groups of phenomena.

Most characteristic by far, however, is Kant's treatment of the Idea of the world in the *Antinomies of Pure Reason.* These antinomies express the fundamental thought of the transcendental dialectic in the sharpest manner, by showing that when the universe is treated as the object of knowledge, propositions which are mutually contradictory can be maintained with equal right, in so far as we follow, on the one hand, the demand of the understanding for a completion of the series of phenomena, and on the other, the demand of the sensuous perception for an endless continuance of the same. Kant proves hence, in the "thesis," that the world must have a beginning and end in space and time, that as regards its substance it presents a limit to its divisibility, that events in it must have free, *i.e.* no longer causally conditioned, beginnings, and that to it must belong an absolutely necessary being, God; and in the antithesis he proves the contradictory opposite for all four cases. At the same time the complication is increased by the fact that the proofs (with one exception) are indirect, so that the thesis is proved by a refutation of the antithesis, the antithesis by refutation of the thesis; each assertion is therefore both proved and refuted. The solution of the antinomies in the case of the first two, the "mathematical," takes the form of showing that the principle of excluded third loses its validity where something is made the object of knowledge, which can never become such, as is the case with the universe. In the case of the third and fourth antinomies, the "dynamical," which concern freedom and God, Kant seeks to show (what, to be sure, is impossible in a purely theoretical way), that it is perhaps thinkable that the antitheses hold true for phenomena, and the theses, on the other hand, for the unknowable world of things-in-themselves. For this latter world, it is at least not a contradiction to think freedom and God, whereas neither is to be met with, it is certain, in our knowledge of phenomena.

§ 39. The Categorical Imperative.

H. Cohen, *Kant's Begründung der Ethik.* Berlin, 1877.
E. Arnoldt, *Kant's Idee vom höchsten Gut.* Königsberg, 1874.
B. Pünjer, *Die Religionsphilosophie Kant's.* Jena, 1874.
[N. Porter, *Kant's Ethics.* Chicago, 1886.]
[J. G. Schurmann, *Kantian Ethics and the Ethics of Evolution.* Lond. 1882.]

The synthetic function in the theoretical reason is the combination of mental presentations into perceptions, judgments, and Ideas. The *practical synthesis* is the relating of the will to a presented content, by which this latter becomes an *end.* This relating Form Kant carefully excluded from the primary conceptions of the knowing understanding; it is instead the *fundamental category of the practical use of the reason.* It gives no objects of knowledge, but instead, objects of will.

1. For the critique of the reason there rises from this the problem, whether there is a *practical synthesis a priori,* that is, whether there are *necessary and universally valid objects of willing;* or whether anything is to be found which the reason makes its end or demands *a priori, without any regard to empirical motives.* This universal and necessary object of the practical reason we call the *moral law.*

For it is clear for Kant from the outset, that the activity of pure reason in proposing ends to itself, if there is any such activity, must appear as a *command,* in the form of the *imperative,* as over against the empirical motives of will and action.   The will directed toward the particular objects and relations of experience is determined by these and dependent upon them; the pure rational will, on the contrary, can be determined only through itself.   It is hence *necessarily directed toward something else* than the natural impulses, and this something else, which the moral law requires as over against our inclinations, is called *duty.*

Hence the predicates of ethical judgment concern only this kind of determination of the will; they refer to the *disposition,* not to the act or to its external consequences.   Nothing in the world, says Kant,[1] can be called good without qualification except a Good Will; and this remains good even though its execution is completely restrained by external causes.   Morality as a quality of man is a *disposition conformable to duty.*

2. But it becomes all the more necessary to investigate as to

---

[1] *Grundlegung zur Metaphysik der Sitten,* I. (W., IV. 10 ff.); Abbott, p. 9.

whether there is such an *a priori* command of duty, and in what consists a law, to which obedience is required by the reason quite independently of all empirical ends.   To answer this question Kant proceeds from the teleological connections of the actual volitional life.   Experience of natural causal connections brings with it the consequence, that we are forced to will according to the *synthetic relation of end and means,* one thing for the sake of another.   From practical reflection on such relations arise (technical) rules of dexterity and ("practical") counsels of prudence.   They all assert, "If you will this or that, then you must proceed thus or so."   They are on this account *hypothetical imperatives.*   They presuppose a volition as actually present already, and demand on the ground of this the further act of will which is required to satisfy the first.

But the moral law cannot be dependent upon any object of will already existing in experience, and moral action must not appear as means in service of other ends.   The requirement of the moral command must be propounded and fulfilled *solely for its own sake.* It does not appeal to what the man already wishes on other grounds, but demands an act of will which has its worth in itself only, and the only truly moral action is one in which such a command is fulfilled without regard to any other consequences.   The moral law is a *command absolute,* a *categorical imperative.*   It holds unconditionally and absolutely, while the hypothetical imperatives are only relative.

If now it is asked, what is the content of the categorical imperative, it is clear that it can contain no empirical element : the demand of the moral law does not stand in relation to the "matter of the act of will."   For this reason happiness is not adapted to be the principle of morals, for the striving after happiness is already present empirically, it is not a demand of reason.   Eudæmonistic morals leads, therefore, to merely hypothetical imperatives ; for it, the ethical laws are only "counsels of prudence or sagacity" advising the best method of going to work to satisfy the natural will. But the demand of the moral law is just for a will other than the natural will; the moral law exists for a higher purpose than to make us happy.   If Nature had wished to place our destiny and vocation in happiness, it would have done better to equip us with infallible instincts than with the practical reason of conscience, which is continually in conflict with our impulses.[1]   The "happiness morals" is even, for Kant, the type of false morals, for in this the law always is that I should do something because I desire something

---

[1] *Grundlegung zur Metaphysik der Sitten,* IV. 12 f.; Abbott, p. 11.

else. Every such system of morals is *heteronomous;* it makes the practical reason dependent upon some thing given outside of itself, and this reproach applies to all attempts to seek the principle of morality in metaphysical conceptions, such as that of perfection. The theological morals is completely rejected by Kant with the greatest energy, for it combines all kinds of heteronomy when it sees the sanction in the divine will, the criterion in utility, and the motive in the expectation of reward and punishment.

3. The categorical imperative must be the expression of the *autonomy of the practical reason, i.e.* of the pure self-determination of the rational will. It concerns, therefore, solely the Form of willing, and requires that this should be a *universally valid law.* The will is heteronomous if it follows an empirically given impulse; it is autonomous only where it carries out a law given it by itself. The categorical imperative demands, therefore, that instead of act-ing according to impulses we should rather act according to *maxims,* and according to such as are adapted for a universal legislation for all beings who will rationally. *"Act as if the maxim from which you act were to become through your will a universal law of nature."*

This purely formal principle of conformity to law gains a mate-rial import by reflection upon the various kinds of worths. In the kingdom of ends that which is serviceable for some end, and can therefore be replaced by something else, has a price, but that only has *worth* or dignity, which is absolutely valuable in itself, and is the condition for the sake of which other things may become valu-able. This worth belongs in the highest degree to the moral law itself, and, therefore, the motive which stimulates man to obey this law must be nothing but *reverence for the law itself.* It would be dishonoured if it were fulfilled for the sake of any external advan-tage. The worth or dignity of the moral law, moreover, passes over to the man who is determined by this alone in the whole extent of his experience, and is able to determine himself by the law itself, to be its agent, and to identify himself with it. Hence *reverence for the worth of man* is for Kant the material principle of moral science. Man should do his duty not for the sake of advantage, but *out of reverence for himself,* and in his intercourse with his fellow-man he should make it his supreme maxim, never to treat him as a mere means for the attainment of his own ends, but always to honour in him the *worth of personality.*

From this Kant deduces a proud and strict system of morals [1] in

---

[1] *Metaphysische Anfangsgründe der Tugendlehre,* W., V. 221 ff.

which, as set forth in his old age, we cannot fail to discern the features of rigourism and of a certain pedantic stiffness. But the fundamental characteristic of the *contrast between duty and inclination* lies deeply rooted in his system. The principle of autonomy recognises as moral, only acts of will done in conformity to duty, and wholly out of regard for maxims; it sees in all motivation of moral action by natural impulses a falsification of pure morality. Only that which is done solely from duty is moral. The empirical impulses of human nature are, therefore, in themselves, ethically indifferent; but they become bad as soon as they oppose the demand of the moral law, and the moral life of man consists in realising the command of duty in the warfare against his inclinations.

4. The self-determination of the rational will is, therefore, the supreme requirement and condition of all morality. But it is impossible in the realm of the experience which is thought and known through the categories : for this experience knows only the determination of each individual phenomenon by others; self-determination, as the power *to begin* a series of the conditioned, is impossible according to the principles of cognition. This power with reference to the will we call *freedom*, as being an action which is not conditioned by others according to the schema of causality, but which is determined only through itself, and is on its part the cause of an endless series of natural processes. Hence if the theoretical reason, whose knowledge is limited to experience, had to decide as to the reality of freedom, it would necessarily deny it, but would thereby reject also the possibility of the moral life. But the *Critique of Pure Reason* has shown that the theoretical reason cannot assert anything whatever as to things-in-themselves, and that, accordingly, there is no contradiction in thinking the possibility of freedom for the supersensuous. But as it is evident that freedom must necessarily be real if morality is to be possible, the *reality of things-in-themselves and of the supersensuous,* which for the theoretical reason must remain always merely problematical, is herewith guaranteed.

This guarantee is, to be sure, not that of a proof, but that of a *postulate.* It rests upon the consciousness; *thou canst, for thou oughtest.* Just so truly as thou feelest the moral law within thee, so truly as thou believest in the possibility of following it, so truly must thou also believe in the conditions for this, viz. autonomy and freedom. Freedom is not an object of knowledge, but an object of faith, — but of a faith which holds as universally and necessarily in the realm of the supersensuous, as the principles of the understanding hold in the realm of experience, — an *a priori faith.*

Thus the practical reason becomes completely independent of the theoretical.   In previous philosophy "the primacy" of the theoretical over the practical reason had prevailed; knowledge had been assigned the work of determining whether and how there is freedom, and accordingly of deciding as to the reality of morality.   According to Kant, the reality of morality is the fact of the practical reason, and, therefore, we must believe in freedom as the condition of its possibility.   From this relation results, for Kant, *the primacy of the practical over the theoretical reason;* for the former is not only capable of guaranteeing that which the latter must decline to vouch for, but it appears also that the theoretical reason in those Ideas of the unconditioned in which it points beyond itself (§ 38, 9) is determined by the needs of the practical reason.

Thus there appears with Kant, in a new and completely original form, *the Platonic doctrine of the two worlds* of the sensuous and the supersensuous, of phenomena and things-in-themselves.   Knowledge controls the former, faith the latter; the former is the realm of necessity, the latter the realm of freedom.   The relation of antithesis and yet of mutual reference, which exists between these two worlds, shows itself best in the nature of man, who alone belongs in like measure to both.   So far as man is a member of the order of Nature he *appears* as *empirical character* — *i.e.* in his abiding qualities as well as in his individual decisions — as a necessary product in the causal connection of phenomena; but as a member of the supersensuous world *he is intelligible character, i.e.* a being whose nature is decided by free self-determination within itself.   The empirical character is only the manifestation, which for the theoretical consciousness is bound to the rule of causality, of the intelligible character, whose freedom is the only explanation of the feeling of responsibility as it appears in the *conscience.*

5. But freedom is not the only *postulate* of *a priori* faith.   The relations between the sensuous and the moral world demand yet a more general bond of connection, which Kant finds in the *conception of the highest good.*[1]   The goal of the sensuous will is happiness; the goal of the ethical will is virtue; these two cannot sustain to each other the relation of means to end.   The striving after happiness does not make an act virtuous; and virtue is neither permitted to aim at making man happy, nor does it actually do so.   Between the two no causal relation exists empirically, and ethically no teleological connection can be permitted to enter.   But since man belongs as well to the sensuous as to the ethical world, the "highest good" must consist for him in the *union of virtue and happiness.*   This

---

[1] *Critique of Prac. Reason,* Dialectic, W., IX. 225 ff.; [Abbott, 202 ff.].

last synthesis of practical conception, however, can be morally thought only in the form that *virtue alone is worthy of happiness.*

The demand of the moral consciousness, here expressed, is nevertheless not satisfied by the causal necessity of experience. Natural law is ethically indifferent, and affords no guarantee that virtue will necessarily lead to happiness; on the contrary, experience teaches rather that virtue requires renunciation of empirical happiness, and that want of virtue is capable of being united with temporal happiness. If, therefore, the ethical consciousness requires the *reality of the highest good,* faith must reach beyond the empirical life of man, and beyond the order of Nature, on into the supersensuous. It postulates a reality of personality which extends beyond the temporal existence — the *immortal life* — and a *moral order of the universe,* which is grounded in a Supreme Reason — in God.

Kant's *moral proof* for freedom, immortality, and God is, therefore, not a proof of knowledge, but of faith. Its postulates are the conditions of the moral life, and their reality must be believed in as fully as the reality of the latter. But with all this they remain knowable theoretically, as little as before.

6. *The dualism of Nature and morality* appears with Kant in its baldest form in his *Philosophy of Religion,* the principles of which, agreeably to his theory of knowledge, he could seek only in the practical reason; universality and necessity in relation to the supersensuous are afforded only by the ethical consciousness. Only that can be *a priori* in religion, which is based upon morals. Kant's religion of reason is, therefore, not a natural religion, but "moral theology." Religion rests upon *conceiving moral laws as divine commands.*

This religious form of morality Kant develops once more from the twofold nature of man. There are in him two systems of impulses, the sensuous and the moral; on account of the unity of the willing personality neither can be without relation to the other. Their relation should be, according to the moral demand, that of the subordination of the sensuous impulses to the moral; but as a matter of fact, according to Kant, the reverse relation naturally obtains with man,[1] and since the sensuous impulses are evil as soon as they even merely resist the moral, there is in man a *natural bent*

---

[1] The pessimistic conception of man's natural essence doubtless has with Kant its occasion in his religious education; but he guards himself expressly against the identification of his doctrine of the radical evil with the theological conception of hereditary sin; cf. *Rel. innerh. d. Grenze d. r. V.*, I. 4; W., VI. 201 ff. ⸱ ⌜Abbott, p. 347⌝.

to evil. This "radical evil" is not necessary; for otherwise there would be no responsibility for it. It is inexplicable, but it is a fact; it is a deed of intelligible freedom. The task which follows from this for man is the *reversal of the moving springs*, which is to be brought about by the warfare between the good and evil principle within him. But in the above-described perverted condition, the brazen majesty of the moral law works upon man with a terror that dashes him down, and he needs, therefore, to support his moral motives, *faith in a divine power*, which imposes upon him the moral law as its command, but also grants him the help of *redeeming love* to enable him to obey it.

From this standpoint Kant interprets the essential portions of Christian doctrine into a "pure moral religion," viz. the ideal of the moral perfection of man in the Logos, redemption through vicarious love, and the mystery of the new birth. He thus restores to their rightful place, from which they had been displaced by the rationalism of the Enlightenment, the truly religious motives which are rooted in the *felt need of a redemption*, — though he does this in a form which is free from the historical faith of orthodoxy. But the true Church, for him also, is only the invisible, the moral king-dom of God, the ethical community of the redeemed. The historical manifestations of the moral community of men are the Churches; they need the means of revelation and of "statutory" faith. But they have the task of putting this means into the service of the moral life, and if instead of this they lay the main weight upon the statutory, they fall into service for a reward, and into hypocrisy.

7. It is connected with his restriction of ethical judgment by making it apply only to the disposition, that in his *Philosophy of Right* Kant pursued that direction which treats the same, so far as possible, independently of morals. Kant distinguished (even with regard to ethical valuation) between *morality of disposition* and *legality of action*, between voluntary obedience to the moral law and external conformity of action to what is demanded by posi-tive law. Actions are subject to compulsion, dispositions never. While morals speaks of the duties of the disposition, law or right is employed with the external duties of action which can be en-forced, and does not ask as to the disposition with which they are fulfilled or broken.

And yet Kant makes *freedom*, which is the central conception of his whole practical philosophy, the basis also of his science of right. For right or law is also a demand of the practical reason, and has in this its *a priori*, valid principle: it cannot therefore be deduced as a product of empirical interest, but must be understood from the general rational vocation or destiny of man. This latter is the vocation to freedom. The community of men consists of those beings that are destined for ethical freedom, but are yet in the natural state of caprice or arbitrary will, in which they mutually disturb and check each other in their spheres of activity. Law has for its task to establish the conditions under which the will of the one can be united with the will of another according to a universal law of freedom, and, by enforcing these conditions, to make sure the freedom of personality.

From this principle follows analytically, according to Kant's deduction, all private law, public law, and international law. At the same time, it is interesting to observe how the principles of his theory of morals are everywhere authoritative in this construction. Thus, in private law it is a far-reaching principle — corresponding to the categorical imperative — that man must never be used as a thing. So, too, the penal law of the state is grounded not by the task of maintaining the state of right, but by the ethical necessity of retribution.

Law in a state of nature is therefore valid only in a provisory way; it is completely, or, as Kant says, peremptorily, valid, only when it can be certainly enforced, that is, in the state. The supreme rule for justice in the state, Kant finds in this, that nothing should be decreed and carried out which might not have been resolved upon if the state had come into existence by a *contract*. The contract theory is here not an explanation of the empirical origin of the state, but a norm for its task. This norm can be fulfilled with any kind of constitution, provided only law really rules, and not arbitrary caprice. Its realisation is surest if the three public functions of legislation, administration and judicial procedure are independent of each other, and if the legislative power is organised in the "republican" form of the representative system, — a provision which is not excluded by a monarchical executive. It is only by this means, Kant thinks, that the freedom of the individual will be secured, so far as this can exist without detriment to the freedom of others; and not until all states have adopted this constitution can the state of Nature in which they now find themselves in their relations to each other, give place to a state of law. Then, too, the law of nations, which is now only provisory, will become "peremptory."

Upon foundations of philosophy of religion and philosophy of law is built up, finally, Kant's theory of *history*.[1] This took form

---

[1] Cf. besides the treatises cited on pp. 417–422, the treatises, *Idea of a Universal History from a Cosmopolitical Point of View* (1784) [tr. by Hastie in

in dependence upon the theories of Rousseau and Herder, a dependence which follows from the antithesis between those authors. Kant can see in history neither the aberration from an originally good condition of the human race, nor the necessary, self-intelligible development of man's original constitution. If there ever was a primitive paradisiacal state of humanity, it was the *state of innocence* in which man, living entirely according to his natural impulses, was as yet entirely unconscious of his ethical task. The *beginning of the work of civilisation*, however, was possible only through a break with the state of Nature, since it was in connection with its transgression that the moral law came to consciousness. This (theoretically incomprehensible) *"Fall"* was the beginning of history. Natural impulse, previously ethically indifferent, now became evil, and was to be opposed.

Since then the *progress of history* has consisted *not in a growth of human happiness*, but in approximation to ethical perfection, and in the extension of the *rule of ethical freedom*. With deep earnestness Kant takes up the thought that the development of civilisation succeeds only at the cost of individual happiness. He who takes this latter for his standard must speak only of a retrogression in history. The more complicated relations become, the more the vital energy of civilisation grows, by so much the more do individual wants increase, and the less is the prospect of satisfying them. But just this refutes the opinion of the Enlighteners, as if happiness were man's vocation. The ethical development of the whole, the control of practical reason, grows in an *inverse ratio* to the empirical satisfaction of the individual. And since history represents the outer social life of humanity, its goal is the completion of right and law, the establishing of the best political constitution among all peoples, perpetual peace — a goal whose attainment, as is the case with all ideals, lies at an infinite distance.

§ 40. Natural Purposiveness.

A. Stadler, *Kant's Teleologie.* Berlin, 1874.
H. Cohen, *Kant's Begründung der Æsthetik.* Berlin, 1889.
[J. H. Tufts, *The Sources and Development of Kant's Teleology.* Chicago, 1892.]

By his sharp formulation of the antithesis of Nature and Freedom, of necessity and purposiveness (or adaptation to ends), the theoretical aud practical reason diverge so widely in Kant's system, that the unity of the reason seems endangered. The critical philosophy needs, therefore, in a manner that prefigures the methodical development of its system,[1] a *third principle* that shall afford a definitive mediation, and in which the synthesis *of the above opposites* shall be effected.

1. *Psychologically,* the sphere in which this problem is to be solved can, in accordance with the triple division adopted by Kant (cf. § 36, 8), be only the *faculty of feeling or "approval."* This, in fact, takes an intermediate position between ideation and desire. Feeling or approval presupposes a complete idea of the object, — complete in the theoretical sense, — and sustains a synthetic relation to this; and this *synthesis* as a feeling of pleasure or pain, or as approval or disapproval, always expresses in some way that the object in question is felt by the subject to be either *purposive, i.e.* adapted to its end, or not to the purpose.

The standard of this valuation may have existed beforehand as a conscious design, forming thus a case of intentional volition, and in such cases the objects are termed *useful* or injurious; but there are also feelings which, without being referred to any conscious purposes whatever, characterise their objects immediately as *agreeable* or disagreeable, and in these also a determination with reference to an end must be somehow authoritative.

The critique of the reason, accordingly, has to ask, Are there *feelings a priori,* or *approvals that have universal and necessary validity?* and it is clear that the decision upon this case is dependent upon the nature of the ends which determine the feelings and approvals in question. With regard to the purposes of the will, this question has been already decided by the *Critique of the Practical Reason;* the only end of the conscious will which has *a priori* validity is the fulfilling of the categorical imperative, and on this side, therefore, only the feelings of approval or disapproval in which we employ the ethical predicates "good" and "bad," can be regarded as necessary and universally valid. For this reason the new problem restricts itself to the *a priori* character of those feelings in which no conscious purpose or design precedes. But these, as may be seen from the beginning, are the feelings of the *Beautiful* and the *Sublime.*

2. But the problem widens upon another side, when we take into consideration the *logical* functions which are concerned in all feel-

---

[1] Cf. note at the close of the Introduction of the *Critique of Judgment,* W.-VII. 38 f.

ings and approvals. The judgments in which these are expressed are evidently all synthetic. Predicates such as agreeable, useful, beautiful, and good, are not analytically contained in the subject, but express the worth of the object with reference to an end; they are estimations of adaptation, and contain in all cases the *subordination of the object to its end.* Now in the psychological scheme which lies at the basis of the *Critique of Pure Reason,* Kant designates the faculty of subsuming the particular under the general by the name *Judgment.* And this, too, was regarded as playing among the theoretical functions, also, the mediating part between Reason and Understanding, in such a sort that the former gives principles, the latter objects, while the Judgment performs the task of applying the principles to the objects.

But in its theoretical use the Judgment is analytical, since it determines its objects by general conceptions according to rules of formal logic; the attainment of a correct conclusion depends only on finding the appropriate minor for a given major, or *vice versa.* In contrast with this determining Judgment, which thus needs no "Critique," Kant sets the *reflecting* Judgment, in the case of which the synthesis consists just in subordination to an end. And accordingly the problem of the *Critique of the Judgment* takes this formulation : *Is it a priori possible to judge Nature to be adapted to an end?* Evidently this is the highest synthesis of the critical philosophy; the *application of the category of the practical reason to the object of the theoretical.* It is clear from the outset that this application itself can be neither theoretical nor practical, neither *a knowing nor a willing :* it is only a *looking at Nature from the point of view of purposiveness or adaptation to ends.*

If the reflecting Judgment gives to this contemplation the direction of judging Nature with regard to her adaptation to the contemplating subject as such, it proceeds *æsthetically, i.e.* having regard to our mode of feeling or sensibility ;[1] if, on the contrary, it regards Nature as if she were purposive in herself, then it proceeds *teleologically* in the narrower sense, and so the *Critique of the Judgment* is divided into the investigation of æsthetic and teleological problems.

3. In the first part Kant is primarily concerned to separate the *æsthetic judgment* with exactness from the kinds of judgments of feeling or approval which border upon it on both sides, and to this end he proceeds from the point of view of the feeling of the *beauti-*

---

[1] *Empfindungsweise;* thus Kant justifies his change in terminology, W., VII. 28 ff. ; cf. II. 60 f. and above, p. 483 f.

ful. The beautiful shares with the good the *a priori* character, but the good is that which agrees with the end presented as a norm in the moral law, while the beautiful, on the contrary, pleases *without a conception.* For this reason, also, it is impossible to set up a universal criterion which shall contain a content according to which beauty shall be judged with logical clearness. An æsthetic doctrine is impossible; there is only a "*Critique of the Taste,*" that is, an investigation as to the possibility of the *a priori* validity of æsthetic judgments.

On the other hand, the beautiful shares with the agreeable its conceptionless quality, the absence of a conscious standard of judgment, and, therefore, the immediacy of the impression. But the distinction here lies in the fact that the agreeable is something individually and contingently gratifying, whereas the beautiful forms the object of universal and necessary pleasure.[1] The principle that there is no disputing over tastes, is true only in the sense that in matters of taste nothing is to be effected by proofs with conceptions, but this does not exclude the possibility of an appeal to universally valid feelings.

Finally, the beautiful distinguishes itself from both the good and the agreeable, in that it is the object of a *completely disinterested pleasure.* This appears in the circumstance that the *empirical reality* of its object is a matter of complete indifference for the æsthetic judgment. The hedonic feelings all presuppose the material presence of the phenomena which excite them; ethical approval or disapproval concerns just the realisation of the moral end in willing and acting; the æsthetic feelings, on the contrary, require as their condition a *pure delight in the mere represented image* of the object, whether the same is objectively present for knowledge or not. The æsthetic life lacks the power of the feelings of personal weal and woe, just as it lacks the earnestness of a universally worthy work for ethical ends; it is the mere *play* of ideas in the imagination.

Such a delight which relates *not* to the object, but only to the *image of the object,* cannot concern the objective material of the object, —for this always stands in relation to the interests of the subject, — but only the *form* in which the object is *presented to the mind;* and in this, therefore, if anywhere, is to be sought the ground of the *a priori* synthesis which belongs to the æsthetic judgments. The purposiveness of æsthetic objects cannot consist in their adaptation to some interest or other; it can be only in their adaptation to the

---

[1] Cf. F. Blencke, *Kant's Unterscheidung des Schönen vom Angenehmen* (Strassburg, 1889), where the analogy to the judgments of perception and of experience is emphasised.

knowing Forms, by the aid of which they are imaged in the mind. But the faculties which are active in presenting every object are sensibility and understanding. The *feeling of beauty* arises, therefore, in connection with those objects in the apprehension of which in the imagination sensibility and understanding co-operate in harmonious manner. Such objects are purposive with regard to their working upon our ideational activity, and to this relates the disinterested delight which manifests itself in the feeling of their beauty.[1]

But this relation to the formal principles of objective ideation has its ground, not in merely individual activities, but in the "consciousness in general," in the "supersensuous substrate of humanity." On this account the feeling of a fitness or purposiveness of objects with reference to this consciousness in general is *universally communicable*, though not capable of proof by conceptions, and from this is explained the *a priori* character of the æsthetic judgments.

4. While the "undesigned fitness" or appropriateness of the beautiful is thus set in relation with the working of the object upon the cognitive functions, Kant conceives the nature of the *sublime* from the point of view of an adaptation of the working of the object to the relation between the sensuous and supersensuous parts of human nature.

While the beautiful signifies a delightful rest in the play of the knowing faculties, the impression of the sublime is effected through the medium of a painful feeling of inadequacy. In the presence of the immeasurable greatness or overpowering might of objects, we feel the inability of our sensuous perception to master them, as an oppression and a casting down; but the supersensuous power of our reason raises itself above this our sensuous insufficiency. If here the imagination has to do only with extensive magnitudes, — the mathematically sublime, — then the firmly shaping activity of the theoretical reason gains the victory; but if, on the contrary, it has to do with the relations of power, — the dynamically sublime, — then the superiority of our moral worth to all the power of Nature comes to consciousness. In both cases the discomfort over our sensuous inferiority is richly outweighed and overcome by the triumph of our higher rational character. And since this is the appropriate

---

[1] [A fragment published by Reicke in his *Lose Blätter aus Kant's Nachlass* (B. II. p. 112) shows that Kant at one time connected this adaptation with the psychological and physiological conception of a general furtherance of life, whether through the senses or through the play of intellectual faculties. Cf. J. H. Tufts, *op. cit.*, p. 35 f.]

relation of the two sides of our being, these objects have an exalting, "*subliming*" effect, and produce the feeling of a delight of the reason, and this feeling, again, because it is based only upon the relation of our ideational Forms, is universally communicable and of *a priori* operation.

5. Kant's æsthetic theory, accordingly, in spite of its "subjective" point of departure, takes essentially the course of an explanation of the beautiful and the sublime *in Nature;* and determines the same through the relation of the *ideational Forms.* Hence the philosopher finds *pure* beauty only where the æsthetic judgment relates solely to forms that have no meaning. Where with the delight there is mingled a regard for the meaning of the forms for any norm whatever, however indefinite, there we have *dependent* beauty. This appears everywhere where the æsthetic judgment is directed toward objects in which our thought puts a reference to an end. Such norms of dependent beauty rise necessarily as soon as we contemplate in the individual phenomenon the relation to the class which it represents. There is no norm of beauty for landscapes, arabesques, or flowers, but there may be such perhaps for the higher types of the organic world. Such norms are æsthetic *ideals,* and the true ideal of the æsthetic judgment is *man.*

The presentation of the ideal is *art,* the power of æsthetic production. But while this is a function of man which is performed with reference to an end, its product will make the impression of the beautiful only when it appears as undesigned, disinterested, and free from the attempt to represent a conception, as is the case with the beauty of Nature. *Technical art* produces structures corresponding to definite ends according to rules and designs, — structures which are adapted to satisfy definite interests. *Fine art* must work upon the feeling as does a purposeless product of Nature; it must "be able to be regarded as Nature."

This, therefore, is the secret of artistic creation, and the characteristic element in it, viz. that the mind which builds with a purpose works, nevertheless, in the same way as Nature, which builds without designs and disinterestedly. The great artist does not create according to general rules; he creates the rules themselves in his involuntary work; he is original and prototypal. *Genius* is an *intelligence that works like Nature.*

In the realm of man's rational activity the desired synthesis of freedom and nature, of purposiveness and necessity, of practical and theoretical function, is then represented by genius, which with undesigning purposiveness or appropriateness creates the work of fine art.

6. In the Critique of the *Teleological* Judgment the most prominent task is to establish the relations which, from the points of view of transcendental idealism, exist between the scientific explanation of Nature and the consideration of the adaptation that dwells within her. The *theory of natural science* can in all lines be only *mechanical.* "End" (*Zweck*) is not a category or a constitutive principle of objective knowledge: all explanation of Nature consists in pointing out the causal necessity with which one phenomenon produces another; a phenomenon can never be made intelligible by emphasising its adaptation or fitness. Such "lazy" teleology is the death of all philosophy of Nature. The apprehension of purposiveness can, therefore, never profess to be an act of knowledge.

But, on the other hand, the standpoint of the mechanical explanation of Nature would give us the right to completely reject teleological consideration of Nature, only in case we were in a position to make intelligible with the aid of scientific conceptions the whole system of experience, even to the last remnant, in principle at least. But should points be found where scientific theory is inadequate for the explanation of the given material, not indeed on account of the limited nature of the material hitherto available in human experience, but on account of the permanent form of the principle which determines this material, then in these points the possibility of supplementing our knowledge by a teleological consideration must be conceded, if, at the same time, it appears that that which is mechanically inexplicable makes upon us the inevitable impression of the purposive. Critical teleology can, therefore, concern only the *limiting conceptions of the mechanical explanation of Nature.*

The first of these is *Life.* A mechanical explanation of the organism has not only not yet succeeded, but it is, according to Kant, impossible in principle. All life can be explained only through other life. We are to understand the individual functions of organisms through the mechanical connection of their parts with each other and with the environment; but we shall always be obliged to bring into our account the peculiar nature of organised matter and its capacity of reaction, as a factor incapable of further reduction. An archæologist of Nature may trace back the genealogy of life, the origination of one species from another according to mechanical principles as far as possible;[1] he will always be obliged to stop with an *original organisation* which he cannot explain through the mere mechanism of inorganic matter.

---

[1] The passages, in which Kant anticipated the latter theory of descent, are collected in Fr. Schultze, *Kant und Darwin* (Jena, 1874).

This explanation is impossible because the essential nature of an organism is, that the whole is determined by the parts just as the part is determined by the whole, — that every member is both cause and effect of the whole. This *reciprocal causality* is incomprehensible mechanically : the organism is the miracle in the world of experience.[1] It is just this inter-related play of forms and forces which in the organism makes the *impression of the purposive,* or of adaptation to an end. Therefore the teleological view of organisms is *necessary and universally valid.* But it must never profess to be anything else than a mode of consideration. Thought must never be satisfied with this in an individual case ; but the insight into this purposeful activity must rather serve as a *heuristic principle* for seeking out the mechanical connections by which this purposeful vitality realises itself in each particular case.

7. A second limit of the knowledge of Nature Kant designates by the name of the *Specification of Nature.* From pure reason arise the general Forms of the uniformity of Nature [*i.e.* causality, etc.], but only these. The *particular laws of Nature* do indeed range themselves beneath those general laws, but do not follow from them. Their particular content is only empirical, *i.e.* from the standpoint of pure reason it is contingent, and has only the force and validity of an actual matter of fact,[2] [not that of *a priori* necessity]. It is never to be understood why there is just this and not some other content. But at the same time, this particular aspect of Nature proves completely purposive ; on the one hand, with reference to our knowledge, since the wealth of the matter of fact in our experience shows itself to be adapted to be ordered under the *a priori* Forms of experience, — and on the other hand, as purposive in itself, also, inasmuch as the whole varied multiplicity of the given fits together to form a concrete world of reality, which is objectively unitary.

In this lie the reasons *a priori for regarding Nature as a whole from the point of view of purposiveness,* and for seeing in the vast mechanism of her causal connections the realising of a *supreme end of reason.* But in accordance with the primacy of the practical reason, this end can be none other than the *moral law,* and thus the teleological consideration issues in the moral faith in the divine world-order.

Finally, if we consider Nature as purposive, in the sense that in

---

[1] Cf. above, p. 480.

[2] Here Kant joins on in an extremely interesting manner to the latest speculations of the Leibnizian Monadology ; cf. above, p. 425 [cf. further on this point *Ueber eine Entdeckung, etc.,* and J. Dewey, *Leibniz's New Essays,* last chapter].

it the universal Forms and the particular contents completely harmonise with each other, then the divine mind, as the reason which creates the content at the same time with its Forms, appears as *intellectual perception or intuitive understanding.*[1]   In this conception the ideas of the three Critiques run together.

---

[1] *Critique of Judg.*, § 77.   Cf. G. Thiele, *Kant's Intellectuelle Anschauung* (Halle, 1876).

CHAPTER II.

THE DEVELOPMENT OF IDEALISM.

R. Haym, *Die romantische Schule.* Berlin, 1870.
[A. Seth, *From Kant to Hegel.* Lond. 1882.]

THE development of the principles won by Kant, to the comprehensive systems of German philosophy, took place under the co-operation of very different kinds of circumstances. Externally, it was of primary importance that the doctrine of criticism, after at first experiencing the fortune of being neglected and misunderstood, was first raised as a standard by the leading spirits of the University of *Jena*, and made the centre of a brilliant teaching activity. But in this lay the incitement to build out a unified and impressive *system of instruction*, the foundations of which Kant had laid by a careful separation and fine arrangement of philosophical problems. The systematic impulse ruled philosophical thought at no period so energetically as at this, and this was due in good part to the desires of an audience in a state of high and many-sided excitement, which demanded from the teacher a complete scientific *Weltanschauung.*

But in Jena philosophy found itself close by *Weimar*, the residence of Goethe, and the main literary city of Germany. In constant personal contact, *poetry and philosophy* mutually stimulated each other, and after Schiller had joined the thoughts of the two, their interaction became constantly more intimate and deep with their rapid forward movement.

A third factor was of a purely philosophical nature. A coincidence that was rich in results willed that just at the time when the Critique of Reason of the "all-crushing" Königsberger began to break its path, the most firmly articulated and most influential of all metaphysical systems, the type of "dogmatism," became known in Germany — *Spinozism.* Through the strife between Jacobi and Mendelssohn, which related to Lessing's attitude to Spinoza, the latter's doctrine was brought into the most lively interest, and thus, in spite of the deep opposition which prevails between the two, Kant and Spinoza became the two poles about which the thought of the following generation moved.

The predominance of the Kantian influence may be chiefly recognised in that the common character of all these systems is *idealism ;*[1] they all develop out of the antagonistic thoughts which were interwoven in Kant's treatment of the *conception thing-in-itself.* After a short time of critical hesitation, *Fichte, Schelling,* and *Hegel* took the lead in the unresting effort to understand the world as a *System of Reason.* Over against the bold energy of metaphysical speculation of these thinkers, which was extended by numerous disciples to a many-coloured variety, there appears in men like *Schleiermacher* and *Herbart* the Kantian reminder of the limits of human knowledge; while, on the other hand, the same motive unfolded in the construction of a *Metaphysics of the Irrational* in *Schelling's* later doctrine, and with *Schopenhauer.*

Common to all these systems, however, is the all-sidedness of philosophical interest, the wealth of creative thoughts, the fineness of feeling for the needs of modern culture, and the victorious power of an elaboration from the point of view of a principle, of the historical material of ideas.

The *Critique of the Pure Reason* found little regard at first, and then later violent opposition. The most important impetus to this was given by Friedrich Heinrich **Jacobi** (1743–1819, finally President of the Munich Academy). His main treatise bears the title, *David Hume über den Glauben, oder Idealismus und Realismus* (1787); in addition to this the treatise *Ueber das Unternehmen des Kriticismus die Vernunft zu Verstande zu bringen* (1802). The treatise *Von den göttlichen Dingen und ihrer Offenbarung* (1811) was directed against Schelling. Cf. also his introduction to his philosophical writings in the second volume of the complete edition (6 vols., Leips. 1812–1825). His main disciple was Fr. **Köppen** (1775–1858 ; *Darstellung des Wesens der Philosophie*, Nuremberg, 1810 ; cf. on him the art. *K.* by W. Windelband in *Ersch u. Gruber's Enc.*).

As further opponents of Kant are to be named Gottlob Ernst **Schulze** (1761–1823), the author of the anonymous writing, *Ænesidemus oder über die Fundamente der Elementarphilosophie* (1792), and of a *Kritik der theoretischen Philosophie* (Hamburg, 1801) ; J. G. **Hamann** (cf. above, p. 510), whose "review" of the *Critique* was first printed in 1801 in Reinhold's *Beiträgen,*

---

[1] Let it be remarked here at the outset that not only the main series of the development from Reinhold to Fichte, Schelling, Krause, Schleiermacher, and Hegel is idealistic, but also the series which is usually opposed to this, Herbart and Schopenhauer, in so far, that is, as by "idealism" is understood the dissolution or resolution (*Auflösung*) of the world of experience in the process of consciousness. Herbart and Schopenhauer are "idealists" in the same degree as Kant; they posit things-in-themselves, but the world of the senses is to them also a "phenomenon of consciousness." With Schopenhauer this is usually noted. With Herbart, on the contrary, the circumstance that he called the things-in-themselves "Reals" (*Realen*), in connection with the fact that for entirely other reasons he opposed the Fichte-Hegel line of thought, has led to the completely distorted and misleading mode of expression which has run through all previous text-books of the history of philosophy, of terming his doctrine "realism," and him in opposition to the "idealists" a "realist."

and G. **Herder** in his treatise, *Verstand und Vernunft, eine Metakritik zur Kritik der reinen Vernunft* (1799), also in the *Kalligone*, 1800.

Jac. Sig. **Beck** (1761–1842 ; *Einzig möglicher Standpunkt, aus welchem die kritische Philosophie beurtheilt werden muss*, Riga, 1796) worked more positively in the development of the Kantian doctrine, as did also Salomon **Maimon** (died 1800 ; *Versuch einer Transscendentalphilosophie*, 1790 ; *Versuch einer neuen Logik*, 1794 ; *Die Kategorien des Aristoteles*, 1794 ; cf. J. Witte, *S. M.*, Berlin, 1876).

In Jena the Kantian philosophy was introduced by Professor Erh. **Schmid** ; its main organ was the *Allgemeine Litteraturzeitung*, which appeared there after 1785, edited by Schütz and Hufeland. The greatest success for extending the doctrine of Criticism was gained by K. L. **Reinhold's** *Briefe über die kantische Philosophie*, which first appeared in Wieland's *Deutscher Merkur* (1786).

The same author begins also the series of re-shapings and transformations of the doctrine. Karl Leonh. Reinhold (1758–1823 ; fled from the cloister of the Barnabites in Vienna ; 1788, Professor in Jena ; from 1794 Professor in Kiel) wrote *Versuch einer neuen Theorie des menschlichen Vorstellungsvermögens* (Jena, 1789) and *Das Fundament des philosophischen Wissens* (1791). Later, after many changes in his standpoint, he fell into fantasticalness and was forgotten. His teaching presented in his Jena period gave in crude outlines a superficially systematic exposition, which soon became the school-system of the "Kantians." To tear from forgetfulness the names of these numerous men is not for this place.

Much finer, richer, and more independent was the work which Fr. **Schiller** gave to Kant's ideas. Of his philosophical writings are here principally to be named *On Grace and Dignity*, 1793 ; *On the Sublime*, 1793 ; *Letters upon the Æsthetical Education of Man*, 1795 ; *On Naïve and Sentimental Poetry*, 1796 [Eng. tr. Bohn Library]. In addition to these the philosophical poems such as *Die Künstler*, *Ideal und Leben*, and the correspondence with Körner, Goethe, and W. v. Humboldt. Cf. K. Tomaschek, *Sch. in seinem Verhältniss zur Wissenschaft*, Vienna, 1862 ; K. Twesten, *Sch. in seinem Verhältniss zur Wissenschaft*, Berlin, 1863 ; Kuno Fischer, *Sch. als Philosoph*, 2d ed., 1891 ; Fr. Ueberweg, *Sch. als Historiker und Philosoph*, pub. by Brasch, Leips. 1884.

Johann Gottlieb **Fichte**, born 1762, at Rammenau in Lusatia, educated in the "Princes' School" at Pforta and at the University of Jena, after he had experienced many changes of fortune as a private teacher and had become famous by his *Kritik aller Offenbarung*, which appeared by chance anonymously, and was universally ascribed to Kant (1792), was called in 1794, while living in Zurich, to become Reinhold's successor as Professor at Jena. After a brilliant activity there, he was dismissed in 1799, on account of the "atheism controversy " (cf. his *Appellation an das Publicum* and the *Gerichtliche Verantwortungsschrift*), and went to Berlin, where he came into connection with the Romanticists. In 1805 he was for a time assigned to the University of Erlangen ; in 1806 he went to Königsberg, and then returned to Berlin, where in the winter of 1807 to 1808 he delivered the *Reden an die deutsche Nation.* At the newly founded Berlin University he acted as Professor and as the first Rector. He died, 1814, of hospital fever. His main writings are *Grundlage der gesammten Wissenschaftslehre*, 1794 ; *Grundriss des Eigenthümlichen der Wissenschaftslehre*, 1795 [these two, together with other minor works, are translated by A. E. Kroeger, under the title *The Science of Knowledge*, Lond. 1889] ; *Naturrecht*, 1796 [tr. by A. E. Koeger, *The Science of Rights*, Lond. 1889] ; the two *Introductions to the Wissenschaftslehre*, 1797 ; *System der Sittenlehre*, 1798 ; *Die Bestimmung des Menschen*, 1800 ; *Der geschlossene Handelsstaat*, 1801 ; *Ueber das Wesen des Gelehrten*, 1805 ; *Grundzüge des gegenwärtigen Zeitalters*, 1806 ; *Anweisung zum seligen Leben*, 1806 [of the last five all but the second are trans. by W. Smith, *Fichte's Popular Works*, Lond. 1889. There are also translations and criticisms in *Jour. of Spec. Phil.*] ; Works, 8 vols., Berlin, 1845 f. ; Post. works, 3 vols., Bonn, 1834 ; *Life and Correspondence*, Sulzbach, 1830 ; *Correspondence with Schelling*, Leips. 1856 ; cf. J. H. Löwe, *Die Philos. Fichte's*, Stuttgart, 1862 ; R. Adamson, *Fichte*, Lond. 1881 ; [also art. in *Enc. Brit.* ; C. C. Everett, *Fichte's Science of Knowledge*, Chicago, 1883].

Friedrich Wilhelm Joseph **Schelling**, born, 1775, at Leonberg in Würtemberg, came to Leipsic in 1796 after his education in Tübingen, was made Professor in Jena in 1798, and in Würzburg in 1803.   Called in 1806 to the Munich Academy, and for a time (1820–1826) active at the Erlangen University, he entered in 1827 the newly founded University of Munich.   From here he accepted, in 1840, a call to Berlin, where he soon gave up his activity as a teacher. He died in 1854 in Ragaz.   Cf. *Aus Sch.'s Leben in Briefen*, ed. by Plitt, Leips. 1869 f. ; *Caroline, Briefe*, etc., ed. by G. Waitz, Leips. 1871.   Schelling's development as philosopher and author falls into five periods : (1) Philosophy of Nature, *Ideen zu einer Philos. der Natur*, 1797 ; *Von der Weltseele*, 1798 ; *Erster Entwurf eines Systems der Naturphilosophie*, 1799 ; (2) Æsthetic Idealism, *Der transcendentale Idealismus*, 1800 ; *Vorlesungen über die Philosophie der Kunst;* (3) Absolute Idealism, *Darstellung meines Systems der Philosophie*, 1801 ; *Bruno, oder über das natürliche und göttliche Princip der Dinge*, 1802 ; *Vorlesungen über die Methode des akademischen Studiums*, 1803 ; (4) his Doctrine of Freedom, *Philosophie und Religion*, 1804 ; *Untersuchungen über das Wesen der menschlichen Freiheit*, 1809 ; *Denkmal der Schrift Jacobi's von den göttlichen Dingen*, 1812 ; (5) Philosophy of Mythology and Revelation, *Lectures* in Part II. of the writings ; Collected works, 14 vols., Stuttg. and Augsb. 1856–1861 ; [J. Watson, *Schelling's Transcendental Idealism*, Chicago, Griggs series].

Among the thinkers who stood in close relation to Schelling may be noticed, of the Romantic School, Fr. **Schlegel** (1772–1829 ; Characteristics and Criticisms in the "Athenæum," 1799 f. ; *Lucinde*, 1799 ; *Philosophical Lectures*, in the years 1804–6, ed. by Windischmann, 1836 f. ; Complete writings, 15 vols., Vienna, 1846 [Eng. tr. of the *Philosophy of History* and of the *Philosophy of Life and of Language* in Bohn Library]) and **Novalis** (Fr. v. Hardenberg, 1772–1801), also K. W. F. **Solger** (1780–1819 ; *Erwin*, 1815 ; *Philosophische Gespräche*, 1817 ; *Vorlesungen über Æsthetik*, ed. by Heyse, 1829) ; further, Lor. **Oken** (1779–1851 ; *Lehrbuch der Naturphilosophie*, Jena, 1809 ; cf. A. Ecker, *L. O.*, Stuttgart, 1880) ; H. **Steffens** (1773–1845 ; a Norwegian, *Grundzüge der philosophischen Naturwissenschaft*, 1806), G. H. **Schubert** (1780–1860 ; *Ahndungen einer allg. Geschichte des Lebens*, 1806 f.), Franz **Baader** (1765–1841 ; *Fermenta Cognitionis*, 1822 ff. ; *Speculative Dogmatik*, 1827 ff. Complete writings with a biography ed. by Fr. Hoffmann, Leips. 1851 ff.) ; and finally, K. Chr. Fr. **Krause** (1781–1832 ; *Entwurf des Systems der Philosophie*, 1804 ; *Urbild der Menschheit*, 1811 ; *Abriss des Systems der Philosophie*, 1825 ; *Vorlesungen über das System der Philosophie*, 1828.   Some years since an inexhaustible body of material has appeared from his literary remains, ed. by P. Hohlfeld and A. Wünsche.   Cf. R. Eucken, *Zur Erinnerung an K.*, Leips. 1881).

Georg Wilhelm Friedrich **Hegel**, Schelling's older friend. was born, 1770, in Stuttgart, studied in Tübingen, was a private teacher in Berne and Frankfort, and began, in 1801, his activity as a teacher in Jena, where, in 1805, he became Professor Extraordinary.   After 1806 he became editor of a review in Bamberg, and in 1808 Gymnasium Director in Nuremberg.   In 1816 he went as Professor to Heidelberg ; in 1818 from there to Berlin, where he worked until his death in 1831 as the head of a school which extended with greater and greater brilliancy.   Besides the articles published in the *Kritische Journal der Philosophie*, which he edited in connection with Schelling, he published *Phänomenologie des Geistes* (1807) [tr. of chs. 1, 2, and 3 in *Jour. Spec. Phil.*, Vol. II. ; tr. in prep. by J. Royce, Holt & Co., N.Y.] ; *Wissenschaft der Logik* (1812 ff.) [tr. of Vol. II. by W. T. Harris, *Hegel's Doctrine of Reflection*] ; *Encyclopädie der philosophischen Wissenschaften* (1817) [of this the *Logic* is trans. with *Prolegomena* by W. Wallace, Clar. Press, 1874, 2d ed., in 2 vols., 1892] ; *Grundlinien der Philosophie des Recht's* (1821).   After 1827 the *Jahrbücher für wissenschaftliche Kritik* was the organ of his school.   His works, including his lectures edited by his students, were published in 18 vols. (Berlin, 1832 ff.) [trans. of the *Philosophy of History*, by J. Sibree, Bohn Library ; of the *Introd. to Phil. of Art*, by B. Bosanquet (Lond. 1886) ; of the *Phil. of Art*, abr. by W. Hastie (Edin.), and of the second part of the same in *Jour. Spec. Phil.*, Vols. V.–XIII. ; of the *History of Philosophy*, by E. S. Haldane, in 3 vols.,

Vol. I. (Lond. 1892) ; of the *Phil. of Religion and of the State*, in part in *Jour. Spec. Phil.*, Vols. XV.–XXI.]. From the very extensive literature we may name C. Rosenkranz, *H.'s Leben* (Berlin, 1844), and *H. als deutscher Nationalphilosoph* (Berlin, 1870) [part. trans. G. S. Hall, St. Louis, 1876] ; R. Haym, *H. und seine Zeit* (Berlin, 1857) ; K. Köstlin, *H.* (Tübingen, 1870) ; J. Klaiber, *Hölderlin, Schelling und Hegel in ihren schwäbischen Jugendjahren* (Stuttgart, 1877) [*The Secret of Hegel*, by J. H. Stirling (Lond. 1865), 2 vols. ; *Hegel*, by E. Caird (Edin. and Lond. 1883) ; *Hegelianism and Personality*, by Seth (Edin. and Lond., 2d ed., 1893) ; *Critical Expositions* in Griggs series (Chicago) ; of the *Æsthetics*, by J. S. Kedney (1885) ; of the *Philosophy of the State and of History*, by G. S. Morris (1887) ; and of the *Logic*, by W. T. Harris (1890) ; numerous articles in the *Jour. Spec. Phil.* cited in last-named work].

Friedrich Ernst Daniel **Schleiermacher**, born, 1768, in Breslau, educated at the Herrnhuter educational institutions in Niesky and Barby, and at the University of Halle, after private positions took a vicarship in Landsberg, and in 1796 began his duties as preacher at the Berlin Charité. In 1802 he went as court preacher to Stolpe ; in 1804 as Professor Extraordinary to Halle ; in 1806 returned to Berlin, where in 1809 he became preacher at the *Dreifaltigkeitskirche ;* and in 1810 Professor at the University. He acquitted himself well in both offices, occupying at the time a successful position in the ecclesiastical movement (Union) until his death in 1834. His philosophical writings form the third part of his works collected after his death (Berlin, 1835 ff.). They contain his lectures on *Dialectic, Æsthetic*, etc. ; among his writings are to be mentioned : *Reden über die Religion an die Gebildeten unter ihren Verächtern* (1799) ; *Monologen* (1800) ; *Grundlinien einer Kritik der bisherigen Sittenlehre* (1803). The most important work, the *Ethik*, is given in the coll. works, in the edition by Al. Schweizer ; it is also published in an edition by A. Twesten (Berlin, 1841).— Cf. *Aus Sch.'s Leben in Briefen*, ed. by L. Jonas and W. Dilthey, 4 vols. (Berlin, 1858–1863) ; W. Dilthey, *Leben Schleiermacher's*, Vol. I. (Berlin, 1870) [art. *S.* in *Enc. Brit.*, J. F. Smith].

Johann Friedrich **Herbart**, born, 1776, at Oldenburg, educated there and at the Jena University, for a time private teacher in Berne and acquainted with Pestalozzi, became in 1802 Privatdocent in Göttingen, was from 1809 to 1833 Professor in Königsberg, and then returned to Göttingen as Professor, where he died, 1841. His main writings are : *Hauptpunkte der Metaphysik* (1806) ; *Allgemeine praktische Philosophie* (1808) ; *Einleitung in die Philosophie* (1813) ; *Lehrbuch zur Psychologie* (1816) [Eng. tr. by M. K. Smith, N.Y. 1891] ; *Psychologie als Wissenschaft* (1824 f.). Complete edition by G. Hartenstein, 12 vols. (Leips. 1850 ff.) ; in process of appearance, ed. by K. Kehrbach, since 1882. The pedagogical writings have been edited by O. Willmann in 2 vols. (Leips. 1873 and 1875). Cf. G. Hartenstein, *Die Probleme und Grundlehren der allgemeinen Metaphysik* (Leips. 1836) ; J. Kaftan, *Sollen und Sein* (Leips. 1872) ; J. Capesius, *Die Metaphysik Herbart's* (Leips. 1878) [Ward, art. *Herbart*, in *Enc. Brit.*].

Arthur **Schopenhauer**, born 1788 in Danzic, passed over somewhat late to philosophical life, studied in Göttingen and Berlin, received his degree in 1813 at Jena with his treatise on the *Fourfold Root of the Principle of Sufficient Reason*, lived for a time at Weimar and Dresden, habilitated as Privatdocent in Berlin in 1820, but withdrew after he had won no success in a work as teacher which was frequently interrupted by journeys, and spent the rest of his life in private, after 1831, in Frankfort on the Main, where he died in 1860. His main work is *Die Welt als Wille und Vorstellung*, 1819 [*The World as Will and as Idea*, tr. by R. B. Haldane and J. Kemp, Lond. and Boston, 3 vols., 1884–86]. To this were attached *Ueber den Willen in der Natur*, 1836 ; *Die beiden Grundprobleme der Ethik*, 1841 ; finally, *Parerga und Paralipomena*, 1851. Complete edition in 6 vols. (Leips. 1873 f.), and since then frequently edited. [Tr. of the *Fourfold Root* and of *On the Will in Nature*, by K. Hillebrand, Bohn Library, 2d ed., 1891 ; of selected essays by Bax, Bohn Library, also by T. B. Saunders, 5 vols., Lond. and N.Y., 3d ed., 1892.] Cf. W. Gwinner, *Sch.'s Leben*, 2d ed. (Leips. 1878) ; J. Frauenstädt, *Briefe über die Sch.'sche*

Philosophie (Leips. 1854) ; R. Seydel, *Sch.'s System* (Leips. 1857) ; A. Haym, *A. Sch.* (Berlin, 1864) ; G. Jellinek, *Die Weltanschauungen Leibniz' und Schopenhauer's* (Leips. 1872) [H. Zimmern, *Schopenhauer, His Life and Phil.*, Lond. 1876 ; J. Sully, *Pessimism*, 2d ed., Lond. 1891 ; Adamson in *Mind*, 1876].

By the side of the main metaphysical development runs a **psychological side-line,** a series of schools which, in an eclectic way, frequently approached the doctrines of the great systems by the path of the psychological method. Such is the relation to Kant and Jacobi of J. Fr. **Fries** (1773–1843 ; *Reinhold, Fichte und Schelling*, 1803 ; *Wissen, Glaube und Ahndung*, 1805 ; *Neue Kritik der Vernunft*, 1807 ; *Psychische Anthropologie*, 1820 f. Cf. Kuno Fischer, *Die beiden kantischen Schulen in Jena*, Acad. Address, Stuttg. 1862), — to Kant and Fichte of Wilh. Traug. **Krug** (1770–1842 ; *Organon der Philosophie*, 1801 ; *Handwörterbuch der philos. Wissenschaften*, 1827 ff.), — to Fichte and Schelling of Fried. **Bouterwek** (1766–1828 ; *Apodiktik*, 1799 ; *Æsthetik*, 1806), — and finally, to Herbart of Fr. **Beneke** (1798–1854 ; *Psychologische Skizzen*, 1825 and 1827 ; *Lehrbuch der Psychologie, als Naturwissenschaft*, 1832 ; *Metaphysik und Religionsphilosophie*, 1840 ; *Die neue Psychologie*, 1845).

§ 41. The Thing-in-Itself.

The compelling power which Kant's philosophy gained over the minds and hearts of men was due chiefly to the earnestness and greatness of its ethical conception of the world; [1] the progress of thought, however, attached itself primarily to the new form which had been given to the principles of the theory of knowledge in the *Critique of the Pure Reason.* Kant took the antithesis of phenomena and noumena from earlier philosophy ; but by his transcendental analytic he widened the realm of phenomena to include the whole compass of human knowledge, and the thing-in-itself survived only as a problematical conception, like a rudimentary organ, which might be indeed characteristic for the historical genesis of this theory of knowledge, but which performed no living function in it.

1. This was first seen by *Jacobi*, when he confessed that without the presupposition of realism one could not enter the Kantian system, and with the same could not remain in it; [2] for the conception of the sensibility introduced at the beginning involves the causal relation of being affected by things-in-themselves, — a relation which, according to the doctrine of the analytic that categories must not be applied to things-in-themselves, it is forbidden to think. In this contradiction of professing to think things-in-themselves and yet of not being permitted to think them, the whole critique of the reason moves ; and at the same time this contradictory assumption does not at all help to guarantee to our knowledge of phenomena even the slightest relation to truth. For, according to Kant, the mind presents to itself in thought "neither itself nor

---

[1] This is especially to be recognised from Reinhold's *Briefen über die kant. Ph.*

[2] Jacobi, W., II. 304.

other things, but solely and alone that which is neither what the mind is itself, nor what other things are." [1] The faculty of cognition hovers between a problematical X of the subject and an equally problematical X of the object. The sensibility has nothing behind it, and the understanding nothing before it; "in a twofold enchanter's smoke, called space and time, rise the ghostly forms of phenomena or appearances in which nothing appears." [2] If we assume things, Kant teaches that knowledge has not the least to do with them. The critical reason is a reason busy about pure nothing, *i.e.* only about itself. If, therefore, criticism will not fall into nihilism or absolute scepticism, the transcendental idealist must have the courage to assert the " strongest " idealism; [3] he must declare that only phenomena are.

In the claim that what Kant calls the object of knowledge is in truth "nothing," inheres as a presupposition the same naïve realism, the destruction of which was the great service of the transcendental analytic; and the same realism determines also the epistemology of *Faith*, which Jacobi opposes to "the transcendental uncertainty," not without being entirely dependent upon it. All truth is knowledge of the actual; but the actual asserts itself in human consciousness not through thought, but through feeling; just Kant's experiment proves that thought alone moves in a circle out of which there is no access to actuality, in an endless series of the conditioned in which no unconditioned is to be found. The fundamental law of causality may indeed be formulated in exactly this manner, viz. there is nothing unconditioned. *Knowledge*, therefore, or thought that can be demonstrated, is in its very nature, as Jacobi says, Spinozism, — a doctrine of the mechanical necessity of all that is finite: and it is the interest of science that there be no God, — indeed, a God who could be known would be no God. [4] Even he who is in his heart a Christian must be in his head a heathen; he who will bring into his intellect the light which is in his heart quenches it. [5] But this knowledge is only a *mediate* knowing; the true, *immediate knowing* is *feeling;* in this we are truly one with the object, [6] and possess it as we possess ourselves in the certainty of a *faith* that has no proof. [7] This feeling, however, as regards its objects, is of a twofold kind: the reality of the sensuous reveals itself to us in *perception*, that of the supersensuous in the "*reason.*"

---

[1] *Allwill*, XV.; W., I. 121.   [2] W., III. 111 f.
[3] W., II. 310.   [4] W., III. 384.
[5] To *Hamann*, I. 367.   [6] W., II. 175.
[7] Hume's conception of belief and his distinction of impressions and ideas (here called *Vorstellungen*) experience in this a noteworthy transformation.

For this *supra-natural sensualism,* therefore, "reason" signifies the immediate feeling of the reality of the supersensuous, of God, freedom, morality, and immortality.   In this limitation Kant's dualism of theoretical and practical reason and of the primacy of the latter return in Jacobi,[1] to be placed in the service of a mystical extravagance of feeling, which manifests itself also in the character of a style which is warm and full of spirit, but rhapsodical and more given to assertion than to proof.

This same fundamental conception, brought somewhat nearer to Kant, appears with *Fries.*   In demanding that the knowledge of the *a priori* forms to which the critical philosophy aspired must itself arise *a posteriori,* through *inner experience,* and therefore that Kant's results must be established or set right by an "anthropological" critique, he rested upon the conviction that the immediate, proper cognitions of the reason are given originally in an obscure form through the feeling,[2] and transformed into intellectual knowledge only by means of *reflection.*   This Leibnizian body ends, however, in the critical tail, since the perceptional and conceptional Forms of this reflection are regarded as only an expression of the phenomenal mode in which the above original truth [as experienced in feeling] appears ; on the other hand, the body received a Kant-Jacobi head, when the limitation of knowledge to these phenomenal Forms had set over against it the immediate relation of moral faith to things-in-themselves, while at the same time — with a decided attachment to the *Critique of Judgment* — the æsthetic and religious feelings had ascribed to them the significance of a *presage* (*Ahndung*) that the Being which lies at the basis of phenomena is just that to which the practical reason relates.

2. The untenability of the Kantian conception of the thing-in-itself, so keenly recognised by Jacobi, became palpable to a certain extent when *Reinhold* in his *Elementary Philosophy* made the attempt to present the critical doctrine in a systematic unity.   He admired Kant and adopted entirely his solutions of the individual problems, but missed in him the formulation of a simple, fundamental principle from which all particular insights might be deduced.   Through the fulfilment of this (Cartesian) demand,[3] opposing private opinions would be at last replaced by *the* philosophy, — Philosophy without any surname.   He himself believed that he had found this principle in the principle which he supposed to be quite free from presuppositions, — that in consciousness every idea is distinguished by the

---

[1] W., III. 351 ff.   [2] Fries, *Neue Kritik,* I. 206.
[3] Reinhold, *Beiträge,* I. 91 ff.

consciousness of subject and object, and is related to both (*Principle of Consciousness*).[1] Hence there inheres in every idea something that belongs to the subject and something that belongs to the object. From the object comes the manifold of the *material*, from the subject the synthetic unity of the *Form*. From this it follows that neither the object in itself, nor the subject in itself, is knowable, but only the world of consciousness which hovers between the two ; from this results further the opposition of the (sensuous) *material impulse* and of the (ethical) *Form impulse ;* in the former the heteronomy of the dependence of the will upon things may be recognised ; in the latter the autonomy of the will directed toward the formal conformity to law.

In this crude form the *Kantian School* propagated the doctrine of the master ; all the fineness and profound meaning of the analytic of the "object " had become lost, and the only substitute was Reinhold's effort to find in the "ideational faculty " (*Vorstellungsvermögen*), or "consciousness," the deeper unity of all the different cognitive powers which Kant had separated from each other as Sensibility, Understanding, Judgment, and Reason. In so far the "fundamental philosophy " opposed with a positive hypothesis the objections which the sharp *separation of the sensibility and the understanding* in the Kantian doctrine encountered with many contemporaries. This separation presented itself in the exposition determined by the after-working of the *Inaugural Dissertation* (cf. p. 538, note 4), still more strongly than the spirit of the *Critique of Reason* required, and became at the same time still more palpable by the dualism of the practical philosophy. So the tendency was awakened to replace the sensibility again in its rights as against Kant, and the Leibnizian doctrine of the gradual transition from the functions of sense to those of reason proved the source of a powerful counter-current against Kant's "dissection" of the soul, — a dissection more apparent than serious. *Hamann* in his review, and in conjunction with him, *Herder* in his *Metakritik,* urged this against the *Critique of Pure Reason.* Both lay chief emphasis upon language as the fundamental, unitary, sensuous-intellectual work of the reason, and seek to show how from the first "splitting apart " of sensibility and understanding all the other chasms and dualisms of the critical philosophy necessarily followed.[2]

---

[1] *Neue Theorie des Vorst.*, pp. 201 ff.

[2] Herder, *Metakritik,* 14, 111. Works in 40 vols., XXXVII. 333 ff. Moreover, this thought as Herder presented it in the *Metakritik,* a silly composition of personal irritation, was for a long time a positively impelling moment in the development. Cf. § 42.

3. The weak points in Reinhold's system could not escape the sceptics, but their attacks applied at the same time to Kant himself. They were united most effectively in Schulze's *Ænesidemus.* He shows that the critical method ensnares itself by setting for itself a task, the solution of which is according to its own results impossible. For if the *Critique* seeks the conditions which lie at the basis of experience, these conditions are yet not themselves objects of experience (a conception which certainly corresponded better with Kant's meaning than did Fries' attempt at a psychological discovery of the *a priori*) *:* the critical method demands, therefore, that philosophical knowledge, at all events a thinking in categories, shall go beyond experience; and just this the *Analytic* declares impermissible. In fact, the "reason" and each of the knowing faculties, as sensibility, understanding, etc., is a thing-in-itself, an imperceptible ground of the empirical activities of the kind of cognition in question; and of all these things-in-themselves and their relations to each other and to experience, the critical philosophy — the metaphysics of knowledge — offers a very circumstantial body of information. To be sure, this information is, if closely examined, very slight; for such a "faculty" is ultimately thought only as an unknown common cause of empirical functions, and is to be characterised only through these its workings.

"Ænesidemus" develops this criticism in connection with Reinhold's conception of the "ideational faculty";[1] he shows that we explain nothing at all, when we postulate over again the content of that which is to be explained, provided with the problematical mark "power" or "faculty." Schulze thus turned against the "faculty theory," which was employed by the empirical psychologists of the Enlightenment in rather a thoughtless manner. It is only descriptively that there is any sense in comprehending like phenomena of the psychical life under one generic conception; but to hypostatise this conception to a metaphysical power — this is a mythological treatment of psychology. With this watch-word Herbart[2] extended the criticism of Schulze to the whole earlier psychological theory, and Beneke also saw in the bringing into prominence of this conception the essential progress towards a natural science of the soul; *i.e.* the associational psychology.[3]

For Schulze, this is only one of the elements in a proof that the critical philosophy, while aiming to prove the authority of the causal conception as against Hume, professes to limit the same

---

[1] *Ænesid.*, p. 98.
[2] Herbart, *Lehrb.*, *z. Psych.*, § 3 ; W., V. 8 and elsewhere.
[3] Beneke, *Neue Psych.*, pp. 34 ff.

to experience, and yet everywhere makes the assumption of a causal relation between experience and that which "lies at its basis." Here, too, belongs of course the contradiction, already exhibited by Jacobi, in the conception of the thing-in-itself by which the "sensibility" is said to be affected. Every attempt of the *Critique of Pure Reason* to go beyond the circuit of experience, even merely problematically, is judged in advance by itself.[1]

4. The first attempt to transform the conception of the thing-in-itself, untenable in its Kantian shape, proceeded from Salomon *Maimon*. He saw that the assumption of a reality to be placed outside of consciousness involves a contradiction. What is thought is in consciousness; to think of a something outside of consciousness is as imaginary as it would be mathematics to regard the requirement $\sqrt{-a}$ as a real quantity. *The thing-in-itself is an impossible conception.* But what was the inducement to form it? It lay in the need of explaining the *given* in consciousness.[2] It meets us, that is to say, in our ideas of the antithesis between the *Form* which we ourselves create and are conscious of creating, and the *material* which we only find present in us, without knowing how we come by it. Of the Forms we have, therefore, a *complete* consciousness; of the matter, on the contrary, only an *incomplete consciousness;* it is something that is in consciousness, without being produced with consciousness. But since nothing outside of consciousness is thinkable, the given can be defined only by the lowest grade of the completeness of consciousness. Consciousness can be thought as diminishing through an infinite number of intermediate stages down to nothing, and the idea of the limit of this infinite series (comparable to the $\sqrt{2}$) is that of the merely-given, the thing-in-itself. Things-in-themselves are, therefore, as Maimon says with direct reference to Leibniz —*petites perceptions;* cf. p. 424 —*differentials of consciousness.*[3] The thing-in-itself is the limiting conception for the infinite decreasing series from complete consciousness down—an *irrational* quantity. The consequence of this fundamental assumption with Maimon is, that of the given there can always be only an incomplete knowledge, as there is only an incomplete consciousness,[4] and that complete

---

[1] The author of the *Ænesidemus* repeated the thoughts of his polemic in most concise and comprehensive manner in his *Kritik der theoretischen Philosophie* (II. 549 ff.),—a work, moreover, which contains not only an analysis of the *Critique of Pure Reason* (I. 172–582), which is one of the best even to the present day, but also a criticism of the same, supported by deep historical understanding (found II. 126–722). Cf. on the relation to *Leibniz*, II. 176 ff.

[2] Maimon, *Transscendentalphilos.*, pp. 419 f.

[3] Ib. 27 ff.

[4] Cf. the contingency of the world with Leibniz and the specification of Nature with Kant, pp. 398 f., 566.

knowledge is limited to the knowledge of the autonomous Forms of the theoretical consciousness, to mathematics and logic. In his esteem for these two demonstrative sciences Maimon's critical scepticism is in harmony with Hume; with regard to their theories of the knowledge of that which is empirically given they diverge diametrically.

With this, however, it had become clear that the investigations of the *Critique of Pure Reason* require a new conception of the *relation of consciousness and Being. Being is to be thought only in consciousness, only as a kind of consciousness.* Thus the prophecy of Jacobi begins to be fulfilled; Kant's doctrine urges toward the "strongest idealism."

This is seen in a disciple who stood in the closest relations to Kant himself: Sigismund *Beck.* He found[1] the "Only Possible Standpoint for Estimating the Critical Philosophy" in this, that the datum of the individual consciousness, given it as "object," is made the content of an "*original,*" supra-individual[2] consciousness, which for this reason is authoritative for the truth of the empirical knowing process. In the place of the things-in-themselves he set Kant's "consciousness in general." But he explained to himself in this way the *a priori* character of the pure conceptions and categories: the given in the sensuous manifold remained for him also the unsolved remnant of the Kantian problem.

5. The full idealistic disintegration of the conception of the thing-in-itself was the work of *Fichte.* We may best understand the matter by following the course of thought in his introductions to his *Science of Knowledge,*[3] which attaches itself directly, in a free reproduction, to the most difficult part of the Kantian doctrine, — the transcendental deduction, — and illumines with complete clearness the culmination of the movement of thought here considered.

The fundamental problem of philosophy — or, as Fichte calls it, just on this account, of the *Wissenschaftslehre* [lit. "doctrine of science," where science has the twofold meaning of knowledge as a mental act, and knowledge as a body of truth = philosophy (cf. p. 94, note 2,)] — is given in the fact, that in contrast with the ideas of individual consciousness, which may come and go in a voluntary and contingent manner, another set of our ideas maintain themselves there, and these latter are characterised by a *feeling of necessity* that can be distinguished with entire certainty. To make this necessity intelligible is the chief task of philosophy or the Science

---

[1] 3d vol. of his *Erläuternder Auszug,* from Kant's writing (Leips. 1796).
[2] Ib. p. 120 ff.   [3] *Fichte's W.,* I. 419 ff.

of Knowledge. We call the system of those ideas which emerge with the feeling of necessity experience; the problem runs, therefore, "What is the ground of experience?" To its solution there are only two paths. Experience is an activity of consciousness directed toward objects; it can therefore be derived only from things or from the consciousness. In the one case the explanation is dogmatic, in the other idealistic. *Dogmatism* regards consciousness as a product of things; it traces the activities of intelligence also back to mechanical necessity of the causal relations; if consistently thought, therefore, it cannot end otherwise than fatalistically and materialistically. *Idealism,* on the contrary, sees in things a product of consciousness, of a free function determined only by itself; it is the system of freedom and of deed. These two modes of explanation, each of which is consistent in itself, are in such thorough-going contradiction to each other and so irreconcilable that Fichte regards the attempt of *syncretism,* to explain experience by dependence both upon things-in-themselves and upon the reason, as a failure from the outset. If one will not fall a victim to sceptical despair, he must choose between the two.

This choice, since both present themselves logically as equally consistent systems, will primarily depend "on what sort of a man one is"[1] (*"was für ein Mensch man ist"*); but while the ethical interest thus already speaks for idealism, there is still a theoretical consideration which comes to its aid. The fact of experience, in the constant reciprocal relation of *"being"* and *"being conscious"* (*Sein und Bewusstsein*), consists in this, that the *"real series"* of objects is perceived in the *"ideal"* series of mental representations.[2] This "doubleness" dogmatism cannot explain; for the causality of things is only a simple series (of "mere being posited"). The repetition of Being in consciousness (or in the being conscious) is incomprehensible, if the being is to serve as a ground of explanation for being conscious. On the contrary, it belongs to the very *nature of intelligence "to see itself."* Consciousness, in that it acts or functions, knows also that it acts and what it does; in conjunction with the real (primary) series of its own functions it produces always at the same time the ideal (secondary) series of the knowledge of these functions. If, therefore, consciousness yields the sole ground of explanation for experience, it does this only in so far as it is the

[1] *Fichte's W.,* I. 434.

[2] If the antithesis of dogmatism and idealism points back to the Kantian antithesis of Nature and Freedom, in which connection, moreover, the system of the necessity of things already appears with a strong Spinozistic character, the systematic influence of Spinoza's doctrine concerning the two attributes asserts itself for the first time in this relation of the two series.

activity which perceives itself and is reflected back into itself, *i.e.* as *self-consciousness*. The science of knowledge has to show that all consciousness (of experience) which is directed toward something else — toward a Being, toward objects, toward things — has its root in the original relation of consciousness to itself.

The principle of idealism is self-consciousness; in a subjective, methodical aspect, in so far as the science of knowledge aims to develop all of its insights from the *intellectual perception* alone, with which consciousness accompanies its own activities, from *reflection* upon that which consciousness knows of its own deed, — in objective, systematic aspect, in so far as in this way those functions of intelligence are to be pointed out, by means of which that which in common life is called thing and object, and in the dogmatic philosophy thing-in-itself, is produced. This last conception, that of the thing-in-itself, which is through and through contradictory, is thus resolved to its last remnant; all Being is comprehensible only as product of reason, and the subject-matter of philosophical knowledge is the *system of the reason* (cf. § 42).

For Fichte and his successors, the conception of the thing-in-itself thus became indifferent, and the old antithesis between Being and consciousness sank to the secondary significance of an immanent relation within the activities of the reason. An object exists only for a subject; and the common ground of both is the reason, the *I* which perceives itself and its action.[1]

6. While the main development of German metaphysics followed this Fichtean tendency, the syncretism above mentioned did not remain without supporters whom the *Wissenschaftslehre* had thrust from the threshold. Its metaphysical type had been stamped out by Reinhold; but it was likewise close at hand for all who took their point of departure from the individual consciousness with the psychological method, and believed that they found the individual consciousness equally dependent upon the Real and upon the universal essence of the intellect. The "*transcendental synthetism,*" which *Krug* taught, may be conceived of as an example of this mode of view. For him, philosophy is an explanation of self by means of the reflection of the "I" upon the "facts of consciousness." But in this the primitive fact proves to be the transcendental synthesis, that real and ideal are posited in consciousness as equally original and in relation to each other.[2] We know Being only in so far as it appears in consciousness, and consciousness only in so far as it refers to Being;

---

[1] Cf. also Schelling's youthful opuscule, *Vom Ich als Princip der Philosophie,* W., I. 151 ff.

[2] Krug, *Fundamentalphilosophie,* pp. 106 ff.

but both are objects of an immediate knowledge just as is the community existing between them in our world of ideas.

These thoughts found a finer turn given them in *Schleiermacher's* dialectic. All knowledge has as its end to establish the *identity of Being and thinking;* for the two emerge in human consciousness separate, as its *real and ideal factors,* perception and conception, organic and intellectual functions. Only their complete adjustment would give knowledge, but they remain always in a state of difference. In consequence of this, science is divided with reference to its subject matter into physics and ethics, with reference to its methods into empirical and theoretical disciplines; natural history and natural science, history of the world, and science of morals. In all these particular disciplines one or the other of the two factors has the *predominance,*[1] materially or formally, although the opposites strive toward each other — the empirical branches of knowledge toward rational articulation, the theoretical towards an understanding of the facts, physics towards the genesis of the organism and of consciousness out of the corporeal world, ethics towards the control and inter-penetration of the sensuous by the will, which acts according to ends. But the complete adjustment of the real and the ideal is nowhere attained in actual cognition; it forms rather the absolute, unconditioned, infinitely removed goal of the thinking which desires to become knowledge, but will never completely succeed.[2] Hence philosophy is the science not of knowledge, but of knowledge in a perpetual state of becoming, — *dialectic.*

But just for this reason it presupposes the reality of this goal which is never to be attained in human knowledge; the *identity of thought and Being.* This Schleiermacher, with Spinoza (and Schelling), calls *God.* It cannot be an object of the theoretical reason, and just as little can it be such of the practical reason. We do not know God, and therefore we cannot order our ethical life with reference to him. Religion is more than knowing and right-doing; it is the community of life with the highest reality, in which Being and consciousness are identical. This communion, however, emerges only in the feeling, in the "pious" (*frommen*) feeling of an "absolute" dependence upon the infinite world-ground which cannot be exhausted by thought (cf. § 42, 6). Spinoza's God and Kant's thing-in-itself coincide in the infinite, but thus are raised above all human knowledge and will, and made the objects of a *mystical* feeling whose delicate vibrations harmonise in Schleiermacher (as in

---

[1] This relation in Schleiermacher's *Dialectic* appears copied after the metaphysical form of Schelling's *System of Identity;* cf. § 42, 8.

[2] *Dialektik*, W., III. 4 b 68 f.

a somewhat different form in Fries, also) with the inwardness of the religious life among the *Moravians*.

Thus the traditions of Mysticism pass through Pietism — in which the orthodox tendency toward a coarser view became more and more prominent after Spener and Francke, and so called forth the opposition of the Brothers of the Common Life — up to the summits of the idealistic development; and indeed the doctrine of Eckhart and the transcendental philosophy are in close touch in the spirit which desires to transpose all the outer into the inner; both have a genuinely Germanic savour, they seek the world in the " *Gemüth* " [the mind as the seat of the feeling and sentiments].

7. In putting aside the possibility of a scientific knowledge of the world-ground Schleiermacher remained nearer to Kant, but the intuition of religious feeling which he substituted was all the more dependent upon Spinoza and upon the influences which the latter had exercised upon the idealistic metaphysics after Fichte's Science of Knowledge. This monism of the reason (cf. the development in § 42) *Herbart* combated by an entirely different re-shaping of the Kantian conception of the thing-in-itself. He desired to oppose the dissolution of this conception, and found himself forced thereby to the paradox of a metaphysics of things-in-themselves, which yet should hold fast to their unknowableness. The contradictions of the transcendental analytic appear here grotesquely magnified.

This is the more noteworthy as the retrogressive tendency which has been ascribed to Herbart's doctrine, perhaps in contrast with the idealistic innovations, developed itself in his attack upon Kant's transcendental logic (cf. § 38, 5). Herbart saw in this with right the roots of idealism. It teaches, indeed, the Forms with which the "Understanding" produces the world of objects, and in Fichte's " I " we only have in a completely developed form that which in germ was in Kant's "consciousness in general " or " transcendental apperception." Herbart's inclination toward the earlier philosophy consists in this, that he denies the creative spontaneity of consciousness, and, like the associational psychologists, finds it determined and dependent in both Form and content from without. He opposes also the virtual innateness which had propagated itself from Leibniz on through the *Inaugural Dissertation* into the *Critique of Pure Reason :* the forms of relation expressed in the categories are for him, like space and time, products of the ideational mechanism. As regards the psycho-genetic questions, he stands entirely upon the platform of the philosophy of the Enlightenment. For this reason he knows no other logic than the formal logic whose principle is the principle of contradiction, *i.e.* the prohibition to commit a contra-

diction. The supreme principle of all thought is, that which contradicts itself cannot be truly real or actual.[1]

Now it is evident that the conceptions in which we think experience are full of internal contradictions; we assume *things,* which
are to be identical with themselves and yet made equal to a variety
of attributes ; we speak of *alterations* in which that which is equal
to itself is successively different ; we trace all inner experience back
to an "*I*" or "*self*" which as that "which mentally represents
itself" (*sich selbst Vorstellende*) involves an infinite series in the
subject as well as in the object, — we trace all outer experience
back to a *matter,* in the idea of which the attributes of the discrete
and the continuous are at variance. This experience can be only
phenomenon; but this phenomenon must have at its basis something
real which is free from contradictions, seeming things must have
absolute "*Reals*" (*Reale*), seeming occurrence and change a real
occurrence and change. Whatever seeming there is, there is just so
much indication of Being. To discover this is the task of philosophy; it is a *working over of the conceptions of experience* which are
given and which must be re-shaped according to the rules of formal
logic, until we know the reality that has no internal contradictions.

The general means to this end is the *method of relation.* The
fundamental form of contradiction always is, that something simple
is thought as having differences (the synthetic unity of the manifold in Kant). This difficulty can be removed only by assuming a
plurality of simple beings, through the relation of which to each
other the "illusion" of the manifold or changeable is produced in
any individual object. Thus the conception of substance can be
maintained only if we suppose that the various qualities and changing states which substance is said to unite, concern not substance
itself, but only the relation in which it successively stands to other
substances. The things-in-themselves must be many ; from a single
thing-in-itself the multiplicity of qualities and states could never be
understood. But each of these metaphysical things must be thought
as entirely *simple and unchangeable;* they are called by Herbart,
"*Reals*" (*Realen*). All qualities which form the characteristics of
things in experience are relative, and make these characteristics

---

[1] Cf. *Einleitung in die Philos.*, W., I. 72–82. The historical stimulus to this
sharp presentation of the principle of contradiction was no doubt the depreciation which this principle found in the dialectic method (cf. § 42, 1) ; logically,
however, Herbart's doctrine (with the exception of his treatment of the "I"
conception) is entirely independent of it. The *Eleatic* element in the Herbartian philosophy (cf. I. 225) is given with the postulate of *Being void of contradictions,* and to this circumstance the philosopher, who otherwise had little
historical disposition, owed his fineness of feeling for the metaphysical motive
in the Platonic doctrine of Ideas. Cf. I. 237 ff. and XII. 61 ff.

appear only in relation to other things ; the *absolute qualities* of the Reals are, therefore, *unknowable.*

8. But they must be thought as the ground which determines the qualities that appear ; and likewise we must assume as ground of the seeming changes which the mutation of qualities exhibits in the case of empirical things, an *actual process or occurrence*, a change of relations between the Reals. Here, however, this whole artificial construction of that which lies beyond experience began to waver. For the Eleatic rigidity of these Reals in nowise permits us to form an idea of the kind of "actual relations" which are held to obtain between them. First of all, these cannot be spatial;[1] space and time are products of the series formed by ideas, products of the psychical mechanism, and hence phenomenal for Herbart in almost a higher degree than for Kant. Only in a transferred sense can the changing relations of substances be termed a "coming and going in the intelligible space"; what they are themselves the Herbartian doctrine has no term to express. Only, in a negative direction it is obliged to make a questionable concession. Every Real has only simple and unchangeable determinations : the relation, therefore, which exists or arises between two Reals is not essential to either, and has not its basis in either. A *tertium quid*, however, which this relation would postulate, is not to be discovered in this metaphysics.[2] Hence the relations which the Reals sustain to each other, and from which the appearance of things and their relations are said to follow, are called "contingent views" (*zufällige Ansichten*) of the Reals; and Herbart's meaning in several passages is scarcely to be understood otherwise than that *consciousness* is the intelligible space in which the above relations between the Reals obtain, that the real process or occurrence, also, is some thing which itself only "takes place for the spectator" as "objective seeming."[3] If we add to this, that the "Being" of the Reals or absolute qualities is

---

[1] Not only in this point do Herbart's Reals distinguish themselves from the atoms of Democritus, with which they have the common basis of a *pluralistic re-shaping of the Eleatic conception of Being*, but also by the difference in (unknowable) quality, in the place of which atomism allows only quantitive differences. Just as little are the Reals to be confused with Leibniz's monads, with which indeed they share their absence of windows, but not the attribute of being a unity of the manifold. With the Platonic Ideas, they have in common the attributes of the Eleatic Being, but not the character of class-concepts.

[2] In this gap of his metaphysics *Herbart* inserted his *philosophy of religion;* for since there is no knowledge of the real ground of the relations between the Reals, from which the world of phenomena proceeds, the impression of purposiveness which the latter makes permits us to believe, in a manner which is theoretically unassailable, upon a supreme intelligence as the ground of these relations, — a very pale revival of the old physico-theological proof.

[3] Cf. W., IV. 93 ff., 127–132, 233, 240 f., 248 ff.; see also E. Zeller, *Gesch. d. deutsch. Philos.*, 844.

defined by Herbart as "*absolute position*," *i.e.* as a "*Setzung*,"[1] a pos-
iting in which Being is at rest, and which is not taken back, we have
opening before us the perspective into an "absolute" idealism.

This was, indeed, carried out by Herbart still less than by Kant;
here, too, it would have led to absolute contradiction. For the
theory of Reals aims to deduce consciousness also, as a consequence,
emerging in the realm of phenomena, of the "co-existence of the
Reals." The Reals are held to reciprocally "disturb" each other,
and to call forth in each other as reactions against these disturbances, inner states which have the significance of *self-preservations.*"[2] Such self-preservations are immediately known to us as
those by the aid of which the unknown Real of our *soul* maintains
itself against disturbance by other Reals; they are *ideas* (*Vorstellungen*). The soul as a simple substance is naturally unknowable;
psychology is only the science of its self-preservations. These, the
ideas, sustain within the soul, which simply furnishes the indifferent stage for their co-existence, once more the relations of Reals;
they disturb and *inhibit* each other, and the whole course of the
psychical life is to be explained from this *reciprocal tension of ideas.*
By their tension the ideas lose in intensity; and the consciousness
depends upon the degree of intensity. The lowest degree of
strength, which the ideas can have and still be regarded as actual,
is the *threshold of consciousness.* If the ideas are pressed by others
below this threshold, they change into *impulse.* Hence the essential
nature of those psychical states which are called feeling and will is
to be sought in the inhibitory relations of ideas. All these relations
must be developed as a "statics and mechanics of ideas,"[3] and since
we have to do here essentially with the determining of differences of
force, this metaphysical psychology must take on the form of a *mathematical theory of the mechanism of ideas.*[4] Herbart lays particular

---

[1] Cf. W., IV. 71 ff.

[2] The "*suum esse conservare*," with Hobbes and Spinoza the fundamental instinct of individuals, appears with Herbart as the metaphysical activity of the
Reals, by virtue of which they produce the world of seeming, *i.e.* experience.

[3] On this metaphysical basis Herbart erected the structure of an immanent
associational psychology. The assumption of a mechanical necessity of the
ideational process, and the view that the volitions follow from this as likewise
necessary relations, proved a fortunate basis for a scientific theory of *pedagogics,* — a discipline which Herbart made also dependent upon ethics, since the
latter teaches the goal of education (the formation of ethical character), while
psychology teaches the mechanism through which this is realised. In a similar
way Beneke, who took the standpoint of associational psychology without Herbart's metaphysics, found the path to a systematic pedagogics.

[4] In carrying out this thought Herbart assumed that ideas in their reciprocal
inhibitions lose in intensity in as much as the weakest of them possesses, and that
this inhibition-sum is divided among the individual ideas in inverse ratio to
their original strength, so that if in the simplest case, $a > b$, a is reduced by

weight upon the investigation of the process by which newly entering ideas are "assimilated," ordered, formed, and in part altered, by the ideas already present; he employs for this the expression *apperception* (first coined by Leibniz; cf. p. 463), and his theory of this takes the form of an explanation of the "I" or "self" by associational psychology. The "I" is thought as the moving point in which the apperceiving and apperceived ideas continually converge.

While the self-preservation of the Real which constitutes the soul, against disturbance by other Reals thus produces the phenomena of the ideational life, the reciprocal self-preservation and "partial inter-penetration" of several Reals produce for the consciousness of the spectator the "objective seeming or illusion" of *matter*. The various physical and chemical phenomena are here tortured out of the metaphysical presuppositions with an unspeakably toilsome deduction,[1] — an attempt forgotten to-day, which remained as destitute of results in natural science as in philosophy.

9. Another Göttingen professor, *Bouterwek*, attacked the thing-in-itself with other weapons. He showed in his *Apodiktik*, that if the doctrines of the Critique of Pure Reason are to be taken in earnest, nothing remains for the "object to which the subject necessarily relates" except a completely inconceivable X. We cannot talk of a thing-in-itself or of things-in-themselves; for in this are involved already the categories of Inherence, of Unity and Plurality,[2] and of Reality, which hold good only for phenomena. The transcendental philosophy must become "negative Spinozism."[3] It can teach only that to the "consciousness in general" a "something in general" corresponds, concerning which nothing whatever is to be affirmed in absolute knowledge. (Cf. with regard to Spinoza, above, pp. 408 f.). On the other hand, this absolutely real asserts itself in all *relative knowledge* through the *consciousness of willing*.[4] For this shows everywhere the *living force of individuality*. We know of the subject because it wills something, and of the object because it furnishes

---

the inhibition to $\dfrac{a^2 + ab - b^2}{a + b}$, and b to $\dfrac{b^2}{a + b}$. Cf. on this arbitrarily axiomatic assumption and on the mistaken nature of the whole "psychological calculus," A. Lange, *Die Grundlegung der mathematischen Psychologie*, Duisburg, 1865.

[1] *Allgem. Metaphysik*, §§ 240 ff., 331 ff.; *W.*, IV. 147 ff., 327 ff. In Herbart's metaphysics the branching out of general ontology into the beginnings of psychology and natural philosophy is designated by the names *Eidology* and *Synechology*.

[2] Cf. esp. *Apodiktik*, I. 261, 392 ff.

[3] Ib. 385 ff.

[4] Following the example of Kant and Fichte, Bouterwek ends his theoretical *Apodiktik* in scepticism or in completely abstract-formal, absolute knowledge; it is the "practical" apodictic which first gains a relation of its content to reality.

resistance to this will. The antithesis of *force and resistance* thus furnishes a common basis to the knowledge of the reality of our-selves, and to that of the reality of other things, — of the I and the Not-I.[1] This doctrine Bouterwek would have called *absolute Virtu-alism.* We know our own reality in that we will, and the reality of other things in that our will finds in them a resisting force. The feeling of resistance refutes pure subjectivism or solipsism, but this relative knowledge of the particular forces of the real is supple-mented by the consciousness of our own willing to form a merely empirical science.[2]

This thought of his Göttingen teacher was developed by *Schopen-hauer,* under the influence of Fichte, to a metaphysics. With a bold leap he swings himself up from the position of Virtualism to the knowledge of the essential nature of all things. We recognise the will within us as the true reality, and the resistance from which we know the reality of other things must, therefore, be likewise will. This is demanded by the " *metaphysical need* " of a unitary explana-tion for all experience. The world "as idea" can be only phenome-non; an object is possible only in the subject and determined by the Forms of the subject. Hence the world in man's idea or mental representation (as " phenomenon of the brain," as Schopenhauer has often said with a dangerously contradictory laxity of expression) appears as a manifold ordered in *space* and *time,* a manifold whose connection can be thought only in accordance with the principle of *causality,* — the only one of the Kantian categories which Schopen-hauer can admit to an originality of the same rank as that which belongs to the pure perceptions. Bound to these Forms, conceptional knowledge can have for its object only the necessity which prevails between individual phenomena: for causality is a relation of phe-nomena to each other; science knows nothing absolute, nothing unconditioned; the guiding thread of causality, which leads from one condition to the other, never breaks off and must not be broken off arbitrarily.[3] The conceptional work of science can, therefore, in nowise raise itself above this infinite series of phenomena; only an *intuitive interpretation* of the whole world of ideas, a look of genius over experience, an immediate apprehension, can penetrate to the true essence, which appears in our ideas as the world determined in space and time and by causality. This intuition, however, is that by which the knowing subject is given *immediately* through itself as *will.* This word solves, therefore, the mystery of the outer world

---

[1] *Apodiktik* II. 62 ff.   [2] Ib. II. 67 f.

[3] In this Schopenhauer is in complete agreement with Jacobi (cf. above, p. 574).

also. For we must apprehend the significance of all that is given to us immediately in space and time as idea,[1] according to this analogy of the only thing which is immediately given. *The thing-in-itself is the Will.*

The word "will" as here used must indeed be taken in an extended sense. In men and in animals the will appears as *motivation* determined through ideas, in the instinctive and vegetative life of the organism as *susceptibility to stimulation*, in the rest of the world of experience as *mechanical processes*. The meaning which is common to these different internal or external kinds of causality, should be designated *a potiori* as will, in accordance with that form in which alone it is immediately known to us. Accordingly the philosopher emphasises expressly the point, that the particular peculiarities with which the will is given in human self-perception, *i.e.* its motivation through ideas and conceptions, must be kept quite apart from our notion of the will as thing-in-itself, — a requirement which it was, indeed, hard enough for Schopenhauer himself to fulfil.

At the same time, however, the relation between thing-in-itself and phenomenon must not be thought according to the rule of the understanding, *i.e.* causally. *The thing-in-itself is not the cause of phenomena.* Even in the case of man the will is not the cause of his body or of the bodily activities; but the same reality, which is given us mediately, through our ideas in space and time perception, as body, and which in cognition is conceived as something causally necessary and dependent upon other phenomena, — this is immediately given as will. Because the thing-in-itself is not subject to the principle of sufficient reason, we have the paradox, that man feels himself as will immediately free, and yet in idea knows himself to be necessarily determined. So Schopenhauer adopts Kant's doctrine of intelligible and empirical character. In the same way, however, phenomenal Nature must everywhere be regarded as *objectification ;* that is, as the perceptional and conceptional mode of representation of the will or the immediately real, and must not be regarded as the product of the latter. The relation of essence to phenomenon is not that of cause and effect.

Further, the will as thing-in-itself can be only the *one, universal* "*world-will.*" All plurality and multiplicity belong to perception in space and time; these latter are the *principium individuationis.* Hence things are different and separate from each other only as phenomena — in idea and cognition; in their true essence they are

---

[1] Cf. *World as Will*, etc., II. §§ 18–23.

all the same. The will is the ἓν καὶ πᾶν. Here lies for Schopenhauer the metaphysical root of morals. It is the deception of the
phenomenal that makes the individual distinguish his own weal
and woe from that of other individuals, and brings the two into
opposition : in the fundamental moral feeling which feels another's
sorrows as one's own — in *sympathy*, the transcendental unity of will
of all reality comes to light.

Finally, the will can have for its object no particular content that
can be empirically presented in consciousness; for every such
content belongs already to its "objectivity." The world-will has
only itself for its object; it wills only to will. It wills only to be
actual; for all that actually is, is itself only a willing. In this
sense Schopenhauer calls it the *will to live*. It is the thing-in-itself
which ever gives birth to itself in timeless, eternal process, and as
such it is represented in the restless mutation of phenomena.

§ 42. The System of Reason.

The direction which the main line of the idealistic development
was to take was prescribed by the principle from which Fichte
made bold to throw overboard the conception of the thing-in-itself.
The relation of Being and consciousness can be explained only out
of consciousness, and by the fact that consciousness "looks at its
own action" and creates thereby at once the real and the ideal
series of experience — objects and the knowledge of them. The
problem of the *Wissenschaftslehre* is, therefore, to comprehend the
world as a necessary connected whole of rational activities, and
the solution can proceed only by reflection on the part of the philosophising reason upon its own action and upon that which *is requisite* therefor. The necessity, therefore, which prevails in this
system of reason is *not causal, but teleological*. The dogmatic system
understands the intelligence as a product of things, the idealistic
develops intelligence as an inherently purposeful connection of acts,
some of which serve to produce objects. The progress of philosophical thought should not take the form, that because something
is, therefore something else is also, but should rather shape itself
after the guiding principle that *in order that something may take
place, something else must take place also*. Every act of reason has
a task; to perform this it needs other acts and thus other tasks;
the connected series of all activities for the fulfilment of all tasks,
taken as a purposeful unity, is the system of the reason, the
"history of consciousness." The ground or reason of all Being lies

in the ought; that is, in the activity of self-consciousness directed toward an end.

The schema for carrying out this thought is the *dialectical method.* If the world is to be comprehended as reason, the system of reason must be developed from an original task; all particular acts of intelligence must be deduced as means to its performance. This act [lit. "deed-act," *Thathandlung*] is *self-consciousness.* A beginning without assumptions, such as philosophy needs, is not to be found by means of an assertion or proposition, but by means of a *demand,* which every one must be able to fulfil: "*Think thyself!*" And the whole business of philosophy consists in making clear what takes place in this act, and what is requisite for it. But this principle can lead on farther, only so long as it is shown that between that which should take place and that which does take place to this end, there is still a contradiction, out of which the new task results, and so on. The dialectical method is a system in which every problem or task creates a new one. There is in the reason itself a resistance to the result it seeks to achieve, and to overcome this resistance it unfolds a new function. These *three momenta* are designated as *Thesis, Antithesis,* and *Synthesis.*

If Kant had maintained the necessity of insoluble problems of reason for his explanation and criticism of metaphysics, the idealistic metaphysics now makes this thought a positive principle. By this means the reason's world becomes an infinity of self-production, and the *contradiction* between the task and the actual doing is declared to be the real nature of the reason itself. This contradiction is necessary and cannot be abolished. It belongs to the essential nature of the reason; and since only the reason is real, the contradiction is thus declared to be real. Thus the dialectical method, this metaphysical transformation of Kant's transcendental logic, came into stronger and stronger opposition to formal logic. The rules of the understanding, which have their general principle in the principle of contradiction, are adequate, perhaps, for the ordinary elaboration of perceptions into conceptions, judgments, and conclusions; for the intellectual perception of the philosophising reason they do not suffice, before the problems of "speculative construction" they sink to a relative importance.

This doctrine asserts itself already in the first exposition which Fichte gave to his Science of Knowledge;[1] it was then spoken out more and more boldly by disciples and associates like Fr. Schlegel, and, ultimately, the speculative reason affected a superiority to the

---

[1] *Grundlage der ges. W.-L.,* § 1; W., I. 92 ff. [Kroeger's tr., pp. 63 ff.].

"reflective philosophy of the understanding" hemmed in within the principle of contradiction. Schelling[1] appealed to the *coincidentia oppositorum* of Nicolaus Cusanus and Giordano Bruno, and Hegel[2] sees in the triumph of the "narrow understanding" over the reason the hereditary error of all earlier philosophy.[3] Metaphysics, of which Kant has shown that it is not possible for the understanding, seeks an organ of its own in *intellectual perception or intuition*, and a form of its own in the dialectical method. The *productive* synthesis of the manifold must keep its unity above the antitheses into which it divides itself. It is the essential nature of mind or spirit to disunite itself, and from this state of being rent apart, to return back to its original unity.

This *triplicity* rests entirely upon the above (Fichtean) fundamental characterisation of the mind as that which beholds itself. The reason is not only "in-itself" as a simple ideal reality, but also "for-itself"; it appears to itself as "something other, alien"; it becomes for itself an object different from the subject, and this otherness is the principle of *negation*. The doing away with this difference, the negation of the negation, is the synthesis of the two moments above named. These are annulled or sublated ["*aufgehoben*," which has no exact English equivalent; Bosanquet suggests "put by"] in the threefold aspect that their one-sided force is overcome, their relative meaning is preserved, and their original sense transmuted into a higher truth. Following this scheme of the "in-itself," "for-itself," and "in-and-for-itself" (*An-sich, Für-sich, An-und-für-sich*). *Hegel* developed his dialectical method with great virtuosoship by making each conception "turn into its opposite," and from the contradiction of the two making the higher conception proceed, which then experienced the same fortune of finding an antithesis which required a still higher synthesis, and so on. The Master himself, in his employment of this method, particularly in the *Phænomenology* and in the *Logic*, worked in an astonishing wealth of knowledge, a quite unique fineness of feeling for conceptional connections, and a victorious power of combining thought, while occasionally his profundity passed over into obscurity and schematic word-building. In the case of his disciples, a philosophical jargon grew out of this, which pressed all thought into the triple scheme, and by the thoughtless externality with which it was used,—

---

[1] Sixth *Vorl. über Meth. d. ak. St.*, W., V. 267 ff.

[2] Cf. esp. his article on *Glauben und Wissen*, W., I. 21 ff.

[3] It is from this point of view that we best can understand Herbart's polemic against absolute idealism. He, too, finds contradictions in the fundamental conceptions of experience, but just on this account they ought to be worked over until the contradictionless reality is recognised ; cf. above. § 41, 7.

and used for a time in widely extended circles, — it was all too well adapted to discredit philosophy as an empty bombast.[1]

2. The system of reason with *Fichte,* in the first period of his philosophical activity (about 1800), is, in its content also, in full accord with the above method. The original "act" (*Thathandlung*) of self-consciousness, which is determined by nothing except itself, is that the "*I*" or self can only be "posited" by being distinguished from a "*Not-I*" or "not-self." Since, however, the not-self is posited only in the self, — *i.e.* historically expressed, the object posited only in consciousness, — the self and the not-self (*i.e.* subject and object) must reciprocally determine each other within the "I" or self. From this results the theoretical or the practical series of self-consciousness, according as the Not-I or the "I" is the determining part.

The functions of the *theoretical* reason are now developed by Fichte in the following manner: The particular stages result from the reflection of consciousness upon its own previously determined action. By virtue of its own activity, which is limited by nothing external, it presses beyond every bound which the "I" has set for itself in the Not-I as object. The pure perceptions, space and time, the categories as rules of the understanding, and the principles of the reason, are treated as the several forms of this self-determining. In place of the antitheses which Kant had set up between these particular strata, Fichte set the principle, that in each higher stage the reason apprehends in purer form what it has accomplished in the lower stage. Knowing is a process of self-knowledge on the part of the reason, beginning with sense perception and ascending to complete knowledge.[2] But this whole series of the theoretical reason presupposes an original "self-limitation" of the I. If this is given, the entire series is comprehensible in accordance with the principle of self-perception; for every activity has its object and its reason in the preceding. The first self-limitation has its ground in no preceding act, and therefore, theoretically, no ground whatever. It is a *groundless, free activity,* but as such, the ground of all other activities. This groundless [undetermined] free act is *sensation.* It falls into consciousness, therefore, only in its content, which is to be taken up into perception; as act it is, like all that has

---

[1] Cf. the humorous portrayal in G. Rümelin, *Reden und Aufsatze,* pp. 47–50, Freiburg, 1888.

[2] Without any directly visible influence from Leibniz, his conception of the relation of the different knowing faculties asserts itself here in contrast with the Kantian separation. Only it is to be noted that this "history of the development of reason" is, with Leibniz, determined causally, with Fichte teleologically. What Hamann and Herder (cf. above, p. 576) demanded as a requirement of the unity of intelligence in the Leibnizian sense, Fichte and Schelling had meanwhile performed in quite another sense.

no ground, *unconscious.*[1] In this consists its "givenness," by virtue of which it appears as foreign and coming "from without." In place of the thing-in-itself comes, therefore, the *unconscious self-limitation of the I.* Fichte calls this activity *the productive imagination.* It is the world-producing activity of the reason.

For sensation there is then no *ground* which determines it; it is there with absolute freedom, and determines on its part all knowledge as regards content. Hence it can be comprehended only through its *end* — in the *practical Wissenschaftslehre*, which has to investigate to what end the self limits itself. This is only to be understood if we regard the I or self, not as resting Being, but as in its nature *infinite activity* or *impulse.* For since all action is directed toward an object in connection with which it develops, so the self, which finds its object not given to it, as is the case with the empirical will, must, in order to remain impulse and action, *set objects* for itself. This takes place in sensation: sensation has no *ground,* but only the *end* of creating for the impulse of the self a limit beyond which the self passes in order to become object for itself. The actual world of experience, with all its things, and with the "Reality" which it has for the theoretical consciousness, is only the *material for the activity of the practical reason.*

The inmost essence of the ego, therefore, is its action, directed only toward itself, determined only by itself, — the *autonomy of the ethical reason.* The system of reason culminates in the categorical imperative. The I is the ethical will, and the world *is the material of duty put into sensuous form.* It is there, to the end that we may be active in it. It is not that Being is the cause of doing, but Being is brought forth for the sake of the doing. All that *is,* is only to be understood or explained from the point of view of that which it *ought to be (soll).*

The demand of the *Wissenschaftslehre*, so paradoxical for the ordinary consciousness,[2] amounts, accordingly, to robbing the *category*

---

[1] The paradox of the "unconscious activities of consciousness" lies in the expression, not in the thing. German philosophers have frequently been very unfortunate in their terminology, most unfortunate precisely where they wished to give German words a new meaning. Fichte not only uses consciousness and self-consciousness promiscuously, but he understands by consciousness, on the one hand, the actual idea or mental presentation of the individual or the empirical ego (hence in this sense "unconscious," *bewusstlos*), and on the other hand, the functions of the "consciousness in general," of the transcendental apperception or the "universal ego or self" (in this sense he speaks of "history of consciousness"). In these verbal relations rests a good part of the difficulty of Fichte's exposition and of the misunderstanding which it has called forth.

[2] In this spirit Fr. H. Jacobi protested against this knitting, not indeed of the stocking, but of the knitting (W., III. 24 ff.). Cf., on the other hand, C. Fortlage, *Beiträge zur Psychologie* (Leips. 1875), pp. 40 f.

of substantiality of the fundamental significance which it has in the naïve, sensuous view of the world. In this a something that "is," a "Being" ("*Seiendes*") is always thought as support and cause of activities; in Fichte's thought the "doing" or action is conceived as the original, and Being is regarded as only the means posited for that end. This antithesis came sharply to light in the atheism controversy, which had so important consequences for Fichte personally. The *Wissenschaftslehre* could not allow *God* to be regarded as "substance"; in this case he would necessarily be something derived; it could seek the metaphysical conception of God only in the "Universal Ego or Self" (*allgemeinen Ich*), in the absolutely free, world-creating action; and in clear contrast to the *natura naturans* of dogmatism it calls God the *Moral World-order*,[1] the *ordo ordinans*.

Accordingly, the chief philosophical discipline for Fichte is *moral science*. Projected before Kant's Metaphysics of Morals, Fichte's system takes from the same the categorical imperative in the formula "act according to thy conscience," for the starting-point of a strictly carried out science of duties, which develops the general and particular tasks of man from the opposition appearing in the empirical self between the natural impulse and the moral impulse. At the same time, the Kantian rigour is softened by the fact, that man's sensibility, also, is permitted to assert its rights as product of reason. The dualism still survives, but it is already on the way toward being overcome, and in the thought that the purposeful connected whole of the reason assigns each of its members a vocation prescribed by its natural manifestation, ethical theory is brought to an elaboration of the "material for the fulfilment of duty," which is much more penetrating and gives a deeper value to the data of experience. This shows itself in Fichte's exposition of professional duties, in his nobler conception of marriage and family life, in the finer penetration of his ethical investigations into the manifold relations of human life.

The like is true, also, of Fichte's treatment of the problems of public life. A youthful energy masters the Kantian fundamental thoughts here, and gives them a much more impressive formulation than they could receive from Kant himself, who undertook the systematic carrying out of these thoughts, only in his old age. The reciprocal limitation of spheres of freedom in the outer social life of individuals is, for Fichte also, the principle of Natural Right. As "primitive rights" he regarded the claims of the individual to

---

[1] Fichte, W., V. 182 ff., 210 ff.

freedom of his body as the organ for performance of duty, of his property as being the external sphere of operation to this end, and finally of his self-preservation as personality. But these primitive rights become efficient as compulsory rights or laws only through the authority of (positive) laws in the state. The idea of the compact which is at the basis of the state, Fichte analyses into the citizen, the property, and the defence contract. It is interesting in this connection to see how these thoughts culminate in his politics in the principle, that the state has to make provision that every one may be able to live by his work, — the doctrine, named after him, of the so-called *right to work*.[1] Work is the duty of the moral personality, the condition of existence of the physical; it must unconditionally be furnished by the state. Hence the regulation of the relations of labour must not be left to the natural working of supply and demand (as according to Adam Smith), and the profits of labour must not be left to the mechanism of society's war of interests, but the rational law of the state must enter here. From the point of view of this thought, with a careful consideration of the conditions given by experience,[2] Fichte projected his *ideal of the socialistic state* as "the complete industrial state" (*geschlossenen Handelsstaates*), which itself takes in hand all production and manufacturing, and all trade with foreign countries, in order to assign to each citizen his work and also the full revenue for his work. The powerful idealism of the philosopher did not shrink from a deep system of compulsion, if he could hope to assure to every individual thereby a sphere for the free fulfilment of duty.

3. The problem of conceiving the universe as a system of reason was solved in the main in the Science of Knowledge by the method of deducing the external world of the senses as a product, appearing in the empirical ego, of the "consciousness in general"; in this sense Fichte's doctrine, like Kant's, was later characterised as "subjective idealism." Fichte's meaning in this, however, was throughout that "Nature," which it was his intention to have posited as an organic whole,[3] should possess the full significance of an objective product of reason, in contrast with the ideas of individuals; to set this forth he lacked the penetrating knowledge of his subject which he possessed in the case of the relations of human life. Thus it was a supplementing of this work, that was welcome to Fichte also,

---

[1] *Naturrecht*, § 18; W., III. 210 ff.; *Geschl. Handelsst.*, I. 1; W., III. 400 ff.

[2] Cf. G. Schmoller, *Studie über J. G. Fichte* in Hildebrand's *Jahrb. f. Nat. u. Stat.*, 1865; also W. Windelband, *Fichte's Idee des deutschen Staates* (Freiburg, 1890).

[3] Fichte, W., IV. 115.

when *Schelling* undertook to solve the other part of the problem and took up in earnest the thought of constructing or deducing *Nature as the objective system of reason.*   According to the Science of Knowledge and Kant's Philosophy of Nature this was possible only if Nature could be successfully comprehended as a connected whole of forces, having their ultimate end in a service toward the realisation of the reason's command.   The starting-point for this construction was necessarily Kant's *dynamic* theory, which derived the existence of *matter* from the relation of the forces of attraction and repulsion (cf. § 38, 7), and its goal was given by that manifestation of Nature in which alone the practical reason evinces itself — the human *organism.*   Between the two the whole wealth of Nature's forms and functions must be spread out as a *life in unity,* whose rational meaning was to be sought in the organic growth of the final goal out of the material beginnings.   *Nature is the ego, or self, in process of becoming* — this is the theme of Schelling's *Philosophy of Nature.*   This task, which had its basis in philosophical premises, seemed at the same time set by the condition of *natural science,* which had once again reached the point where scattered detail-work craved a living conception of Nature as a whole.   And this craving asserted itself the more vigorously, as the progress of empirical science gave little satisfaction to the highly pitched expectations which had been set upon the principle of the mechanical explanation of Nature after the seventeenth century.   The derivation of the organic from the inorganic remained, as Kant stated, problematical, to say the least; a genetic development of organisms on this basis was a vexed question; for the theory of medicine, which was then passing through a great movement, no key had as yet been found by which it could be fitted into the mechanical conception of the world; now came, also, the discoveries of electric and magnetic phenomena, for which at that time it could not be anticipated that it would be possible to subsume their peculiar mysterious qualities under the point of view of the Galilean mechanics.   In contrast with this, *Spinoza* had made his powerful impression upon the minds of men just because he thought all Nature, man not excluded, as a connected unity, in which the divine Being manifests itself in all its fulness, and for the development of German thought it became of decisive importance that *Goethe* made this conception his own. The poet, indeed, as we find it best expressed in his splendid aphorisms *Die Natur,* reinterpreted this view in his own way; in the stead of the "mathematical consequence" and its mechanical necessity he set the concrete idea of a *living unity of Nature,* in which the *Weltanschauung* of the Renaissance was revived, though without a formulation in abstract thought. This *poetic Spinozism*[1] became an essential link in the development of the idealistic systems.

All these motives come into play in Schelling's *Philosophy of Nature:* as a result its central conception is *life,* and it makes the attempt to consider Nature from the point of view of the *organism,* and to understand the connection of its forces from the ultimate end of the production of organic life. Nature is not to be described and measured, but the meaning and *significance* which belong to its particular phenomena in the purposeful system of the whole are to be understood. The "categories of Nature" are the forms or shapes in which the reason sets itself as objective to itself; they form a system of development in which every particular phenomenon finds its logically determined place. In carrying out this idea Schelling was of course dependent upon the condition of the natural science of his time. Of the connection of forces, of their transformation into each other, which was the principal point of interest for his purpose, ideas at that time were still very imperfect, and the philosopher did not hesitate to fill out the gaps of knowledge by hypotheses, which he took from the *a priori* construction of the teleological system. In many cases these theories proved valuable heuristic principles (cf. above, p. 566), in others they proved false paths by which investigation could attain no useful results.

The element in the *Philosophy of Nature,* which is of historical significance, is its opposition to the dominance of the Democritic-Galilean principle of the purely mechanical explanation of Nature. Quantitative determination is here again regarded as only external form and appearance, and the causal mechanical connection as only the mode of representation which conforms to the understanding. The meaning of the structures of Nature is the significance which they have in the system of the development of the whole. If, therefore, Schelling turned his look toward the relationship of forms in the organic world, if he used the beginnings of comparative morphology, in which *Goethe* played so important a role, in order to exhibit the *unity of the plan* which Nature follows in the succession of animate beings, yet this connected system was not for him, or for his disciples such as *Oken,* properly a causal genesis in time, but the expression of a gradually succeeding fulfilment of the end. In the different orders of animate beings we see in separate forms, according to Oken, what Nature intends with the organism, and what she first reaches completely in man. This teleological interpretation

---

[1] It took Herder prisoner also, as is proved by his conversations on Spinoza's system under the title *Gott* (1787).

does not exclude a causal relation in time, but, with Schelling and Oken at least, it does not include it.   It is not their point to ask whether one species has arisen from another; they only wish to show that one is the preliminary stage for that which the other accomplishes.[1]

From this we can understand why the mechanical explanation of Nature, which has again attained the victory in the nineteenth century, is wont to see in the period of the Philosophy of Nature, only a fit of teleological excess, now happily overcome, which checked the quiet work of investigation.   But the chronicles of the controversy, which since the time of Democritus and Plato has filled the history of the mode of conceiving Nature, are not yet closed, even to-day.   The reduction of the qualitative to the quantitative, which presses forward victoriously under the flag of mathematics, has repeatedly encountered the need which seeks behind motions in space a reality of rational meaning.   This felt need of a living content of Nature Schelling's theory aimed to meet, and for this reason the great poet, who endeavoured to demonstrate as the true reality in the charming play of colours not a vibration of atoms, but a something that is originally qualitative, felt drawn toward it.   This is the philosophical meaning of Goethe's " Theory of Colours."

With Schelling the system of *Nature* is ruled by the thought that in it the objective reason struggles upward from its material modes of manifestation, through the multitude of forms and transformations of forces, up to the organism in which it comes to *consciousness.*[2]   *Sensitive* beings form the termination of the life of Nature ; with sensation the system of the Science of Knowledge begins. The devious way which Nature pursues to this goal is frequently altered in details in the various remodellings which Schelling gave to his Philosophy of Nature, but in its main outlines it remained the same.   In particular, it was the conception of *duality*, of the opposition of forces which negate each other in a higher unity, that formed the fundamental schema of his "construction of Nature," — a conception due to the Science of Knowledge, — and from this point of view the *polarity* in electric and magnetic phenomena which

---

[1] The " interpretation " of phenomena was, to be sure, a dangerous principle from a scientific point of view ; it opened the gates of the Philosophy of Nature to poetic fancy and brilliant flashes.   These guests forced their way in even with Schelling, but still more with his disciples, such as *Novalis, Steffens,* and *Schubert.*   In the case of Novalis especially we have a magical, dreamy symbolism of Nature in a play which is admirable in poetry but questionable in philosophy.

[2] The poetry of this fundamental thought was expressed in most characteristic form by Schelling himself in the beautiful verses which are printed in *Sch.'s Leben in Briefen,* I. 282 ff.

busied Schelling's contemporaries as a newly found enigma was particularly significant for him.

4. When Schelling wished to place beside his Philosophy of Nature an elaboration of his own of the Science of Knowledge, under the name of "Transcendental Idealism," an important change had taken place in the common thought of the Jena idealists, to which he now gave the first systematic expression. The impetus to this came from *Schiller,* and from the development which he had given to the thoughts of the *Critique of Judgment.* It had become plainer step by step that the system of reason must become perfected for idealism in the æsthetic function, and in place of the ethical idealism which the Science of Knowledge taught, and the physical idealism which the Philosophy of Nature presented, appeared now *æsthetic idealism.*

The re-shaping, so rich in results, which Kant's thoughts experienced through Schiller, by no means concerned merely the æsthetic questions which lay nearest the poet, but likewise the ethical questions and those pertaining to the history of philosophy, and therewith the whole system of reason. For Schiller's thoughts, even before his acquaintance with Kant, — as is shown among other things by his poem, *Die Künstler,* — had been turned to the problem of the significance of art and the beautiful in the whole connected system of man's rational life and its historical development, and by solving this problem with Kantian conceptions he gave to the idealism of the Science of Knowledge a decisive turn.

This began with the new Forms which Schiller found for Kant's conception of beauty. The synthesis of the theoretical and the practical in the æsthetic reason (cf. § 40, 2) could perhaps find no more fortunate expression than in Schiller's definition of *beauty as freedom in phenomenal appearance.*[1] It asserts that æsthetic contemplation apprehends its object without subjecting it to the rules of the cognising understanding; it is not subsumed under conceptions, and we do not ask for the conditions which it has in other phenomena. It is perceived *as if* it were free. *Schopenhauer* afterwards expressed this in the form that the enjoyment of the beautiful is the contemplation of the object in independence of the principle of sufficient reason. Schiller later laid still more weight upon the point that the æsthetic process is as independent of the practical reason as of the theoretical. The beautiful (in distinction from the agreeable and the good) is as little an object of the sensuous as it

---

[1] Cf. chiefly the letters to Körner of February, 1793, also the sketch on " The Beautiful in Art," printed with the letter of the 20th of June of that same year, — all fragments of the dialogue *Kallias* which was not completed.

is of the moral impulse; it lacks that quality of want or need which belongs to the life of empirical impulse, just as it lacks the earnestness of the practical reason. In the æsthetic life the *play impulse* unfolds itself;[1] every stirring of the will is silent in disinterested contemplation. In this, too, Schiller was followed by Schopenhauer, when the latter found the happiness of the æsthetic condition in the overcoming of the unhappy will to live, in the activity of the pure, willess subject of knowledge.[2]

From this Schiller concluded in the first place that wherever we have to do with educating man, subject to his sensuous nature, to a condition where he shall will morally, the æsthetic life offers the most effective means to this end. Kant had designated the "reversal of motives" as the ethical task of man (cf. above, § 39, 6); for the transition from the sensuous to the ethical determination of the will he offered man, as an aid, religion; Schiller offered art.[3] Faith and taste cause man to act legally, at least, when he is not yet ripe for morality. In intercourse with the beautiful the feelings become refined, so that natural rudeness vanishes, and man awakes to his higher vocation. Art is the fostering soil for science and morality. Such was the teaching of Schiller in the *Artists;* his *Letters on the Æsthetic Education of the Human Race* go deeper. The æsthetic condition, or state (*Staat*), because it is the completely disinterested state, destroys the sensuous will, also, and thus makes room for the possibility of the moral will; it is the necessary point of transition from the physical state, ruled by needs, into the moral state. In the physical state man endures the power of Nature; in the æsthetic state he frees himself from it; and in the moral state he controls it.

But already in the *Artists* the beautiful had been assigned a second higher task of ultimately giving also the culmination and completion to moral and intellectual cultivation, and in building this thought into the critical system the poet passes over from supplementing to transforming the Kantian doctrine. The two sides of human nature are not reconciled if the moral impulse is obliged to overcome the sensuous impulse. In the physical and in the "moral" state one side of human nature is always suppressed in favour of the

---

[1] The attempt which Schiller makes in his *Letters concerning Æthestic Education* (11 f.) to lay a basis for this in transcendental psychology remind us strongly of the Reinhold-Fichte time when "Jena whirred with the buzz of Form and Matter."

[2] *World as Will*, etc., I. §§ 36–38. In this connection Schopenhauer no doubt claims the same value for scientific knowledge. Cf. § 43, 4.

[3] Cf. the conclusion of the essay, *Ueber den moralischen Nutzen ästhetischer Sitten.*

other. We have a complete manhood only where neither of the two impulses prevails over the other. Man is truly man, only where he plays, where the war within him is silent, where his sensuous nature is exalted to so *noble a sentiment or sensibility* that it is no longer needful for him to will loftily. The Kantian rigorism holds where-ever sensuous inclination stands over against duty : but there is the higher ideal of the *" schöne Seele "* — the *beautiful soul* — which does not know this internal conflict because its nature is so ennobled that it fulfils the moral law from its own inclination. And just this ennobling is gained by man, only through æsthetic education. Through it alone is the sensuous-supersensuous discord in human nature abolished; in it alone does complete, full manhood come to realisation.

5. In the ideal of the *" schöne Seele "* the *" virtuosoship "* of Shaftesbury overcomes the Kantian dualism. The completion of man is the æsthetic reconciliation of the two natures which dwell within him; *culture* is to make the life of the individual a *work of art*, by ennobling what is given through the senses to full accord with the ethical vocation. In this direction Schiller gave expression to the ideal view of life characteristic of his time in antithesis to the rigorism of Kant, and the *æsthetic Humanism* which he thus wrested from abstract thought found besides his, a wealth of other characteristic manifestations. In them all, however, *Goethe* appeared as the mighty personality, who presented in living form this ideal height of humanity in the æsthetic perfection of his conduct of life, as well as in the great works of his poetic activity.

In this conception of the genius Schiller was first joined by *William von Humboldt*.[1] He sought to understand the nature of great poems from this point of view; he found the ideal of man's life in the harmony of the sensuous and the moral nature, and in his treatise which laid the foundations for the *science of language*[2] he applied this principle by teaching that the nature of language is to be understood from the organic interaction of the two elements.

An attitude of sharper opposition to the Kantian rigorism had already been taken, in the Shaftesbury spirit, by *Jacobi* in his romance patterned after Goethe's personality, *" Allwill's Briefsammlung."* The moral genius also is " exemplary " ; he does not subject himself to traditional rules and maxims, he lives himself out and thereby gives himself the laws of his morality. This " ethical Nature " is the highest that the circuit of humanity affords.

---

[1] Born 1767, died 1835. Works, 7 vols. (Berlin, 1841 ff.). Aside from the correspondence, especially that with Schiller, cf. principally the *Æsthetischen Versuche* (Brunswick, 1799). Also Rud. Haym, *W. v. H.* (Berlin, 1856).

[2] *Ueber die Kawi-Sprache* (Berlin, 1836).

Among the *Romantic School* this ethical "geniality" in theory and practice came to its full pride of luxuriant efflorescence. Here it developed as an *æsthetic aristocracy of culture* in opposition to the democratic utility of the Enlightenment morals. The familiar word of Schiller's as to the nobility in the moral world was interpreted to mean, that the Philistine, with his work ruled by general principles, has to perform his definite action determined by ends, while the man of genius, free from all external determination by purposes and rules, merely lives out his own important individuality as a something valuable in itself, — lives it out in the disinterested play of his stirring inner life, and in the forms shaped out by his own ever-plastic imagination. In his morals of genius, the sensibility (*Sinnlichkeit*) in the narrowest significance of the word is to come to its full, unstunted right, and by æsthetic enhancement is to become equal in rank to the finest stirrings of the inner nature, — a sublime thought, which did not prevent its carrying out in Schlegel's *Lucinde* from running out into sensual though polished vulgarity.

Schleiermacher's ethics brought back the Romantic morals to the purity of Schiller's intention.[1] It is the complete expression of the life-ideal of that great time. All ethical action seems to it to be directed toward the unity of Reason and Nature. By this is determined in general the moral law, which can be none other than the natural law of the reason's life; by this is also determined in detail the task of every individual, who is to bring this unity to expression in a special way, proper only for him. In the systematic carrying-out of this thought, Schleiermacher distinguishes (according to the organic and the intellectual factors of intelligence, cf. § 41, 6) the organising and the symbolising activities, according as the unity of Nature and Reason is procured by striving, or is presupposed, and thus result in all four fundamental ethical relations, to which correspond as goods, the state, society, the school, and the Church. From these the individual has to develop in self-activity to a harmonious life of his own.

Finally, *Herbart*, also, reduced ethical theory to the æsthetic reason in a completely independent manner; for him, morals is a branch of general æsthetics. Besides the theoretical reason, which contains the principles for knowledge of Being, he recognises as original only the *judging or estimation of the existent in accordance with æsthetic Ideas.* This estimation has to do with the will and the needs of the empirical self as little as has the knowing activity; "Judgments of taste" hold necessarily and universally with direct self-evidence,

---

[1] Cf. also Schleiermacher's *Vertraute Briefe über die Lucinde* (1800).

and always refer to the *relations in the existent:* these have an original pleasure or displeasure inherent in them. The application of these principles to the narrower field of the æsthetic is only indicated by Herbart : ethics, on the contrary, is regarded by him as the science of the judgments of taste pronounced upon the relations of human will. It has not to explain anything — that is the business of psychology ; it has only to settle the norms by which the judgment mentioned above is passed. As such norms, Herbart finds the five *ethical Ideas,* — Freedom, Affection, Benevolence, Right, and Equity, — and according to these he seeks to arrange the systems of the moral life, while for his genetic investigation he always employs the principles of the associational psychology, and thus in the statics and mechanics of the state undertakes to set forth the mechanism of the movements of the will, by which the social life of man is maintained.

6. From *Schiller's* æsthetic morals resulted, also, a *philosophy of history,* which made the points of view of Rousseau and Kant appear in a new combination. The poet unfolded this in an entirely characteristic manner in his essays on *Naïve and Sentimental Poetry,* by gaining the fundamental æsthetic conceptions from bringing forward historical antitheses, and constructing a general plan of their movement. The different ages and the different kinds of poetry are characterised, in his view, by the different relations sustained by the spirit to the realm of Nature and the realm of Freedom. As the "Arcadian" state, we have that where man does what is in accordance with the moral order instinctively, without commandment, because the antithesis of his two natures has not yet unfolded in consciousness: as the Elysian goal, we have that full consummation in which his nature has become so ennobled that it has again taken up the moral law into its will. Between the two lies the struggle of the two natures, — the actual life of history.

Poetry, however, whose proper task it is to portray man, is everywhere determined by these fundamental relations. If it makes the sensuous, natural condition of man appear as still in harmonious unity with his spiritual nature, then it is *naïve;* if, on the contrary, it sets forth the contradiction between the two, if in any way it makes the inconsistency between the reality and the ideal in man appear, then it is *sentimental,* and may be either satirical or elegiac or, also, in the form of the idyl. The poet who is himself Nature presents Nature naïvely ; he who possesses her not has the sentimental interest in her of calling back, as Idea in poetry, the Nature that has vanished from life. The harmony of Nature and Reason is given in the former, set as a task in the latter — there as reality,

here as ideal.   This distinction between the poetic modes of feeling
is, according to Schiller, characteristic also for the contrast between
the ancient and the modern.   The Greek feels naturally, the modern
man is sensible of Nature as a lost Paradise, as the sick man is
sensible of convalescence.   Hence the ancient and naïve poet gives
Nature as she is, without his own feelings; the modern and sentimental only in relation to his own reflection: the former vanishes
behind his object, as the Creator behind his works; the latter shows
in the shaping of his material the power of his own personality
striving toward the ideal.   There realism is dominant; here idealism; and the last summit of art would be the union in which the
naïve poet should set forth the sentimental material.   So Schiller
sketched the form of his great friend, the modern Greek.

These principles were eagerly seized upon by the *Romanticists.*
Virtuosos of the reviewer's art, such as were the *Schlegels,* rejoiced
in this philosophical schema for criticism and characterisation, and
introduced it into their comprehensive treatment of the history of
literature.   In this *Frederick* Schlegel gave Schiller's thoughts the
specifically romantic flavour, for which he knew how to use Fichtean
motifs with ready superficiality.   While he designated the antithesis propounded by Schiller with the new names *classic* and *romantic,*
he remodelled it materially, also, by his doctrine of *irony.*   The
classic poet loses himself in his material; the romantic poet hovers
as a sovereign personality above it; he annuls matter by the form.
In going with his free fancy beyond the material which he posits,
he unfolds, in connection with it, merely the play of his genius,
which he limits in none of its creation.   Hence the romantic poet
has a tendency to the infinite, toward the never complete: he himself is always more than any of his objects, and just in this the
irony evinces itself.   For the infinite doing of the ethical will, of
which Fichte taught, the Romanticist substitutes the endless play
of the fancy, which creates without purpose, and again destroys.

The elements in Schiller's doctrine that concern the *philosophy
of history* found their full development in *Fichte,* from whom they
borrowed much.   As the result of their influence he allowed the
antitheses of his *Wissenschaftslehre* to become reconciled in the
æsthetic reason.   Already in his Jena lectures on the Nature of
the Scholar, and in the treatment which the professional duties
of the teacher and the artist found in the "*System of Ethics*" we
hear these *motifs*; in his Erlangen lectures they have become the
ruling theme.   When he proceeded to draw the "*Characteristics of
the Present Age,*" he did it in the pithy lines of a construction of
universal history.   As the first ("Arcadian") state of mankind

appears that of *rational instinct* or *instinctive reason* ("*Vernunftin-stinct*"), as the representatives of which a normal people is assumed. In this age the universal consciousness is dominant over and in individuals with immediate, uncontested certainty of natural neces-sity; but it is the vocation of the free individual ego to tear himself loose from this government of custom and tradition, and follow his own impulse and judgment. With this, however, begins the age of sinfulness. This sinfulness becomes complete in the intel-lectual and moral crumbling of social life, in the anarchy of opin-ions, in the atomism of private interests. With clear strokes this "*complete sinfulness*" is characterised as the theory and practice of the Enlightenment. The community of mankind has here sunk to the "state based upon needs" ("*Nothstaat*"), which is limited to making it externally possible for men to exist together, — and ought to be so limited, since it has nothing to do with any of man's higher interests, — morality, science, art, and religion, — and must leave them to the sphere of the individual's freedom. But for this reason the individual has no living interest in this "actual" state; his home is the world, and perhaps also at any moment the state which stands at the summit of civilisation.[1] This civilisation, how-ever, consists in the subordination of individuals to the known law of reason. Out of the sinful, arbitrary free-will of individuals must rise the autonomy of the reason, the self-knowledge and self-legisla-tion of the universally valid, which is now consciously dominant in the individual. With this the age of the *rule of reason* will begin, but it will not be complete until all the powers of the rationally matured individual are placed at the service of the whole in the "true state," and so the commandment of the common conscious-ness is again fulfilled without resistance. This ("Elysian") final state is that of *rational art* or *artistic reason* ("*Vernunftkunst*"). It is the ideal of the "*schöne Seele*" carried over to politics and history. To bring about this age, and in it to lead the community, the "kingdom," by reason, is the task of the "teacher," the scholar, and the artist.[2]

The "beginning of the rule of reason" Fichte's vigorous idealism saw just where sinfulness and need had risen to the highest point. In his "*Addresses to the German Nation*" he praised his people

---

[1] The classical passage for the cosmopolitanism of the culture of the eighteenth century is found in Fichte, W., VII. 212.

[2] In the religious turn which Fichte's thought takes at the close, this picture of the ideal civilised state of the future takes on more and more theocratic features: the scholar and artist have now become the priest and seer. Cf. W., IV. 453 ff., and *Nachgel. Werke*, III. 417 ff.

as the only one that still preserves its originality and is destined to create the true civilised state. He cries to his people to bethink itself of this its vocation, on which the fate of Europe is hanging, to raise itself from within by a completely new education to the kingdom of reason, and to give back freedom to the world.

7. The point of view of the *æsthetic reason* attained full mastery in the whole system of the idealistic philosophy through *Schelling*. In his working out of the " *Transcendental Idealism* " he developed the Fichtean antithesis of the theoretical and practical *Wissenschaftslehre* by the relation between the conscious and unconscious activity of the self (cf. above, No. 2). If the conscious is determined by the unconscious, the self is theoretical; in the reverse case it is practical. But the theoretical self, which looks on at the productiveness of the unconscious reason, manifested in feeling, perceiving, and thinking, never comes to an end with this, and the practical self, also, which re-shapes and transforms the unconscious reality of the cosmos in the free work of individual morality, of political community, and of historical progress, has the goal of its activity in the infinite. In neither series does the whole essential nature of the reason ever come to its full realisation. This is possible only through the *unconscious-conscious activity of the artistic genius,* in which the above antitheses are abolished. In the undesigned appropriateness of the creative activity, whose product is freedom in phenomenal appearance, the highest synthesis of all activities of reason must be sought. Kant had defined genius as the intelligence that works like Nature; Schiller had characterised the æsthetic condition of play as the truly human; Schelling declared the æsthetic reason to be the capstone of the idealistic system. The work of art is that phenomenon in which the reason attains purest and fullest development; *art* is the true organon of philosophy. It is in art that the "spectator thought" has to learn what reason is. Science and philosophy are one-sided and never completed series of the development of the subjective reason; only art is complete in all its works as entirely realised reason.

After he had written the *Transcendental Idealism* Schelling delivered in Jena his lectures on the *Philosophy of Art,* which carried out this fundamental thought with an intelligent appreciation for artistic character and mode of production, that showed admirable fineness and acuteness especially in its treatment of poetry. These lectures, not printed at that time, determined the whole subsequent development of æsthetics by their influence upon the Jena circle. As published later they present that form which Schelling gave them some years after, when delivering them in

Würzburg.   In this later form[1] the change in general point of view,
to which the philosopher had meanwhile advanced, asserts itself
still more.

8. The æsthetic *motif* was active also, at least formally, in that
a common systematic basis was sought for the Philosophy of Nature
and the Transcendental Philosophy.   The former treated the objective, the latter the subjective reason; the two, however, must be
indentical in their ultimate essence; whence this phase of idealism
is called the *System of Identity* (*Identität-system*).   According to
this, a common principle is required for Nature and the self.   In
the treatise which Schelling entitled "Exposition of my System
of Philosophy," this common principle is called the "*Absolute
Reason*" or the "*Indifference* of Nature and Spirit, of object and
subject"; for the highest principle can be determined neither as
real nor as ideal; in it all antitheses must be obliterated.   The
"Absolute" is here as undetermined in its content,[2] with Schelling,
as in the old "negative theology," or as in Spinoza's "substance."
With the latter conception it has in common the property, that its
phenomenal manifestation diverges into two series, the real and the
ideal, Nature and Spirit or Mind.   This kinship with Spinoza as
regards his thought, Schelling strengthened by formal relationship,
imitating in his *Exposition* the schematism of the *Ethics.*
Nevertheless this idealistic Spinozism is different throughout from
the original in its conception of the world.   Both desire to set forth
the eternal transmutation of the Absolute into the universe; but
in this Spinoza regards the two attributes of materiality and consciousness as completely separate, and each finite phenomenon as
belonging solely to one of the two spheres.   Schelling, however,
requires that "Reality" and "Ideality" must be contained in every
phenomenon, and construes particular phenomena according to the
degree in which the two elements are combined.   The dialectical
principle of *absolute idealism* is the *quantitative difference between the
real and the ideal factors ;* the Absolute itself is just for this reason
complete indifference.[3]   The *real series* is that in which the objective
factor predominates ("*überwiegt*"); it leads from matter through
light, electricity, and chemism to the *organism* — the relatively
spiritual manifestation of Nature.   In the ideal series the subjective
factor predominates.   In it the development proceeds from morality

---

[1] In the coll. works, V. 353 ff., first printed 1859.

[2] Schelling's disciple, Oken, expressed this very characteristically when he
placed the Absolute, already called God by him, $= \pm 0$.

[3] Schelling illustrates this schematically by the example of the magnet, in
the different parts of which north and south magnetism are present with varying intensities.

and science to the *work of art*, the relatively most natural appearance in the realm of Spirit.   And the total manifestation of the
Absolute, the *universe*, is, therefore, at once the most perfect organism and the most perfect work of art.[1]

9. In this system Schelling would comprehend the entire issue of
the investigations which had previously diverged in various directions.   The different stages of the self-differentiation of the Absolute
he termed at first, " potencies," but soon introduced another name,
and at the same time another conception of the matter.   This was
connected with the *religious turn* which the thinking of the Romanticists took at about the close of the last and the beginning of the
present century.   The incitement to this came from *Schleiermacher*.
He proved to the " Cultured Despisers of Religion," that the *system
of reason can become complete only in religion*.   In this, too, was a
victory for the *æsthetic* reason.   For what Schleiermacher then
preached as religion (cf. § 41, 6) was not a theoretical or practical
behaviour of man, but an æsthetic relation to the World-ground, the
feeling of absolute dependence.   Therefore, religion, too, was in his
view limited to pious feeling, to the complete permeation of the
individual by this inward relation to the universal, and put aside all
theoretical form and practical organisation.   For the same reason
religion was held to be an individual matter, and positive religion
was traced back to the " religious genius " of its founder.   In view
of this kinship we can understand the influence which Schleiermacher's " *Reden* " exercised upon Romanticism : to this is due the
inclination of the latter to expect from religion the unitary solution
of all problems of mankind, to desire to bring in it the separated
spheres of the activity of civilisation into inner and intimate union
again, and, finally, to seek the eternal welfare of all in that rule of
religion over all spheres of life, which obtained in the Middle
Ages.   As Schiller created an idealised Greece, so the later Romanticists created an idealised Middle Ages.

Schelling followed this line of thought with great acuteness and
fineness of feeling.   Like Spinoza, he now named the Absolute " *God* "
or the " Infinite," and likewise as Spinoza had inserted the attributes and the " infinite modes " (cf. p. 409 f.) between " substance " and
the particular finite realities, so the " potencies " are now regarded as
the eternal forms of the phenomenal manifestation of God, while
the empirical particular phenomena are the finite copies of these.
But when in this sense they were also termed by Schelling
Ideas (in his *Bruno* and in his *Method of Academical Study*)

---

[1] W., I. 4, 423.

another influence still comes to light in this. Schleiermacher and
Hegel, the latter of whom had exerted a personal influence upon
Schelling since 1801, both pointed to *Plato;* but the philosophical
knowledge of that time[1] still saw Plato's doctrine through the spec-
tacles of *Neo-Platonism,* which conceived of the *Ideas as God's vision
or intuition of himself* (*Selbstanschauung Gottes*). And so Schelling's
doctrine turned back into a *Neo-Platonic Idealism,* according to
which the "Ideas" formed the intermediate link through which
the Absolute became transformed into the world.

This religious idealism of Schelling's doctrine of Ideas has a
number of parallel and succeeding phenomena. The most interesting of these personally is *Fichte's* later doctrine, in which he paid to
the victory of Spinozism the tribute of making the infinite impulse
of the I proceed forth from an "absolute Being" (*Sein*) and be directed toward the same. For finite things, he held fast to his deduction of them as products of consciousness; but the infinite activity
of this consciousness he now deduced from the end of "imitating"
an absolute Being, the deity, and hence the vocation and destiny of
man appeared to him no longer the restless activity of categorical
imperative, but the "blessed life" of sinking into a contemplation
of the divine original, — a mystical dying note of the mighty
thinker's life, which makes the victory of the æsthetic reason
appear in its full magnitude.

The religious *motif* was followed still farther by Schelling's disciple *Krause.* He wished to combine the pantheistic *Weltanschauung*
of idealism, which Schelling even at that time still defended (in
Spinozistic fashion), with the conception of divine personality. He,
too, regards the world as the development of the divine "essence,"
which is distinctly stamped out in the Ideas; but these ideas are
the *intuition which the supreme personality has of himself.* Essence
(*Wesen*)—this is Krause's term for God — is not indifferent Reason, but the personal, living ground of the world. In his farther
carrying out of the system, which was characterised as "Panen-
theism," Krause has scarcely any other originality than the very
objectionable one of presenting the thoughts common to the whole
idealistic development in an unintelligible terminology, which he
himself invented, but declared to be pure German. He carries
out, especially, his conception of the entire life of reason from the
point of view of the "*Gliedbau*" (in German, organism). He not
only, like Schelling, regards the universe as a "*Wesengliedbau*"

---

[1] On Herbart's independent position, the importance of which becomes clear
just in antithesis to that of Schelling and Hegel, see above, p. 584, note 1.

(divine organism), but also regards the structures of society as continuations of the organic vital movement beyond the individual man ; every union (*Bund*) is such a "*Gliedbau,*" and inserts itself again into a higher organism as a member (*Glied*), and the course of history is the process of the production of more and more perfect and comprehensive unions.

For the *Romantic œsthetics,* finally, Schelling's new doctrine gave rise to the result that the Neo-Platonic conception of beauty, as phenomenal manifestation of the Idea in the sensuous, became again recognised as authoritative. The relation of inadequacy between the finite appearance and the infinite Idea agreed with Schlegel's principle of irony, and these thoughts *Solger,* especially, made the basis of his theory of art.

10. The consummation of this whole rich and varied development is formed by *Hegel's logical idealism.* He signifies in the main a return from Schelling to Fichte, a giving up of the thought that the living wealth of the world can be derived or deduced from the "Nothing"[1] of absolute indifference, and the attempt to raise this empty substance again to *spirit,*[2] — to the self-determined *subject.* Such knowledge, however, cannot have the form of intuition or immediate perception (*Anschauung*), which Fichte and Schelling had claimed for the Ego or the Absolute, but only that of the *conception or notion (Begriff).* If all that is real or actual is the manifestation of spirit or mind, then metaphysics coincides with the logic[3] which has to develop the creative self-movement of spirit as a dialectical necessity. The conceptions into which mind or spirit takes apart and analyses its own content are the *categories of reality,* the forms of the cosmic life; and the task of philosophy is not to describe this realm of forms as a given manifold, but to comprehend them as the *moments* of a single unitary development. The dialectical method, therefore, serves, with Hegel, to determine the essential nature of particular phenomena by the *significance* which they have as members or links in the self-unfolding of spirit. Instead of Spirit (*Geist*) Hegel also uses Idea or God. It is the highest task that has ever been set philosophy, to comprehend the world as a development of those principles or determinations which form the content of the divine mind.

---

[1] Hegel, *Phänomen. Vorr.*, W., II. 14.

[2] [*Geist*, as in § 20, has the connotation of both "mind" and "spirit." The former seems more appropriate where logical relations are under consideration, though the latter is usually retained for the sake of uniformity.]

[3] This metaphysical logic is of course not formal logic, but in its determining principle is properly Kant's transcendental logic. The only difference is that the "phenomenon" is for Kant a human mode of representation, for Hegel an objective externalising of the Absolute Spirit.

In this, Hegel sustains not only to the German philosophy, but to the whole earlier intellectual movement, a relation similar to that of Proclus to Greek thought: [1] in the "schema of trinities" of Position, Negation, and Sublation or Reconciliation, all conceptions with which the human mind has ever thought reality or its particular groups, are woven together into a unified system. Each retains its assigned place, in which its necessity, its relative justification, is said to become manifest: but each proves by this same treatment to be only a *moment* or factor which receives its true value only when it has been put in connection with the rest and introduced into the whole. It is to be shown that the antitheses and contradictions of conceptions belong to the nature of mind itself, and thus also to the essential nature of the reality which unfolds from it, and that their truth consists just in the systematic connection in which the categories follow from one another. "The phenomenon is the arising and passing away, which itself does not arise and pass away, but 'is' in-itself, and constitutes the reality and movement of the life of truth." [2]

Hegel's philosophy is, therefore, essentially *historical, a systematic elaboration of the entire material of history*. He possessed both the necessary erudition and also the combining power and fineness of feeling for the discovery of those logical relations which were of importance for him. The interest in his philosophy lies less in the individual conceptions, which he took from the intellectual labours of two thousand years, than in the systematic *combination* which he brought about between them: and just by this means he knew how to portray in masterly manner the meaning and significance of individual details, and to throw a surprising light upon long-standing structures of thought. He, indeed, displayed in connection with his data the *arbitrariness* (*Willkür*) of [*a priori*] *constructive thought*, which presents the actual reality, not as it offers itself empirically, but as it ought to be in the dialectical movement, and this violation of the actual matter of fact might be objectionable where the attempt was made to bring empirical material into a philosophical system, as in the philosophy of Nature, the history of philosophy, and history in general. All the more brilliant did the power of the thinking saturated by the historical spirit prove in those fields where it is the express province of philosophical treatment, merely to reflect on

---

[1] Cf. above, § 20, 8.
[2] This *Heracliteanism*, which was inherent already in Fichte's doctrine of action (cf. above, p. 594 f.), found its most vigorous opponent in Herbart's Eleaticism (cf. § 41, 7 f.). This old antithesis constitutes the essential element in the relation of the two branches of German idealism (cf. above, p. 584, note).

undoubted data, but not to give any account of empirical reality. So Hegel gave as æsthetics a historical structure built up of the *æsthetic ideals of mankind.* Following Schiller's method, and attaching himself also materially to Schiller's results, he displayed all the fundamental systematic conceptions of this science in the well-arranged series of the symbolic, the classic, and the romantic, and likewise divided the system of the arts into architecture, sculpture, painting, music, and poetry. So, too, from the fundamental conception of *religion* as being the relation of the finite to the absolute Spirit in the form of imaginative representation (*Vorstellung*) his philosophy of religion develops the *stages of its positive realisation* in the natural religion of magic, fire worship, and animal symbolism, in the religion of spiritual individuality of the sublime, the beautiful, and the intellectual, and finally in the absolute religion which represents God as what he is, the triune Spirit. Here, with a deep-going knowledge of his material, Hegel has everywhere drawn the main lines in which the empirical treatment of these same subjects later moved, and set up the philosophical categories for the general consideration of historical facts as a whole.

The same is true, also, of his treatment of universal history. Hegel understood by *Objective Spirit* the active and influential living body of individuals, which is not created by these, but rather forms the source from which they proceed as regards their spiritual life. The abstract form of this body is called *Right;*[1] it is the Objective Spirit "in itself." The subjection of the subjective disposition of the individual to the commands of the common consciousness the philosopher calls "*morality,*" while he retains the name of " *Sittlich-keit* " [social morality or the moral order] for the realisation of the common consciousness in the *State.* In the immanent living activity of the human reason the state is the highest; beyond this are only art, religion, and science, which press forward to the Absolute Spirit. The state is the realisation of the ethical Idea; it is the spirit of the people become visible; it is in its Idea the living work of art, in which the inwardness of the human reason comes forth into outer manifestation. But this Idea, from which the system of the forms and functions of political life derives, appears in the actual world only in the individual structures of the states which arise and pass away. Its only true and full realisation is *universal history,* in which the peoples enter successively, to live out their spirit in the work of state formation, and then retire from the stage.

---

[1] Hence Hegel treats the doctrine of Objective Spirit under the title *Philoso-phy of Right* (*Rechtsphilosophie*).

So every epoch is characterised by the spiritual predominance of a definite people, which imprints the sign of its peculiar character upon all the activities of civilisation.   And if it is the task of *history* as a whole to understand this connected order, then *politics*, too, must not suppose that it can construct and decree a political life from abstract requirements; it must, rather, seek in the quiet development of the national spirit the motives of its political movement.   So in Hegel, the "Philosopher of the Restoration," the *historical Weltanschauung* turns against the revolutionary doctrinairism of the Enlightenment.

Hegel is less successful in the treatment of questions of natural philosophy and psychology; the energy of his thought lies in the domain of history.   The external scheme of his system, as a whole, is in large the following: the Spirit in itself (*Geist an sich*), *i.e.* in its absolute content, is the realm of the categories; this is treated by the *Logic* as the doctrine of Being, of Essence, and of Conception or Notion.   Spirit for itself (*Geist für sich*), *i.e.* in its otherness and self-estrangement or externalisation, is Nature, the forms of which are treated in Mechanics, Physics, and Organics.   The third main part treats, as *Philosophy of Spirit*, the Spirit in and for itself (*an und für sich*), *i.e.* in its conscious life as returning to itself; here three stages are distinguished, viz. the Subjective (individual) Spirit; the Objective Spirit as Right, Morality, State, and History; finally, the Absolute Spirit as pure perception (*Anschauung*) in Art, as imaginative representation (*Vorstellung*) in Religion, as conception (*Begriff*) in the History of Philosophy.

He repeats, in all these parts of his philosophy, not only the formal dialectic of the construction of his conceptions, but also the material which constitutes the contents of the successive conceptions.   So the *Logic* in its second and third parts develops already the fundamental categories of the Philosophy of Nature and of Spirit; so the development of the æsthetic ideals constantly points toward that of the religious *Vorstellungen;* and so the whole course of the *Logic* is parallel to his History of Philosophy.   Just this relation belongs to the essential nature of the *system of reason*, which here embraces not only, as with Kant, the Forms, but also the content, and aims to unfold before its view this content in the variety of the "forms of the actual world of reality," although this content is ultimately everywhere the same with itself.   The course of development is always the same, viz. that the "Idea," by differentiating and becoming at variance with itself, "*comes to itself.*" Hence the categories progress from the Being which has no content to the inner Essence, and from there to the Idea which understands itself; hence the forms of the empirical world ascend from matter to the imponderables, then to the organism, consciousness, self-consciousness, reason, right, morality, and the social morality of the state, successively, to apprehend the Absolute Spirit in art, religion, and science; hence the history of philosophy begins with the categories of material existence, and becomes complete after all its fortunes in the doctrine of the self-comprehending Idea; hence, finally, the entrance into this "system of the reason," also, will best be found by making it clear to one's self how the human mind begins with the sensuous consciousness, and by the contradictions of this is driven to an ever higher and deeper apprehension of itself, until it finds its rest in philosophical knowledge, in the science of the conception. The inter-relation of all these developments Hegel has set forth with obscure language and many mysterious and thoughtful intimations, in his *Phenomenology.*

In this system of reason every particular has its truth and reality only in its being a *moment* in the development of the whole. Only as such is it real *in concreto,* and only as such is it comprehended by philosophy. But if we take it abstractly, if we think it in its isolation, in which it exists not *realiter,* but only according to the subjective apprehension of the understanding, then it loses that connection with the whole, in which its truth and actual reality consists: then it appears as accidental and without reason. But as such, it exists only in the limited thinking of the individual subject. For philosophical knowledge, the principle holds, that what is reasonable is real, and what is real is reasonable.[1] The System of Reason is the sole reality.

§ 43. The Metaphysics of the Irrational.

The "dialectic of history" willed it that the System of Reason should also change into its opposite, and that the insight into the insurmountability of the barriers which the attempt to deduce all phenomena from one fundamental principle necessarily encounters, caused other theories to arise close beside the idealistic doctrines already treated; and these other theories found themselves thereby forced to maintain the *unreason of the World-ground.* The first to pass through this process was the many-sided agent of the main development, the Proteus of idealism, Schelling. The new in this movement is not the knowledge that the rational consciousness always has ultimately something for its content, which it simply

---

[1] *Vorrede zur Rechtsphilos.,* W., VIII. 17.

finds present within itself, without being able to give any account of it : such limiting conceptions were the transcendental X as thing-in-itself, with Kant ; as differential of consciousness, with Maimon; as a free act without rational ground, in Fichte. The new was, that this which could not be comprehended by the reason, and which resisted its work, was now also to be thought as something *irrational.*

1. Schelling was forced upon the path of irrationalism, remarkably enough, by taking up the religious *motif* into his absolute idealism (§ 42, 9). If "the Absolute" was thought no longer merely in Spinozistic fashion, as the universal, indifferent essence of all phenomena, if the divine and the natural principle of things were distinguished, so that the eternal Ideas as the Forms of the divine self-perception were assigned a separate existence beside finite things, then the transmutation of God into the world must again become a problem. This was really Hegel's problem also, and the latter was right when he taught later that, in his view, philosophy has the same task as theology. He aided himself with the dialectical method which aimed to show in the form of a higher logic, how the Idea agreeably to its own conceptional essence releases itself to "otherness" (*Anderssein*), *i.e.* to Nature, to finite phenomenal appearance.

Schelling sought to solve the same problem by the method of *theosophy, i.e.* by a mystico-speculative doctrine, which transposed philosophical conceptions into religious intuitions. His happening upon this method was due to the fact that the problem met him in the form of an attempt to limit philosophy by religion. He obligated himself, in a vigorous reaction against this in the name of philosophy, to solve the religious problem also. This, indeed, could only be done if philosophy passed over into theosophical speculations.

A disciple of the System of Identity, Eschenmayer,[1] showed that philosophical knowledge can indeed point out the reasonableness of the world, and its agreement with the divine reason, but cannot show how this world attains the self-subsistent existence with reference to the deity, which it has in finite things. Here philosophy ceases and religion begins. In order to vindicate this domain also for philosophy, and restore the old unity between philosophy and religion, Schelling lays claim to specifically religious intuitions as philosophical conceptions, and so re-shapes them in accordance with this claim that they appear usable for both disciplines : in doing which he makes a copious use of Kant's philosophy of religion.

---

[1] Eschenmayer (1770–1852), *Die Philosophie in ihrem Uebergange zur Nicht-philosophie* (1803).

In fact,[1] there is no continuous transition from the Absolute to the concrete reality; the origin of the world of sense from God is thinkable only by a *leap (Sprung)*, a breaking off from the condition of absoluteness.   A ground for this — Schelling still teaches here — is to be found neither in the Absolute nor in the Ideas : but in the nature of the latter the possibility at least is given.   For to the Ideas as the "antitype" or counterpart of the Absolute, in which it beholds itself, the self-subsistence of the archetype communicates itself, — the *freedom* of that which is in itself (*"In-sich-selbst-seins"*). In this lies the possibility of the *falling away of the Ideas from God,* of their assuming metaphysical independence, by which they become actual and empirical, *i.e.* finite.   But this falling away is not necessary and not comprehensible : it is a *fact without rational ground;* not, however, a single event, but as timeless and eternal as the Absolute and the Ideas.   We see that the religious colouring of this doctrine comes from Kant's theory of the radical evil as a deed of the intelligible character, while the philosophical, on the contrary, comes from Fichte's conception of the free acts of the ego, which have no rationale.   On this apostasy, therefore, rests the actualisation of the Ideas in the world.   Hence the *content* of the actual reality is rational and divine ; for it is God's Ideas that are actual in it : their *being actual,* however, is apostasy, sin, and unreason.   This reality of the Ideas external to God is *Nature.*   But its divine essence strives back to the original ground and archetype, and this *return of things into God* is *history,* the epic composed in the mind of God, whose Iliad is the farther and farther departure of man from God, and whose Odyssey is his return to God.   Its final purpose is the *reconciliation of the apostasy,* the reuniting of the Ideas with God, the cessation of their self-subsistence.   Individuality also experiences this change of fortunes : its selfness (*Ichheit*) is intelligible freedom, self-determination — breaking loose from the Absolute : its deliverance is a submergence in the Absolute.

In similar manner *Frederick Schlegel*[2] made the "triplicity" of the infinite, the finite, and the return of the finite to the infinite, the principle of his later theory, which professed to maintain the contradictions of the actual as a fact, to explain them from the fall, and to reconcile them through subjection to divine revelation ; but merely concealed, with great pains, the philosophical impotence of its author under the exposition employed.

---

[1] Schelling, *Religion und Philosophie*, W., I. 6, pp. 38 ff.
[2] In the *Philosophische Vorlesungen*, edited by Windischmann (1804–1806), and likewise later in the *Philosophie des Lebens* and the *Philosophie der Geschichte* (1828–1829).

2. The subtlety of *Schelling*, on the contrary, could not free itself from the once-discovered problem. The monism, which had always controlled his thought, forced him to the question, whether the ground of the falling away was not ultimately to be found in the Absolute itself: and this could be affirmed only if the *irrational* was transferred *to the essence of the Absolute itself.* From the point of view of this thought, Schelling became friendly to the mysticism of *Jacob Boehme* (cf. p. 374 f.). This was brought near to him by his intercourse with Franz von *Baader.* The latter himself had received his stimulus both from Boehme and from Boehme's French prophet *St. Martin*,[1] and, holding fast to the Catholic faith, had elaborated his mysticism with obscure fantastic genius and un-methodical appropriation of Kantian and Fichtean thoughts. The original idea that stirred within him was, that the course of the life of man, who is the image of God, and who can know of himself only so much as God knows of him, must be parallel to the self-development of God. Since, now, man's life is determined by the fall as its beginning and redemption as its goal, the *eternal self-generation of God* must consist in God's unfolding himself out of his dark, irrational, primitive essence, through self-revelation and self-knowledge, to absolute reason.

Under such influences Schelling also began in his treatise[2] on freedom (1809) to speak of an *Urgrund, Ungrund,* or *Abgrund* [primordial ground, unreason, or abyss] in the divine nature, which is depicted as mere Being, and absolute primordial accident (*"Urzu-fall"*), as a dark striving, an infinite impulse. It is the unconscious will, and all actual reality is in the last instance will. This will, directed only toward itself, creates as its self-revelation the Ideas, the image in which the will beholds itself — the reason. Out of the interaction of the ever dark and blind urgency and its ideal self-beholding proceeds the world, which as Nature permits us to recognise the conflict between purposive formation and irrational impulse, and as historical process has for its content the victory of the universal will revealed in reason, over the natural

---

[1] *St. Martin* (1743–1803), "Le philosophe inconnu," the stern opponent of the Enlightenment and of the Revolution, was seized through and through by Boehme's teachings, and translated his *Aurora.* Of his writings, the most important are *L'Homme de Désir* (1790), *Le Nouvel Homme* (1796), and *De l'Esprit des Choses* (1801) ; the most interesting perhaps is the strange work, *Le Crocodile, ou guerre du bien et du mal arrivée sous la règne de Louis XV., poème épicomagique* (1799). Cf. A. Franck, *La Philosophie Mystique en France* (Paris, 1866) ; also v. Osten-Sacken, *Fr. Baader und St. Martin* (Leips. 1860).

[2] This later doctrine of Schelling's is accordingly usually called the Doctrine of Freedom, as the earlier is called the System of Identity. Schelling, *Unters. über die Freiheit,* W.. I. 7, 376

unreason of the particular will. In this way the development of the actual leads from the unreason of the primordial will (*deus implicitus*) to the self-knowledge and self-determination of reason (*deus explicitus*).[1]

3. Thus at last religion became for Schelling the "organon of philosophy," as art had been earlier. Since the process of God's self-development goes on in the revelations, with which in the human mind he beholds himself, all *momenta* of the divine nature must appear in the succession of ideas which man in his historical development has had of God. Hence in the *Philosophy of Mythology and Revelation*, the work of Schelling's old age, the *knowledge of God is gained from the history of all religions:* in the progress from the natural religions up to Christianity and its different forms the self-revelation of God makes its way from dark primordial will to the spirit of reason and of love. God develops or evolves in and by revealing himself to men.[2]

In its methodical form this principle reminds us strongly of Hegel's conception of the history of philosophy, in which "the Idea comes to itself," and the happy combination and fineness of feeling with which Schelling has grouped and mastered the bulky material of the history of religions in these lectures shows itself throughout akin and equal in rank to the Hegelian treatment. But the fundamental philosophical conception is yet entirely different. Schelling terms the standpoint of this his latest teaching, *metaphysical empiricism*. His own earlier system and that of Hegel he now calls negative philosophy: this philosophy may indeed show that if God once reveals himself, he does it in the forms of natural and historical reality which are capable of dialectical *a priori* construction. But *that* he reveals himself and thus transmutes himself into the world, dialectic is not able to deduce. This cannot be deduced at all; it is only to be *experienced*, and experienced from the way *in which God reveals himself in the religious life of mankind*. To understand from this process God and his self-evolution into the world is the task of *positive philosophy*.

Those who both immediately and later derided Schelling's Philosophy of Mythology and Revelation as "*Gnosticism*" scarcely knew, perhaps, how well founded the comparison was. They had in mind only the fantastic amalgamation of mythical ideas with philosophical conceptions, and the arbitrariness of cosmogonic and theogonic constructions. The true resemblance, however, consists

---

[1] Cf. above, p. 290 f.

[2] Cf. Constantin Frantz, *Schelling's Positive Philosophie* (Cöthen, 1879 f.).

in this, that as the Gnostics gave to the warfare of religions, in the midst of which they were standing, the significance of a history of the universe and the divine powers ruling in it, so now Schelling set forth the development of human ideas of God as the development of God himself.

4. Irrationalism came to its full development in *Schopenhauer* by the removal of the religious element. The dark urgency or instinct directed only toward itself appears with him under the name of the *will to live*, as the essence of all things, as the thing-in-itself (cf. § 41, 9). In its conception, this will, directed only towards itself, has a formal resemblance to Fichte's "infinite doing," just as was the case with Schlegel's irony (cf. § 42, 5) : but in both cases the real difference is all the greater. The activity directed solely toward itself is with Fichte the autonomy of ethical self-determination, with Schlegel the arbitrary play of fancy, with Schopenhauer the *absolute unreason of an objectless will.* Since this will only creates itself perpetually, it is the never satisfied, the *unhappy* will : and since the world is nothing but the self-knowledge (self-revelation —objectification) of this will, it must be a world of misery and suffering.

Pessimism, thus grounded metaphysically, is now strengthened by Schopenhauer[1] by means of the hedonistic estimate of life itself. All human life flows on continually between willing and attaining. But to will is pain, is the ache of the "not-yet-satisfied." Hence *pain is the positive feeling*, and pleasure consists only in the removal of a pain. Hence pain must preponderate in the life of will under all circumstances, and actual life confirms this conclusion. Compare the pleasure of the beast that devours with the torture of the one that is being devoured — and you will be able to estimate with approximate correctness the proportion of pleasure and pain in the world in general. Hence man's life always ends in the complaint, that the best lot is never to be born at all.

If life is suffering, then only sympathy can be the fundamental ethical feeling (cf. § 41, 9). The individual will is immoral if it increases the hurt of another, or also if it is merely indifferent toward it ; it is moral if it feels another's hurt as its own and seeks to alleviate it. From the standpoint of sympathy Schopenhauer gave his psychological explanation of the ethical life. But this alleviation of the hurt is only a palliative ; it does not abolish the will, and with the will its unhappiness persists. "The sun burns perpetual noon." The misery of life remains always the same ;

---

[1] *World as Will and Idea*, I. §§ 56 ff. ; II. ch. 46 ; *Parerga*, II. ch. 11 f.

only the form in which it is represented in idea alters. The special shapes change, but the content is always the same. Hence there can be no mention of a progress in history; intellectual perfecting alters nothing in the will which constitutes the essential nature of man. History shows only the endless sorrow of the will to live, which with an ever-new cast of characters constantly presents the same tragi-comedy before itself.[1] On this ground the philosophy of Schopenhauer has no interest in history; history teaches only individual facts; there is no rational science of it.

A deliverance from the wretchedness of the will would be possible only through the *negation or denial of the will itself.* But this is a mystery. For the will, the ἓν καὶ πᾶν — the one and all — the only Real, is indeed in its very nature self-affirmation; how shall it deny itself? But the Idea of this deliverance is present in the mystical asceticism, in the mortification of self, in the contempt of life and all its goods, and in the peace of soul that belongs to an absence of wishes. This, Schopenhauer held, is the import of the Indian religion and philosophy, which began to be known in Europe about his time. He greeted this identity of his teaching with the oldest wisdom of the human race as a welcome confirmation, and now called the world of idea the veil of Maia, and the negation of the will to live the entrance into *Nirvana.* But the unreasonable will to live would not let the philosopher go. At the close of his work he intimates that what would remain after the annihilation of the will, and with that, of the world also, would be for all those who are still full of will, certainly *nothing;* but consideration of the life of the saints teaches, that while the world with all its suns and milky ways is nothing to them, they have attained blessedness and peace. "In thy nothing I hope to find the all."

If an absolute deliverance is accordingly impossible, — were it ever possible, then in view of the ideality of time there could be no world whatever of the affirmation of the will, — there is yet a relative deliverance from sorrow in those intellectual states in which the pure willess subject of knowing is active, viz. in disinterested contemplation and disinterested thought. The object for both of these states he finds not in particular phenomena, but in the eternal

---

[1] Hence the thought of grafting the optimism of the Hegelian development system on this will-irrationalism of Schopenhauer's after the pattern of Schelling's *Doctrine of Freedom* was as mistaken as the hope of reaching speculative results by the method of inductive natural science. And with the organic combination of the two impossibilities, even a thinker so intelligent and so deep and many-sided in his subtle investigations as *Edward von Hartmann,* could have only the success of a meteor that dazzles for a brief period (*Die Philosophie des Unbewussten,* Berlin, 1869) [Eng. tr. *The Philosophy of the Unconscious,* by E. C. Coupland, Lond. 1884].

Forms of the objectification of the will — the *Ideas.*   This Platonic (and Schellingian) element, however (as is the case also with the assumption of the intelligible character), fits with extreme difficulty into Schopenhauer's metaphysical system, according to which all particularising of the will is thought as only an idea in space and time; but it gives the philosopher opportunity to employ Schiller's principle of disinterested contemplation in the happiest manner to complete his theory of life.   The will becomes free from itself when it is able to represent to itself in thought its objectification without any ulterior purpose.   The misery of the irrational World-will is mitigated by morality; in art and science it is overcome.

PART VII.

THE PHILOSOPHY OF THE NINETEENTH CENTURY.

M. J. Monrad, *Denkrichtungen der neueren Zeit.* Bonn, 1879.

A. Franck, *Philosophes Modernes, Étrangers et Français.* Paris, 1873.

R. Eucken, *Geschichte und Kritik der Grundbegriffe der Gegenwart.* Leips. 1878. 2d ed. 1892.

E. v. Hartmann, *Kritische Wanderung durch die Philosophie der Gegenwart.* Leips. 1890.

W. Dilthey, *Archiv für Geschichte der Philosophie.* Vol. XI. pp. 551 ff.

H. Siebert, *Geschichte der neueren deutschen Philosophie seit Hegel.* Göttingen, 1898.

Ph. Damiron, *Essai sur l'Histoire de la Philosophie en France au 19ᵉ Siècle.* Paris, 1834.

H. Taine, *Les Philosophes Classiques Français au 19ᵉ Siècle.* Paris, 1857.

F. Ravaisson, *La Philosophie en France au 19ᵉ Siècle.* Paris, 1868.

L. Ferraz, *Histoire de la Philosophie en France au 19ᵉ Siècle,* 3 vols. Paris, 1880–1889.

P. Janet, *Les Maitres de la Pensée Moderne.* Paris, 1883.

E. De Roberty, *La Philosophie du Siècle.* Paris, 1891.

Ch. Adam, *La Philosophie en France, pr. Moitie du 19ᵉ Siècle.* Paris, 1894.

L. Liard, *Les Logiciens Anglais Contemporains.* Paris, 1878.

Th. Ribot, *La Psychologie Anglaise Contemporaine.* Paris, 1870.

D. Masson, *Recent English Philosophy,* 3d ed. Lond. 1877.

Har. Höffding, *Einleitung in die englische Philosophie der Gegenwart.* Leips. 1890.

L. Ferri, *Essai sur l'Histoire de la Philosophie en Italie au 19ᵉ Siècle.* Paris, 1869.

K. Werner, *Die italienische Philosophie des 19. Jahrhunderts.* Vienna, 1884 ff.

[O. Pfleiderer, *The Development of Rational Theology since Kant.* Lond. and N.Y. 1891.]

[L. Stephen, *The English Utilitarians,* 3 vols. Lond. and N.Y. 1900.]

[J. T. Merz, *A History of European Thought in the 19th Century,* Vol. I. 1896.]

The history of philosophical principles is *closed* with the development of the German systems at the boundary between the eighteenth and the nineteenth centuries. A survey of the succeeding development in which we are still standing to-day has far more of literary-historical than of properly philosophical interest. For nothing essentially and valuably new has since appeared. The nineteenth century is far from being a philosophical one; it is, in this respect perhaps, to be compared with the third and second centuries B.C. or the four-teenth and fifteenth A.D. To speak in Hegel's language, one might say that the *Weltgeist* of our time, so busy with the concrete reality and drawn toward the outer, is kept from turning inward and to itself, and from enjoying itself in its own peculiar home.[1] The philosophical literature of the nineteenth century is, indeed, exten-sive enough, and gives a variegated play of all the colours; the seed of Ideas, which has been wafted over to us from the days of the flower of the intellectual life, has grown luxuriantly in all spheres of science and public life, of poetry and of art; the germinant thoughts of history have been combined in an almost immeasurable wealth of changing combinations into many structures of personally impressive detail, but even men like Hamilton and Comte, like Rosmini and Lotze, have their ultimate significance only in the energy of thought and fineness of feeling with which they have surveyed the typical con-ceptions and principles of the past, and shaped them to new life and vigour. And the general course of thought, as indicated by the problems which interest and the conceptions that are formed in our century,[2] moves along the lines of antitheses that have been trans-mitted to us through history, and have at most been given a new form in their empirical expression.

For the decisive factor in the philosophical movement of the nineteenth century is doubtless the question as to the degree of importance which the natural-science conception of phenomena may claim for our view of the world and life as a whole. The influence which this special science had gained over philosophy and the intellectual life as a whole was checked and repressed at the begin-ning of the nineteenth century, to grow again afterwards with all the greater power. The metaphysics of the seventeenth, and there-fore the Enlightenment of the eighteenth century, were in the main under the dominance of the *thinking of natural science.* The con-ception of the universal conformity to law on the part of all the actual world, the search for the simplest elements and forms of occurrence and cosmic processes, the insight into the invariable necessity which lies at the basis of all change, — these determined theoretical investigation. The "natural" was thus made a general standard for measuring the value of every particular event or expe-

---

[1] Hegel, *Berliner Antrittsrede,* W., VI., XXXV.
[2] To the literary-historical interest in this field, which is so hard to master on account of its multiplicity, the author has been devoting the labor of many years. The product of this he is now permitted to hope soon to present as special parts of the third (supplementary) volume of his *Geschichte der neueren Philosophie* (2d ed. Leips. 1899). In this can be carried out in detail and proved what here can only be briefly sketched.

rience. The spread of this mechanical way of regarding the world was met by the German Philosophy with the fundamental thought, that all that is known in this way is but the phenomenal form and vehicle of a purposefully developing inner world, and that the true comprehension of the particular has to determine the significance that belongs to it in a purposeful connected whole of life. The *historical Weltanschauung* was the result of the work of thought which the System of Reason desired to trace out.

These two forces contend with each other in the intellectual life of our century. And in the warfare between them all arguments from the earlier periods of the history of philosophy have been presented in the most manifold combinations, but without bringing any new principles into the field. If the victory seems gradually to incline toward the side of the principles of Democritus, there are two main *motifs* favourable to this in our decades. The first is of essentially intellectual nature, and is the same that was operative in the times of intellectual life of previous centuries: it is the *simplicity and clearness to perception or imagination* (*anschauliche Einfachheit*), the certainty and definiteness of the natural-science knowledge. Formulated mathematically and always demonstrable in experience, this promises to exclude all doubt and opinions, and all trouble of interpretative thought. But far more efficient in our day is the evident *utility* of natural science. The mighty transformation in the external relations of life, which is taking place with rapid progress before our eyes, subjects the intellect of the average man irresistibly to the control of the forms of thought to which he owes such great things, and on this account we live under the sign of *Baconianism* (cf. above, p. 386 f.).

On the other hand, the heightened culture of our day has kept alive and vital all questions relating to the value which the social and historical life has for the individual. The more the political and social development of European humanity has entered upon the epoch when the influences of masses make themselves felt in an increasing degree, and the more pronounced the power with which the collective body asserts its influence upon the individual, even in his mental and spiritual life, the more does the individual make his struggle against the supremacy of society, and this also finds expression in the philosophic reflections of the century. The contest between the views of the world and of life which spring respectively from history and from natural science, has gone on most violently at the point where the question will ultimately be decided, in what degree the individual owes what makes his life worth living to himself, and in what degree he is indebted to the influences of the environing whole.   Universalism and individualism, as in the time of the Renaissance, have once more clashed in violent opposition.

If we are to bring out from the philosophical literature of this century and emphasise those movements in which the above characteristic antithesis has found its most important manifestation, we have to do primarily with the question, in what sense the psychical life can be subjected to the methods and concepts of natural science; for it is in connection with this point that the question must first be decided of the right of these methods and concepts to absolute sovereignty in philosophy.   For this reason the question as to the task, the method, and the systematic significance of *psychology* has never been more vigorously contested than in the nineteenth century, and the limitation of this science to a purely empirical treatment has appeared to be the only possible way out of the difficulties.   Thus psychology, as the latest among the special disciplines, has completed its separation from philosophy, at least as regards the fundamental principles of its problem and method.

This procedure had more general presuppositions.   In reaction against the highly strained idealism of the German philosophy, a broad stream of *materialistic Weltanschauung* flows through the nineteenth century.   This spoke out about the middle of the period, not indeed with any new reasons or information, but with all the more passionate emphasis.   Since then it has been much more modest in its claims to scientific value, but is all the more effective in the garb of sceptical and positivist caution.

To the most significant ramifications of this line of thought belongs without doubt the endeavour to regard the social life, the historical development, and the relations of mental and spiritual existence, from the points of view of natural science.   Introduced by the unfortunate name of *Sociology*, this tendency has sought to develop a peculiar kind of the philosophy of history, which aims to extend upon a broader basis of fact the thoughts which were suggested toward the close of the philosophy of the Enlightenment (see § 37).

But on the other hand, the historical view of the world has not failed to exercise its powerful influence upon natural science.   The idea of a history of the organic world, which was postulated in the philosophy of nature, early in the century, has found a highly impressive realization in empirical investigation.   The methodical principles, which had led to the philosophy of Nature, extended as if spontaneously to other fields, and in the theories of evolution the historical and the scientific views of the world seem to approximate as closely as is possible without a new philosophic idea, which shall reshape and reconstruct.

From the side of the individual, finally, the suggestions which were inherent in the problem of civilization as this was treated by the eighteenth century, temporarily brought the question as to the worth of life into the centre of philosophic interest. A pessimistic temper had to be overcome in order that from these discussions the deeper and clearer question as to the nature and content of values in general should be separated and brought to clear recognition. And so it was that philosophy, though by a remarkably devious path, was enabled to return to Kant's fundamental problem of values which are universally valid.

From the philosophical literature of the nineteenth century the following main points may be emphasized : —

In **France Ideology** divided into a more physiological and a more psychological branch. In the line of Cabanis worked principally the **Paris physicians,** such as Ph. **Pinel** (1745–1826; *Nosographie Philosophique,* 1798), F. J. V. **Broussais** (1772–1838; *Traité de Physiologie,* 1822 f.; *Traité de l'Irritation et de la Folie,* 1828), and the founder of *Phrenology,* Fr. Jos. **Gall** (1758–1828 : *Recherches sur le Système Nerveux en général et sur celui du Cerveau en particulier,* 1809, which was edited in conjunction with **Spurzheim**). — The antithesis to this, physiologically, was formed by the school of **Montpellier** : **Barthez** (1734–1806 ; *Nouveaux Éléments de la Science de l'Homme,* 2d ed., 1806). Associated with this school were M. F. X. **Bichat** (1771–1802 ; *Recherches Physiologiques sur la Vie et la Mort,* 1800). **Bertrand** (1795–1831 ; *Traité du Somnambulisme,* 1823), and **Buisson** (1766–1805 ; *De la Division la plus Naturelle des Phénomènes Physiologiques,* 1802). Corresponding to this was the development of Ideology with **Daube** (*Essai d'Idéologie.* 1803), and especially with Pierre **Laromiguière** (1756–1837 ; *Leçons de Philosophie,* 1815–1818) and his disciples, Fr. **Thurot** (1768–1832; *De l'Entendement et de la Raison,* 1830) and J. J. **Cardaillac** (1766–1845 ; *Etudes Élémentaires de Philosophie,* 1830). — Cf. Picavet, *Les Idéologues* (Paris, 1891).

A line of extensive historical study and of deeper psychology begins with M. J. **Degérando** (1772–1842 ; *De la Génération des Connaissances Humaines,* Berlin, 1802 ; *Histoire Comparée des Systèmes de Philosophie,* 1804) and has its head in Fr. P. Gonthier **Maine de Biran** (1766–1824 ; *De la Décomposition de la Pensée,* 1895 ; *Les Rapports du Physique et du Moral de l'Homme,* printed 1834 ; *Essai sur les Fondements de la Psychologie,* 1812 ; *Œuvres Philosophiques,* edited by V. Cousin, 1841 ; *Œuvres Inédites,* edited by E. Naville, 1859 ; *Nouvelles Œuvres Inédites,* edited by A. Bertrand, 1887). The influences of the Scottish and German philosophy discharge into this line (represented also by A. M. Ampère) through P. **Prévost** (1751–1839), **Ancillon** (1766–1837), **Royer-Collard** (1763–1845), **Jouffroy** (1796–1842), and above all, **Victor Cousin** (1792–1867 ; *Introduction à l'Histoire Générale de la Philosophie,* 7th ed., 1872 ; *Du Vrai, du Beau et du Bien,* 1845 ; complete works. Paris, 1846 ff. ; cf. E. Fuchs, *Die Philos. V. C.'s,* Berlin, 1847 ; J. Elaux, *La Philosophie de M. Cousin,* Paris, 1864). The numerous school, founded by Cousin, which was especially noted through its historical labours, is called the *Spiritualistic* or *Eclectic* School. It was the official philosophy after the July Revolution, and is in part still such. To its adherents who have been active in the historical field, where their work has been characterised by thoroughness and literary taste, belong Ph. Damiron, Jul. Simon, E. Vacherot, H. Martin, A. Chaignet, Ad. Franck, B. Haureau, Ch. Bartholmèss, E. Saisset, P. Janet, E. Caro, etc. F. **Ravaisson** has risen from the school to a theoretical standpoint which is in a certain sense his own. (*Morale et metaphysique,* in the *Revue de Met. et de Mor.* 1893).

Its principal opponents were the philosophers of the *Church party,* whose theory is known as **Traditionalism.** Together with Chateaubriand (*Le Génie du Christianisme,* 1802), Jos. **de Maistre** (1753–1821 ; *Essai sur le Principe*

Générateur des Constitutions Politiques, 1810 ; *Soirées de St. Petersbourg*, 1821 ; *Du Pape*, 1829; cf. on him Fr. Paulhan, Paris, 1893) and J. **Frayssinons** (1765–1841; *Défense du Christianisme*, 1823), V. G. A. **de Bonald** (1753–1841; *Théorie du Pouvoir Politique et Religieux*, 1796 ; *Essai Analytique sur les Lois Naturelles de l'Ordre Social*, 1800 ; *Du Divorce*, 1801 ; *De la Philosophie Morale et Politique du 18e siècle;* complete works, 15 vols., Paris, 1816 ff.) stands here in the foreground. The traditionalism of P. S. **Ballanche** is presented in a strangely fantastic fashion (1776–1847 ; *Essai sur les Institutions Sociales*, 1817 ; *La Palingénésie Sociale;* complete works, 5 vols., Paris, 1883). In the beginning H. F. R. de **Lamennais** (1782–1854) also supported this line in his *Essai sur l'Indifférence en Matière de Religion* (1817) ; later, having fallen out with the Church (*Parole d'un Croyant*, 1834), he presented in the *Esquisse d'une Philosophie* (4 vols., 1841–1846) a comprehensive system of philosophy, which had for its prototype partly the Schellingian System of Identity and partly the Italian Ontologism.

Among the philosophical supporters of **Socialism** (cf. L. Stein, *Geschichte der socialen Bewegung in Frankreich*, Leips. 1849 ff.) the most important is Cl. H. de **St. Simon** (1760–1825 ; *Introduction aux Travaux Scientifiques du 19e siècle*, 1807 ; *Réorganisation de la Société Européenne*, 1814 ; *Système Industriel*, 1821 f. ; *Nouveau Christianisme*, 1825 ; *Œuvres choisies*, 3 vols., 1859). Of his successors may be mentioned, **Bazard** (*Doctrine de St. Simon*, 1829), B. **Enfantin** (1796–1864 ; *La Religion St. Simonienne*, 1831), Pierre **Leroux** (1798–1871 ; *Réfutation de l'Eclecticisme*, 1839 ; *De l'Humanité*, 1840), and Ph. **Buchez** (1796–1866 ; *Essai d'un Traité Complet de Philosophie au Point de Vue du Catholicisme et du Progrès*, 1840).

Aug. **Comte** occupies a most interesting position apart. He was born in Montpellier in 1798 and died alone in Paris in 1857 : *Cours du Philosophie Positive* (6 vols., Paris, 1840–1842) [Eng. tr., or rather a condensation and reproduction by H. Martineau, *The Positive Philosophy of A. Comte*, 2 vols., Lond. 1853] ; *Système de Politique Positive* (Paris, 1851–1854) ; *The Positive Polity* and certain earlier works, trans. by various authors, 4 vols., Lond. 1876–1878; *Catéchisme Positiviste* (1853) ; cf. Littré, *C. et la Philosophie Positive*, Paris, 1868 ; J. S. Mill, *C. and Positivism*, Lond. 1865 ; J. Rig, *A. C. La Philosophie Positive Résumée*, Paris, 1881 ; E. Caird, *The Social Philosophy and Religion of C.*, Glasgow, 1885.

In the following period Comte's position became more influential and in part controlling. E. **Littré** (1801–1881 ; *La Science au Point de Vue Philosophique*, Paris, 1873) defended his positivism in systematic form. A freer adaptation of positivism was made by such writers as H. **Taine** (1828–1893 ; *Philosophie de l'Art*, 1865 ; *De l'Intelligence*, 1870 ; cf. on him G. Barzellotti, Rome, 1895) and Ernest **Renan** (1823–1892 ; *Questions Contemporaines*, 1868 ; *L'Avenir de la Science*, 1890). Under Comte's influence, likewise, has been the development of empirical psychology. Th. **Ribot**, editor of the *Revue Philosophique*, is to be regarded as the leader in this field. In addition to his historical works on English and German psychology, his investigations with regard to heredity and abnormal conditions of memory, will, personality, etc., may be noted.

In part also **Sociology** stands under Comte's influence, as R. Worms, G. Tarde, E. Durkheim, and others have striven to work it out (cf. *Année Sociologique*, pub. since 1894). Finally, evolutionary theories belong in this connection, which have been especially carried out by J. M. **Guyau** (1854–1888 ; *Esquisse d'une Morale*, 1885 ; *L'irreligion de l'avenir*, 1887 ; *L'art, au point de vue sociologique*, 1889) [*Problèmes de l'Esthétique Contemporaine*, 1897].

By far the most important among the present representatives of philosophy in France is Ch. **Renouvier** (born 1818 ; *Essais de Critique Générale*, 2d ed., 1875–96 ; *Esquisse d'une Classification Systematique des Doctrines Philosophiques*, 1885 ; *La Philosophie Analytique de l'Histoire*, 1896 ; *La Nouvelle Monadologie*, 1899). The synthesis of Kant and Comte which he has sought to effect has its literary organ in the *Année Philosophique* (published since 1889).

In England the **Associational Psychology** continues through Thomas Brown to men like Thomas **Belsham** (1750–1829 ; *Elements of the Philosophy of the Human Mind*, 1801), John **Fearn** (*First Lines of the Human Mind*,

1820), and many others ; finds support here also in physiological and phreno-logical theories as with G. **Combe** (*A System of Phrenology*, Edin. 1825), Sam. **Bailey** (*Essays on the Pursuit of Truth*, 1829 ; *The Theory of Reasoning*, 1851 ; *Letters on the Philosophy of the Human Mind*, 1855) and Harriet **Martineau** (*Letters on the Laws of Man's Nature and Development*, 1851), and reaches its full development through **James Mill** (*Analysis of the Phenomena of the Human Mind*, 1829), and his son, **J. Stuart Mill** (1806–1873 ; *System of Logic Ratiocinative and Inductive*, 1843 ; *Principles of Political Economy*, 1848 ; *On Liberty*, 1859 ; *Utilitarianism*, 1863 ; *Examination of Sir W. Hamilton's Philosophy*, 1865 ; *Autobiography*, 1873; Posthumously, *Essays on Religion*, 1874 ; *Collected Dissertations and Discussions*, N. Y., 1882 ; Useful ed. of Ethical Writings by Douglas, Edin. 1897. Cf. H. Taine, *Le Positivisme Anglais*, Paris, 1864 [Eng. tr. by Haye ; Courtney, *Life of M.*, and *Metaphysics of J. S. M.* ; Bain, *J. S. M.* 1882], Douglas, *J. S. M.*, *A Study of his Philos.*, Edin. 1895). Closely connected with this line of thought stands Alex. **Bain** (*The Senses and the Intellect*, 1856, 3d ed. 1868 ; *Mental and Moral Science*, 1868, 3d ed. 1872, Pt. II, 1872 ; *The Emotions and the Will*, 1859, 3d ed. 1875 ; *Mind and Body*, 3d ed. 1874.

The related **Utilitarianism** is represented by T. **Cogan** (*Philosophical Treatise on the Passions*, 1802 ; *Ethical Questions*, 1817), John **Austin** (1790–1859 ; *The Philosophy of Positive Law*, 1832), G. Cornwall **Lewis** (*A Treatise on the Methods of Observation and Reasoning in Politics*, 1852). [As representatives of Utilitarianism, in addition to Mill, and Bain, *op. cit.* above, H. **Sidgwick**, *Methods of Ethics*, Lond. 1874, 6th ed. 1901, and T. **Fowler**, *Principles of Morals*, Lond. 1886 f., should also be mentioned.

Scottish Philosophy, after Dugald Stewart and James **Mackintosh** (1764–1832 ; *Dissertation on the Progress of Ethical Philosophy*, 1830), had at first unimportant supporters like **Abercrombie** (1781–1846 ; *Inquiry concerning the Intellectual Powers*, 1830 ; *Philosophy of the Moral Feelings*, 1833) and **Chalmers** (1780–1847), and was especially as academical instruction brought into affiliation with the eclecticism of Cousin by Henry **Calderwood** (*Philosophy of the Infinite*, 1854), S. **Morell** (*An Historical and Critical View of the Speculative Philosophy of Europe in the 19th Century*, 1846), also H. **Wedgwood** (*On the Development of the Understanding*, 1848).

The horizons of English thought were widened by acquaintance with the German literature, to which Sam. Tayl. **Coleridge** (1772–1834), W. **Wordsworth** (1770–1850), and especially Thomas **Carlyle** (1795–1881 ; *Past and Present*, 1843 [the articles on various German thinkers and the *Sartor Resartus* belong here also]) contributed. In philosophy this influence made itself felt primarily through Kant, whose theory of cognition influenced J. **Herschel** (*On the Study of Natural Philosophy*, 1831), and especially W. **Whewell** (*Philosophy of the Inductive Sciences*, 1840).

In intelligent reaction against this influence, Scottish philosophy experienced a valuable re-shaping at the hands of **Sir William Hamilton** (1788–1856 ; *Discussions on Philosophy and Literature*, 1852 ; *On Truth and Error*, 1856 ; *Lectures on Metaphysics and Logic*, 1859 ; *Editions of Reid's and Stewart's Works* ; cf. J. Veitch, *S. W. H., The Man and his Philosophy*, Edin. and Lond. 1883 [Memoir in 2 vols., 1869, by same author]). In his school *Agnosticism* proper, supported principally by H. L. **Mansel** (1820–1871 ; *Metaphysics or the Philosophy of Consciousness*, 1860), is separated from a tendency inclining toward eclectic metaphysics : J. **Veitch**, R. **Lowndes** (*Introduction to the Philosophy of Primary Beliefs*, 1865), **Leechman**, **McCosh**, and others.

Following a suggestion from one aspect of Hamilton's thought, a movement arose which sought to develop formal logic as a calculus of symbols. To this movement belong G. **Boole** (*The Mathematical Analysis of Logic*, 1847 ; *An Analysis of the Laws of Thought*, 1854) ; De Morgan (*Formal Logic*, 1847) ; Th. Spencer **Baynes** (*An Essay on the New Analytic of Logical Forms*, 1850) ; W. Stanley **Jevons** (*Pure Logic*, 1864 ; *Principles of Science*, 1874) ; J. **Venn** (*Symbolic Logic*, 1881 ; *Logic of Chance*, 1876 ; *Principles of Logic*, 1889) [C. S. Peirce, *Algebra of Logic*, 1867 ; Ladd and Mitchell, in *Studies in Logic*, ed. by Peirce, Boston, 1883]. Compare on this A. Riehl (*Vierteljahrsschr. f. wiss. Philos.* 1877) and L. Liard (*Les Logiciens Anglais Contemporains*, 1878).

The combined influence of Kant and the later German theism impressed the philosopher of religion, James **Martineau** (who is also the most prominent recent representative of intuitionist ethics [*Types of Ethical Theory*, 1885 ; *A Study of Religion*, 1888 ; *Seat of Authority in Rel.*, 1890]; cf. A. W. Jackson, *J. M.*, Boston, 1900), and likewise F. W. Newman (*The Soul*, etc., 1849 ; *Theism*, 1858), A. C. Fraser and others.   Since Hutchinson **Stirling** (*The Secret of Hegel*, 1865 ; *What is Thought ?* 1900) German idealism in its whole development and in its metaphysical aspect, particularly in the Hegelian form, has called forth a vigorous idealistic movement, of which the leading representative was the late Thomas Hill **Green** (1836–1882), Professor at Oxford.   [His *Introd. to Hume* was followed by criticisms on Lewes and Spencer and (posthumously) by the *Prolegomena to Ethics*, 1883, and complete works (except the *Proleg.*), 3 vols., Lond. and N. Y. 1885, 1886, 1888; cf. W. H. Fairbrother, *The Philosophy of T. H. G.*, Lond. 1896.]   In sympathy with this idealistic and more or less Hegelian interpretation of Kantian principles are F. H. **Bradley** (*Logic*, Lond. 1883 ; *Ethical Studies*, 1876 ; Appearance and Reality, 1893), B. **Bosanquet** (*Logic*, 2 vols., 1888 ; *Hist. of Æsthetics*, 1892 ; *Philos. of the State*, 1899, etc.) ; **J. Caird** (*Introduction to the Philosophy of Religion*, 1880) ; **E. Caird** (*Critical Phil. of Kant*, 2 vols., 1889 ; *Essays*, 2 vols., 1892 ; *Evolution of Religion*, 1893); Seth and Haldane (*Essays in Phil. Criticism*, 1883) ; J. **Mackenzie** (*Social Philosophy*, 1890).   Cf. A. Seth, *Hegelianism and Personality*, 1887, and the review of this in *Mind*, by D. G. Ritchie.

These movements above noted stand under the principle of **Evolution**; the same principle became authoritative for the investigation of organic nature through Charles **Darwin** (*Origin of Species by Means of Natural Selection*, 1859 ; *Descent of Man*, 1871 ; *The Expression of the Emotions*, 1872).   The same principle was formulated in more general terms and made the basis of a comprehensive System of Synthetic Philosophy by **Herbert Spencer** (born 1820), *First Principles*, 1862, 6th ed. 1901; *Principles of Psychology*, 1855, 5th ed. 1890 ; *Principles of Biology*, 1864–1867, 4th ed. 1888 ; *Principles of Sociology*, 1876–1896 ; *Principles of Ethics*, 1879–1893.   Cf. on him O. Gaupp, Stuttgart, 1897 [T. H. Green, in *Works*; F. H. Collins, *Epitome of the Synthetic Philosophy*, 1889.]   Huxley, Wallace, Tyndall, G. H. Lewes (*Problems of Life and Mind*, 3d ed. 1874), belong in the main to this tendency.

[Other works in evolutionary ethics are, L. **Stephen**, *The Science of Ethics*, Lond. 1882 ; S. **Alexander**, *Moral Order and Progress*, Lond. 1889 ; C. M. **Williams**, *The Ethics of Evolution*, Lond. and N.Y. 1893.   This last contains useful summaries of the chief works.]

[In America idealistic lines of thought were introduced (in opposition to the prevalent Scottish philosophy) through the medium of Coleridge's interpretation of Kant, by James **Marsh** (1829) and Henry's trans. of V. Cousin's *Lectures on Locke* (1834), more directly from Germany by L. P. **Hickok** (*Rational Psychology*, 1848 ; *Emp. Psych.*, 1854 (rev. ed. by J. H. **Seelye**, 1882) ; *Moral Science*, 1853 (rev. ed. by J. H. Seelye), etc.).   W. T. **Harris**, in the *Jour. Spec. Philosophy*, and elsewhere, has done an important work in the same line. Of more recent writers, J. **Royce** (*The Religious Aspect of Philosophy*, 1885 ; *Spirit of Modern Philos.*, 1892 ; *The World and the Individual*, 1900), J. **Dewey** (*Psychology*, 1886 ; *Outlines of Ethics*, 1891), are closer to the school of Green, while G. T. **Ladd** (*Phys. Psychology*, 1887 ; *Introd. to Phil.*, 1891 ; *Psychology Descriptive and Explanatory*, 1894 ; *Philos. of Mind*, 1895 ; *Philos. of Knowledge*, 1897 ; *A Theory of Reality*, 1899) and B. P. **Bowne** (*Metaphysics*, *Psychological Theory*, *Ethical Theory*, etc.) stand nearer to Lotze. Ormond (*The Foundations of Knowledge*, 1900) combines idealistic motives with those of Scottish thought.   The extremely suggestive work of W. **James** (*Psychology*, 2 vols., 1890) should also be mentioned, and as representatives of the modern treatment of this science, in addition to the works of Ladd and Dewey cited above, J. M. **Baldwin** (*Psychology*, 2 vols., 1890 f. ; *Mental Development*, 1895–1897) and G. S. **Hall** (in *Am. Jour. Psychology*) may be named as American writers, and Jas. **Ward** (art. *Psychology* in *Enc. Brit.*), S. H. **Hodgson** (*Time and Space*, 1865 ; *The Philosophy of Reflection*, 1878 ; *Metaphysics of Experience*, 1898), James **Sully** (*The Human Mind*, 2 vols., 1892), and G. F. **Stout** (*Analytic Psychology*, 1896) as Englishmen.   Darwin, **Romanes**, and **Lloyd Morgan** have treated comparative psychology.   The *Dictionary of Psychology and Philosophy*, ed. by J. M. Baldwin with coöperation of British and American writers, will give historical material as well as definitions (in press).]

The **Italian** philosophy of the nineteenth century has been determined still more than the French by political motives, and in the content of the thoughts that have been worked over for these ends, it has been dependent partly upon French, partly upon German, philosophy. At the beginning the Encyclopædists' view of the world, both in its practical and its theoretical aspects, was dominant in men like **Gioja** (1766–1829) or his friend, **Romagnosi** (1761–1835), while as early as Pasquale **Galuppi** (1771–1846 ; *Saggio Filosofico sulla Critica delle Conoscenze Umane*, 1320 ff. ; *Filosofia della Volontà*, 1832 ff.) Kantian influences assert themselves,— to be sure, under the psychologistic form of the Leibnizian virtual innateness.

At a later period philosophy, which was mainly developed by the clergy, was influenced essentially by the political alliance of the Papacy with democratic Liberalism, inasmuch as Rationalism wished to unite itself with revealed faith. The most characteristic representative of this tendency and the most attractive personally was Antonio **Rosmini-Serbati** (1797–1855; *Nuovo Saggio sull' Origine delle Idee*, 1830 ; *Principii della Scienza Morale*, 1831 ; Posthum, *Teosofia*, 1859 ff. ; *Saggio Storico-Critico sulle Categorie e la Dialettica*, 1884) [Eng. tr. of the first, *Origin of Ideas*, 3 vols., Lond. 1883 f. ; also *R.'s Philos. System*, by T. Davidson, with int. bibliog., etc., Lond. 1882 ; *Psychology*, 3 vols., Lond. and Boston, 1884–1889]. Cf. on him F. X. Kraus (*Deutsche Rundschau*, 1890). The combination of Platonic, Cartesian, and Schellingian ideas proceeds in still more pronounced lines to an **Ontologism**, *i.e.* an *a priori* science of Being, in Vincenzo **Gioberti** (1801–1852 ; *Degli Errori Filosofico di Rosmini*, 1842; *Introduzione alla Filosofia*, 1840 ; *Protologia*, 1857. Cf. B. Spaventa, *La Filosofia di G.*, 1863). Terenzo **Mamiani** passed through this entire development (1800–1885 ; *Confessioni di un Metafisico*, 1865) ; Luigi Ferri (1826–1895), Labanca, Bonatelli, and others followed it, though influenced also by German and French views.

As opponents this tendency found, on the one hand, the rigid **Orthodoxism** of **Ventura** (1792–1861), **Tapparelli** and **Liberatore** (*Della Conoscenza Intelletuale*, 1865), and, on the other hand, politically radical **Scepticism**, as represented by Guiseppe **Ferrari** (1811–1866 ; *La Filosofia delle Revoluzioni*, 1851) and Antonio **Francki** (*La Religione del 19. Secolo*, 1853). The Kantian philosophy was introduced by Alf. **Testa** (1784–1860 ; *Della Critica della Ragione Pura*, 1849 ff.), and more successfully by C. **Cantoni** (born 1840 ; cf. above, p. 532), F. Tocco, S. Turbiglio, and others. Hegel's doctrine was introduced by A. **Vera** (1813–1885), B. **Spaventa** (1817–1883), and Fr. Fiorentino, and Comte's positivism by Cataneo, Ardigo, and Labriola. [Cf. for this Italian thought the App. in Ueberweg's *Hist. Phil.*, Eng. tr., Vol. II. 461 ff.]

In **Germany** (cf. J. E. Erdmann, *History of Phil.* [Eng. tr. Vol. III.] § 331 ff.) the first development was that of the great philosophic schools in the third and fourth decades of the century. **Herbart's** following proved the most complete in itself and firmest in its adherence. In it were prominent : M. **Drobisch** (*Religionsphilosophie*, 1840 ; *Psychologie*, 1842 ; *Die moralische Statistik und die menschliche Willensfreiheit*, 1867), R. **Zimmermann** (*Æsthetik*, Vienna, 1865), L. **Strümpell** (*Hauptpunkte der Metaphysik*, 1840 ; *Einleitung in die Philosophie*, 1886), T. **Ziller** (*Einleitung in die Allgemeine Pädagogik*, 1856). A special divarication of the school is formed by the so-called **Völkerpsychologie** [Comparative or Folk-Psychology], as opened by M. **Lazarus** (*Leben der Seele*, 1856 f.) and H. **Steinthal** (*Abriss der Sprachwissenschaft*, I. ; *Einleitung in die Psychologie und Sprachwissenschaft*, 1871) ; cf. their common programme in Vol. I. of the *Zeitschrift für Völkerpsychologie und Sprachwissenschaft*.

The **Hegelian** School had rich experience in its own life of the blessing of dialectic ; it split even in the Thirties upon religious antitheses. The important historians of philosophy, **Zeller** and **Prantl**, **Erdmann** and **Kuno Fischer**, went their way, not confused by this. Between the two parties, with a considerable degree of independent thinking, stand K. **Rozenkranz** (1805–1879; *Wissenschaft der logischen Idee*, 1858 f.) and Friedrich Theodor **Vischer** (1807–1887 ; *Æsthetik*, 1846–1858; *Auch Einer*, 1879).

The "right wing" of the Hegelian school, which resisted a pantheistic inter
pretation of the master, and emphasised the metaphysical importance of per
sonality, attracted those thinkers who stood in a freer relation to Hegel, and
maintained Fichtean and Leibnizian motifs. Such were I. H. **Fichte** (son of
the creator of the *Wissenschaftslehre*, 1797–1879 ; *Beiträge zur Characteristik
der neueren Philosophie*, 1829 ; *Ethik*, 1850 ff. ; *Anthropologie*, 1856), C. Fortlage (1806–1881 ; *System der Psychologie*, 1855), Christ. **Weisse** (1801–1866 ;
System der Æsthetik, 1830 and 1871 ; *Grundzüge der Metaphysik*, 1835 ; *Das
philosophische Problem der Gegenwart*, 1842 ; *Philosophie des Christenthums*,
1855 ff.), H. **Ulrici** (1806–1884 ; *Das Grundprincip der Philosophie*, 1845 f. ;
Gott und die Natur, 1861 ; *Gott und der Mensch*, 1866); further, E. Trahn-
dorf (1782–1863 ; *Æsthetik*, 1827), Mor. Carriere (1817–1895 ; *Æsthetik*, 1859,
3d ed. 1885 ; *Die Kunst im Zusammenhang der Kulturentwickelung*, 5 vols.)
Related to these was, on the one side, R. **Rothe** (1797–1867 ; *Theologisch*
Ethik, 2d ed. 1867–1871 ; cf. on his speculative system, H. Holtzmann, 1899),
who interwove many suggestions from the idealistic development into an original mysticism, and on the other side A. **Trendelenburg**, who set the conception of "Motion" in the place of Hegel's dialectical principle, and thought
thereby to combat Hegel's philosophy. His merit, however, lies in the stimulus
which he gave to Aristotelian studies (1802–1872 ; *Logische Untersuchungen*,
1840 ; *Naturrecht*, 1860).

To the "Left" among the Hegelians belong Arnold **Ruge** (1802–1880 ; joint
editor with Echtermeyer of the *Halle'sche Jahrbücher*, 1838–1840, and of the
Deutsche Jahrbücher, 1841 f. ; coll. writings in 10 vols., Mannheim, 1846 ff.),
Ludwig **Feuerbach** (1804–1872 ; *Gedanken über Tod und Unsterblichkeit*, 1830 ;
Philosophie und Christenthum, 1839 ; *Wesen des Christenthums*, 1841 ; *Wesen
der Religion*, 1845 ; *Theogonie*, 1857 ; Works, 10 vols., Leips. 1846 ff.). Cf. K.
Grün (*L. F.*, Leips. 1874), David Friedrich **Strauss** (1808–1874 ; *Das Leben
Jesu*, 1835 ; *Christliche Glaubenslehre*, 1840 f. ; *Der Alte und der neue Glaube*,
1872 ; Works, 12 vols., Berlin, 1876 ff.). Cf. A. Hausrath, *D. F. Str. und die
Theologie seiner Zeit* (Heidelberg, 1876 and 1878).

From the **Materialism controversy** are to be mentioned : K. **Moleschott**
(*Kreislauf des Lebens*, 1852), Rudolph **Wagner** (*Ueber Wissen und Glauben*,
1854 ; *Der Kampf um die Seele*, 1857), C. **Vogt** (*Köhlerglaube und Wissenschaft*, 1854 ; *Vorlesungen über den Menschen*, 1863), L. **Büchner** (*Kraft und
Stoff*, 1855) [*Force and Matter*, Lond.].

Related to this materialism was the development of the extreme **Sensualism**
in the form in which it was presented by H. **Czolbe** (1819–1873 ; *Neue Darstellung des Sensualismus*, 1855 ; *Grundzüge der extensionalen Erkenntnisstheorie*, 1875), and by F. **Ueberweg** (1826–1871), who was originally more
closely related to Beneke (cf. A. Lange, *History of Materialism*, II.). In a
similar relation stood the so-called Monism which E. **Haeckel** (born 1834 ;
Natürliche Schöpfungsgeschichte, 1868 ; *Welträthsel*, 5th ed. 1900 : cf. Loofs,
Anti-Haeckel, 1900, and Fr. Paulsen, *E.' H. als Philosoph*. Preuss. *Jahrb*.
1900) has attempted to develop, and finally the socialistic Philosophy of History, whose founders are Fr. **Engels** (*Ludwig Feuerbach und der Ausgang der
klassischen deutschen Philosophie*, 1888 ; *Der Ursprung der Familie, des Pri-
vateigenthums und des Staates*, 1884) and Karl **Marx** (*Das Kapital*, 1867 ff.,
Capital, 1891) ; cf. on Engels and Marx, R. Stammler, *Wirthschaft und Recht*,
1896 ; L. Wolfmann, *Der historische Materialismus*, 1900.

By far the most important among the epigones of the German Philosophy
was Rudolph Herm. **Lotze** (1817–1881 ; *Metaphysik*, 1841 ; *Logik*, 1842 ; *Medi-
cinische Psychologie*, 1842 ; *Mikrokosmus*, 1856 ff. ; *System der Philosophie*, I.
Logik, 1874 ; II. *Metaphysik*, 1879) [*Microcosmus*, tr. by Hamilton and Jones,
Edin. and N. Y. 1885 ; *Logic and Metaphysics*, 2 vols. each, tr. ed. by B. Bosan-
quet, Oxford, 1884, also 1888 ; *Outlines*, ed. by G. T. Ladd, Boston, 1885 ff.].
Cf. O. Caspari, *H. L. in seiner Stellung zur deutschen Philosophie* (1883) ;
E. v. Hartmann, *L.'s Philosophie* (Berlin, 1888); II. Jones, *Philos. of L.*, 1895.

Interesting side phenomena are : G. T. **Fechner** (1801–1887 ; *Nanna*, 1848 ;
Physical. und philos. Atomenlehre, 1855 ; *Elemente der Psychophysik*, 1860 ;
Drei Motive des Glaubens, 1863 ; *Vorschule der Æsthetik*, 1876 ; *Die Tagesan-
sicht gegenüber der Nachtansicht*, 1879) and Eug. **Dühring** (born 1833 ; *Natürliche Dialektik*, 1865 ; *Werth des Lebens*, 1865 ; *Logik und Wissenschaftstheorie*.

1878). — The following from the Catholic side have taken part in the development of philosophy : Fr. **Hermes** (1775–1831 ; *Einleitung in die christkatholische Theologie*, 1819), Bernh. **Bolzano** (1781–1848 ; *Wissenschaftslehre*, 1837), Anton **Günther** (1785–1863 ; *Ges. Schriften*, Vienna, 1881), and Wilhelm **Rosenkrantz** (1824–1874 ; *Wissenschaft des Wissens*, 1866).

Philosophic interest in Germany, which was much crippled about the middle of the century, has strongly revived, owing to the union of the study of Kant with the demands of natural science. The former, called forth by Kuno Fischer's work (1860), evoked a movement which has been characterized in various aspects as **Neo-Kantianism**. To it belong, as principal members, A. **Lange** (1828–1875 ; *History of Materialism*, 1866) and O. **Liebmann** (born 1840 ; *Analysis der Wirklichkeit*, 3 Aufl., 1900). In theology it was represented by Alb. **Ritschl** (*Theologie und Metaphysik*, 1881). [A. T. Swing, *Theol. of A. R.* 1901.]

Theoretical Physics became significant for philosophy through the work principally of Rob. **Mayer** (*Bemerkungen über die Kräfte der unbelebten Natur*, 1845 ; *Ueber das mechanische Æquivalent der Wärme*, 1850 ; cf. on him A. Riehl in the *Sigwart-Abhandlungen*, 1900) and H. **Helmholtz** (*Physiologische Optik*, 1886 ; *Sensations of Tone*, 1875 ; *Thatsachen der Wahrnehmung*, 1879).

Beginning with physiology, Willhelm **Wundt** (born 1837) has developed a comprehensive system of philosophy. From his numerous writings may be mentioned *Grundzüge der physiologischen Psychologie*, 1873 f., 4th ed. 1893 [*Outlines of Physiological Psychology*, Eng. tr. in prep. by E. Titchenor] ; *Logik*, 1880 f. ; *Ethik*, 1886 [Eng. tr. by Titchenor, Washburn, and Gulliver] ; *The Facts of the Moral Life*, *Ethical Systems*, 1897 ; *Principles of Morality*, 1901 ; *System der Philosophie*, 1889 ; *Grundriss der Psychologie*, 1897 [Eng. tr. by Judd, *Outlines of Psychology*, 1897] ; *Völkerpsychologie*, 1900.

The Kantian theory of knowledge was met by **Realism** in J. v. Kirchmann (*Philosophie des Wissens*, 1804), and by **Positivism** in C. **Göring** (*System der kritischen Philosophie*, 1874 f.), E. **Laas** (*Idealismus und Positivismus*, 1879 ff.), and in part too in A. **Riehl** (*Der philosophische Kriticismus*, 1876 ff. [Eng. tr. of Part III. by A. Fairbanks, 1894, *Science and Metaphysics*]). A similar tendency was followed by R. **Avenarius** (*Kritik der reinen Erfahrung*, 1888–1890 ; *Der menschliche Weltbegriff*, 1891).

As in the first-named authors the concepts of natural science were especially authoritative, so on the other hand the interests of the historical view of the world have normative value for investigators such as Rudolf **Eucken** (*Die Einheit des Geisteslebens*, 1888 ; *Der Kampf um einen geistigen Lebensinhalt*, 1896), H. **Glogau** (*Abriss der philosophischen Grundwissenschaften*, 1880), and W. **Dilthey** (*Einleitung in die Geisteswissenschaften*, 1883).

A mediating standpoint is taken by Christian **Sigwart** (*Logik*, 2d ed. 1893 ; [Eng. tr. by Helen Dendy, 1895]).

Two authors who occupy a position in closer relation to general literature are : —

E. v. **Hartmann** (born 1842), who excited general attention by his *Philosophy of the Unconscious*, 1869 [Eng. tr. by Coupland, 1884]. This was followed by a long series of writings, of which the most important are *Das Unbewusste vom Standpunkt der Descendenztheorie*, 1872 ; *Phänomenologie des sittlichen Bewusstseins*, 1879 ; *Die Religion des Geistes*, 1882 ; *Æsthetik*, 1886 f. ; *Kategorienlehre*, 1897 ; *Geschichte der Metaphysik*, 1900. These works represent a more and more completely scientific standpoint. As representing a popular philosophy, in part pessimistic, in part mystical, may be named as typical, **Mainländer** (*Philosophie der Erlösung*, 1874 f.) on the one hand, and on the other, **Duprel** (*Philosophie der Mystik*, 1884 f.).

Fr. Wilh. **Nietzsche** (1844–1900), whose development in its changing stages is characterised by the following selection from his numerous writings, of which the complete edition is published in Leipsic, 1895 ff. : *Die Geburt der Tragödie aus dem Geiste der Musik*, 1872 ; *Unzeitgemässe Betrachtungen*, 1873–1876 ; *Menschliches — Allzumenschliches*, 1876–1880 ; *Also sprach Zarathustra*, 1883 f. ; *Jenseits von Gut und Böse*, 1886 ; *Zur Genealogie der Moral*, 1887 ; *Götzendämmerung*, 1889. [Eng. tr. by A. Tille, 1896 ff., *Thus spake Zarathustra* ; *Beyond Good and Bad* ; *Genealogy of Morals*.] Cf. Al. Riehl, *Nietzsche*, Stuttgart, 2d ed. 1897. [P. Carus in *The Monist*, IX. 572 ff. ; G. N. Dolson in *Cornell Cont. to Phil.*, III.]

§ 44. The Controversy over the Soul.

A characteristic change in the general scientific relations during the nineteenth century has been the constantly progressing *loosening and separation of psychology from philosophy*,[1] which may now be regarded as in principle complete. This followed from the rapid decline of metaphysical interest and metaphysical production, which appeared in Germany, especially, as a natural reaction from the high tension of speculative thought. Robbed thus of a more general base of support, in its effort to give itself a firm footing as purely empirical science, psychology had at first but little power of resistance against the inroad of the method of natural science, according to which it should be treated as a special province of physiology or general biology. About this question a number of vigorous movements grouped themselves.

1. At the beginning of the century a brisk interchange of thought obtained between the French Ideology and the later developments of the English Enlightenment philosophy which had split into associational psychology and the common sense doctrine: in this interchange, however, France bore now the leading part. Here the antithesis which had existed in the French sensualism from the beginning between Condillac and Bonnet (cf. p. 458), came out more sharply. With Destutt de Tracy, and even as yet with Laromiguière, it does not come to a sharp decision. On the other hand, Cabanis is the leader of the *materialistic* line: his investigation as to the interconnection of the physical and the psychical (moral) nature of man, after considering the various influences of age, sex, temperament, climate, etc., comes to the result that the psychical life is everywhere determined by the body and its physical relations. With the organic functions thus reduced solely to mechanical and chemical processes, at least in principle, it seemed that the soul, now superfluous as vital force, had also outlived its usefulness as the agent and supporter of consciousness.

In carrying out these thoughts other physicians, for example Broussais, gave to materialism a still sharper expression: the intellectual activity is " one of the results" of the brain functions. Hence men eagerly seized upon the strange hypothesis of *phrenology*, with which Gall professed to localise at definite places in the brain all the particular " faculties," which empirical psychology had provided up to that time. It was not merely an interesting diversion to hear in public that a more or less vigorous development of special psychical powers could be recognised in the skull; the

---

[1] Cf. W. Windelband, *Ueber den gegenwärtigen Stand der psychologischen Forschung* (Leips. 1876).

thought was connected with this, especially among physicians, that now the materiality of the so-called soul-life was discovered, without doubt. In England especially, as is shown by the success of *Combe's* writings, the phrenological superstition called out very great interest and promoted a purely physiological psychology, in the line of that of Hartley. It was John Stuart *Mill* who first brought his countrymen back to Hume's conception of associational psychology. Without asking what matter and mind are in themselves, the student should proceed from the fact that the corporeal and mental states form two domains of experience, completely incapable of comparison, and that *psychology as the science of the laws of mental life* must study the facts of the latter in themselves, and may not reduce them to the laws of another sphere of existence. Alexander Bain, attaching himself to Mill's standpoint, developed the associational psychology farther. His especial contribution was to point out the significance of the muscular sensations, in which the fundamental facts of the mental life which correspond to spontaneous bodily motion are to be found. This associational psychology has thus nothing in common with a materialistic view of the soul; nevertheless the mechanism of ideas and impulses is the only principle recognised for the purpose of explaining the mental processes.

2. The opposition to the materialistic psychology comes much more sharply to the fore in those lines of thought which emphasise the activity of consciousness as a unity. Following de Tracy's example *Laromiguière's* Ideology distinguished carefully between the "modifications," which are the mere consequence of bodily excitations, and the "actions" of the soul, in which the soul proves its independent existence, even in perception. In the school of Montpellier they still believed in the "vital force." *Barthez* regarded this as separate from body and soul, as a something completely unknown: *Bichat* distinguished the "animal" from the "organic" life by the characteristic of spontaneous "reaction." This element in psychology came to full development through *Maine de Biran.* The acute, subtle mind of this philosopher received many suggestions from English and German philosophy; with reference to the latter his acquaintance with Kant's and Fichte's doctrines — though only a superficial one — and with the virtualism of Bouterwek, who was named with remarkable frequency in Paris, is to be emphasised.[1]

---

[1] The lines of communication were here not merely literary (Villers, Degérando, etc.), but in a strong degree personal. Of great importance among other things was the presence of the Schlegels in Paris, especially the lecturer of Frederick Schlegel. In Paris itself the society of Auteuil, to which also the Swiss embassador Stapfer, a prominent medium of influence, belonged, was of importance.

The fundamental fact on which Maine de Biran bases his theory, later called *spiritualism*, is that in the *will* we immediately experience at once our own activity and the *resistance* of the *"Non-Moi"* (primarily our own body). The reflection of personality upon this its own activity forms the starting-point of all philosophy: inner experience furnishes the form, experience of that which resists furnishes the matter. From this fundamental fact the conceptions force, substance, cause, unity, identity, freedom, and necessity are developed. Thus Maine de Biran builds upon psychology a metaphysical system, which frequently reminds of Descartes and Malebranche, but replaces the *cogito ergo sum*, by a *volo ergo sum;* just for this reason he exerts himself especially to fix securely the boundary lines between psychology and physiology, and particularly to exhibit the conception of *inner experience (sens intime)* as the clear and self-evident basis of all mental science, of which the self-consciousness of the willing and choosing personality appeared to him to be the fundamental principle. These significant thoughts, directed against the naturalistic one-sidedness of the eighteenth century, were supplemented by Maine de Biran for his own faith by a mystical turn, which finds the highest form of life in the giving up and losing of personality in the love of God. This supplementation was made especially toward the close of his life. His scientific doctrine, on the contrary, found further points of contact, in part with the Scottish, and in part with the German philosophy, through his friends, such as Ampère, Jouffroy, and Cousin. In this process, much of the original character was lost in consequence of the eclectic appropriation of material. This was shown externally in the fact that his theory, as thus modified, especially in the instructional form which it received through Cousin, was freely called Spiritualism. In fact, the original character of the theory, which might better have been called Voluntarism, was changed by the intellectualistic additions which Cousin especially brought to it from the German philosophy of identity. At a later time, Ravaisson, and in a still more independent fashion, closely related to the Kantian criticism, Renouvier, sought to hark back from eclecticism to Maine de Biran.[1]

3. Voluntarism has been on the whole, perhaps, the most strongly marked tendency of the psychology of the nineteenth century. It is the form in which empirical science has appropriated Kant's and

---

[1] A similar position is occupied in Italy by Gallupi. Among the "facts of consciousness" which he makes the basis of philosophy, he regards the autonomy of the ethical will as the determining factor, while Rosmini has retained the older intellectualism.

Fichte's transfer of the standpoint of philosophy from the theoretical over to the practical reason.   In Germany the principal influences on this side have been Fichte's and Schopenhauer's metaphysics.   Both these authors make the essential nature of man to consist in the will, and the colouring which such a point of view gives to the whole theory of the world could only be strengthened by the course of German history in our century, and by the transformation in the popular mind which has accompanied it.   The importance of the practical, which has been enhanced to the highest degree, and the repression of the theoretical, which is not without its dangers, have appeared more and more as the characteristic features of the age.

This tendency made its appearance in a scientific form with *Beneke,* who in spite of his dependence in part upon English philosophy and in part upon Herbart, gave a peculiar turn to his exposition of the associational psychology (cf. above, p. 586) by conceiving the elements of the mental life as active processes or impulses (*Triebe*).   He called them "elementary faculties" (*Urvermögen*), and maintained that these, originally set into activity by stimuli, bring about the apparently substantial unity of the psychical nature by their persistence as traces (*Spuren*), and by their reciprocal adjustment in connection with the continual production of new forces.   The soul is accordingly a bundle — not of ideas, as with Hume, but — of impulses, forces, and "faculties."   On the other hand, all real significance is denied to the faculties in the older sense of classifications of the mental activities (cf. above, p. 577).   To establish this doctrine inductively by a methodical elaboration of the facts of inner perception is regarded by Beneke as the only possible presupposition for the philosophical disciplines, such as logic, ethics, metaphysics, and the philosophy of religion.   In this procedure he passes on to a *theory of the values* which belong to stimuli (the so-called "things"), on account of the increase or diminution of the impulses.

Fortlage gave metaphysical form to the psychological method and theory of Beneke, by incorporating it into Fichte's Science of Knowledge.   He, too, conceives of the soul and all things in their relations as a system of impulses or forces, and perhaps no one has carried through so sharply as he the conception that the source of substantial existence is the activity of the will, — an activity which is devoid of any substrate.[1]   He regarded the essential nature of the psychical processes as follows : From original functions arise contents which grow into synthetic union, remain, become established, and thus produce the forms of psychical reality.   He thus pointed out once more the way

---

[1] Cf. C. Fortlage, *Beiträge zur Psychologie* (Leips. 1875), p. 40.

by which alone metaphysics can be freed from the schema of material processes which are conceived as movements of unchangeable substances, such as atoms. But, at the same time, there were in these theories suggestions for the thought that the processes of ideation, of attention, and of evaluation in judgments, must be regarded as functions of the "impulse" which issues in question and assent or rejection. In the later development, indeed, the psychological analysis of the thinking process has penetrated even to the realm of logic, and here has often averted attention from the proper problems of that science. In the last decades especially, psychology as method and theory has had a luxurious development similar to that in the eighteenth century, and in its degenerate forms it has led to the same manifestations of the most superficial popular philosophy.

4. In England, also, the traditional psychological method and standpoint remain in control; nor was this dominance essentially affected by the transformation which Hamilton gave to the Scottish tradition under the influence of German philosophy and particularly of Kant. He, too, defends the standpoint of inner experience and regards it as affording the standard for all philosophical disciplines. Necessity and universality are to be found only in the simple, immediately intelligible facts of consciousness which are present in every one. But in these facts — and to these belong also all individual perceptions of the presence of an external thing — it is only the finite, in finite relations and conditions, which comes to our knowledge. It is in this sense, and without reference to the Kantian conception of the phenomenal, that human knowledge is regarded by Hamilton as limited to experience of the finite. Of the Infinite and Absolute, *i.e.*, of God, man has only a moral certainty of faith. Science, on the contrary, has no knowledge of this " Unconditioned," because it can think only what it first distinguishes from another in order then to relate it to another (cf. Kant's conception of synthesis). Mansel brought this " Agnosticism " into the service of revealed theology, making a still stronger and more sceptical employment of the Kantian theory of knowledge. He shows that religious dogmas are absolutely incomprehensible for human reason, and maintains that just on this account they are also incapable of attack. The unknowableness of the " Absolute " or the " Infinite," as Hamilton had taught it, still plays an important rôle in other philosophical tendencies in England; *e.g.* in Herbert Spencer's system (cf. below, § 45).

As set over against psychology, which has to do only with the facts of consciousness, Hamilton treats logic, æsthetics, and ethics, which correspond to the three classes of psychical phenomena, as the theory of the laws under which facts stand; yet he does not attain complete clearness as to the normative character of this legislation, and so the philosophical disciplines also remain entangled in the method of psychology. In working out his system, Hamilton's logical theory became one of the most clearly defined productions of formal logic. The problem of logic for him is to set forth systematically the relations which exist between concepts, and he limits the whole investigation to relations of quantity, going quite beyond the principle of the Aristotelian analysis (cf. above, pp. 135 f.). Every judgment is to be regarded as an equation, which declares what the relation is between what is comprised in the one concept, and what is comprised in the other. For example, a judgment of subordination, "the rose is a flower," must take the form : " All S = some P," "all roses = some flowers." The peculiarity of this is that the predicate is "quantified," whereas previous logical theory has quantified the subject only. When all judgments were thus reduced to the form of equations, obtaining between the contents of two concepts, inferences and conclusions appeared to be operations of reckoning, performed with given magnitudes. This seemed to be the complete carrying through of the principle of the terministic logic, as it was formulated by Occam (cf. above, p. 342), Hobbes (p. 404), and Condillac (p. 478). The new analysis or logical calculus has spread since the time of Hamilton, and become a broad field for the intellectual gymnastics of fruitless subtlety and ingenuity. For it is evident that such a logic proceeds from only a single one among the numerous relations which are possible between concepts and form the object of judgments. Moreover, the relation in question is one of the least important; the most valuable relations of logical thought are precisely those which fall outside this kind of analysis. But the mathematical exactness with which this logic has seemed to develop its code of rules has enlisted in its behalf a series of vigorous investigators, and that not merely in England. They have, however, overlooked the fact that the living, actual thought of man knows nothing of this whole formal apparatus, so neatly elaborated.

5. In the debates over these questions in France and England the religious or *theological interest* in the conception of the *substance of the soul* is naturally always a factor : the same interest stood in the foreground in the very violent controversies which led in Germany to the dissolution of the Hegelian school. They turned essentially about the *personality of God* and the *immortality of the soul.* Hegelianism could not continue as "Prussian state-philosophy" unless it maintained the "identity of philosophy with religion." The am-

biguous mode of expression of the master, who had no direct interest in these questions, enveloped as it was in the dialectical formalism, favoured this contest as to the orthodoxy of his teaching. In fact, the so-called "right wing" of the school, to which prominent theologians like Gabler, Göschel, and Hinrichs belonged, tried to keep this orthodoxy : but while it perhaps might remain doubtful how far the " coming-to-itself of the Idea " was to be interpreted as the personality of God, it became clear, on the other side, that in the system of perpetual Becoming and of the dialectical passing over of all forms into one another, the finite personality could scarcely raise a plausible claim to the character of a " substance " and to immortality in the religious sense.

This motive forced some philosophers out of the Hegelian school to a *" theistic "* view of the world, which, like that of Maine de Biran, had for its centre the conception of *personality,* and with regard to finite personalities inclined to the Leibnizian Monadology. The younger *Fichte* termed these mental or spiritual realities *Urpositionen* [prime-positions]. The most important carrying-out of the thought of this group was the philosophical system of Chr. *Weisse,* in which the conception of the possible is placed ontologically above that of Being, to the end of deriving all Being from freedom, as the self-production of personality (Fichte).

In the relation between the possible and the actual, we have here repeated the antithesis set up by Leibniz, between the *vérités éternelles,* and the *vérités de fait,* and likewise the problems which Kant brought together in the conception of the " specification of Nature " (cf. above, p. 566). Within the " possibilities " which cannot be thought away, the actual is always ultimately such that it might be conceivably otherwise; *i.e.* it is not to be deduced, it must be re-garded as given through freedom. Law and fact cannot be reduced to each other.

Carrying out this view in a more psychological manner, *Ulrici* regarded the self as the presupposition for the distinguishing activity, with which he identified all consciousness, and out of which he developed his logical, as well as his psychological, theory.

6. The orthodoxy, which at the time of the Restoration was grow-ing in power and pretension, was attacked by the counter-party with the weapons of Hegelianism, and in this contest Ruge served as leader in public support of both religious and political liberalism. How pantheistically and Spinozistically the idealistic system was apprehended by this wing is best seen from *Feuerbach's Thoughts on Death and Immortality,* where the divine infinitude is praised as the ultimate ground of man's life, and man's disappearance in the same

as the true immortality and blessedness. From this ideal pantheism Feuerbach then rapidly advanced to the most radical changes of his doctrine. He felt that the panlogistic system could not explain the individual things of Nature : though Hegel had called Nature the realm of the accidental or contingent, which is incapable of keeping the conception pure. This inability, thought Feuerbach, inheres rather in the conception which man makes to himself of things : the general conceptions in which philosophy thinks are no doubt incapable of understanding the real nature of the individual thing. Therefore Feuerbach now inverts the Hegelian system, and the result is a *nominalistic materialism.* The actual reality is the individual known to the senses ; everything universal, everything mental or spiritual, is but an illusion of the individual. Mind or spirit is " Nature in its otherness." In this way Feuerbach gives his purely *anthropological explanation of religion.* Man regards his own generic nature — what he wishes to be himself — as God.

This " theory of the wish," is to free humanity from all superstition and its evil consequences, after the same fashion as the theory of Epicurus (cf. above, p. 188). The epistemology of this " philosophy of the future " can be only sensualism; its ethics only eudæmonism: the impulse to happiness is the principle of morals, and the sympathetic participation in the happiness of another is the fundamental ethical feeling.

After materialism had shown so illustrious a metaphysical pedigree, others employed for its advantage the anthropological mode of argument which had been in use in French literature since Lamettrie, and which seemed to become still stronger through the progress of physiology. Feuerbach had taught: man is what he eats (*ist was er isst*) ! And so once more the dependence of the mind upon the body was interpreted as a materialising of the psychical activity ; thinking and willing were to be regarded as secretions of the brain, similar to the secretions of other organs. A companion for this theory appeared in the guise of a purely sensualistic theory of knowledge, as it was developed by Czolbe independently of metaphysical assumptions; although at a later time Czolbe himself reached a view of the world which bordered closely upon materialism. For, since he regarded knowledge as a copy of the actual, he came ultimately to ascribe to ideas themselves spatial extension, and, in general, to regard space as the supporter of all attributes, giving it the place of Spinoza's substance.

So the materialistic mode of thought began to spread in Germany also, among physicians and natural scientists, and this condition of affairs came to light at the convention of natural scientists at Göttingen in 1854. The contradiction between the inferences of natural science and the " needs of the heart " (*Gemüth*) became the theme of a controversy which was continued in writing also, in which Carl *Vogt* championed the absolute sovereignty of the mechanical view of the world, while Rudolph *Wagner*, on the contrary, professed to gain at the bounds of human knowledge the possibility for a faith that rescued the soul and its immortality. This effort,[1] which with extreme unaptness was termed " book-keeping by double entry," had subsequently its chief effect in creating among natural scientists who saw through the one-sidedness of materialism, but could not befriend the teleology of idealism, a growing inclination toward *Kant*, into whose thing-in-itself they thought the needs of the heart and soul might be permitted to make their escape. When, then, in 1860, Kuno Fischer's brilliant exposition of the critical philosophy appeared, then began the " return to Kant" which was afterwards destined to degenerate into literary-historical micrology. To the natural-science temper, out of which it arose, Albert Lange's *History of Materialism* gave expression.

Many misunderstandings, to be sure, accompanied this movement when even great natural scientists like Helmholtz[2] confused transcendental idealism with Locke's theory of signs and doctrine of primary and secondary qualities. Another misunderstanding appeared somewhat later, when a conspicuous school of theology, under the leadership of Ritschl, adopted the doctrine of the "thing-in-itself," in a form analogous to the position of English agnosticism.

The philosophical revival of Kantianism, which has permeated the second half of the century, especially since Otto Liebmann's impressive book, *Kant and the Epigones* (1865), presents a great variety of views, in which we find repeated all shades of the opposing interpretations which Kant's theory met at its first appearance. The empirical and the rationalistic conceptions of knowledge and experience have come again into conflict, and their historical, as well as their systematic, adjustment has been the ultimate ground of the pragmatic necessity which has brought about gradually a return to Fichte. To-day there is once more an idealistic metaphysics in process of formation, as the chief representative of which we may regard Rudolf Eucken.

---

[1] It is not without interest to note the fact that this motif was not far removed from the French materialists. Of Cabanis and of Broussais we have expressions, made at the close of their life, which are in this spirit, and even of a mystical tendency.

[2] Cf. H. Helmholtz, *Physiologische Optik*, 25, and, especially, *The Facts of Perception* (Berlin, 1879).

But in all these forms, this Neo-Kantian movement, with its earnest work upon the problem of knowledge, has had the result of rendering the superficial metaphysics of materialism evidently inadequate and impossible, and hence has led to its rejection. Even where Kant's doctrine was given an entirely empirical, and indeed positivistic turn, or even in the fantastic reasonings of so-called "solipsism," the thought of regarding consciousness as an accessory function of matter was rejected as an absurdity. Rather we find the opposite one-sided view that primary reality is to be ascribed only to inner perception, in contrast with outer perception.

Materialism was thus overcome in science; it lives in popular expositions, such as Büchner's "Force and Matter" (*Kraft und Stoff*), or in the more refined form of Strauss's "Old and New Faith"[1] (*Alter und neuer Glaube*); it lives on also as theory of life in just those circles which love to enjoy the "results of science" from the most agreeable hand. For this superficial culture, materialism has found its characteristic exposition in Haeckel's works and his so-called "monism."

For psychology as science, however, it became necessary to renounce the conception of a soul-substance for the basis as well as for the goal of its investigation, and as a science of the laws of the psychical life to build only upon inner or outer experience. So we came by our "psychology without a soul," which is free from all metaphysical assumptions — or means to be.

7. A deeper reconciliation of the above antitheses was given by *Lotze* from the fundamental thoughts of German idealism. The vital and formative activity which constitutes the spiritual essence of all this real world has as its end, the good. The mechanism of nature is the regular form in which this activity works in the realisation of its end. Natural science has doubtless no other principle than that of the mechanical, causal connection, and this principle is held to apply to organisms also; but the beginnings of metaphysics, like those of logic, lie only in ethics. In carrying out this *teleological idealism, motifs* from all the great systems of German philosophy accord to a new, harmonious work; every individual real entity has its essential nature only in the living relations in which it stands to other real entities; and these relations which constitute the connected whole of the universe are possible only if all that is, is grounded as a partial reality in a substantial unity, and if thus all

---

[1] The evidence of descent from the Hegelian dialectic is seen also in this, the most ingenious form which materialism can find, — L. Knapp's *Rechtsphilosophie* (1857) might perhaps be classed with it, — for all higher forms of mental life are treated as the striving of nature to go beyond herself.

that takes place between individuals is to be apprehended as purposeful realisation of a common life goal. By the powerful universality with which he mastered the material of facts and the forms
of scientific elaboration in all the special disciplines Lotze was
specially fitted to carry out fully this fundamental metaphysical
thought, and in this respect, also, his personality as well as what he
taught, joins worthily on to the preceding epoch. His own attitude
is best characterised by its conception of knowledge as a vital and
purposive interaction between the soul and the other "substances."
The "reaction" of the soul is combined with the excitation which
proceeds from "things." On the one side, the soul develops its own
nature in the forms of perception, and in the general truths which
come to consciousness with immediate clearness and evidence on the
occasion of the stimulus from things; on the other hand, the participation of the subject makes the world of ideas a phenomenal appearance. But this appearance or phenomenal manifestation, as the
purposive inner life, is by no means mere illusion. It is rather a
realm of worths or values, in which the good is realising itself. The
coming to actual reality of this world of consciousness is the most
important result of the interaction of substances. It is the ultimate and truest meaning of the world-process. From these fundamental thoughts, Lotze, in his *Logic*, has conceived the series of
forms of thought as a systematic whole, which develops out of the
problems or tasks of thinking. In his *Metaphysics*, he has developed
and defined his view of the world with fineness and acuteness in his
treatment of conceptions, and with most careful consideration in all
directions. The view is that of teleological idealism. The third
part of the system, the ethics, has unfortunately not been completed
in this more rigorous form. As a substitute, we have the convictions of the philosopher and his mature comprehension of life and
history presented in the fine and thoughtful expositions of the
Microcosmus.

8. Another way of escape from the difficulties of the natural-
science treatment of the psychical life was chosen by *Fechner*. He
would look upon body and soul as the modes of phenomenal manifestation — completely separated and different in kind, but in constant
correspondence with each other — of one and the same unknown
reality ; and follows out this thought in the direction, that every
physical connection has a mental series or system of connections
corresponding to it, although the latter are known through perception only in the case of our own selves. As the sensations which
correspond to the excitation of particular parts of the nervous system, present themselves as surface waves in the total wave of our

individual consciousness, so we may conceive that the consciousness of a single person is in turn but the surface wave of a more general consciousness, — say that of the planetary mind : and if we continue this line, we come ultimately to the assumption of a *universal total-consciousness in God,* to which the universal causal connection of the atoms corresponds. Moreover, according to Fechner, the connection of inner and outer experience in our consciousness makes it possible to investigate the laws of this correspondence. The science of this is *psycho-physics.* It is the first problem of this science to find out *methods for measuring psychical quantities,* in order to obtain laws that may be formulated mathematically. Fechner brings forward principally the *method of just perceptible differences,* which defines as the unit of mass the smallest difference that is still perceptible between intensities of sensation, and assumes this to be equal everywhere and in all cases.

On the basis of this assumption, which to be sure is quite arbitrary, it seemed possible to give a mathematical formulation to the so-called " Weber-Fechner law." This was stated as follows : The intensities of different sensations are to each other as the logarithms of the intensities of their stimuli. The hope was thus awakened by Fechner that through the indirect measurement of psychical magnitudes a mathematical statement could be given by scientific methods for the psycho-physical, perhaps even for the psychological laws, and in spite of the numerous and serious objections which it encountered, this hope has had great success in promoting experimental study during the past decades in many laboratories established for this purpose. Yet it cannot be said that the outcome for a new and deeper comprehension of the mental life has kept pace with the activity of experimentation.[1]

The revival of the Spinozistic parallelism has likewise met greater and greater difficulties. With Fechner it was dogmatically intended since he claimed complete metaphysical reality for the contents of sense-perception. He called this view the " day view," and set it over against the " night view " of the phenomenalism which is found in natural science and philosophy. Others, on the contrary, conceived the parallelism in a more critical fashion, assuming that mind and body, with all their states and activities, are only the different manifestations of one and the same real unity. But as a result of the vigorous discussions which this question has awak-

---

[1] With reference to controversies upon these points, it is simplest to refer to Fechner himself, *Revision der Hauptpunkte der Psychophysik* (Leips. 1882). In addition we may refer especially to H. Münsterberg, *Ueber Aufgaben und Methoden der Psychologie* (Leips. 1891) [*Psychologie,* 1900].

ened,[1] it has become increasingly evident that such a parallelism is untenable in any form.

This is seen in the case of the investigator who has been most active in the extension of psycho-physical study, Wilhelm Wundt. He has gone on in the development of his thought from a "Physiological Psychology" to a "System of Philosophy." This latter work regards the world as an interconnected whole of active *individualities* which are to be conceived in terms of *will*. Wundt employs in his metaphysics the conception of activity without a substrate, which we have met in Fichte and Fortlage, and limits the application of the conception of substance to the theories of natural science. The interaction between the activities of these wills produces in organic beings higher unities of will, and at the same time, various stages of central consciousness; but the idea of an absolute world-will and world-consciousness, which arises from these premises in accordance with a regulative principle of our thought, lies beyond the bounds of the capacity of human knowledge.

9. Voluntarism has thus grown stronger and stronger, especially in its more general interpretation, and has combated the intellectualism which was regarded as a typical feature in the most brilliant period of German neo-humanism. As a result of this conflict we find emerging the same problem as to the relative primacy of the will or the intellect which occupied so vigorously the dialectical acuteness of the scholastics (cf. above, § 26). That this problem actually arose from the antagonistic development within the system of idealism was seen most clearly by *Eduard von Hartmann*. His "Philosophy of the Unconscious" proceeds from a synthesis of Hegel, on the one hand, with Schopenhauer and the later thought of Schelling, on the other. Its purpose was to bring together once more the rational and irrational lines of idealism. Hartmann attempts by this means to ascribe to the one World-Spirit *both will and idea* (the logical element), as coördinated and interrelated attributes. In calling the absolute spirit the "Unconscious," Hartmann attributes to the concept of consciousness an ambiguity like that which Schopenhauer ascribed to the will; for the activities of the "Unconscious" are functions of will and ideation which are indeed not given in any empirical consciousness, but yet presuppose some other consciousness if we are to think of them at all. This

---

[1] A critical survey of the literature on the question is given by E. Busse in the *Philos. Abhandlungen zur Sigwart's 70. Geburtstag* (Tübingen, 1900). Cf. also especially the investigation by H. Rickert in the same volume. [Cf. also the arts. by Erhardt, Busse, Paulsen, König, and Wentscher, in *Zeitschr. f. Philos.*, Vols. 114–117, and A. K. Rogers, in *Univ. of Chicago Cont. to Phil.*, 1899.]

higher consciousness, which is called Unconscious, and is to form the common ground of life in all conscious individuals, Hartmann seeks to exhibit as the active essence in all processes of the natural and psychical life; it takes the place of Schopenhauer's and Schelling's Will in Nature, and likewise of the vital force of former physiology and the "Entelechies" of the System of Development. The Unconscious unfolds itself above all in the teleological inter-relations of organic life. In this respect Hartmann has controverted materialism very efficiently, since his theory everywhere points to the unitary mental or spiritual ground of things. To this end he employed a wealth of knowledge in the fields of natural science, and that too in the most fortunate manner, although it was an illusion to suppose that he was winning his "speculative results by the inductive methods of natural science." At all events, the interest which he borrowed from the natural sciences in combination with an attractive and sometimes brilliant exposition, contributed much to the extraordinary, though transient, success of the "Philosophy of the Unconscious"; its greatest attractiveness lay in the treatment of pessimism (cf. below, § 46), and along this line it was followed by a train of popular philosophical literature which was for the most part of very inferior quality.

Hartmann himself made extensive historical studies, and with their aid extended his fundamental metaphysical thoughts to the fields of ethics, æsthetics, and philosophy of religion; then he proceeded to work out a rigorous dialectic system in his *Theory of the Categories*. This is the most systematic work of a constructive character in the field of abstract concepts which has appeared during the last decades in Germany, — a work which has been supplemented by a historical and critical basis in his *History of Metaphysics*.[1]

The *Theory of the Categories*, which is no doubt Hartmann's main work from a scientific standpoint, seeks to gain a common formal basis for the disciplines of philosophy by tracing all the relating principles employed by the intellect, whether in perception or in reflection, through the subjective ideal field of the theory of knowledge, the objective real field of the philosophy of nature, and the metaphysical realm. In the fineness of its dialectical references, and in the wealth of interesting outlooks upon the fields of reality, it presents a unique counterpart to Hegel's *Logic*. As Hegel developed dialectically the whole process in which the Idea changes over into Nature, in which the concept leaves itself and becomes "other," so Hartmann shows, in the case of every category, the transforma-

---

[1] *Geschichte der Metaphysik* (2 parts, Leips. 1899–1900).

tion which the "logical" experiences by its relation to the "non-logical" element of reality, which arises from the Will. Here, too, the world appears as divided within itself, as the conflict of Reason against will.

§ 45. Nature and History.

The dualism of the Kantian *Weltanschauung* is reflected in the science of the nineteenth century by the peculiar tension in the relation between *science of Nature and science of mind*. At no earlier time has this antithesis been so current as respects both material and methods, as in ours; and from this circumstance a number of promising new shiftings have arisen. If from the domain of mental science we take, as has been shown, the contested province of psychology, we then have remaining over against "Nature," what corresponds still more to Kantian thought—the *social life and its historical development* in its full extent in all directions. The thinking of natural science, pressing forward in its vigorous career of annexation, from the nature of the case easily found points in the social phenomena as it had previously found in the psychological, where it might set the levers of its mode of consideration, so that a struggle became necessary upon this field, similar to that which had taken place on account of the soul; and thus the earlier antithesis culminated in that between *natural science and historical science*.

1. The first form in which the struggle between the natural science and the historical *Weltanschauung* was fought out, was the successful opposing of the Revolution Philosophy by the *French Traditionalism*. After St. Martin and de Maistre had set forth the Revolution as the judgment of God upon unbelieving mankind, *de Bonald* proceeded to oppose to the social theories of the eighteenth century, which he too held responsible for the horrors of the Reign of Terror, the theory of the clerical-legitimist Restoration. Unschooled in abstract thought, a dilettante, especially in his predilection for etymology, he was influential by the warmth of his presentation and by the weight of the principle which he defended. It was the mistake of the Enlightenment, he taught, to suppose that the reason could from its own resources find out truth and organise society, and to leave to the liking of individuals the shaping of their social life. But in truth all intellectual and spiritual life of man is a product of *historical tradition*. For it is rooted in *language*. Language, however (and just here Condillacism is most vigorously opposed), was given man by God as the first revelation; the divine "Word" is the source of all truth. Human knowledge is always only a participating in this truth; it grows out of conscience, in which we make that which holds universally, our

own. But the bearer of the tradition of the divine word is the
Church : her teaching is the God-given, *universal reason,* propagated
on through the centuries as the great tree on which all the genuine
fruits of human knowledge ripen. And therefore this revelation is
the only possible foundation of society. The arrogance of the individuals who have rebelled against this has found its expiation in the
dissolution of society, and it is now in point to build society once
more upon the eternal basis : this was also the thought which held
loosely together the obscure and strange fancies of *Ballanche.*

2. The philosophical factor in this church-political theory was,
that the generic reason realising itself in the historical development
of society was recognised as the ground of the intellectual and spiritual life of individuals : if the theological views were distracted
from this Traditionalism, the reader found himself hard by *Hegel's*
conception of the *Objective Spirit.* Hence it was extremely humorous when Victor *Cousin,* while adopting German philosophy on just
this side, to a certain extent took from the Ultra-montanes the cream
of their milk. Eclecticism also taught a universal reason, and was
not disinclined to see in it something similar to the Scottish " common sense," to which, however, it still did not deny a metaphysical
basis, fashioned according to Schelling and Hegel. When, therefore, *Lamennais,* who at the beginning had been a traditionalist and
had then passed through the school of the German philosophy, treated
the doctrine of Ideas in his *Esquisse d'une Philosophie,* he could fully
retain the above theory of the conscience, so far as its real content
was concerned.

Quite another form was assumed by the doctrine of Objective
Spirit, where it was apprehended purely psychologically and empirically. In the mental life of the individual, numerous processes go
on, which rest solely upon the fact that the individual never exists
at all except as member of a psychical interconnected whole. This
interacting and overreaching life, into which each one grows, and
by virtue of which he is what he is, evinces itself not by conformity
to natural laws, as do the general forms of the psychical processes :
it is rather of a historical character, and the general mind which lies
at the basis of individual life expresses itself objectively in language,
in customs and morals, and in public institutions. Individual psychology must be broadened to a *social psychology* by a study of these.
This principle has been propounded by *Lazarus* and *Steinthal,* and
the eminently historical character which this must have when carried out they have indicated by the otherwise less fortunate name
of *Völkerpsychologie* [Folk or Comparative Psychology].

3. One must take into account the fundamental social thought of

Traditionalism to understand the religious colouring which is characteristic of *French socialism* since *St. Simon,* in contrast with the
social-political theories of the last century. St. Simon's theory,
however, stands not only under the pressure of the religious zeal
which was growing to become a new social and political power, but
also in lively relations to German philosophy, and indeed to its
dialectic.   All this passed over to his disciple, Auguste *Comte,*
whose thought passed through an extremely peculiar course of
development.

He aims at nothing more or less than a complete reform of human
society.   He, too, regards it as an evident conclusion that with the
Revolution, the Enlightenment, which was its cause, has become
bankrupt.   Like the Traditionalists, he fixes the responsibility for
this upon the independence of individuals, upon free investigation
and autonomy in the conduct of life.   From these follow anarchy
of opinions and anarchy of public life.   The salvation of society is
to be sought only in the dominance of scientific knowledge.   We
must find once more, and along securer lines, that subordination of
all the activities of life beneath a universally valid principle which
was approximately attained in the grand but premature catholic system of the Middle Ages.   In place of theology we must set positive
science, which tolerates freedom of faith as little as theology tolerated it in the Middle Ages.   This Romantic element determined
Comte's theory throughout.   It is shown not only in his philosophy
of history by his enthusiastic portrayal of the mediæval system of
society, not only in his projected "Religion of Humanity" and its
cultus, but above all in his demand for a concurrent spiritual and
secular authority for the new social order.   The new form of the
social order was to proceed from the creative activity of the *pouvoir
spirituel,* and Comte made fantastic attempts toward this by establishing his " Western Committee."   As he thought of himself as the
chairman of this committee, so he trusted to himself the establish-
ment of the new teaching.   But the positive philosophy on which
the new social order was to arise was nothing other than the ordered
system of the positive sciences.

Comte's projected *positive system of the sciences* first of all pushes
Hume's and Condillac's conception to the farthest point.   Not only
is human knowledge assigned for its province to the reciprocal relations of phenomena, but there is nothing absolute whatever, that
might lie unknown, as it were, at the basis of phenomena.   The only
absolute principle is, that *all is relative.*   To talk of first causes or
ultimate ends of things has no rational sense.   But this relativism
(or, as it has later been termed. "correlativism") is forfeited at once

to the universalistic claim of the thinking of mathematical natural science, when science is assigned the task of explaining all these relations from the point of view that in addition to individual facts we must discover and establish also the order of these facts as they repeat themselves in time and space. This order we may call "general fact," but nothing more. Thus positivism seeks by "laws" — this is Comte's usual name for general facts — not to explain the particular facts, but only to establish their recurrence. From this is supposed to come foresight for the future, as the practical outcome of science, — *savoir pour prévoir*, — although such foresight is quite unintelligible and unjustifiable under his presuppositions. This conception of Comte's has found assent not only with philosophers like *C. Göring*, who appropriated it especially for his theory of causality, but also to some degree among natural scientists, particularly with the representatives of mechanics, such as *Kirchhoff* and *Mach*. Their tendency is to exclude the conception of efficient agency from the scientific theory of nature, and to reach the elimination of "force" on the basis of a mere "description" or discovery of the most adequate "image." This has been attempted by H. Hertz in his *Principles of Mechanics*. Similar thoughts have been spun out into the unspeakably tedious terminologies of his "Empirio-Criticism," by *Richard Avenarius*, who has employed the generalisations of an abstract dialectic, and seeks to demonstrate all philosophical conceptions of the world to be needless variations of one original world-conception of pure experience, which is to be once more restored.

4. Phenomena, according to Comte, both individual and general, are in part simple, in part more or less complicated. Knowledge of the simpler must precede that of the more complex. For this reason he arranges the sciences in a hierarchy which proceeds step by step from the simple to the complex. Mathematics is followed by astronomy, then by physics, chemistry, biology which includes psychology, and finally by " sociology." This relation, nevertheless, is not to be conceived as if every following discipline was supposed to be deduced from the preceding discipline or disciplines; it merely presupposes these in the sense that their more complicated facts include within themselves the more elementary facts; the completely new facts add their own peculiar combination and nature to those more elementary facts. So, for example, biology presupposes physical and chemical processes, but the fact of life is something completely new, and incapable of deduction from these processes; it is a fact which must be verified by biological observation. Such, too, is the relation of sociology to the five preceding disciplines. Following this principle Comte's social statics declines with charac-

teristic emphasis to derive sociality from the individual, as was done in the Enlightenment philosophy. The social nature is an original fact, and the first social phenomenon is the family. Still more independent is his social dynamics, which without psychological explanation sets itself the task of discovering the *natural law of the history of society*. Comte finds this in the *principle of the three stages*, which society necessarily passes through (an *aperçu*, which had been anticipated by d'Alembert and Turgot as well as by Hegel and Cousin). Intellectually, man passes out of the theological phase, through the metaphysical, over into the positive. In the first he explains phenomena by supernatural powers and beings thought in anthropomorphic guise, in the second by general concepts [*e.g.* force, etc.] which he constructs as the essence working behind phenomena; in the positive stage he comprehends the particular only by the actually demonstrable conditions, from which it follows according to a law verifiable experimentally. To this universal law of the mental life are subject all special processes into which the same divides, and likewise the *movement of human history as a whole*. Moreover, the intellectual process is accompanied by a corresponding course of development in the external organisation of society, which passes out of the priestly, warlike condition, through the rule of the jurists (*légistes*), to the "industrial" stage.

The very circumstantial philosophy of history which Comte here carries out, interesting in particular points, but on the whole completely arbitrary and often distorted by ignorance and prejudice, is to be estimated solely as a construction undertaken for his reformatory purpose. The victory of the positive view of the world, and at the same time of the industrial order of life, is the goal of the historical development of European peoples. At this goal "the great Thought, viz.: positive philosophy, will be wedded with the great Power, the proletariate."[1]

But as if the law of the circuit of the three phases was to be first verified in the case of its author, Comte in the last ("subjective") period of his thinking fell back into the theological stage, making mankind as *Grand-être* the object of a religious veneration or worship, as whose high priest he imitated the whole apparatus of worship of the saints, with a positivist remodelling. Among these phantastic products of the imagination the history of philosophy can at most consider only the motive which guided Comte in his later course. He best set this forth in the *General View of Positivism*, which is

---

[1] Cf. on Comte, among recent works, Tschitscherin, *Philosophische Forschungen*, tr. from the Russian (Heidelberg, 1899).

reprinted in the first volume of the *Positive Polity.* This shows him turning aside from the outspoken individualism which had shown itself in his earlier conviction that positive science as such would be sufficient to bring about the reform of society. He has now seen that the positive philosophy may indeed teach how the new order of things is to appear, but that the work of bringing about this new order can be achieved only by the " affective principle "—the *feeling.* Whereas he had formerly taught that the specifically human, as it develops in history, is to be sought in the predominance of the intelligence over the feelings, it is from the predominance of the heart over the intellect that he now expects the fulfilment of his hopes which he formulates as *l'amour pour principe, l'ordre pour base, le progrès pour but.*[1] And since Gall has shown that the preëminence of heart over intellect is a fundamental characteristic of the brain of woman, Comte bases on this his worship of woman, which he would make an essential constituent in the religion of humanity. He who had begun with the proud announcement of a positivist papacy ended with an appeal to the proletariate and the emancipation of woman.

5. It is in accord with the practical, *i.e.* political, ends which Comte followed, that in history also general facts or laws appeared to him more important than particular facts. He believed that in the realm of history a foresight (*prévoyance*) should guide and direct action. But apart from this theory and in spite of the one-sidedness of his education along the lines of mathematics and natural science, Comte was yet sufficiently broad-minded to understand and to preserve the distinctive character of the different disciplines, and as he had already attempted to secure for biology its own distinctive methods, he expressly claimed for his sociology the " historical method." In the biological field the series of successive phenomena in a race of animals is only an external evolution which does not alter or concern the permanent character of the race (hence, Comte was throughout an opponent of Lamarck's theory). In sociology we have to do with an actual transformation of the human race. This has been brought about through the changing vicissitudes of generations and the persisting cumulation of definite life processes which has been made possible thereby. The historical method is to return to general facts, and thus observation is to be guided by theory, so that historical investigation will yield only a construction based upon a philosophy of history. It was thus perhaps not quite in Comte's meaning, but nevertheless it was a consequence of his teaching, when the effort was made here and ther

---

[1] " Love for the principle, order for the basis, progress for the end."

to raise history to the plane of a natural science. *John Stuart Mill* called attention to this in his methodology. Schopenhauer had denied to history the character of a science on the ground that it teaches only the particular and nothing of the universal. This defect seemed now to be remedied in that the effort was made to press forward beyond the description of particular events to the general facts. The most impressive attempt of this sort was made by Comte's English disciple, Thomas Buckle. In his *History of Civilisation in England* (1857), Buckle defined the task of historical science as that of seeking the natural laws of the life of a people. For this purpose Buckle found in those slow changes of the social conditions which are recorded in the statistical tables, much more usable and exact material than in the recital of particular events to which the old chronicle forms of historical writing had been limited.

Here the proper sense of the antithesis is disclosed: on the one hand the life of the masses with the changes taking place conformably to general law — on the other hand the independent value of that which presents itself but once, and is determined within itself. In this respect the essence of the historical view of the world has been by no one so deeply apprehended, and so forcibly and warmly presented, as by Carlyle, who worked himself free from the philosophy of enlightenment by the assistance of the German idealism, and laboured unweariedly for the recognition of the archetypal and creative personalities of history, — for the comprehension and veneration of " heroes."

In these two extremes are seen anew the great antitheses in the conception of the world which were already prevalent in the Renaissance, but which had not at that time attained so clear and methodical an expression. We distinguished in that period a historical century, and a century of natural science, in the sense that the new investigation of nature emerged from the conflict of traditions as the most valuable outcome (cf. Part IV.). From the victory of the methods and conceptions of natural science resulted the great metaphysical systems, and as their sequence the unhistorical mode of thought characteristic of the Enlightenment. In opposition to this the German philosophy set its historical view of the world. It is to be noted that the almost complete counterpart of this antithesis is found in the psychological realm in the antithesis between Intellectualism and Voluntarism. On this account the attempt which has been made during the last decade to introduce the so-called scientific[1] method into history, is not in accord with the development of

---

[1] [*Naturwissenschaftliche.* In English the term "science" is so commonly used as the equivalent of "natural science" that the confusion objected to in

psychology during our century. It is indeed not the great historians who have fallen victims to this mistake, but here and there some who have either been too weak to stand against the watchwords of the day, or have made use of them for popular effect. In this so-called scientific[1] treatment of historical structures or processes the misuse of comparisons and analogies is especially undesirable — as if it were a genuine insight to call society an organism;[2] or as if the effect of one people upon another could be designated as endosmose and exosmose!

The introduction of natural-science modes of thought into history has not been limited to this postulate of method which seeks to ascertain the laws of the historical process; it has also had an influence upon the contents. At the time when Feuerbach's Materialism, which was a degenerate product of the Hegelian dialectic (cf. above, § 44, 6), was yet in its vigour, Marx and Engels created *socialism's materialistic philosophy of history,* in which motives from Hegel and from Comte cross in peculiar manner. The meaning of history they too find in the " processes of social life." This collective life, however, is essentially of an economic nature. The determining forces in all social conditions are the economic relations ; they form the ultimate motives for all activities. Their change and their development are the only conditioning forces for public life and politics, and likewise for science and religion. All the different activities of civilisation are thus only offshoots of the economic life, and all history should be economic history.

6. If history has had to defend its autonomy against the destruction of the boundary lines which delimit it from the sciences, the natural science of the nineteenth century has conversely contained an eminently historical factor which has attained a commanding influence, viz. the *evolutionary* motive. In fact we find the natural science of to-day in its general theories, as well as in its particular investigations, determined by two great principles which apparently stand in opposition to each other, but which in truth reciprocally supplement each other, viz. the principle of the *conservation of energy* and that of *evolution.*

The former has been found by Robert Mayer, Joule, and Helmholtz to be the only form in which the axiom of causality can be used by the physical theory of to-day. The epistemological postulate that there is nothing new in nature, but that every following phenomenon

---

the text is all the more likely to occur. Of course the author is objecting not to scientific methods, but to the assumption that the scientific method for natural science is the proper scientific method for history.]

[2] [But cf. on this, Kant, *Critique of Judgment,* § 65. Cf. also Lapie in *Rev de Met. et de la Morale,* May. 1895.]

is only a transformation of that which precedes, was formulated by Descartes as the law of the Conservation of Motion (cf. above, p. 411), by Leibniz as the law of Conservation of Force (p. 421), by Kant as that of the Conservation of Substance (pp. 545 f.). The discovery of the mechanical equivalent of heat, and the distinction between the concepts of kinetic and potential energy, made possible the formulation that the sum of energy in nature is quantitatively unchangeable, and only qualitatively changeable, and that in every material system which is regarded as complete or closed within itself, the spatial distribution and direction of the kinetic and potential energy at any time is absolutely determined by the law just stated. It is not to be overlooked that in this statement the exclusion of other than material forces from the explanation of nature is made still more sharply than with Descartes; on the other hand, however, signs are already multiplying that a return to the *dynamic* conception of matter has been thereby introduced, such a conception as was demanded by Leibniz, Kant, and Schelling (cf. above, § 38, 7).

7. The principle of evolution had many lines of preparation in modern thought. In philosophic form it had been projected by Leibniz and Schelling, although as a relation between concepts, and not as a process taking place in time (so with Aristotle; cf. § 13); and among Schelling's disciples it was *Oken* who began to regard the ascending of classes and species in the realm of organic life as a process in time. With the aid of comparative morphology, to which also Goethe's studies had contributed, Oken dared that "adventure" in the "archæology of nature" of which Kant had spoken (p. 565). All organisms are regarded as variously formed "protoplasm" (*Urschleim*), and the higher have proceeded from the lower by an increasing multiplication of protoplasmic vesicles. At the same time (1809), in his *Philosophie Zoölogique, Lamarck* gave the first systematic exposition of the theory of descent. He explained the relationship of organisms by descent from a common original form, and their differences, in part by the direct effect of environment, and in part by the indirect effect of environment which operates by calling for a greater use of some organs and a less use of others. This use modifies structures, and the modifications in structure are inherited. The variations in species which become stable were thus explained by the alternating influences of heredity and adaptation. To these factors of explanation *Charles Darwin* added the decisive factor of *natural selection*. Organisms tend to increase at a far higher rate than the available means of nutrition. Hence the struggle for existence. Those plants or animals which vary in a direction that favours them in this struggle will survive.

The presuppositions of the theory, therefore, are the two princi-ples of heredity and variability; an additional element was the assumption of great periods of time for the accumulation of indefi-nitely small deviations, an assumption which was made possible by contemporaneous geological investigations.

This biological hypothesis at once gained more general signifi-cance in that it promised a purely mechanical explanation of the adaptations or purposive elements which constitute the problems of organic life, and it was believed that thereby the necessity of the progress of nature to higher and higher forms had been understood. The "purposive" had been mechanically explained in the sense of that which is capable of survival — that is, of that which can main-tain and propagate itself — and it was supposed that the same explanation could be applied to everything else which appears pur-posive in other relations, especially to that which is purposive in a normative respect. So the theory of selection following Darwin's own suggestions was very soon applied on many sides to psychology, sociology, ethics, and history, and was pressed by zealous adherents as the only scientific method. Few were clear on the point that *nature was thereby placed under a category of history*, and that this category had experienced an essential change for such an applica-tion. For the evolutionary theory of natural science, including the theory of natural selection, can indeed explain alteration but not *progress;* it cannot give the rational ground for regarding the result of the development as a "higher," that is, a *more valuable* form.

8. In its most universal extent the principle of evolution had already been proclaimed before Darwin by his countryman *Herbert Spencer,* and had been made the fundamental conception of the lat-ter's System of Synthetic Philosophy, in which many threads of English philosophy are brought together. He proceeds from agnos-ticism in so far as he declares the Absolute, the Unconditioned, the Unitary Being, which he is also fain to call Force, to be unknowable. Religion and philosophy have laboured in vain to conceive this in definite ideas; for us it is by the very nature of the case incapable of determination. Human knowledge is limited to an interpretation of phenomena, that is, to the manifestations of the Unknowable. Philosophy has only the task of generalising the results of the particular sciences, and putting these generalised results together into the simplest and most complete totality possible.

The fundamental distinction in phenomena Spencer designates as that of the "vivid" and the "faint" manifestations of the Un-knowable, *i.e.* of impressions and ideas. This indicates an attach-ment to Hume which is not fortunate (cf. above, p. 453). From this starting-point, although Spencer rightly rejects the reproach of materialism, he yet introduces a turn in his view of the world which directs preëminent interest to the character of physical phenomena. For an examination of all the particular sciences is supposed to yield the result that the fundamental form in which the Absolute manifests itself is evolution. And by evolution Spencer understands — following a suggestion of the scientist, von Baer — the tendency of all natural structures to pass over from the homogeneous to the heterogeneous. This active variation in which the ever-active force manifests itself consists in two processes, which in coöperation with each other constitute evolution, and which Spencer designates as differentiation and integration. On the one hand, by virtue of the plurality of effects which belong to every cause, the simple passes into a manifold; it differentiates and individualises itself; it divides and determines itself by virtue of the fulness of relations into which it enters. On the other hand, the thus sepa‑ rated individual phenomena come together again to form firm compounds and functional systems, and through these integrations new unities arise which are higher, richer, and more finely articulated than the original. So the animal organism is a higher unity than the cell; society is a higher "individual" than a single man.

This schema is now applied by Spencer to all material and spiritual processes, and with tireless labour he has sought to enforce it in the case of the facts of all the particular sciences. Physics and chemistry are refractory; they stand under the law of the conservation of energy. But astrophysical theory shows the differentiation of the original gas into the suns and the peripheral structures of the planets with their satellites, and likewise the corresponding integration in the articulated and ordered system of motion which all these bodies maintain. It is, however, in biology and sociology that the system attains full unfolding. Life is regarded by Spencer as a progressive adaptation of inner to outer relations. From this the individualising growth of a single organism is explained, and from the necessary variations of the latter according to the method of the theory of selection is explained the alteration of species.

Social life also in its whole historical course is nothing other than the progressive adaptation of man to his natural and plastic environment. The perfecting which the race wins thereby rests upon the dying out of the unfit and upon the survival of the fit functions. From the standpoint of this doctrine Spencer seeks also to decide the old strife between rationalism and empiricism upon both the logical and ethical fields. As against the associational psychology he admits that there are for the individual immediately evident principles, and truths which are innate in the sense that they cannot be explained by the experience of the individual. But the strength with which these judgments assert themselves so that consciousness finds it impossible to deny them, rests upon the fact that they are the intellectual and emotional habits acquired by the race, which have proved themselves to be adapted to further the race, and have maintained themselves on this ground. The *a priori* is everywhere an evolutionary product of heredity. So in particular for morals, everything in the form of intelligent feeling and modes of will survives which is adapted to further the self-preservation and development of the individual, of society, and of the race.

Finally every particular development reaches its natural end when a condition of equilibrium has been gained in which the inner relations are everywhere completely adapted to the outer, so that the capacity for further articulation and variation has been exhausted. It is, therefore, only by external influence that such a system can be destroyed and disturbed, so that its individual parts may enter into new processes of evolution. On the contrary Spencer strives against the assumption of the possibility that the whole universe, with all the particular systems which it contains, can ever come to a perfect and therefore permanent condition of equilibrium. He thus contradicts those investigators who have regarded as theoretically possible such a distribution of energies as to exclude all alterations; this is due ultimately to the fact that Spencer regards the Unknowable as the ever self-manifesting force, and regards evolution itself as the most universal law of the manifestation of the Unknowable.

9. Taken all in all Spencer's development of the principle of evolution is throughout of a cosmological character, and in this is shown just the alteration in this controlling principle which is due to the prevalence of natural science in our century. This is seen most clearly by comparing Hegel and Spencer. With the former, evolution is the nature of the self-revealing spirit; with the latter, it is the law of the successive manifestations of an unknowable force. To speak in Hegel's language (cf. p. 611), the subject has again become substance. In fact the Unknowable of Spencer resembles most that "indifference of real and ideal" which Schelling designated as the Absolute. This analogy would lead us to expect that the cosmological form of the principle of evolution will not be the final one, and that the historical standpoint and method, as the appropriate home of this principle, will give the permanent form which it will take in philosophy. In England itself, and still more in America, a decided turn toward Hegel is to be noticed since the impressive book of Hutchinson Stirling and Wallace's excellent

introduction of Hegel's logic. In Germany, Kuno Fischer's exposition of Hegel's doctrine, which is now just reaching completion, will dissipate prejudices which have hitherto stood in the way of its just valuation, and by stripping off the terminology which has become foreign to us, will cause this great system of evolution to appear in full clearness.

The same tendency to win back the historical form for the thought of evolution is found in the logical and epistemological efforts which have as their goal what Dilthey has denoted with a fortunate expression, a "critique of the historical reason." The aim is to break through that one-sidedness which has attached to logic since its Greek origins, and which prescribes as the goal and norm of logical laws in their formal aspect the relation of the universal to the particular (cf. § 12), and for the content and material of those laws the knowledge of nature. Under these presuppositions stand not only the extreme of mathematical logic (cf. § 44, 4), but also the important works of John Stuart Mill and Stanley Jevons, which are to be characterised essentially as the logical theory of natural science. Over against this, the elaborations of logical science by Lotze and Sigwart, especially in the latter's second edition, show a much more universal stamp, and in connection with the movement of historical idealism which has its attachments to the Fichtean view of the world (cf. § 44, 6), a deeper comprehension of the logical forms of historical science is on the way; such, for example, as we find in Rickert's investigations regarding the limitations of the concepts of natural science.[1]

§ 46. The Problem of Values.

While the end of the century finds us in the yet unadjusted strife between the historical and the natural-science standards, we see just in this continuation of an inherited antithesis how little the philosophy of this period has been able to win a real progress in its principles. Its great and varied industry has been rather at the periphery, and in the work of adjusting relations with the special sciences, while the central development falls prey to a certain stagnation which must be simply put up with as a fact easily comprehensible historically. The exhaustion of metaphysical energy and the high tide of empirical interests give a completely satisfactory explanation. For this reason we can readily understand that the philosophy of the nineteenth century shows a rich development along the bounding provinces in which it comes in contact with the empirical disciplines, as in psychology, philosophy of nature, anthropology,

---

[1] H. Rickert, *Grenzen der naturwissenschaftlichen Begriffsbildung*, 1896.

philosophy of history, philosophy of law and philosophy of religion, while on the contrary it makes the impression of an eclectic and dependent attitude in the fundamental disciplines.   Surely this is the inevitable consequence of the fact that it suffers from the repressive wealth of traditions which have attained complete historical consciousness.   It is in accord with this that no earlier time has seen such a luxuriant and fruitful growth in the study of the history of philosophy.   But there is need of a new central reconstruction if philosophy is to meet in satisfactory manner the wants which in recent time come once more for satisfaction from the general consciousness and from the special sciences.[1]

The direction in which the solution of this problem is to be sought is determined on the one hand by the predominance of that voluntarism which extends from psychology into general metaphysical theories (§ 44), and on the other by the circumstance that the two forms of the principle of evolution (§ 45), viz. the historical and that of natural science, are distinguished from each other by their different attitudes toward the determinations of value.   In addition the mighty upward sweep in the conditions of life which Europeans have experienced in this century has worked at once destructively and constructively upon general convictions.   Civilisation, caught in this movement of rapid enhancement and extension, is urged on by a deeper demand for comprehension of itself, and from the problem of civilisation which made its appearance in the Enlightenment (cf. § 37) a movement has developed for which the " transformation and re-valuation of all values " (*Umwertung aller Werthe*) has become the watchword.

1. The characteristic trait in this is that in the foreground of all ethical considerations the *relation of the individual to society* stands

---

[1] That the Catholic Church has sought to solve this problem by a revival of Thomism is well known, and does not need to be further set forth here.   Nor on this account do we need to cite the numerous Thomists (mostly Jesuits) in Italy, France, Germany, Belgium, and Holland.   In theory they represent no new principles, but at most seek to build out the old doctrine in details so that it may appear in some manner adapted to modern knowledge, in particular to modern science of nature.   But the freer tendencies of Catholic philosophy, which are usually called *Ontologism*, have created nothing new and fruitful.   They attach themselves for the most part to the Platonism of Malebranche, and point back to Augustine, so that the antagonism which we noted in the Middle Ages and in the Renaissance is repeated again (cf. pp. 364, 416.)   The finest presentation of Ontologism was found in the Italians, Rosmini and Gioberti ; the former gave it a sort of psychological basis ; the latter a purely metaphysical form (*L'ente crea l'esistente*).   In Germany Günther introduced into it certain elements of the idealistic speculations, especially of Fichte's doctrine ; in France, Gratry from this standpoint combats especially the eclecticism of Cousin, and in this eclecticism he combats Hegelianism and the " pantheism " which he finds in both (cf. *Étude sur la Sophistique Contemporaine, lettre à M. Vacherot*, Paris, 1851).

forth in much more conscious and explicit form than ever before, — whether in the positive form that the subordination of the individual to society is presented and grounded in some manner as the norm of all valuation, or whether it be in the negative form that the resistance of the individual to the oppressing weight of the species is praised and justified.

The first form is that which has been transmitted from the philosophy of the Revolution and from Utilitarianism, especially in the stamp given to it by Bentham (cf. p. 522). This Utilitarianism goes through the popular literature of the century as a broad stream in which the standard of the public good is taken as a matter of course without deep analysis of its meaning. It is characterised for the most part by limiting its care "for the greatest happiness of the greatest number" to man's earthly welfare; the mental and spiritual goods are not indeed denied, but the measure of all valuation is found in the degree of pleasure or pain which a circumstance, a relation, an act, or a disposition may call forth. Theoretically, this doctrine rests on the unfortunate inference of the associational psychology, that because every satisfied desire is accompanied with pleasure the expectation of the pleasure is, therefore, the ultimate motive of all willing, and every particular object is willed and valued only as means for gaining this pleasure. This formal eudæmonism was earlier forced either to regard the altruistic impulses as equally original with the egoistic, or to make them proceed from the egoistic through the experiences which the individual undergoes in social life. In contrast with this the noteworthy transformation which Utilitarianism has experienced in recent time consists in its combination with the principle of evolution, as has already been mentioned in the case of Spencer's doctrine (cf. § 45, 8). The valuation of altruism from the standpoint of social ethics appears according to this new point of view to be the result of the process of evolution, inasmuch as only those social groups have maintained themselves in the struggle for existence whose individual members have achieved altruistic thought and action in a relatively high degree.[1] The history of morals is a struggle of values or "ideals," from which we may in part explain the relativity of historical systems of morals, and in part their converging development to a universal human ethics. These fundamental thoughts of evolutionary ethics have been carried out in many detailed expositions; among their representatives

---

[1] Benjamin Kidd, *Social Evolution*, London, 1895, has attempted to determine the nature of religion sociologically by considering the part which ideas of the supernatural have played in this evolutionary process — a genuinely English undertaking.

may be mentioned, in France, Fouillée, in Germany, Paul Rée, whose evolutionary theory of conscience excited attention for a time, and G. H. Schneider.

[Before passing to the continental representatives of Utilitarianism it will be instructive to consider more fully the changes which have been effected in British theories both within and without the so-called Utilitarian school.[1] These changes affect the standard of value, the motives to which ethical appeal is made, and the relation which the individual is conceived to sustain to the social body ; their nature shows the influence of the close relation which ethical theory in England has always sustained to social and political conditions. During the century England has seen an almost continuous effort toward social and political reform. This movement has aimed at an extension of political privilege, and at making possible a higher standard of living for the less fortunate members of society. It has thus been democratic in so far as it has insisted upon the widest participation in the goods of civilisation ; but by emphasising not merely material comforts, but also political rights, social justice, and educational opportunities, it has tended to measure human welfare, not so much in terms of feeling as in terms of "dignity" and fulness of life or "self-realisation." The movement along these two directions has been due in part to the influence of German idealism as transmitted through Coleridge, Carlyle, and later through Green and others, but the immanent forces of social progress have had a decisive influence in the same direction.

As has been pointed out (pp. 513 f.), a general tendency of British theory has been to unite a social standard or criterion of moral value with an individualistic, and even egoistic theory of motives. This seemed the more possible to Bentham, because in the individualistic language of his day the community was defined as a "fictitious body composed of individual persons who are considered as constituting, as it were, its members." The interest of the community, then, "is the sum of the interests of the several members who compose it." Hence it might seem that one way to promote the interest of the community would be for every man to seek his own interest. If, however, it should be necessary to bring pressure to bear upon the individual in order to keep him from interfering with the interests of others, Bentham conceived that the principal reliance should be placed upon what he called the four sanctions, which he specified as the physical, political, moral, and religious, meaning by these the

---

[1] The material from this point to the paragraph numbered " 2 " on p. 670 has been added by the translator.

pleasures and pains derived from physical sources, from the penalties of law, from public opinion, or from belief in divine rewards and punishments. It is for pain and pleasure alone "to point out what we ought to do, as well as to determine what we shall do," and the ambiguity in the terms "pain" and "pleasure," according to which they mean in the one case pleasure or pain of the community, and in the other case pleasure or pain of the agent, permits Bentham to suppose that he is maintaining a consistent hedonistic theory. But there were two other important qualifications in this hedonistic and individualistic theory. In the first place he intimates that the individual may seek public pleasure as well as private,[1] thus giving the theoretical statement of the principle which governed his own life, directed as it was toward the public interest. In the next place, the maxim which Bentham used to interpret the phrase, "greatest good of the greatest number," was, "everybody to count for one, nobody for more than one." This, while apparently a principle of extreme individualism, was really a recognition of individual rights, and was based upon fairness rather than upon a purely hedonistic standpoint. It is thus essentially a social principle, and a demand that the pleasure which "determines what we should do" shall be not merely a maximum, but a particular kind of pleasure, regulated not by considerations of quantity, but by principles of fairness and justice. A further inadequacy of Bentham's theory to account for Bentham's practice appears in his famous definition that in estimating pleasures and pains we must consider quantity only, — "push-pin is as good as poetry." But Bentham's own activity, if not primarily directed toward poetry, was at least as little directed toward push-pin for himself or for others. His whole life-work was given toward promoting legislative and social reform, toward securing rights and justice; and although he had little appreciation of certain of the finer values of art and culture, he was at least as little as his successor, Mill, to be explained by the hedonistic formula.

The theoretical individualism of the hedonistic standard for measuring the values of human life and the motives for moral action found vigorous and successful opposition in the work of Coleridge and Carlyle. The former exerted his influence primarily in the religious field, and in special opposition to the theories of motive and obligation propounded by Paley (p. 514, above), which had wide currency in educational and religious circles. According to Paley, the only difference between prudence and duty is that in the one we

---

[1] "Such pleasures seek, if private be thy end. If it be public," etc Cf. J. Dewey, *Study of Ethics.*

consider the gain or loss in the present world; in the other, we consider also gain or loss in the world to come. Obligation, according to
Paley, means to be urged by a violent motive, resulting from the
command of another. Against these positions Coleridge urged that
while man as a mere animal, or as a being endowed merely with
"understanding," may know only motives which spring from the
calculations of pleasures and pains, man as rational may hear another
voice and respond to higher appeals. It is, in fact, in just this
distinction that we find the difference between prudence and true
morality. The written works of Coleridge were few and fragmentary, but his personal influence upon the literary, religious, and
philosophical thought of his own and the succeeding period, in both
Britain and America, has been powerful and far-reaching.

The criticism of Carlyle was directed against "Benthamism." Its
individualism of motive seemed to Carlyle adapted to aggravate
rather than to heal the disease of the age. The economic development had been steadily in the direction of greater individualism. It
had substituted the wage-system for the older personal relation.
What Carlyle felt to be needed was the deeper sense of social unity,
a stronger feeling of responsibility. Now the pursuit of happiness
is essentially an individualising force, — "the man who goes about
pothering and uproaring for his happiness, he is not the man that
will help us to get our knaves and dastards arrested; no, he is rather
on the way to increase the number — by at least one unit." A true
social organisation can be secured only if the individualistic and
commercial theory of interests is abandoned. This leads at once to
the other point of Carlyle's attack, — measurement of value in terms
of pleasure and happiness. Instead of a "greatest happiness principle," a "greatest nobleness principle" must be substituted. Man
cannot be satisfied with the results of attempts to give him pleasure
if these aim simply at pleasure. "Man's unhappiness comes of his
greatness; it is because there is an infinite in him which he cannot
quite bury under the finite. The shoe-black also has a soul quite
other than his stomach, and would require for his permanent satisfaction and saturation *God's Infinite Universe.*" It is to the heroes
that we must look for our ideals of human life. It is in work rather
than in pleasure that the end of human life is to be achieved.

It was in the thought of John Stuart Mill that the fusion of utilitarian and idealistic principles found its most instructive illustration.
The social philosophy of Comte and a personal character actuated by
high ideals of duty and ardent for the promotion of public welfare
conspired with the influences already named to secure this result.
Educated by his father, James Mill, in the principles of associational

psychology, associated with Ricardo, the representative of an individualistic economic theory, and with Bentham, he inherited thus a
theory of human nature and a method of analysis from which he
never completely freed himself; but on the other hand he introduced
into the scheme a new content which led him to transcend the hedonistic position.[1] First as regards the *object of desire*. It had been the
position of the associationalists that the individual desires originally
pleasure, and pleasure only. This is the only intrinsic good. It was
held that other objects, however, might become associated with the
individual's happiness, and thus become independent objects of
desire. In this theory it would be the purpose of moral training so
to associate the public good with the private good of the individual
that he would come to desire the public welfare. Taught by his own
experience that such external associations had no permanent motive
power, Mill was led to reject this theory, and to state the hedonistic
paradox that to find pleasure one must not consciously seek it. Of
greater significance for our present purpose is Mill's theory of the
motives to moral action. On the one hand he retains so much of
the eighteenth century atomistic view of conduct as to affirm that " the
motive has nothing to do with the morality of the action, though
much with the morality of the agent." He still retains the doctrine
of the external sanctions without stating explicitly that however
useful these may be to control the non-moral or immoral, until other
motives get a foothold, they are not moral motives. But on the
other hand he lays far greater stress upon the "internal" sanctions
of duty. This feeling of duty, in turn, though strengthened by education and association, has as its ultimate foundation the "social
feelings of mankind." It is because man naturally "never conceives
himself otherwise than as a member of a body " that the interest of
the community is the interest of the individual. The principle of
sympathy which had served alternately as a means of psychological
analysis and as a term for the broader social impulse, was given its
most important place as that on which rests "the possibility of any
cultivation of goodness and nobleness and the hope of their ultimate
entire ascendency."

Finally, Mill transcends the hedonistic *criterion of value*. While
maintaining that the mental pleasures are superior to the bodily
pleasures on purely quantitative grounds, he asserts that, quite
apart from questions of quantity, some kinds of pleasure are
more desirable and valuable than others. The test for pleasure,

---

[1] In addition to the *Utilitarianism*, the *Autobiography*, the essays on Bentham
and Coleridge and *On Liberty* are of special interest.

whether we seek to measure its intensity or its quality, must in any case be subjective; and the question as to which of two pleasures is the better must be decided by those who have had experience of both. Instead, therefore, of using pleasure as the standard for value, Mill, like Plato, would appeal to "experience and wisdom and reason" as judges. Instead of pleasure as standard, we have rather a *standard for pleasure.* If, then, we ask what these "competent judges" will assign as the highest values, we may find different names, such as love of liberty and love of power, etc., but the most "appropriate appellation is the sense of dignity." "It is better to be a human being dissatisfied than a pig satisfied; better to be Socrates dissatisfied than a fool satisfied." And in the further development of this principle of valuation Mill even goes beyond Carlyle's position by declaring that to do without happiness is now done involuntarily by nineteen-twentieths of mankind, and often has to be done voluntarily by the hero or the martyr, who in sacrificing his own happiness for that of others displays the "highest virtue which can be found in man."

A similar conflict between hedonistic and other standards of value is evident in the ethical system of Herbert Spencer. On the one hand, following the tradition of a hedonistic psychology, Spencer maintains that life is good or bad according as it does or does not bring a surplus of agreeable feeling. The only alternative to this test is to reverse the hypothesis and suppose that pain is good and pleasure is bad. No other standard of value can be admitted. This position is fortified by the biological law that if creatures should find pleasure in what is hurtful, and pain in what is advantageous, they would soon cease to exist. On the other hand, Spencer propounds also a standard of value which does not easily conform to the test of pleasure and pain. According to this standard the highest conduct is that which conduces to "the greatest breadth, length, and completeness of life"; the highest stage in evolution is that reached when "conduct simultaneously achieves the greatest totality of life in self, in offspring, and in fellow-men." The subjective standard of *pleasurable feeling* and the objective standard of *fulness of life* are thus set over against each other. The attempt is made to bring them together by showing that the biological development has necessarily brought about a harmony between pleasure and progress, but on the other hand it is admitted that a condition of progress involves a lack of adaptation between the individual and the environment. It would therefore seem that, however well-suited pleasure might be as a test for the static individual, it cannot be regarded as a test of value for the guidance of a progressive being. Hence Spencer maintains that the perfect application of his test supposes an ideal humanity. A consistent hedonism would require that the test of such an ideal humanity be solely the continuity and intensity of pleasurable feeling attained, but the numerous recognitions of more objective factors make it improbable that Spencer would regard merely sentient beings deprived of all active faculties as the highest type of evolution.

The employment by Spencer of the principles of evolution as affording a moral standard leads to an interesting complication of the problems considered under § 45 with the problem of the individual in relation to society. On the one hand, as already noted (p. 662), the social sentiments and related moral principles are regarded by Spencer as finding their basis in the evolutionary process. These social qualities subserve the welfare of the family or species, and aid it in the struggle for existence. On the other hand, it is maintained that the fundamental law of progress is that "each individual shall take the consequences of his own nature and actions: survival of the fittest being the result." Among gregarious creatures the freedom of each to act has to be restricted by the provision that it shall not interfere with similar freedom on the part of others. Progress is therefore dependent upon giving the greatest possible scope to individual freedom. With Bentham and Mill the maxim "everybody to count for one, nobody for more than one" had represented a socialising of the criterion and ideal. In Spencer's opinion this represents an undue emphasis upon equality; from this to communism the step is only one from theory to practice. "Inequality is the primordial idea suggested" by evolution; equality, as suggested in the need of restriction, is secondary. From this *individualistic interpretation of evolution* Spencer opposes not only communism in property, but the assumption by the State of any functions beyond that of securing "justice" to the individual. The State should keep the individual from interfering with the freedom of other individuals. The State is thus essentially negative in its significance. Man in his corporate capacity may not realise a positive moral value in the pursuit of common good. But while agreeing thus with the views of Gundling and von Humboldt (cf. p. 520), Spencer insists that, in denying the possibility of reaching positive values through the State, he aims to secure these values more efficiently by voluntary and private action. "Beneficence" belongs to the family virtues; "justice" to the State.[1]

---

[1] Cf. *Ethics* Vol. II., *The Man* vs. *the State*, and *Essays*, Vol. III.

The relation of evolutionary processes to the problem of moral values has been most sharply formulated by Huxley.[1] In opposition to certain philosophical writers who find in the evolutionary process a moral standard, Huxley points out with great vigour and incisiveness the distinction between the "cosmic process" and the "ethical process." The attempt to find in the "cosmic process" an ethical standard is based upon the ambiguity in the phrase "survival of the fittest." *Fittest*, it is scarcely necessary to say, is not synonymous with ethically best. If the temperature of the earth should be reduced, the survival of the fittest would mean a return to lichens and diatoms.

The ethical process must find its standard not in the cosmic process, but in the moral ideals of man. Its principle is not that of the survival of the fittest, but that of fitting as many as possible to survive. The duty of man is not to conform to the cosmic process, but to combat it. In a sense it may be admitted that the moral process is a part of the cosmic process, but the important point is that the moral process cannot take its standards from the non-moral parts of the cosmic process, and the theory of government which Spencer would derive from this is characterised by Huxley as "administrative nihilism." [2]

The opposition to an ethical theory based upon the conceptions of natural science, has received its most thorough-going expression in the work of T. H. Green. Previous English sympathisers with German idealism had for the most part appropriated results without attempting for themselves the "labour of the notion." Believing that current theories of evolution and ethics were repeating the fallacies of Hume in another form, Green set himself the task of criticising those fallacies and of re-stating the conditions under which any experience, and especially any moral experience, is possible. The central, fundamental, and determining conception is found in self-consciousness. Questions as to freedom, desire, and ideals must be stated in terms of self-consciousness, and not in physical concepts, if they are to be intelligible. Nor can self-consciousness be explained in terms of the unconscious, or as developing from the unconscious. It seems rather to be comprehensible only as the reproduction in man of an eternal consciousness. This has an important bearing on the determination of the moral ideal. In the first place it requires that the end or ideal shall always be some desirable state of self. In this it seems to

---

[1] In his Romanes lecture, 1893. Reprinted as *Evolution and Ethics*, 1894. Cf. J. Dewey, *Evolution and Ethics*, Monist, VIII. 321 ff.

[2] *Critiques and Addresses.*

approach hedonism, but whereas hedonism holds that pleasure makes
a state or an object desirable, Green insists that the pleasure follows
the attainment of desire, and that what a being desires is determined
by the nature of the being.   Man desires the full realisation of himself, and " in it alone he can satisfy himself."   The good is therefore
a personal good.   It is also a common or social good.   " Without
society, no persons."   While therefore it may not be possible to
state definitely the specific characteristics of the " best state of
man," history shows that man has bettered himself through institutions and habits which make the welfare of all the welfare of
each, and through the arts which make nature the friend of man."
It is in political society that self-consciousness finds fullest development.   The institutions of " civil life give reality to the capacities
of will and reason and enable them to be really exercised." [1]

The ultimate justification of all rights is that they serve a moral
end in the sense that the powers secured in them are essential to the
fulfilment of man's vocation as a moral being, *i.e.* as a being who in
living for himself lives for other selves.   With Green's definition
may be compared Spencer's formulation of the ideal as " completeness of life."   It is a striking illustration of the strong relation
which British ethical theory has always maintained to British life,
that two thinkers from such opposite standpoints should approach
so near in actual statement.

2.   Turning now to continental theories, we note that] the conception of life which corresponds to this utilitarian social ethics is
throughout an optimistic affirmation of the world.   Life as an
evolutionary process is the sum total of all goods, and the progress
to the more perfect is the natural necessity of the actual world; the
strengthening and broadening of life is as well the moral law as the
law of nature.   This consequence has been carried out with the most
refinement and warmth, and not without a religious turn by Guyau.
He finds the highest meaning and enjoyment of individual existence
in the conscious unity of life with society, and beyond this with the
universe.

But even without the evolutionary supplement, naturalism and
materialism had asserted their joyous optimism and directed it
against every kind of morals which avoids or renounces the world,
especially against the religious forms of such ethical theories.   This
was shown already in the case of *Feuerbach*, who set for his philosophical activity the task of making man a " free, self-conscious

---

[1] These principles are further developed by B. Bosanquet, *The Philosophical
Theory of the State*, 1899.

citizen of the earth." [1] The will is for him identical with the impulse to happiness, and happiness is nothing else than "life, normal, sound, without defect." Hence the impulse to happiness is the foundation of morals; the goal, however, consists in the vital and active combination of the striving toward one's own happiness with that toward the happiness of others. In this positive action of willing the welfare of others lies the root of sympathy also. Virtue stands in contradiction with only that form of happiness which seeks to be happy at the expense of others. On the other hand, virtue has a certain degree of happiness as its indispensable presupposition, for the pressure of want forces the impulse to happiness irresistibly and one-sidedly toward the egoistic side. Just on this account human morality can be furthered only by the improvement of mankind's external situation — a thought from which Feuerbach proceeds to very far-reaching demands. His moral sensualism is supported by the firm conviction that historical development lies along the line of his postulates, and with all his pessimistic and often bitter estimate of the present he combines a strongly hopeful optimism for the future. Man, as a bodily personality, with his sensuous feeling and willing, is for him the sole truth; when set over against this truth all philosophic theories, echoes as they are of theological theories, collapse into nothing.

Another optimistic materialist is Eugen *Dühring*, who has made a peculiar "philosophy of reality" the basis of his estimation of the "worth of life." The anti-religious character of this kind of world-affirmation appears here much more clearly than in the case of Feuerbach. Dühring sees in the pessimism of the 60's and 70's, which he has opposed with bitter relentlessness, the romantic continuation of the attitudes of Christianity and Buddhism, which are hostile to the world. He regarded the "superstitious" ideas of the "other world," or the "beyond," as the real ground of the lack of appreciation for the actual world of reality; only when all superstitious belief in supernatural beings has been banished will the true and immanent worth of life be completely enjoyed, in his opinion. True knowledge apprehends reality exactly as it is, just as it lies immediately before human experience; it is delusion to seek still another behind it. And even as with knowledge, so also with values, they must be found in what is given; the only rational is reality itself. Already in the conceptions of infinity Dühring detects — not so incorrectly — a going beyond what is given; for him, therefore, the

---

[1] Cf. particularly the fragment published by K. Grün, *L. Feuerbach in Seinem Briefwechsel und Nachlass.*, II. 253 ff., in which Feuerbach declares his position as against Schopenhauer.

actual world is limited in magnitude and number. But it bears within itself all the conditions of self-satisfying happiness. Even the view that there is a lack of sufficient means of life, on which Darwin grounded his doctrine of the struggle for existence and his theory of selection, is controverted by Dühring in a most vigorous fashion, although he is not hostile to the theory of descent and the principle of evolution. On the basis of these conceptions Dühring seeks to refute pessimism by demonstrating that man's enjoyment of life is spoiled only by the bad arrangements and customs which owe their origin to ideas of the supernatural. It is the mission of the philosophy of reality alone to produce healthy life from healthy thought, and to create the satisfaction of a disposition based on a noble humanity, capacities for which have been given by nature herself in the sympathetic affections. Although Dühring has declaimed thus sharply and with irritation against the present social system, he has enlisted himself energetically in defence of the reasonableness of the actual world as a whole. As he has theoretically maintained the identity of the forms of human perception and thought with the laws of reality, so he has also convinced himself that this same reality contains all the conditions for ultimately realising the values presented in the rational consciousness. For this rational consciousness of ours is in the last analysis nothing more than the highest form of the life of nature.

3. All these kinds of positivistic optimism make the most instructive variations in the Hegelian principle of the identity of the real and the rational (p. 615); all of them show besides a trace of that faith in the goodness of nature which was characteristic of Rousseau, and in their hope for a better future of the human race they incline to give an evolutionary stamp to the thought of man's unlimited capacity for perfection, which the philosophy of the French Revolution had produced (cf. p. 525). All the more characteristic is it that the last factor has given an essentially altered form to the opposite conception, viz. *pessimism*.

In themselves optimism and pessimism, as answers to the hedonic question, whether the world contains more pleasure or pain, are equally pathological phenomena. This is true especially in the form in which these enter as factors into general literature. For science this question is as unnecessary as it is incapable of answer. The controversy gains philosophic significance only because it is brought into connection with the question as to the rationality or irrationality of the world-ground, as it had already been brought by Leibniz along one line and by Schopenhauer along another. But in both cases it was completely impossible to make the hedonistic origin of the problem disappear by the metaphysical transformation which was given to it.

The pessimistic temper which prevailed in Germany in the first decade of the second half of our century had its easily recognisable grounds in political and social relations, and the eager reception and welcome of Schopenhauer's doctrines, supported by the brilliant qualities of the writer, are usually regarded as easily intelligible for that reason. It is more remarkable and serious that this temper has outlasted the year 1870, and indeed that precisely in the following decade it unburdened itself in an unlimited flood of tirades of a popular philosophical sort, and for a time has completely controlled general literature. Considered from the standpoint of the history of civilisation, this fact will be regarded as a manifestation of relaxation and surfeit; the part which the history of philosophy has in the movement is connected with the brilliant and misleading "Philosophy of the Unconscious." *Eduard von Hartmann* found a witty synthesis between Leibniz and Schopenhauer on the basis of his metaphysics, which regarded the world-ground as a complex resultant of the irrational will and of the "logical element" (cf. § 44, 9). This synthesis was that this world is indeed the best of all possible worlds, but nevertheless that it is still so bad that it would have been better if there had been none at all. The mixture of teleological and dysteleological views of nature which had passed by inheritance from Schelling to Schopenhauer (pp. 618 ff.) appears here with Hartmann in grotesque and fanciful development; and the contradiction is to be solved by the theory that after the irrational will has once taken its false step of manifesting itself as life and actual existence, this life-process goes on in a progressive development whose ripest meaning is the insight into the unreason of the "will to live." The rational element in this life-process will then consist in denying that unreason, in retracing the act of world-origination, and in redeeming the will from its own unhappy realisation.

On this account Hartmann found the essential nature of the "rational" consciousness to lie in seeing through the "illusions" with which the irrational pressure of the will produces just what must make it unhappy, and out of this relation he developed the ethical task that each one should co-operate to save the world-will by the denial of illusions. He developed also the thought of fundamental importance for the philosophy of history that all work of civilisation should be directed toward this goal of salvation. The development of the irrational will ought to have the annihilation of this will as its rational goal; hence Hartmann approves all work of civilisation because its ultimate end is the annihilation of life and the redemption of the will from the unhappiness of existence. In this respect he comes into contact with Mainländer, who with him and after him worked out Schopenhauer's theory to an ascetic "Philosophy of Salvation"; but with Hartmann these thoughts take on the colouring of an evolutionary optimism which shows a much deeper intelligence for the earnestness and wealth of historic development than we find with Schopenhauer. And as von Hartmann has anonymously given the best criticism of his "Philosophy of the Unconscious," from the standpoint of the theory of descent, so in his own development the shell of pessimism has been gradually stripped off and the positive principle of evolution has emerged as the essential thing. In him, too, Hegel has triumphed over Schopenhauer.

4. All these theories of life, whose typical extremes were here set over against each other, vary indeed with regard to their recognition and gradation of individual values and goals, but they coincide in recognising on the whole the prevailing moral code, and in particular the altruism which is its chief constituent. Their differences concern rather the general formulation, or the sanction, or the motive of morality, than morality itself. Even the more radical tendencies seek only to free human ethics from the perversions which it is said to have experienced in certain historical systems, or in their survivals and their after effects; and through all the doctrines already mentioned goes a strongly democratic tendency which sets the weal of the whole above everything else, and estimates the worth of the individual much lower than was the case in the great period of German philosophy. A tendency to hero-worship, like that of Carlyle (cf. p. 654), is quite isolated in our century; far more prevalent is the theory of the *milieu* or environment which Taine brought into circulation for the history of the mind, and which is inclined to minimise the part which the individual bears in the historical movement as contrasted with the influence of masses.

We cannot fail to recognise that such theories correspond completely to certain political, social, literary, and artistic conditions and obvious manifestations of modern life; hence it is easier to understand why, here and there, the reaction of individualism in an especially passionate form has made its appearance. We must insist, in the first place, that over against that type of assiduous striving which permits itself to be driven by every tide of influence, the individualistic idea of culture which belongs to that great period, now somewhat depreciatingly denoted Romanticism, has in no wise so completely died out as is supposed. It lives on in many highly developed personalities who do not find it necessary to make a display with it in literature; for the theory of this ideal has been expressed by Fichte, Schiller, and Schleiermacher. And just for this reason it does not make common cause with the artificial paradoxes which radical individualism loves to present on occasion.

The most robust example of such paradoxes came from the Hegelian "left," in the fantastic book of M. Stirner (Kaspar Schmidt, 1806–1856), *The Individual and his Property* [1] (1844). Stirner is related to Feuerbach as Feuerbach is to Hegel: he draws the conclusion which would completely invert the premises. Feuerbach had looked upon "spirit" or the "idea" as the "other-being of Nature," and as abstract and unreal as the theological ghost. He had declared the only reality to be man, living man of flesh and blood; but his ethics aimed toward humanity, active love to humanity. What is mankind? asks Stirner. A general idea, an abstraction — a last shadow of the old ghost which is still walking, even in Feuerbach's system. The true concrete reality is the individual — the autocratic personality. Such a personality makes its world both in its acts of ideation and in its acts of will; therefore its ownership extends as far as its will extends. It recognises nothing above itself; it knows no other weal than its own, and serves no alien law or alien will. For in truth there is nothing for it except itself. Thus by reversing Fichte's doctrine of the "universal ego," Stirner attains to "egoism" in both the theoretical and the practical sense of the word. He plays the "solipsist" [2] and preaches unscrupulous self-seeking, — *Ich hab' mein' Sach' auf nichts gestellt.* [3] All this sounded like an artificial cynicism, and it was a matter of doubt whether the book was intended to be taken seriously. At all events it soon lost the interest which it momentarily excited, and fell into an oblivion from which it has only recently been rescued. But when, as now, there is a disposition to see in it a first cry of distress from the individual repressed by the mass, it ought not to be ignored that the "individual" who was here seeking to emancipate himself from the community did not give any indication of a peculiar value which would have justified him in any such emancipation. His sole originality consisted in the courage of paradox.

5. Another bizarre form of individualism was developed from Schopenhauer's metaphysics of the will, by Julius *Bahnsen.* Here the "unreason" of the will is taken with complete seriousness, but the pantheistic aspect of the "one only will" is stripped away.

---

[1] *Der Einzige und sein Eigenthum.*
[2] Cf. above, p. 471.   [3] I care for nothing.
[4] *Beiträge zur Charakterologie* (1867); *Der Widerspruch im Wissen und Wesen der Welt* (1881–1882).

We know only individuals who will, and Bahnsen sees in them the independent *elementary potencies* of reality, beyond which no higher principle is to be assumed. The separate and self-sufficient existence of finite personalities, which Bahnsen also calls " Henads," has never been so sharply formulated as in this atheistic atomism of the will. Each of these "wills" is, moreover, divided within itself into two, and in this consists its unreason and its unhappiness. This contradiction belongs to the essence of the will ; the will is the "asserted contradiction," and this is the true dialectic, "the real dialectic." This contradiction, however, cannot be grasped by logical thinking; hence all the effort which the will makes to know the world is in vain. Logical thinking which excludes contradiction is incapable of understanding a world which consists of intrinsically contradictory wills. The contradiction between the world and the intellect makes impossible even the partial salvation which Schopenhauer admitted,[1] and the indestructible individual will must therefore endure forever the suffering of self-laceration in ever new existences. At so high a price is the metaphysical dignity purchased, which personality here receives as its "intelligible character." The living out of this "intelligible character," purposeless and futile as it really is, forms the principle of all values.

Since the theory of knowledge involved in this "real dialectic" maintains that logical thinking and reality with its contradictions have no common measure, the fantasies of this "miserableism" make no claim to scientific validity ; they are only the expression of the gloomy mood of the individual who is caught in the conflict of his own will. They form the melancholy counterpart to the pert frivolity of Stirner's individual. Both show what result may be expected if "philosophy" takes moods which constitute the peculiar nature of pessimism and optimism as a basis for serious conclusions.

This is still more recognisable in the case of the great influence which has been exercised in the last decade upon the view of life and its literary expression by the poet, *Friedrich Nietzsche.* Many factors combine to form this influence: the fascinating beauty of language which ensnares and intoxicates even where the content passes over into enigmatic suggestions; a mysterious symbolism which, in "Thus spake Zarathustra," permits the author to revel in obscurity and indefiniteness; the aphoristic form of expression which never requires the reader to think coherently in scientific terms, but rather leaves him to determine for himself how much stimulus and suggestion he will utilise, and thus decide the degree

---

[1] Cf. p. 621.

in which he will expect himself to enjoy the surprising hits, the brilliant formulations, the happy comparisons, and paradoxical combinations. But all these elements are unimportant in comparison with the immediate impression of the personality of the writer. We meet an individual of the highest culture, and of a thoroughly original stamp, who experiences all the tendencies of the time, and suffers from the same unsolved contradictions by which the time itself is out of joint. Hence the echo which his language has found; hence the danger of his influence, which does not heal the sickness of his age, but increases it.

The two factors of the inner antagonism of his own nature Nietzsche himself has called the "Dionysus" and the "Apollo." It is the antithesis between voluntarism and intellectualism, between Schopenhauer's will and Hegel's idea. It appears here in an individual of the highest intellectual culture and æsthetic productiveness, who is able to apprehend history and life with the greatest delicacy and to reproduce them poetically with equal fineness of feeling. But science and art have not saved this individual from the dark "will to live"; deep within stirs a passionate, compelling impulse toward wild deeds, toward the achieving and unfolding of power. His is the case of a nervous professor who would fain be a wild tyrant, and who is tossed back and forth between the quiet enjoyment of the goods of the highest culture on the one hand, and that mysterious, burning demand for a life of passion on the other. Now he luxuriates in serene blessedness of æsthetic contemplation and artistic production; now he casts all this aside and asserts his impulses, his instincts, his passions. Sensual enjoyment, as such, has never been a value for him — this is shown in the height and purity of his nature. The enjoyment which he seeks is either that of knowing or that of power. In the struggle between the two he has been crushed — the victim of an age which is satisfied no longer by the impersonal and superpersonal values of intellectual, æsthetic, and moral culture, but thirsts again for the boundless unfolding of the individual in a life of deeds. Caught in the struggle between its reason inherited from the past and its passion thirsting for the future, it and all of value that it possesses are torn and ground. The artistic expression of a nature thus rent and torn is the charm of Nietzsche's writings.

In his first period, which contains the following in germ, the conflict between the two motive forces has not yet come to open outbreak ; rather we find him applying Schopenhauer's fundamental thoughts to the origin of Greek tragedy and to Richard Wagner's musical drama, and thus presenting art as the source of salvation from the torture of the will.   But even at that time it was his thought that out of this tragic temper a new, a higher culture should be brought forth; a prouder race should emerge, of bold and splendidly audacious will which would victoriously burst the bonds of the present intellectual and spiritual life, and even at that period this bent toward originality and independence threw overboard the ballast of the historic period.   No condition and no authority is to repress this artistic civilisation; æsthetic freedom is to be cramped neither by knowledge nor by life.

It is not difficult to understand that when these thoughts began to clarify themselves the philosophic poet followed for a time along the path of intellectualism.   Science is the free spirit which casts off all fetters and recognises nothing above itself; but she is such only when she makes the "real" man free, placing him on his own feet, independent of everything that is above the senses or apart from the senses.   This science which Nietzsche would now make the bearer of the essence of culture is positive science, — no meta-physics, not even the metaphysics of the will; hence he dedicates his book "for free spirits" to the memory of Voltaire, and while he had earlier turned Wagner from Feuerbach to Schopenhauer, now he himself goes the reverse way.   He comes into agreement with the utilitarian ethics of Paul Rée; he believes in the possi-bility of the purely scientific culture.   He even goes so far as to see in knowledge the highest and best aim of life.   Knowledge is for him the true joy, and the whole freshness of delight in the joys of the world and of life which is found in θεωρία (contemplation) — an enjoyment of the present actual world which is at once æsthetic and theoretical — is the fundamental note of this period, the most fortunate period which was granted to him.

Then the Dionysus element of passion came to expression as an uncontrollable longing for strong, masterful, unsympathetic living out of personality, which throws down all that would stand in its path.   The strongest impulse of man is the *will for power*.   It is for him to assert this.   But this unconditional assertion bursts the system of values in which our civilisation, up to this time, has enmeshed itself; the new ideal is in this sense "beyond good and bad." [1]   The will for power knows no bonds which prescribe what is "permitted"; for it, everything is good which springs from power and increases power; everything is bad which springs from weak-ness and weakens power.   So also in our judgments, in knowledge

---

[1] *Jenseits von Gut und Böse*, the title of one of Nietzsche's books, translated by A. Tille.

and in conviction, the important thing is not whether they are " true," but whether they help us, whether they further our life and strengthen our mind. They have worth only if they make us strong. Hence, conviction also may and must change as life unfolds its changes (as was the case in part with Nietzsche himself). Man chooses what he needs ; the value of knowing also lies beyond true and false. Here begins, therefore, the overturning and re-valuation of all values (*Umwerthung aller Werthe*). Here the philosopher becomes a reformer of morals, the legislator the creator of a new civilisation. In the third period of his development Nietzsche was full of the consciousness of this task.

From this standpoint he sets up the ideal of the over-man (*Uebermensch*) in contrast with the ordinary, everyday man of the common herd. Will for power is will for mastery, and the most important mastery is that of man over man. Hegel once said that of all great things which the world's history shows, the greatest is the mastery of one free will over others. It recalls this saying when Nietzsche develops his new idea of civilisation from the antithesis between the " morals of masters " and " morals of slaves." All the brutality of trampling down those who may be in the way, all the unfettering of the primitive beast in human nature, appear here as the right and duty of the strong. The strong man unfolds and defends the energy of living as against the scantiness and meagreness of renunciation and humility. The morality of slaves, therefore, coincides essentially with the ascetic nature of the supernaturalism which Nietzsche had formerly combated, and the positive connection of the transition period with his third period consists in the " joyous " assertion of a world-conquering thirst for living.

Nevertheless the ideal for the "over-man" remains veiled in poetic dimness and indefiniteness. According to the original tendency, the over-man is the great individuality which asserts its primitive rights over against the mass. The common herd of the " far too many " (*Viel-zu-Viele*) exists only to the end that out of it as rare instances of fortune may rise the over-men. These, from century to century, recognize each other as bearers of all the meaning and worth that is to be found in all this confused driving of disordered forces. The genius is the end and aim of history, and it is in this that his right of mastery as over against the Philistine has its root. But according to another tendency the over-man appears as a higher type of the human race, who is to be bred and trained — as the strong race which enjoys its strength of mastery in the powerful unfolding of life, free from the restraints and self-disturbing tendencies of the slavish morality. In both cases Nietzsche's ideal of the over-man is alike aristocratic and exclusive, and it is a sharp penalty for the poetic indefiniteness and symbolic ambiguity of his aphorisms that his combating of "slavish morality" and of its supernatural foundations has made him popular with just the very ones who would be the first to strike from the over-man the head by which he towers above the common herd of the "too many."

Between the two lines along which the ideal of the over-man develops, the author has not come to a clear decision. Zarathustra mingles them together, with wavering lines of transition. It is clear that the one form is an echo of the romantic ideal of the genius as the other borrows from sociological evolution. But the thought of an elevation of the human type through the agency of philosophy reminds us of the postulates of German idealism.

The remark is quite just that from this conception of the doctrine of the over-man the step to Fichte would not have been a long one. That Nietzsche could not take it was due to the fact that he had in his nature too much of Schlegel's "genius," which treats all experiences from the standpoint of irony (p. 605). This made him unable to find his way back from the individual mind to the "universal ego" — to the conception of values which assert their validity over all.

7. The revolt of boundless individualism culminates in the claim that all values are relative. Only the powerful will of the over-man persists as the absolute value, and sanctions every means which it brings into service. For the "higher" man there is no longer any form or standard, either logical or ethical. The arbitrary will of the over-man has superseded the "autonomy of reason"—this is the course from Kant to Nietzsche which the nineteenth century has described.

Just this determines the problem of the future. Relativism is the dismissal and death of philosophy. Philosophy can live only as the science of values which are universally valid. It will no longer force its way into the work of the particular sciences, where psychology also now belongs. Philosophy has neither the craving to know over again from her standpoint what the special sciences have already known from theirs, nor the desire to compile and patch together generalisations from the "more general results" of the separate disciplines. Philosophy has its own field and its own problem in those values of universal validity which are the organising principle for all the functions of culture and civilisation and for all the particular values of life. But it will describe and explain these values only that it may give an account of their validity; it treats them not as facts but as *norms.* Hence it will have to develop its task as a "giving of laws"—not laws of arbitrary caprice which it dictates, but rather laws of the reason, which it discovers and comprehends. By following the path toward this goal it seems to be the aim of the present movement, divided within itself as it often is, to win back the important conquests of the great period of German philosophy. Since Lotze raised the *conception of value* to a place of prominence, and set it at the summit of logic and metaphysics as well as of ethics, many suggestions toward a "theory of values," as a new foundation science in philosophy, have arisen. It can do no harm if these move in part in the psychological and sociological realm, provided it is not forgotten that in establishing facts and making genetic explanations we have only gained the material upon which philosophy itself must perform its task of criticism.

But a no less valuable foundation for this central work is formed by the *history* of philosophy, which, as Hegel first recognised, must be regarded in this sense as an integrant part of philosophy itself. For it presents the process in which European humanity has embodied in scientific conceptions its view of the world and judgment of human life.

In this process particular experiences have furnished the occasions, and special problems of knowledge have been the instrumentalities, through which step by step reflection has advanced to greater clearness and certainty respecting the ultimate values of culture and civilisation. In setting forth this process, therefore, the history of philosophy presents to our view the gradual attainment of clearness and certainty respecting those values whose universal validity forms the problem and field of philosophy itself.

APPENDIX.

P. 348. To the lit., add :—

W. Windelband, *Geschichte d. neueren Philosophie*, 2d ed. Vols. I. II. 1899 ; H. Höffding, *History of Modern Philosophy* (Eng. tr. by B. Meyer, Lond. and N.Y. 1900) ; K. Lasswitz, *Geschichte der Atomistik vom Mittelalter bis Newton*. 2 vols., Hamburg, 1889–1890 [W. Graham, *English Political Philosophy from Hobbes to Maine*, Lond. and N.Y. 1900].

P. 352. To the lit., add :—

W. Dilthey, *Auffassang und Analyse des Menschen in 15 and 16 Jahr.* (*Arch. f. Gesch. d. Philos.*, IV., V.).

P. 356. Line 5, add :—

H. Maier, *M. als Philosoph* (*Arch. f. Gesch. d. Philos.*, X., XI.).

P. 356. Line 22, from foot, insert :—

The unsettled character of his life was in part due to his own character. He combined a proud flight of imaginative thought and an enthusiastic devotion to the new truth — especially to the Copernican system — for which he had to suffer, with unbridled passionateness, ambitious boastfulness and keen pleasure in agitation. On his Italian and Latin writings, cf. recently, F. Tocco (Florence, 1889, and Naples, 1891) ; cf. also Dom Berti, *G. B., sua Vita e sua Dottrine* (Rome, 1889).

P. 357. Line 3. To the notice of Campanella, add :—

In him, too, we find learning, boldness of thought, and desire of innovation mingled with pedantry, fancifulness, superstition, and limitation. Cf. Chr. Sigwart, *Kleine Schriften*, I. (Freib. 1889).

P. 362. Line 1. After "also," insert :—

Popular Stoicism had a considerable number of adherents among the Renaissance writers on account of its moral and religious doctrines, which were independent of positive religion.

P. 367. Note 1. Add :—

Indeed, the humanistic reaction favoured Stoicism directly as against the more mediæval Neo-Platonism.

P. 378. To the lit., add :—

W. Dilthey, *Das natürliche System der Geisteswissenschaften in 17 Jahrh.* (*Arch. f. Gesch. d. Philos.*, V., VI., VII.).

P. 379. Last line. To the notice of Galileo, add :—

His quiet, unimpassioned advocacy of the investigation of nature, which had been newly achieved and given its conceptional formulation by himself, could not shield him from the attacks of the Inquisition. He purchased peace and the right to further investigation, which was all that he cared for, by extreme subjection. Cf. C. Prantl, *Galileo und Kepler als Logiker* (Munich, 1875).

P. 380. Line 9. To lit. on I. Newton, add :—

F R. Rosenberger, *I N. und seine physikalischen Prinzipien* (Leips. 1895).

P. 380.　　Line 18.　　To the lit. add: —

E. Mach, *Die Mechanik in ihrer Entwicklung* (Leips. 1883).　H. Hertz, *Die Principien der Mechanik*, Introd., pp. 1–47 (Leips. 1894).

P. 380.　　To the notice of Bacon, add: —

The unfavourable aspects of his personal character, which had their origin in political rivalry, fall into the background in comparison with the insight which filled his life, that man's power, and especially his power over nature, lies only in scientific knowledge.　In a grandiloquent fashion, which was in conformity with the custom of his time, he proclaimed it as the task of science to place nature with all her forces at the service of man and of the best development of social life.

P. 380.　　To the notice of Descartes, add: —

A complete edition of his works is appearing under the auspices of the Paris Academy.　The main characteristics of his nature are found in the passion for knowledge, which turns aside from all outer goods of life, in his zeal for self-instruction, in his struggle against self-delusion, in his abhorrence of all public appearance and of the conflicts connected therewith, in the calm pre-eminence of the purely intellectual life, and in the complete earnestness which springs from sincerity.

P. 381.　　To the notice of Spinoza, add: —

In proud independence, he satisfied his modest needs by his earnings from the polishing of optical glasses.　Untroubled by the hatred and opposition of the world, and not embittered by the untrustworthiness of the few who called themselves his friends, he lived a life of thought and disinterested intellectual labour, and found his compensation for the transitory joys of the world, which he despised, in the clearness of knowledge, in the intelligent comprehension of human motives, and in the devoted contemplation of the mysteries of the divine nature.　[J. Freudenthal, *Lebensgeschichte Sp.'s*, Leips. 1899; v. d. Linde, *B. Sp. Bibliographie*, Gravenhage, 1871.]

P. 381.　　Line 24.　　To the lit. on Pascal, add: —

G. Droz (Paris, 1886).

P. 381.　　Line 36.　　To the lit. on Geulincx, add: —

J. P. N. Land, *Arn. Geulincx und seine Philosophie* (The Hague, 1895).

P. 413.　　To the foot-note, add: —

Descartes' conception of these perturbations reminds us in many ways of Stoicism, which was brought to him by the whole humanistic literature of his time.　Just on this account the modern philosopher fell into the same difficulties respecting theodicy and freedom of the will which had vexed the Stoa. Cf. above, § 16.　His ethics was likewise related to that of the Stoics.

P. 425.　　Under § 32.　　As lit. on this topic: —

T. H. Green, *Principles of Political Obligation*, Wks., Vol. II., and separately, 1895; D. G. Ritchie, *Natural Rights*, Lond. and N. Y. 1895; J. H. Tufts and H. B. Thompson, *The Individual and his Relation to Society as reflected in British Ethics* (Chicago, 1898).

P. 440.　　To the notice of Locke, add: —

Plain good sense and sober charity are the main traits of his intellectual personality; but corresponding to these there is also a certain meagreness of thought and a renunciation of the philosophical impulse in the proper sense. In spite of this, the courage of his triviality made him popular, and so made him leader of the philosophy of the Enlightenment.

P. 441. To the notice of Shaftesbury, add: —

He was one of the foremost and finest representatives of the Enlightenment. Humanistic culture is the basis of his intellectual and spiritual nature. In this rests the freedom of his thought and judgment, as well as the taste with which he conceives and presents his subject. He himself is a conspicuous example for his ethical teaching of the worth of personality. [B. Rand has recently published *The Life, Letters, and Philosophical Regimen*, Lond. and N. Y. 1900. The *Regimen* consists of a series of exercises or meditations patterned after those of Epictetus and Marcus Aurelius. It shows a closer dependence upon ancient, particularly Stoic, thought than is manifest in the *Characteristics.*]

P. 441. To the lit. on Adam Smith, add: —

[Hasbach, *Untersuchungen über Adam Smith* (Leips. 1891); Zeyss, *A. S.* (Leips. 1889); Oncken, *Smith und Kant* (1877); Schubert, in *Wundt's Studien*, VI. 552 ff.]

P. 441. To the notice of Hume, add: —

Cool and reflective, clear and keen, an analyst of the first rank, with unprejudiced and relentless thought, he pressed forward to the final presuppositions upon which the English philosophy of modern times rested. And this is the reason why, in spite of the caution of his utterances, he did not at first find among his countrymen the recognition which he deserved.

P. 441. To the lit. on English Moral Philosophy, add: —

[Selby-Bigge, *British Moralists* (Clar. Press, 1897), contains reprints of the most important ethical writings of nearly all the writers of this period, with Introd.]

P. 442. To the lit. on the Scottish School, add: —

McCosh, *The Scottish Philosophy ;* on the preceding development, E. Grimm, *Zur Geschichte des Erkenntniss-problems von Bacon zu Hume* (Leips. 1890).

P. 442. To the notice of Voltaire, add: —

For the history of philosophy, the most important elements in Voltaire's nature are his honest enthusiasm for justice and humanity, his fearless championship for reason in public life, and, on the other hand, the incomparable influence which he exercised upon the general temper of his age through the magic of his animated, striking style. G. Desnoiresterres, *V. et la Société au 18 Siècle* (Paris, 1873).

P. 444. To the notice on Leibniz, add: —

Leibniz was one of the greatest savants who have ever lived. There was no department of science in which he did not work, and that with suggestiveness. This universalism asserted itself everywhere in a conciliatory tendency, as the attempt to reconcile existing oppositions. This, too, was his work in political and ecclesiastical fields.

P. 445. Line 4. Add: —

On Platner's relation to Kant, cf. M. Heinze (Leips. 1880); P. Rohr (Gotha, 1890); P. Bergemann (Halle, 1891); W. Wreschner (Leips. 1893).

P. 445. Line 11 from foot. To the lit. on Empirical Psychology, add: —

M. Dessoir, *Geschichte der neueren deutschen Psychologie.* Vol. I. (Berlin, 1894. New ed. in press

P. 452. To the foot-note, add : —

In the field of demonstrative knowledge, Locke makes far-reaching conces-sions to rationalism, as it was known to him from the Cambridge school ; *e.g.* he even regarded the cosmological argument for the existence of God as possible.

P. 488. Line 24. After "world" insert : —

This theory was, in his case, none other than the imaginative view of Nature which had been taken over from the Italian Renaissance by the English Neo-Platonists. In his *Pantheisticon,* Toland pro-jected a sort of cultus for this natural religion, whose sole priestess should be Science, and whose heroes should be the great historical educators of the human mind.

P. 502. To the lit. under § 36, add : —

J. H. Tufts, *The Individual and his Relation to Society as reflected in British Ethics.* Part II. (Chicago, in press.)

P. 517. Line 7.

[The conception of "sympathy" in the *Treatise* is not the same as in the *Inquiry.* In the *Treatise* it is a psychological solvent like Spinoza's "imitation of emotions," and = "contagiousness of feeling." In the *Inquiry* it is opposed to selfishness, and treated as an impulse = benevolence; cf. on this, Green, *Int.,* Selby-Bigge, *Inquiry.*]

P. 521. Line 6 from foot. To the words "human rights," add the reference : —

G. Jellinek, *Die Erklärung der Menschenrechte* (Heidelb. 1896) ; [D. G. Ritchie, *Natural Rights,* Lond. and N.Y., 1895 ; B. Bosanquet, *The Philos. Theory of the State,* Lond. and N.Y., 1899.]

P. 522. Foot-note 3.

Cf. *Comte rendu des Séances des Écoles Normales.* Vol. 1.

P. 527. Line 11 from foot of text, add : —

By this definition of history the principles of investigation in natural science and those appropriate to history were no longer distinguished, and the contrasts between mechanical and teleological standpoints were obliterated in a way which necessarily called out the opposition of so keenly methodical a thinker as Kant. (Cf. his review of Herder's book, *Ideas toward the Philosophy of the History of Mankind,* in the *Jen. Allg. Litt. Ztg.,* 1785.) On the other hand, a harmonising thought was thus won for the theory of the world, quite in accord with the Leibnizian Monadology, and this has remained as an influential postu-late and a regulative idea for the further development of philosophy.

P. 529. To the lit., add : —

E. von Hartmann, *Die deutsche Aesthetik seit Kant* (Berlin, 1886). Julian Schmidt, *Geschichte der deutschen Litteratur von Leibniz bis auf unserer Zeit.* [Kuno Francke, *Social Forces in German Literature,* 2d ed., N.Y. 1897.]

P. 530. Line 8, add : —

Through this participation in the work of the highest culture, in which litera-ture and philosophy gave each to the other furtherance toward the brilliant cre-ations of the time, the German people became anew a nation. In this it found once more the essence of its genius ; from it sprang intellectual and moral forces through which, during the past century, it has been enabled to assert in the world the influence of this, its newly won nationality.

P. 532. To the lit., add : —

Fr. Paulsen, *I. Kant, sein Leben und seine Lehre,* Stuttgart, 1898.

P. 535. To the notice of Kant, add : —

His activity as a teacher extended not only over philosophical fields, but also to anthropology and physical geography ; and just in these, by his suggestive, discriminating, and brilliant exposition, his influence extended far beyond the bounds of the university. In society he was regarded with respect, and his fel· low-citizens sought and found in him kindly instruction in all that excited general interest.

P. 536. To the lit., add : —

Among the publications of Kant's Lectures the most important are the *Anthropologie* (1798, and by Starcke, 1831) ; *Logik* (1800) ; *Physische Geographie* (1802–1803) ; *Pädagogik* (1803) ; *Metaphysik* (by Pölitz, 1821). [On this last, which is valuable for Kant's development, 1770–1780, see B. Erdmann in *Philos. Monatshefte,* Vol. XIX., and M. Heinze, *K.'s Vorlesungen über Met.,* Leips. 1894.] A critical complete edition, such as has long been needed, is being published by the Berlin Academy of Sciences. [This appears in four parts, comprising, I. Works, published by Kant himself ; II. Correspondence ; III. Unpublished Manuscripts ; IV. Lectures. Vols. I. and II. of the Correspondence have appeared, ed. by Reicke (Berlin, 1900).] The *Kant Studien,* ed. by H. Vaihinger (1896——), gives the most complete information regarding recent literature. [Recent translations are *Kant's Cosmogony* (Glasgow, 1900), by W. Hastie ; *Dreams of a Spirit Seer* (Lond. and N.Y., 1900), by Goerwitz ; *The Inaugural Dissertation of 1770,* by Eckhoff (N.Y., 1894).]

P. 537. To the lit., add : —

E. Adickes, *Kant's Systematik als systembildender Factor* (Berlin, 1887), and *Kantstudien* (1894) ; E. Arnoldt, *Kritische Excurse im Gebiet der Kantforschung,* Königsberg, 1894.
[J. G. Schurmann in *Philos. Review,* Vols. VII., VIII.]

P. 551. To the lit., add : —

A. Hegler, *Die Psychologie in Kant's Ethik,* Freiburg i. Br. 1891.
W. Förster, *Der Entwicklungsgang der kantischen Ethik,* Berlin, 1894.

P. 557. Line 18 from foot, insert as a new paragraph : —

"The Communion of Saints," on the contrary, the ethical and religious union of the human race, appears as the true *highest good* of the practical reason. This reaches far beyond the subjective and individual significance of a combination between virtue and happiness, and has for its content the realisation of the moral law in the development of the human race — the Kingdom of God upon earth. (Cf. *Critique of Judgment,* §§ 85 ff., *Religion within the Bounds of Mere Reason,* 3d part (I. 2 ff.).

P. 559. To the lit. under § 40, add : —

[V. Basch, *Essai critique sur l'Esthétique de Kant,* Paris, 1896.]

P. 564.　Last line.　To "fine art," attach as note :—

On the historical connections of the theories here developed by Kant within the framework of his system, cf. P. Schlapp, *Die Anfänge der Kritik des Geschmacks und des Genies* (Göttingen, 1899).

P. 569.　Line 14 from foot of text, add :—

Jacobi was in youth a friend of Goethe.　He was a typical personality for the development of the German life of feeling in its transition from the time of "Storm and Stress," over into the Romantic movement.　He was the chief representative of the principle of religious sentimentality.　Cf. on his theory Fr. Harms (Berlin, 1876).

P. 570.　Line 6.　Add :—

On Beck, cf. W. Dilthey in *Arch. f. Gesch. d. Philos.*, II. 592 ff.　On Maimon, cf. A. Mölzner (Greifswald, 1890).

P. 570.　Line 18.　To the notice of Reinhold, add :—

He was an ardent, but not an independent, man.　His capacity to appreciate and adopt the work of another, and a certain skill in formulation, enabled him to render the Kantian philosophy a great service which was not, however, without its drawbacks.　In this consisted the importance of his Jena period.

P. 570.　Line 33.　To the lit. on Schiller, add :—

G. Geil, *Sch.'s Verhältniss zur kantischen Ethik*, Strassburg, 1888 ; K. Gneisse, *Sch.'s Lehre von der ästhetischen Wahrnehmung*, Berlin, 1893 ; K. Berger, *Die Entwicklung von Sch.'s Aesthetik*, Weimar, 1893 ; E. Kühnemann, *Kant's und Sch.'s Begründung der Aesthetik*, Munich, 1895.

P. 570.　Line 14 from foot.　To the notice of Fichte, add :—

As he worked his own way out of difficult conditions with great energy, so his whole life was filled with a thirst for achievement and for the improvement of the world.　He seeks to reform life, and especially the life of students and universities, by the principles of Kant's teaching.　It is as orator and preacher that he finds his most efficient activity.　High-flying plans, without regard to the actual conditions and often, perhaps, without sufficient knowledge of the data, form the content of his restless efforts, in which his "Philosophy of the Will" incorporates itself.　The dauntless and self-forgetful character of his idealism is evidenced above all in his "Addresses to the German Nation" (1807), in which he called his people with ardent patriotism to return to their true inner nature, to moral reform, and thereby to political freedom.　[To the Eng. tr. has been added the *Science of Ethics*, by Kroeger, 1897.]

P. 571.　Line 8.　To the notice of Schelling, add :—

In his personality the predominant factor is the combining capacity which is shown by an imagination that received satisfaction and stimulation on every side.　Religion and art, natural science and history, presented to him the rich material through which he was able to vitalise the systematic form which Kant and Fichte had constructed, and to bring it into living and fruitful connection with many other interests.　But this explains the fact that he seems to be involved in a continuous reconstruction of his theory, while he himself supposed that he was retaining the same fundamental standpoint from the beginning to the end of his work.　(Cf. the lectures by K. Rosenkranz, Danzig, 1843) ; L. Noack, *Sch. und die Philos. der Romantik*, Berlin, 1859 ; E. v. Hartmann, *Sch.'s positive Philosophie*, Berlin, 1869 ; R. Zimmermann, *Sch.'s Philosophie der Kunst*, Vienna, 1876; C. Frantz, *Sch.'s positive Philosophie*, Cöthen, 1879 f. ; Fr. Schaper, *Sch.'s Philos. der Mythologie und der Offenbarung*, Nauen, 1893 f.

P. 571. Line 33. Insert : —

J. J. Wagner (1775–1841, *System der Idealphilosophie*, 1804, *Organon der menschlichen Erkenntniss*, 1830).

P. 571. Line 4 from foot. To the notice of Hegel, add : —

Hegel was of a thoroughly didactic nature, with a tendency to schematise. An extremely rich and thorough knowledge, which was deeper and more comprehensive in the realms of history than in those of natural science, was ordered and arranged in his thought according to a great systematic plan. Imagination and practical ends fall far into the background in his life, in comparison with the purely intellectual need of comprehending all human knowledge as a historical necessity and a connected whole. This didactic uniformity appears also in the construction of his terminology, and has both its good and its bad side. Cf. H. Ulrici, *Ueber Princip und Methode der H. Schen Philos.* (Leips. 1841); P. Barth, *Die Geschichtsphilos. H.'s* (Leips. 1890). [Recent translations of *Philosophy of Mind*, by W. Wallace, Clar. Press, 1894 ; *Philosophy of Religion*, by Speirs and Sanderson, Lond. 1895 ; *Philosophy of Right*, by S. W. Dyde, 1896. Cf. J. MacTaggart, *Studies in the Hegelian Dialectic*, 1896 ; G. Noël, *La Logique de H.*, Paris, 1897.] Kuno Fischer's work on Hegel is now in press as the 8th vol. of the "Jubilee Edition" of his *Geschichte der neueren Philosophie*, and has progressed in its brilliant exposition so far as to include the *Logic*.

P. 572. To the notice of Schleiermacher, add : —

Schleiermacher's kindly nature, which was particularly skilful in fine and delicate adjustments, is developed especially in the attempt to harmonise the æsthetic and philosophical culture of his time with the religious consciousness. With delicate hand he wove connecting threads between the two, and removed in the sphere of feeling the opposition which prevailed between the respective theories and conceptions. Cf. D. Schenkel, *Sch.*, Elberfeld, 1868 ; W. Dilthey, *Leben Schl.'s*, Bd. I. Berlin, 1870 ; A. Ritschl, *Sch.'s Reden üb. d. Rel.*, Bonn, 1875 ; F. Bachmann, *Die Entwicklung der Ethik Schl.'s*, Leips. 1892. [Eng. tr. of the *On Religion*, by Oman (Lond. 1893).]

P. 572. To the notice of Herbart, add : —

Herbart's philosophical activity was conspicuous for its keenness in conceptual thought and for its polemic energy. Whatever he lacked in wealth of perceptual material and in æsthetic mobility was made up by an earnest disposition and a lofty, calm, and clear conception of life. His rigorously scientific manner made him for a long time a successful opponent of the dialectical tendency in philosophy.

P. 573. Line 4. To the notice of Schopenhauer, add : —

Of the recent editions of his works the most carefully edited is that of E. Grisebach. Schopenhauer's peculiar, contradictory personality and also his teaching have been most deeply apprehended by Kuno Fischer (9th vol. of the *Gesch. d. neueren Philos.*, 2d ed., 1898).

His capriciously passionate character was joined with a genius and freedom of intellectuality which enabled him to survey and comprise within one view a great wealth of learning and information, and at the same time to present with artistic completeness the view of the world and of life which he had thus found. As one of the greatest philosophical writers, Schopenhauer has exercised the strongest influence through his skill in formulation and his language, which is free from all the pedantry of learning, and appeals to the cultivated mind with brilliant suggestiveness. If he deceived himself as to his historical position in the Post-Kantian philosophy, and thereby brought himself into an almost pathological solitariness, he has nevertheless given to many fundamental thoughts of this whole development their most fortunate and effective form. Cf. W. Wallace, *Sch.* (London, 1891), R. Lehmann, *Sch., ein Beiträg zur Psychologie der Metaphysik* (Berlin, 1894). [W. Caldwell, *S.'s System in its Philosophical Significance* (Lond. and N.Y. 1896). J. Volkelt, *Sch.* (Stuttgart, 1900).]

P. 573.   Line 14.   After the parenthesis, insert : —

—to Schelling of J. P. V. **Troxler** (1780–1866, *Naturlehre des menschlichen Erkennens*, 1828).

P. 585.   Foot-note 2, add : —

Cf. A. Schoel, *H.'s Philos. Lehre von der Religion* (Dresden, 1884).

P. 586.   Note 3.   Line 7.   Insert : —

The theory thus given its scientific foundation and development by Herbart became the point of departure for the whole pedagogical movement in Germany during the nineteenth century, whether the direction taken was one of friendly development or of hostile criticism.   A literature of vast extent has been called out by it, for which histories of pedagogy may be consulted.

P. 588.   Line 14 from foot.   Affix to this the reference : —

Cf. Schopenhauer's essay *On the Fourfold Root of the Principle of Sufficient Reason*, and his *Criticism of the Kantian Philosophy* (in Vol. II. of the Eng. tr.).

P. 592.   Line 9 from foot of the text.   Affix the reference : —

Cf. E. v. Hartmann, *Ueber die dialektische Methode* (Berlin, 1868).

P. 599.   Line 21.

See Jac. Stilling in the *Strassburger Goethevorträgen* (1899), pp. **149 ff.**

INDEX.

References to pages 1–347 refer to the first volume of *A History of Philosophy,* published as a Harper Torchbook with the subtitle *Greek, Roman, and Medieval.*

NOTE. — Figures enclosed in parentheses indicate pages of the text to which supplementary matter has been added in the Appendix. Thus, under "Abelard," 690 (275) indicates that on page 690 will be found material supplementary to that on page 275.

Index.